Elements of
STATISTICAL INFERENCE

FINAL EXAM
Wed. May 1
10:20 - 12:20
Phys. 114

Normal approx to Binomial —
to Two-sample t-test (9.7)

Test Fri Apr. 8

Exclude
Sec 9.8

$H_0 : p_1 = p_2$

Book for Tables

one page of notes

Elements of

STATISTICAL INFERENCE
THIRD EDITION

DAVID V. HUNTSBERGER
Iowa State University

PATRICK BILLINGSLEY
The University of Chicago

Allyn and Bacon, Inc.   Boston

Contents

Preface

Sociology, business and economics, agriculture, engineering, ecology, psychology, education, medicine—these and other disciplines increasingly demand a knowledge of the language and methods of statistics. And increasingly, statistics is set as a requirement in the already-crowded program of students in these disciplines. A statistics course designed to meet the needs of such students should be brief, ordinarily of a single quarter or semester; it should presuppose no technical background; and it should not require that the student learn a great deal of mathematics first.

This book, written with such a course in mind, presents the student with the statistical techniques he is likely to need in his field of study. It aims at giving him an understanding of the reasoning underlying these techniques, for without such an understanding the techniques must be learned by rote and hence soon evaporate. The methods covered are not peculiar to one field of application alone, but apply to all subjects in which statistics is used. The book also provides a base from which the student can proceed to more advanced work, including specialized applications. The mathematical prerequisites have been kept to a minimum: Arithmetic and a little algebra suffice. Chapters 1 through 8 will ordinarily be taken up in sequence; material from Chapters 9 through 13 can then be selected in a variety of ways depending on the length of the course and interests of the class.

In this third edition, the level of mathematical presentation has been kept the same as that of the second edition. The text has been reworked in accordance with the suggestions of students and teachers, and a chapter on nonparametric methods, used increasingly in all fields, has been added.

DAVID V. HUNTSBERGER
PATRICK BILLINGSLEY

Elements of
STATISTICAL INFERENCE

1

Introduction

1.1 WHAT IS STATISTICS?

The word *statistics* often conjures up images of numbers piled upon numbers in vast and forbidding arrays and tables, of volume after volume of figures pertaining to births, deaths, taxes, populations, incomes, debits, credits, and the like, ad infinitum. This is so because in common usage the word *statistics* is synonymous with *data*, as, for example, when we speak of the statistics of a football game, the statistics of an election, or the statistics of highway accidents. This conception of the word does not correspond to the discipline that carries the name statistics, nor does it give a clue to the activities of present-day statisticians, who are no longer to be defined as collectors and tabulators of numerical facts.

In the modern sense of the word, statistics is concerned with the development and application of methods and techniques for collecting, analyzing, and interpreting quantitative data in such a way that the reliability of conclusions based on the data may be evaluated objectively by means of probability statements. It is this use of mathematical probability to evaluate the reliability of conclusions and inferences based on data that is the unique and major contribution of the statistical approach to inductive inference. For this reason the mathematical theory of probability plays a fundamental role in the theory and applications of statistics.

The purpose of statistics is not the exclusive service of any one science alone. Rather, statistics provides a set of methods valuable to research workers in all quantitative sciences. These methods can be used as effectively in engineering as in the biological sciences, and in the physical as well as in the social sciences. The problems may be very different, but the scientific method is common to all, and statistics can be regarded as the technology of the scientific method.

Statistical activities can be broadly classified into two major areas: theoretical or mathematical statistics, and applied statistics. Theoretical statistics is concerned with the mathematical elements of the subject—with lemmas, theorems, and proofs—and in general with the mathematical foundations of statistical methodology. We look to the mathematical statistician for the development of new theories that will provide new methods with which to attack practical problems.

To the applied statistician, statistics is a means to an end. He faces problems in other disciplines and selects from the available statistical methods those best fitted to the job at hand. He may be asked to participate in designing a sample survey or an experiment, or he may be consulted about sampling inspection schemes for statistical quality control. His statistical work directly involves him in the subject whence the problem arose—physiology, traffic engineering, economics, pharmacology, or whatever it may be. Frequently he is presented with a set of data and asked to provide an analysis and interpretation—often a difficult task, since the methods of analysis must depend on the way the data were collected. If the statistician was not consulted on the methods used in obtaining the data, he is too often obliged to say that, owing to the way in which the figures were obtained, they are inadequate, or of the wrong kind, to give the desired information.

In the main, statisticians are consultants to administrators, executives, and research workers in business, in government, in academic institutions, and in industry. We have made a distinction between theoretical and applied statistics, but the majority of statisticians engage in both.

1.2   THE USES OF STATISTICS

Statistical methods are traditionally used for descriptive purposes, for organizing and summarizing numerical data. *Descriptive statistics* deals with the tabulation of data, its presentation in graphical or pictorial form, and the calculation of descriptive measures. Chapters 2 and 3 cover these topics.

Modern uses of statistical methods primarily concern *statistical inference*. As long as we refrain from making generalizations based on our calculated measures, we are only describing what we observed. But as soon as we make an *inductive* generalization, we have passed beyond description and have entered the realm of inference. For example, a newspaper reporter questioned 100 people concerning their opinion of a proposed tax increase. Seventy of them responded in favor of the increase. If the reporter writes that 70 out of the 100 people questioned were in favor, he is merely describing what he observed. If, however, his story says that 70% of the town's citizens favor the increase, he is inferring that the percentage in the whole community that favor the proposition is essentially the same as that in his small sample. Starting from the incomplete information represented by his sample, he passes to a statement about the larger group from which the sample was taken. As a matter of fact, it is perhaps difficult *not* to generalize, at least subconsciously.

This kind of statistical inference is valid if statistical principles have been applied in selecting the sample and deriving the estimates. Suppose the reporter's sample was random—that is, was obtained by drawing 100 names from a hat containing the names of all the town's citizens, or by some scheme equivalent to this but easier to carry out. If 70% of those in the *sample* favor the tax increase, then our reporter can correctly assume that the true fraction in the *entire community* favoring the increase must be somewhere in the vicinity of 70%. It is difficult in this circumstance to believe the true fraction is as low as 30%, say, or as high as 98%. But what about 60%? Or 80%? The reasonableness of these values is more difficult to judge, and the answer depends on probability theory. This is one reason the theory of chance enters into statistics: Probability can tell whether the sample was sufficiently large, and, on the basis of the sample, probability considerations can delimit a reasonable range for the true fraction of those in the community who favor the increase in taxes.

For opinion pollers, market analysts, sociologists, economists, and others in fields where large variability in subjects or materials makes generalizations difficult, and where experimentation is only rarely possible, the statistical design of sampling investigations provides techniques without which these research workers would often be unable to draw any conclusions at all.

Other areas of application correspond to other subdivisions of statistical methodology: statistical quality control, genetic statistics, business statistics, psychological statistics, and so on. To repeat, statistics provides a body of methods applicable in all scientific areas where data are collected, analyzed, and interpreted.

It is not the purpose of this book to make a statistician of the reader. The objective is to give him an understanding of the fundamental principles of the subject and enough of the language of statistics that he may meet with statisticians on common ground. He will learn enough about statistical techniques to be able to handle many common types of problems himself, and he will learn to recognize those more complex problems that require consultation with a professional statistician.

CHAPTER

2

Empirical Frequency Distributions

2.1 FREQUENCY DISTRIBUTIONS

Statistical data obtained by means of census, sample survey, or experiment usually consist of raw, unorganized sets of numerical values. Before these data can be used as a basis for inferences about the phenomenon under investigation or as a basis for decision, they must be summarized and the pertinent information must be extracted. The kind of information required naturally depends on the application. If we were investigating the reliability of electronic components, it might suffice for our purposes simply to observe what percentage of the components tested failed to operate satisfactorily for longer than 1000 hours. If, however, we were interested in improving these components, we would require information concerning the reasons for the observed failures.

One type of information that may be desired of a set of data relates to the pattern or grouping into which the data fall. As a first step in developing this type of information, we could construct an *array*; that is, we could order the numerical values from low to high. An array may help make the overall pattern of the data apparent. However, if the number of values is large, construction of the array is difficult without punched-card equipment.

A more useful method for summarizing a set of data is the construction of a *frequency table* or *frequency distribution*. That is, we divide the overall range of the values in our set of data into a number of classes and count the number of observations that fall into each of these classes. By looking at such a table or distribution we can readily see the overall pattern of the data.

To illustrate the construction of a frequency distribution, we can use the 106 measurements of cranial widths in Table 2.1.*

TABLE 2.1.   106 Cranial Widths (in Millimeters)

146	141	139	140	145	141	142	131	142	140
144	140	138	139	147	139	141	137	141	132
140	140	141	143	134	146	134	142	133	149
140	143	143	149	136	141	143	143	141	140
138	136	138	144	136	145	143	137	142	146
140	148	140	140	139	139	144	138	146	153
148	142	133	140	141	145	148	139	136	141
140	139	158	135	132	148	142	145	145	121
129	143	148	138	149	146	141	142	144	137
153	148	144	138	150	148	138	145	145	142
143	143	148	141	145	141				

Before we can construct our frequency distribution, we must decide how many classes to use. This is to a certain extent arbitrary, but it is common to use from five to twenty classes, with more classes for larger sets of data. Suppose we fix on about ten classes for our data. (For comments on the number of classes to use, see Sections 2.3 and 3.4 and problem 1 at the end of this chapter.)

Having decided to use about ten classes, we now specify the *class intervals* (sizes or widths of the classes) and the *class boundaries*. Referring to Table 2.1, we note that the smallest observation is 121 and the greatest is 158. This means that our class intervals must cover the range from 121 to 158; that is, the combined length of the classes must be at least 158 − 121, or 37. Dividing 37 by 10, the number of classes, gives a class interval of 3.7. It would be very inconvenient to use a class interval that is not a multiple of the basic unit (the millimeter in this case), so we use an interval of 4. We can use ten classes, each of which is 4 units wide. We could instead use thirteen classes of 3 units each, eight classes of 5 units each, or any of several other combinations. Notice that in each case the intervals are of equal width (all 3, all 4, or all 5). Use of equal intervals is not absolutely necessary, and in the case of very lopsided distributions unequal intervals sometimes give a clearer picture of the situation. But equal intervals result in simpler calculations, and it is therefore best to use them when possible.

---

*Typical anthropometric data, these are widths of 106 male skulls unearthed in London during the construction of a whiskey store in 1895; their former owners very likely perished in the Great Plague of 1665–66.

To prevent ambiguity, we select our class boundaries in such a way that there can be no question about which class a given observation belongs to. Suppose we choose a class with boundaries 120 and 124 (which gives an interval of width of 4) and the next class with boundaries 124 and 128. Then an observation of 124 is impossible to classify; we do not know which of the two adjacent classes to put it in. The simplest solution is to select *impossible values* for the boundaries. In the present instance, if a class has boundaries 119.5 and 123.5 (which gives an interval of width of 4) and the next has boundaries 123.5 and 127.5, there can be no ambiguity, since all measurements are to the nearest millimeter.

With these preliminary considerations taken care of we can now construct the frequency distribution. The result is presented in Table 2.2.

TABLE 2.2.   Distribution of Widths (in Millimeters) of 106 Crania

Width (millimeters)	Tally	Number of observations
120–123	/	1
124–127		0
128–131	//	2
132–135	ﾟﾟ﹐﹍ //	7
136–139	ﾟﾟﾟﾟ ﾟﾟﾟﾟ ﾟﾟﾟﾟ ﾟﾟﾟﾟ /	21
140–143	ﾟﾟﾟﾟ ﾟﾟﾟﾟ ﾟﾟﾟﾟ ﾟﾟﾟﾟ ﾟﾟﾟﾟ ﾟﾟﾟﾟ ﾟﾟﾟﾟ ﾟﾟﾟﾟ /	41
144–147	ﾟﾟﾟﾟ ﾟﾟﾟﾟ ﾟﾟﾟﾟ ////	19
148–151	ﾟﾟﾟﾟ ﾟﾟﾟﾟ //	12
152–155	//	2
156–159	/	1
	Total	106

The tally shown in the central portion of the table is for convenience only and would not be displayed in the completed distribution. Notice that each class in this frequency distribution is specified by the greatest and least values that can be attained by a member of the class; these two numbers are called the *class limits*. Thus, a class boundary is midway between the upper limit of the class preceding it and the lower limit of the class following it; see Table 2.3.

It is convenient to select one value from each class to serve as a representative of the class. The value commonly used is the midpoint of the class, the *class mark*. This is the average of the two class limits, or, what amounts to the same thing, the average of the two class boundaries. For the distribution of cranial widths, the class mark of the first class is $(120 + 123)/2 = 121.5$ if computed from class limits, or $(119.5 + 123.5)/2 = 121.5$ if computed from class boundaries.

The number of observations in any class is the *class frequency* of that class. It is sometimes convenient to present the data in a *relative frequency distribution*. The relative class frequencies are found by dividing the class frequencies by the total number of observations. A *percentage distribution* is obtained by multiplying the relative class frequencies by 100 to convert them to percentages. For example, for the fifth class in Table 2.2, the class frequency is 21, so the relative frequency is 21/106, or .198, and the percentage is .198 × 100, or 19.8%.

All these concepts are illustrated in Table 2.3 for the cranial data. In practice, not all the columns are displayed.

TABLE 2.3.   Distribution of Widths (in Millimeters) of 106 Crania

Class limits	Class boundaries	Class mark	Class Frequency	Relative frequency	Percentage of observations
120–123	119.5–123.5	121.5	1	0.009	0.9
124–127	123.5–127.5	125.5	0	0.000	0.0
128–131	127.5–131.5	129.5	2	0.019	1.9
132–135	131.5–135.5	133.5	7	0.067	6.7
136–139	135.5–139.5	137.5	21	0.198	19.8
140–143	139.5–143.5	141.5	41	0.387	38.7
144–147	143.5–147.5	145.5	19	0.179	17.9
148–151	147.5–151.5	149.5	12	0.113	11.3
152–155	151.5–155.5	153.5	2	0.019	1.9
156–159	155.5–159.5	157.5	1	0.009	0.9
		Totals	106	1.000	100.0

Sometimes it happens that our data contain a few observations whose numerical values are much smaller or much larger than the rest. If we include these values in the ordinary way we may find that a number of our class frequencies are equal to zero. The frequency distribution for the waiting times between failures of a certain type of airborne radio equipment is given in Table 2.4. Because of the one extreme value, five of the class frequencies are equal to zero.

We can obtain a clearer picture of the distribution of the time to failure of these equipments without increasing the number of classes if we make use of an *open-ended interval*, one that has no upper boundary, for the last class. The resulting distribution is given in Table 2.5.

Open-ended intervals permit the inclusion of a wide range of extreme values, but, unhappily, the actual numerical value is lost and we do not know how much larger or smaller the extremes actually were unless some indication is given in a footnote or elsewhere. Open-ended intervals also present difficulties when we want to calculate the descriptive measures of later chapters.

7

TABLE 2.4.   Waiting Times between Failures of
Equipments

Times between failures (hours)	No. of failures
At least 0 but less than 50	3
" " 50 " " " 100	7
" " 100 " " " 150	13
" " 150 " " " 200	18
" " 200 " " " 250	22
" " 250 " " " 300	21
" " 300 " " " 350	12
" " 350 " " " 400	8
" " 400 " " " 450	0
" " 450 " " " 500	0
" " 500 " " " 550	0
" " 550 " " " 600	0
" " 600 " " " 650	0
" " 650 " " " 700	1
Total	105

In Table 2.4, the second class technically has limits 50 and 99 and
boundaries 49.5 and 99.5, and the class mark is $(50 + 99)/2$, or 74.5. But
in a case like this, where the unit of measurement is small in comparison
with the class interval, the distinction between class limits and class boundaries becomes largely irrelevant, and the class mark may more conveniently
be taken as 75.

TABLE 2.5.   Waiting Times between Failures of
Equipments

Times between failures (hours)	No. of failures
At least 0 but less than 50	3
" " 50 " " " 100	7
" " 100 " " " 150	13
" " 150 " " " 200	18
" " 200 " " " 250	22
" " 250 " " " 300	21
" " 300 " " " 350	12
" " 350 " " " 400	8
400 or more	1
Total	105

2.2 CUMULATIVE FREQUENCY DISTRIBUTIONS

Frequency distributions as described in Section 2.1 are valuable aids for organizing and summarizing sets of data and for presenting data in such a way that the outstanding features are readily apparent. Sometimes, however, we require information on the number of observations whose numerical value is less than a given value, and this information is contained in the *cumulative frequency distribution.*

From Table 2.2 we see that, of the craniums measured, none had a width of less than 120 millimeters, one had a width of less than 124 millimeters, one (1 + 0) had a width of less than 128, three (1 + 0 + 2) a width of less than 132, and so on. To obtain the cumulative frequency of widths less than the lower limit or boundary of a specified class, we add the class frequencies of all the preceding classes. The completed distribution is presented in Table 2.6.

TABLE 2.6. Cumulative Distribution for Cranial Widths

Width (millimeters)	Number of observations
Less than 120	0
" " 124	1
" " 128	1
" " 132	3
" " 136	10
" " 140	31
" " 144	72
" " 148	91
" " 152	103
" " 156	105
" " 160	106

This table contains further information: The number of widths equal to or greater than 140 is, of course, 106 − 31, or 75. And the number of widths that measure at least 140 and less than 148 is 91 − 31, or 60.

Cumulative distributions may be constructed for relative frequencies and percentages as well as for the absolute frequencies. The procedures are identical except that we add the relative frequencies or percentages, as the case may be, instead of the absolute frequencies.

2.3 GRAPHIC PRESENTATION

Though frequency distributions are effective in presenting the salient features of a set of data and are indispensable for computations, pictorial representation of the same information often makes the important characteristics more immediately apparent. We shall here consider only the most basic pictorial forms: histograms and ogives. Horizontal bar charts, compound bar charts, pictographs, and pie diagrams are, in general, adaptations of these basic forms (see reference 2.3).

A *histogram* is a graphic presentation of a frequency distribution and is constructed by erecting bars or rectangles on the class intervals. Along the horizontal scale we record the values of the variable concerned, marking off the class boundaries. Along the vertical scale we mark off frequencies. If we have equal class intervals, we erect over each class a rectangle whose height is proportional to the frequency of that class. For the distribution of the cranial widths, we obtain the histogram of Figure 2.1. It shows very plainly that the widths tend to be in the vicinity of 140 millimeters and are generally within 10 millimeters of this central value.

The class interval used in constructing the frequency table has a marked effect on the appearance of the histogram. The cranial data of Table 2.1 are, in Table 2.2, sorted into classes having a class interval of 4. If a class interval of 2 or of 8 is used, the distributions of Table 2.7 result.

The top and bottom histograms in Figure 2.2 come from the two distributions in Table 2.7, and the middle histogram is a repeat of Figure 2.1. The horizontal scale is the same in each case. When raw data are grouped into classes, a certain amount of information is lost, since no distinction is made between observations falling in the same class. The larger the class interval is, the greater is the amount of information lost. For the cranial data, a class interval of 8 is so large that the corresponding histogram gives very little idea of the shape of the distribution. A class interval of 2, on the

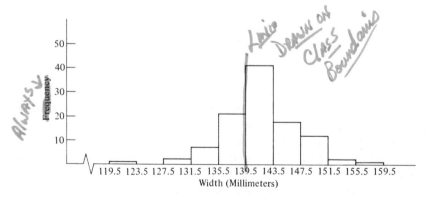

FIGURE 2.1. *Histogram of cranial widths*

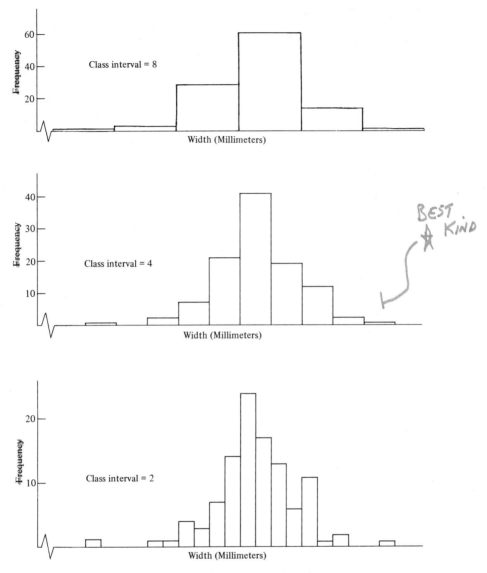

FIGURE 2.2. *Histograms of cranial widths*

other hand, gives a ragged-looking histogram. Little information has been lost in the bottom histogram of Figure 2.2, but the presentation of information is somewhat misleading because the small irregularities in the histogram merely reflect the accidents of sampling. A class interval of 4 represents a reasonable compromise in this case.

Figure 2.3 shows the histogram for the times between failures given in Table 2.5. Observe that although the open class in this distribution cannot

11

TABLE 2.7. Distribution for Cranial Widths

Class interval = 2		Class interval = 8	
Width (millimeters)	Number of observations	Width (millimeters)	Number of observations
120–121	1	116–123	1
122–123	0	124–131	2
124–125	0	132–139	28
126–127	0	140–147	60
128–129	1	148–155	14
130–131	1	156–163	1
132–133	4	Total	106
134–135	3		
136–137	7		
138–139	14		
140–141	24		
142–143	17		
144–145	13		
146–147	6		
148–149	11		
150–151	1		
152–153	2		
154–155	0		
156–157	0		
158–159	1		
Total	106		

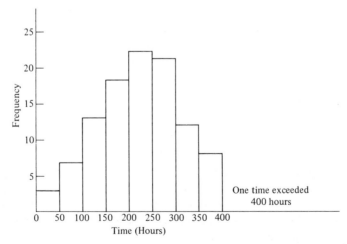

FIGURE 2.3. *Histogram for times between failures of airborne radio equipments*

be represented by a bar in the histogram, we indicate by a note in the histogram that there was an extreme value.

One advantage of equal class intervals is that the areas of the bars will be proportional to the heights of the bars. We therefore can draw the bars so that height is proportional to frequency. This is not correct if the class intervals are unequal. Suppose that in the distribution of cranial widths we were to combine the last four classes, as shown in Table 2.8. Now the rule

TABLE 2.8. Distribution of
Cranial Widths with the Last
Four Classes Combined

Width (millimeters)	Number of observations
120–123	1
124–127	0
128–131	2
132–135	7
136–139	21
140–143	41
144–159	34

for constructing a histogram is that the *area* of the bar over a class interval must be proportional to the frequency of the class. In the case of equal class intervals, this is the same as requiring that the height of the bar be proportional to the class frequency. Not so if the class intervals are unequal. If the histogram for the distribution in Table 2.8 were drawn with height proportional to frequency, we would obtain the result shown in Figure 2.4. Here, because we have not followed the area rule, the thirty-four values in the range 144–159 are given an undue emphasis, and the histogram gives the

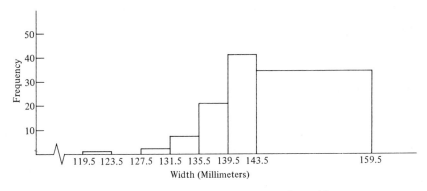

FIGURE 2.4. *Incorrectly drawn histogram for Table 2.8*

impression that a very large proportion of the widths exceed 143. The correct representation is that in Figure 2.5, where the areas of the bars are proportional to the frequencies (the height of the rightmost bar is one-quarter what it was in Figure 2.4). This is correct because the eye naturally interprets size by area.

Just as a frequency distribution can be represented graphically by a histogram, a cumulative frequency distribution can be represented graphically by an *ogive*. To construct an ogive, we first lay out the class boundaries on the horizontal scale, just as for a histogram. Above each class boundary we plot a point at a vertical distance proportional to the cumulative frequency—proportional, in other words, to the number of observations whose numerical value is less than that class boundary. These points are then connected by straight lines. Using Table 2.6 in this way leads to the ogive shown in Figure 2.6.

FIRST No. ALWAYS ZERO

LAST ALWAYS No. of total No. of observations

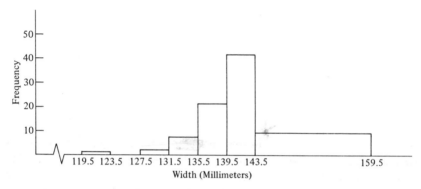

FIGURE 2.5.   *Correctly drawn histogram for Table 2.8*

It is proper to interpolate graphically from an ogive. From the ogive for cranial widths we may, for example, get an approximation to the number of observations whose numerical value is less than 145.5 by finding the height of the curve over that point—see the upper dotted line in Figure 2.6. Thus we *estimate* that eighty-two craniums are less than 145.5 millimeters in width (the actual number is eighty-five).

2.4   DATA AND POPULATIONS

It must be stressed that the material of this and the next chapter concerns empirical data—data obtained by selecting a sample or performing an experiment. The actual data in hand are usually only a very small part of some much larger whole. The 105 failure times recorded in Table 2.4, for example, constitute only a fraction of the totality of failure times for all radio equipment of that kind.

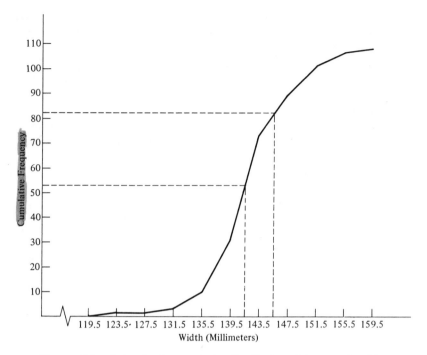

FIGURE 2.6. *Ogive for the cumulative distribution of the cranial widths*

Conceptually, we could construct a frequency distribution for the totality of possible values which might have been obtained. Such conceptual distributions we refer to as *theoretical* or *population* distributions; they are to be distinguished from the *empirical* distributions of this chapter and the next. (Theoretical distributions are discussed in detail in Chapter 5.) An empirical distribution *estimates* the corresponding theoretical distribution.

PROBLEMS

1. One rule that has been advanced (see reference 2.4) for choosing the number of classes best suited to represent the data of a particular frequency distribution is this: If n is the number of observations and k is the number of classes, then k should be about equal to the next integer larger than the base-2 logarithm of n. That is to say,

$$\text{If } 2^3 = 8 < n \le 2^4 = 16, \text{ then } k \text{ should be about 4,}$$

$$\text{If } 2^4 = 16 < n \le 2^5 = 32, \text{ then } k \text{ should be about 5,}$$

$$\text{If } 2^5 = 32 < n \le 2^6 = 64, \text{ then } k \text{ should be about 6,}$$

etc.

(*Continued*)

15

With this rule, about how many classes would be appropriate for a frequency distribution for (a) 40 observations, (b) 200 observations, (c) 1000 observations, (d) 5000 observations?

2. Given 200 numbers such that the smallest is 10.5 and the largest is 75.3, set up a table that would be suitable for grouping the data. Give the class marks as well as the boundaries.

3. If the class limits in a frequency distribution are 25–28, 29–32, 33–36, and 37–40, what are the boundaries of the classes? What are the class marks?

4. Given below are the gains in weight (lb) of forty-eight steers on an experimental ration.
   a. Construct the frequency distribution.
   b. Construct the cumulative distribution.
   c. Draw the histogram and the ogive.

181	182	184	193	125	70
168	172	161	149	77	123
115	114	135	136	115	97
112	109	104	108	184	117
80	64	128	115	132	92
123	120	75	131	118	161
84	100	106	71	56	148
111	128	83	114	112	135

5. Given the following data,
   a. Construct the frequency distribution.
   b. Construct the cumulative distribution.
   c. Draw the histogram and the ogive.

2786	3217	2618	2845
2832	2524	2427	2838
2312	2697	2220	3010
3218	2855	3137	2581
2426	3346	2978	2714

6. Given the following frequency distribution,
   a. Construct the cumulative distribution.
   b. Give the class boundaries and class marks.
   c. Obtain the percentage distribution.
   d. Draw the histogram and the ogive.

Class	Frequency
25– 49	15
50– 74	25
75– 99	30
100–124	20
125–149	10

7. As an experiment, toss four coins fifty times and construct the frequency distribution for the number of heads per toss. Draw the histogram and the ogive.

8. For the following histogram (the numbers in the bars are the frequencies),
   a. What are the boundaries and class marks?
   b. Draw the ogive.

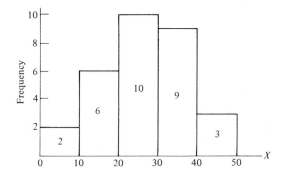

9. Given the following relative frequency distribution for $n = 50$ observations, find the absolute frequencies.

Class	Relative frequency
20–39	.12
40–59	.28
60–79	.36
80–99	.24

10. The following data are the amounts, in parts per million, of a nitrogen compound found in eighty soil samples.
   a. Construct a frequency distribution.
   b. Construct the cumulative distribution.
   c. Draw the histogram and ogive.

3.64	5.08	3.87	3.52	3.05	4.98	3.30	3.64
3.20	2.55	4.40	4.61	3.74	4.42	2.76	3.20
3.30	3.63	5.05	2.87	4.50	4.44	4.40	4.74
3.64	3.81	4.61	4.04	3.40	4.74	3.52	5.06
2.76	3.87	3.39	4.39	5.50	3.52	3.86	4.74
3.40	3.05	2.63	3.08	4.48	5.74	3.64	4.08
4.54	3.72	4.50	3.98	3.96	2.74	3.74	2.76
3.30	5.51	3.07	4.42	4.62	4.10	4.30	2.98
2.76	3.22	2.53	2.98	6.06	3.40	4.50	3.42
5.38	3.73	3.06	5.42	3.98	3.66	4.18	6.08

11. The following is the distribution for the number of defective items found in 100 lots of manufactured items.
  a. What percentage of the lots contained more than five defective items?
  b. What is the relative frequency of the lots that contained two or fewer defectives?
  c. What are the class limits? The class boundaries?
  d. Draw the histogram and ogive.

Number defective	Frequency
0	23
1	25
2	19
3	14
4	11
5	5
6	2
7	1

12. Given the following distribution,
  a. Draw the histogram. Note that the class intervals are not equal.
  b. Draw the ogive to scale.
  c. From the ogive, estimate the age such that 50% are older; that 75% are younger.

Estimated Number of Females in the Labor Force of the United States, 1972

Age	Number of females (thousands)
15 to 19	2212
20 to 24	3503
25 to 29	1313
30 to 34	939
35 to 39	3490
40 to 44	3005
45 to 54	5096
55 to 64	2904
65 to 80	885

13. The following data are the differences in cutoff voltages between the two halves of forty-eight dual-triode electron tubes of a given type.
  a. Construct a frequency distribution. Between -1 and 1 use intervals equal to 1/2 volt. Less than -1 and greater than 1 use intervals equal to 1 volt.
  b. Construct the relative frequency distribution and the percentage distribution.
  c. Construct the cumulative relative frequency distribution.

d. Draw the histogram and the ogive.

e. From the ogive, estimate the proportion of tubes of this type with difference in cutoff less than zero, greater than .50, less than -1.

$-.30$	.24	.25	$-.10$	.53	$-.16$
$-.37$	$-.83$	.48	1.25	.67	.22
.28	$-.15$	-2.02	-1.22	.65	$-.08$
$-.34$	$-.52$	1.55	$-.18$	.15	$-.12$
.86	.06	.56	$-.88$	-1.16	-1.02
2.07	1.02	-1.43	.72	.08	1.10
$-.75$	$-.32$	.08	$-.61$	$-.25$	-1.35
.02	$-.05$	.61	$-.80$	.04	$-.22$

14. The following data are the amounts of impurities in percent found in ninety-six samples of a given compound.

a. Construct a frequency distribution.

b. Construct the cumulative percentage distributions.

c. Sketch the histogram and the ogive.

7.78	6.02	9.68	6.14	7.28	6.23	4.64	7.41
6.75	4.51	8.42	7.92	6.84	5.81	4.67	7.38
5.43	11.28	7.96	6.38	5.92	4.80	10.72	6.17
6.17	9.54	7.82	5.33	5.79	4.76	9.78	5.84
6.00	5.23	6.48	6.53	5.46	4.83	9.51	6.82
7.26	10.90	10.82	9.81	10.73	10.46	10.63	7.79
6.54	9.72	9.74	10.62	4.87	5.23	4.68	7.19
5.28	10.62	7.24	8.38	5.05	4.98	8.62	6.76
5.03	8.41	8.65	8.37	8.46	7.93	7.19	6.53
4.29	8.62	8.50	8.83	7.78	7.64	5.39	7.21
5.31	7.76	6.42	5.13	6.49	6.31	7.72	4.15
4.97	6.13	5.29	6.34	7.82	6.68	6.44	4.68

REFERENCES

2.1 CROXTON, FREDERICK E., DUDLEY J. COWDEN, and BEN W. BOLCH. *Practical Business Statistics*, 4th edition. Prentice-Hall, Englewood Cliffs, 1969. Chapter 2.

2.2 HUFF, DARRELL. *How to Lie with Statistics*. Norton, New York, 1965. Chapters 5 and 6.

2.3 NETER, JOHN, and WILLIAM WASSERMAN. *Fundamental Statistics for Business and Economics*, 2nd edition. Allyn and Bacon, Boston, 1961. Chapters 4 and 5.

2.4 STURGES, H. A. "The Choice of a Class Interval," *J. Am. Stat. Assoc.*, March, 1926.

CHAPTER

3

Descriptive Measures

[handwritten annotations: "Where is it (location) ~)" "How wide is it (dispersion)"]

3.1 INTRODUCTION

In the last chapter we saw how tabular and graphical forms of presentation may be used to summarize and describe quantitative data. Though these techniques make clear important features of the distribution of the data, statistical methods for the most part require concise numerical descriptions. These are arrived at through arithmetic operations on the data which yield *descriptive measures* or *descriptive statistics*. The basic descriptive statistics are the measures of central tendency or location and the measures of dispersion or scatter.

Discussion of these descriptive measures requires some familiarity with the mathematical shorthand used to express them. Since we are concerned with masses of data and since the operation of addition plays a large role in our calculations, we need a way to express sums in compact and simple form. The summation notation meets this requirement.

3.2 SYMBOLS AND SUMMATION NOTATION

If our data consist of measurements of some characteristic of a number of individuals or items such as the annual incomes of some group of persons, the weights of a number of pigs, or the transconductances of a batch of electron tubes, we designate the characteristic of interest by some letter or symbol, say, X. If we have measured two or more characteristics we use

20

different letters or symbols for each. If, in addition to obtaining annual income, we also record the age of each person interviewed we could represent income by X and age by Y. A third characteristic, such as educational level, we could represent by the letter Z, and so on.

In order to differentiate between the same kind of measurements made on different items or individuals, or between similar repeated measurements made on the same element, we add a subscript to the corresponding symbol; thus X_1 stands for the income of the first person interviewed, X_2 for that of the second, X_{23} for that of the twenty-third, and so on. In general, any arbitrary observed value would be represented by X_i, where the subscript i is variable in the sense that it represents any one of the observed items and need only be replaced by the proper number in order to specify a particular observation. The income, age, and educational level of the ith, or general, individual would be represented by X_i, Y_i, and Z_i, respectively.

Given a set of n observations which we represent by $X_1, X_2, X_3, \ldots,$ X_n, we can express their sum as

$$\sum_{i=1}^{n} X_i = X_1 + X_2 + X_3 + \cdots + X_n$$

where $\sum$ (uppercase Greek sigma) is the summation operator, the subscript i is the index of summation, and the 1 and n that appear respectively below and above the operator $\sum$ designate the range of the summation. The combined expression says, "add all X's whose subscripts are between 1 and n, inclusive." In place of i we sometimes use j as the summation index; any letter will do.

If we want the sum of the squares of the n observations we write:

$$\sum_{i=1}^{n} X_i^2 = X_1^2 + X_2^2 + X_3^2 + \cdots + X_n^2$$

which says, "add the squares of all observations whose subscripts are between 1 and n, inclusive." The sum of the products of two variables X and Y would be written as:

$$\sum_{i=1}^{n} X_i Y_i = X_1 Y_1 + X_2 Y_2 + X_3 Y_3 + \cdots + X_n Y_n$$

If we want a partial sum, the sum of some but not all the quantities involved, the range of the summation is adjusted accordingly. For example:

$$\sum_{i=4}^{8} Y_i^2 = Y_4^2 + Y_5^2 + Y_6^2 + Y_7^2 + Y_8^2$$

$$\sum_{i=2}^{5} Y_i^2 f_i = Y_2^2 f_2 + Y_3^2 f_3 + Y_4^2 f_4 + Y_5^2 f_5$$

and

$$\sum_{i=1}^{3} (Y_i - X_i) = (Y_1 - X_1) + (Y_2 - X_2) + (Y_3 - X_3)$$

21

In those cases where the context makes it clear that *the sum is to be taken over all the data* we sometimes simplify the summation notation by omitting the range of summation. Thus $\sum X_i$ is the sum of all of the numbers and $\sum X_1^2$ is the sum of the squares of all of the numbers.

We now look at some of the algebraic rules that apply to summations:

RULE 1: *The summation of a sum (or difference) is the sum (or difference) of the summations:*

$$\sum_{i=1}^{n} (X_i + Y_i - Z_i) = \sum_{i=1}^{n} X_i + \sum_{i=1}^{n} Y_i - \sum_{i=1}^{n} Z_i \qquad (3.1)$$

RULE 2: *The summation of the product of a variable and a constant is the product of the constant and the summation of the variable:*

$$\sum_{i=1}^{n} cY_i = c \sum_{i=1}^{n} Y_i \qquad (3.2)$$

RULE 3: *The summation of a constant is the constant multiplied by the number of terms in the summation:*

$$\sum_{i=1}^{n} c = nc \qquad (there\ are\ n\ terms) \qquad (3.3)$$

For example,

$$\sum_{i=3}^{8} c = 6c \qquad (there\ are\ 6\ terms)$$

Working through some numerical examples makes it clear that these rules are correct.

Each summation must be read with care, so that its meaning is exactly understood. If one reads summations from the inside out, so to speak, many common errors can be avoided. Consider the summation

$$\sum_{i=1}^{n} (X_i - c)^2$$

Read from the inside out, it tells us to

1. subtract the constant c from each X,
2. square each of the differences obtained in step 1,
3. sum the squares obtained in step 2.

Two important but sometimes misread sums are the *sum of squares*

$$\sum X_i^2 = X_1^2 + X_2^2 + \cdots + X_n^2$$

and the *square of the sum*

$$(\sum X_i)^2 = (X_1 + X_2 + \cdots + X_n)^2$$

The former is found by squaring each X and then adding the squares, the latter by adding up the X's and then squaring the sum. These two expressions are usually unequal and often occur together in the same mathematical statement.

3.3   MEASURES OF LOCATION

When we work with numerical data and their frequency distributions, it soon becomes apparent that in most sets of data there is a tendency for the observed values to group themselves about some interior value; some central value seems to be characteristic of the data. This phenomenon, referred to as *central tendency*, may be used to describe the data in the sense that the central value locates the "middle" of the distribution. The statistics we calculate for this purpose are *measures of location*, also called measures of central tendency. For a given set of data, the measure of location we use depends upon what we mean by *middle*, different definitions giving rise to different measures. We consider here three such measures and their interpretations: the mean, the median, and the mode.

3.4   THE MEAN

All of us are familiar with the concept of the mean or average value. We read and speak of batting averages, grade-point averages, mean annual rainfall, the average weight of a catch of fish, and the like. In most cases, the term *average* used in connection with a set of numbers refers to their *arithmetic mean*. For the sake of simplicity we call it the *mean*.

For a given set of n values, $X_1, X_2, X_3, \ldots, X_n$, the mean is their sum divided by n, the number of values in the set. It is denoted by $\overline{X}$ and may be expressed as

$$\overline{X} = \frac{1}{n} \sum_{i=1}^{n} X_i \tag{3.4}$$

If, for example, I catch three fish and their lengths are 10, 13, and 16 inches, their mean length is

$$\overline{X} = \frac{10 + 13 + 16}{3} = \frac{39}{3} = 13 \text{ inches}$$

The 106 cranial widths of Table 2.1 have a sum equal to 15,005 and their mean is

$$\overline{X} = \frac{15,005}{106} = 141.56 \text{ millimeters}$$

Notice that the unit for the mean is the same as the unit for the observations themselves (inches, millimeters, dollars, etc.).

If we are faced with finding the mean for a very large number of observed values and do not have calculating machines available, we can materially decrease the labor involved by grouping the data into a frequency distribution and then finding the mean for the grouped data. It should be borne in mind that by grouping the data we have lost information and that the mean obtained from the grouped data will therefore only approximate the mean of the ungrouped data. If the number of observations is large and the class intervals are small the approximation will be very good.

To illustrate the calculation of the mean for grouped data we apply the procedures to the data summarized in Table 3.1.

TABLE 3.1. Annual Earnings of 300 Part-time Employees

Annual earnings	Class mark	Number of employees
$ 500 but less than 700	$ 600	12
700 ″ ″ ″ 900	800	21
900 ″ ″ ″ 1100	1000	52
1100 ″ ″ ″ 1300	1200	70
1300 ″ ″ ″ 1500	1400	68
1500 ″ ″ ″ 1700	1600	36
1700 ″ ″ ″ 1900	1800	16
1900 ″ ″ ″ 2100	2000	11
2100 ″ ″ ″ 2300	2200	9
2300 ″ ″ ″ 2500	2400	5
	Total	300

To find the mean of this distribution, we operate as if each observed value in a given class were equal to the class mark for that class. Now the observations are $X_1, X_2, \ldots, X_n$, where $n = 300$ for this set of data, and these are grouped into k classes, where $k = 10$ in this case. Let v_j denote the class mark for the jth class, and let f_j denote the class frequency for that class. Now if each observation X_i falling into the jth class had value exactly v_j (instead of having value approximately v_j), the sum of all the observations in the jth class would be $v_j f_j$. In Table 3.1, the class mark of the fourth class (1100 but less than 1300) is $v_4 = 1200$ and the class frequency is $f_4 = 70$. If each employee in the fourth class made *exactly* $1200, the sum of the earnings for these 70 employees would be $v_4 f_4 = 1200 \times 70 = \$84,000$, and this will *approximate* their total earnings even if their individual earnings are spread out over the range 1100–1300. The total earnings for all 300 employees is approximated by summing the individual class totals:

$$\sum_{j=1}^{k} v_j f_j = v_1 f_1 + v_2 f_2 + \cdots + v_k f_k$$

Notice that, since each of the n observations goes into exactly one of the k classes, the class frequencies f_j must add to the total number of observations n:

$$\sum_{j=1}^{k} f_j = f_1 + f_2 + \cdots + f_k = n$$

The mean for the grouped data is thus given by

$$\bar{X} = \frac{\sum v_j f_j}{\sum f_j} = \frac{1}{n} \sum_{j=1}^{k} v_j f_j \tag{3.5}$$

For the data of Table 3.1, we calculate the mean as follows:

Class mark v_j	Frequency f_j	Product $v_j f_j$
$ 600	12	7,200
800	21	16,800
1000	52	52,000
1200	70	84,000
1400	68	95,200
1600	36	57,600
1800	16	28,800
2000	11	22,000
2200	9	19,800
2400	5	12,000
$n = \sum f_j = 300$		$\sum v_j f_j = 395,400$

$$\bar{X} = \frac{395,400}{300} = \$1318$$

For a second example, consider the distribution of the 106 cranial widths of Chapter 2 (see Table 2.3 and the table at the top of page 26).

The difference between the mean width of 141.77 millimeters obtained from the grouped data and that calculated from the ungrouped data, the figure 141.56 given earlier in this section, is due to the loss of information through the grouping. The individual widths lost their identities in the process, and we assumed that every width in a given class was equal to the class mark. Grouping according to a class interval of 2 rather than 4 (see Table 2.7) gives a grouped mean of 141.57, which is closer to the ungrouped mean, and a class interval of 8 gives a grouped mean of 142.07, which is farther away. The greater the class interval, the farther the grouped mean tends to be from the ungrouped mean.

The mean is the middle of a set of data in the sense that it is the center of gravity. If we draw the histogram on some stiff material of uniform density, such as plywood or metal, cut it out, and balance it on a knife-edge arranged perpendicular to the horizontal scale, as shown in Figure 3.1, the X-value corresponding to the point of balance is the mean $\bar{X}$.

Widths (millimeters)	Class mark v_j	Frequency f_j	Product $v_j f_j$
120–123	121.5	1	121.5
124–127	125.5	0	0.0
128–131	129.5	2	259.0
132–135	133.5	7	934.5
136–139	137.5	21	2,887.5
140–143	141.5	41	5,801.5
144–147	145.5	19	2,764.5
148–151	149.5	12	1,794.5
152–155	153.5	2	307.0
156–159	157.5	1	157.5
		$\sum f_j = 106$	$\sum v_j f_j = 15{,}027.5$

$$\bar{X} = \frac{15{,}027.5}{106} = 141.77 \text{ millimeters}$$

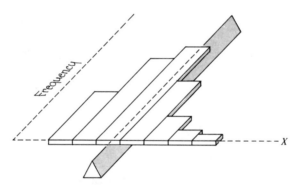

FIGURE 3.1.   *The mean as a center of gravity*

A variant of this physical way of looking at the mean is illuminating in connection with grouping. Suppose we have four observations 1, 8, 7, and 1, with a mean of $(1 + 8 + 7 + 1)/4$, or 4.25. Imagine a seesaw with a scale marked off along its edge, and imagine, for each of the four observations, a one-pound weight positioned according to this scale, as shown in the top half of Figure 3.2. The mean 4.25 is the point at which the fulcrum of the seesaw must be placed in order to make it balance. Now suppose the observations are grouped as follows:

Class	Mark	Frequency
0–2	1	2
3–5	4	0
6–8	7	2

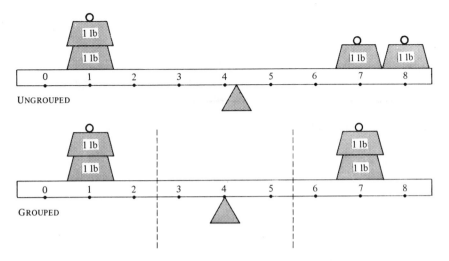

FIGURE 3.2.   *The mean as a center of gravity*

And now imagine weights of 2, 0, and 2 pounds placed at the class marks 1, 4, and 7, respectively. The grouped mean

$$\frac{1 \times 2 + 4 \times 0 + 7 \times 2}{4} = 4$$

is the balance point for this arrangement of weights, as shown in the bottom half of Figure 3.2. The rightmost weight, originally at 8, has been moved to the class mark 7, changing the balance point from 4.25 to 4. The same kind of arrangement of weights can be imagined for more complicated sets of data. The point is that, if the class interval is small, no weight travels very far when it is moved from its original position to its class mark, which means that the balance point cannot travel very far either.

3.5   THE WEIGHTED MEAN

When we compute the simple arithmetic mean of a set of data we assume that all the observed values are of equal importance and we give them equal weight in our calculations. In situations where the numbers are not equally important we can assign to each a weight which is proportional to its relative importance and calculate the *weighted mean.*

Let $X_1, X_2, X_3, \ldots, X_n$ be a set of n values, and let $w_1, w_2, w_3, \ldots, w_n$ be the weights assigned to them. The weighted mean is found by dividing the sum of the products of the values and their weights by the sum of the weights; that is,

$$\overline{X} = \frac{w_1 X_1 + w_2 X_2 + w_3 X_3 + \cdots + w_n X_n}{w_1 + w_2 + w_3 + \cdots + w_n}$$

27

or, in summation notation,

$$\bar{X} = \frac{\sum w_i X_i}{\sum w_i} \tag{3.6}$$

Every student is familiar with the concept of the weighted mean, for his quality-point average is such a measure. It is the mean of the numerical values of the letter grades weighted by the numbers of credit hours in which the various grades are earned. If a student makes A's in two 3-credit courses, a B in a 5-credit course, a C in a 4-credit course, and a D in a 2-credit course, and if the numerical values of the letter grades are A = 4, B = 3, C = 2, and D = 1, his quality-point average for the term is

$$\bar{X} = \frac{3 \times 4 + 3 \times 4 + 5 \times 3 + 4 \times 2 + 2 \times 1}{3 + 3 + 5 + 4 + 2} = \frac{49}{17} = 2.882$$

When we calculate the mean for a grouped set of data by equation (3.5) of Section 3.4, we are actually finding the weighted mean of the class marks. The weights in this case are the class frequencies.

The weighting procedure is also used to find the mean when several sets of data are combined. Suppose we have three sets of data consisting of n_1, n_2, and n_3 observed values and having means $\bar{X}_1, \bar{X}_2$, and $\bar{X}_3$, respectively. The mean for the combined data is the weighted average of the individual means, the respective weights being the sample sizes n_1, n_2, and n_3:

Weighted mean formula

$$\bar{X} = \frac{n_1 \bar{X}_1 + n_2 \bar{X}_2 + n_3 \bar{X}_3}{n_1 + n_2 + n_3} \tag{3.7}$$

Failure to weight the means when combining data is not an uncommon error. Imagine the male student body of a school split into two groups. In the first group the mean height is 75 inches, and in the second group the mean height is 69 inches. The average $(75 + 69)/2 = 72$ is not the mean height of male students in the school, because the first group consists of the 15 members of the basketball team, and the second group consists of the remaining 568 male students in the school. The true mean is

$$\frac{15 \times 75 + 568 \times 69}{583} = 69.15 \text{ inches}$$

in accordance with equation (3.7) for two (rather than three) means.

3.6   THE MEDIAN

Roughly speaking, the *median* of a set of data is a number such that about half the observations are less than that number and about half the observations are greater than that number. To be specific, suppose there are n observed values and that n is an odd number. The array is formed (the values are lined up in increasing order), and the median is by definition the observation in the middle position. For example, in the array

$$1 \quad 1 \quad 2 \quad 3 \quad 3 \quad \mathbf{8} \quad 11 \quad 14 \quad 19 \quad 19 \quad 20$$

the median is 8 (there are five observations to its left and five to its right). If n is even, there is no one observation in the middle position. In this case, we take the median to be the average of the *pair* of observations occupying the two central positions. In the array

$$2 \quad 5 \quad 5 \quad 6 \quad 7 \quad \mathbf{10} \quad \mathbf{15} \quad 21 \quad 21 \quad 23 \quad 23 \quad 25$$

the observations 10 and 15 occupy the two center positions (there are five observations to the left of 10 and five to the right of 15), and so the median is $(10 + 15)/2$, or 12.5.

Since we often have our data in the form of a grouped frequency distribution, we need a way of estimating the median for grouped data. Recall that when raw data are grouped into classes, information is lost because the distinction between the various observations in each individual class is lost. The following method assumes that the observations in each class are more or less evenly spread over that class, so that this loss of information is of little importance.

The method is most easily understood and carried out on the ogive. Consider the ogive in Figure 2.6 for the 106 cranial widths. The height of the curve over a given value on the horizontal scale represents approximately the number of observations whose numerical value is less than that given. Since we want the value for which about 53 (half of 106) observations are less than it, we should look for that value on the horizontal scale for which the height of the curve above it is 53. The way to do this is to locate the cumulative frequency 53 on the vertical scale, trace horizontally over to the curve and then vertically down to the scale at the bottom (see the lower and inside dotted lines in Figure 2.6), and read off the value of the point where the traced line intersects the horizontal scale: 141.5 (approximately). Thus, the median is about 141.5. The actual median according to the above definition, obtained by forming the array, is 141.

There is an arithmetic procedure equivalent to this graphical one; it is less convenient if the ogive has been constructed, but it does not require the ogive. From the cumulative frequency distribution for the cranial widths, as given in Table 2.6, we see that there are 31 observations less than 140 and 72 observations less than 144; therefore, since 53 lies between 31 and 72, the median must lie in the class 140–143. Now there are $72 - 31$, or 41, observations in this class, and of these $53 - 31$, or 22, are less than or equal to the median. The two class boundaries are 139.5 and 143.5 (see Table 2.3). We need for the median a value, call it m, such that 53 out of all 106 observations are less than or equal to m, which is the same thing as a value m such that 22 of the observations in the range 139.5–143.5 are less than or equal to m. If the 41 observations in this range are essentially evenly

29

spread out, then m should be about 22/41 of the distance from the lower class boundary to the upper class boundary, that is,

$$m = 139.5 + \tfrac{22}{41} \times 4 = 141.6$$

This value should be the same as the value arrived at with the graphical procedure; the difference in the answers, 141.6 as opposed to 141.5, is due merely to the difficulty of reading the scale in Figure 2.6 with great accuracy. Since the median according to our original definition is 141, the discrepancy is immaterial anyway.

The formula for this arithmetic procedure is

$$m = b + \frac{d}{f} \times c \qquad\qquad (3.8)$$

where
m = median,
b = lower boundary of the class containing the median,
c = length of the class containing the median,
f = frequency of the class containing the median,
d = $n/2$ minus the cumulative frequency at the lower boundary b of the class containing the median, n being the total number of observations.

As a second example of the arithmetic procedure, consider the cumulative frequency distribution for the earnings of part-time employees in Table 3.1.

Annual earnings			No. of employees	Cumulative frequency
$ 500 but less than	700		12	12
700 ” ” ”	900		21	33
900 ” ” ”	1100		52	85
1100 ” ” ”	1300		70	155
1300 ” ” ”	1500		68	223
1500 ” ” ”	1700		36	259
1700 ” ” ”	1900		16	275
1900 ” ” ”	2100		11	286
2100 ” ” ”	2300		9	295
2300 ” ” ”	2500		5	300
		Total	300	

Since 150 (half of 300, the number of employees) is between 85 and 155, the median must fall in the fourth class. The lower boundary for that class is 1100, the length of the class is 200, its frequency is 70, $n/2$ is 150, and the cumulative frequency at the lower boundary of the fourth class is 85. Thus,

$$b = 1100 \qquad c = 200 \qquad f = 70 \qquad d = 150 - 85 = 65$$

The formula gives

$$m = 1100 + \tfrac{65}{70} \times 200 = 1100 + 185.7 = 1285.7$$

so the median earnings is about $1286.

3.7 THE MODE

When data are grouped, we often find that there is one class which has maximum frequency and that the frequencies of the other classes tend to fall away continually as we move away from the maximum class in either direction. This class is called the *modal class*, and we define the *mode* as the class mark of that class.

For example, for the distribution of cranial widths given in Table 2.2, the class with the greatest frequency is 140–143, the frequency being 41. Moreover, as a glance at the histogram in Figure 2.1 shows, the frequencies taper off on either side of this one with the trivial exception that the frequency of the first class exceeds that of the second. This is therefore the modal class, and its midpoint or class mark 141.5 is the mode M:

$$M = 141.5$$

If there is such a class with maximum frequency, then the distribution is said to be *unimodal*. If there is no such class, the distribution is said to be *multimodal*, and the mode is undefined. In a histogram like that in Figure 3.3, the distribution is multimodal; A is the major mode, and B and C are minor modes. The concentration of values is greatest around A, and there are secondary concentrations around B and C.

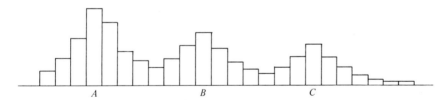

FIGURE 3.3. *A histogram showing major and minor modes*

3.8 SELECTING A MEASURE OF LOCATION

In deciding which measure of location to report for a set of data, a primary consideration is the use to which the results are to be put. In addition, we need to know the advantages and disadvantages of each measure of location as regards its calculation and interpretation.

If the distribution of the data is symmetric and unimodal, then the mean $\overline{X}$, the median m, and the mode M will all coincide; but as the distribution becomes more and more skewed (lopsided), the differences among these measures will become greater. This is illustrated in Figure 3.4.

The mean is sensitive to extreme values. If in a small town the average annual income of the 100 heads of household is reported as $5990, this figure is correct but very misleading if one head of household is a multimillionaire with an income of $500,000 and the remaining 99 are paupers with incomes of $1000. A few extreme values have little or no effect on the median and the mode. For the numbers

$$1, 3, 4, 6, 6, 9, 13$$

we have $\overline{X} = 6$, $m = 6$, and $M = 6$. If we add the number 70 to this set the mean will be equal to 14, a shift of eight units, but the median and mode remain unchanged. For this reason, when the data are skew the median or the mode may be more characteristic and therefore provide a better description.

With the increasing availability of calculating machinery, ease of calculation is a less important consideration. It should be noted, however, that ungrouped data must be arrayed to find the median; hence, if an adding machine or desk calculator is at hand it may be easier to find the mean. Once the data have been grouped, both the median and the mode are calculated more simply than the mean.

The effects of grouping must also be considered. If the frequency distribution includes open-ended classes, the mean cannot be evaluated accurately, if at all. Open-ended classes, in general, will not affect the median and mode. If the classes have unequal widths all three measures may be found, but they will usually be poorer approximations to the values obtained

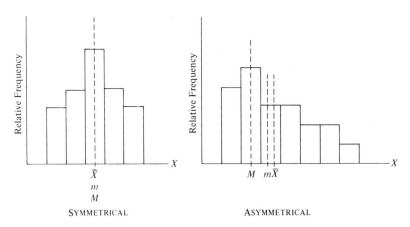

FIGURE 3.4 *Mean, median, and mode for symmetrical and asymmetrical distributions*

from the ungrouped data. The mode is especially sensitive to grouping in that alternative sets of class intervals may result in modes that differ considerably.

If we want to combine measures for several sets of data, the algebraic properties of the mean give it a distinct advantage. We have seen that we can use the weighted mean for this purpose. The median and the mode are not subject to this type of algebraic treatment.

If the evaluation of a measure of location is a first step toward making inferences about the source of the data, the mathematical and distributional properties of the mean give it a distinct advantage. In the realm of statistical inference a primary consideration is statistical stability. It can be shown that if a large number of sets of data are taken from the same source and all three measures are calculated for each set, there will be less variation among the means than among the medians or among the modes; hence the mean is more stable. This, coupled with the fact that it is more amenable to mathematical and theoretical treatment, makes the mean an almost universal choice for all but purely descriptive purposes.

3.9   MEASURES OF VARIATION

The measures of location discussed in the preceding sections serve to describe one aspect of numerical data; but they tell us nothing about another aspect of equal importance, the amount of variation or scatter among the observed values. In any set of statistical data, the numerical values will not be identical but will be scattered or dispersed to a greater or lesser degree. The statistics we calculate to measure this characteristic of the data we refer to as *measures of variation* or *measures of dispersion*. Since several sets of data could have the same, or nearly the same, mean, median, and mode, but vary considerably in the extent to which the individual observations differ from one another, a more complete description of the data results when we evaluate one of the measures of variation in addition to one or more of the measures of location. Several such measures are considered in the following sections.

3.10   THE RANGE

The *range* is the difference between the largest and smallest values in the data. Referring again to the cranial widths, Table 2.1, we find that the smallest width was 121 and the greatest was 158; hence the range is 158 − 121, or 37, millimeters.

Although the range is easy to calculate and is commonly used as a rough-and-ready measure of variability, it is not generally a satisfactory measure of variation for several reasons. In the first place, its calculation

33

involves only two of the observed values regardless of the number of observations available; therefore, it utilizes only a fraction of the available information concerning variation in the data, and reveals nothing with respect to the way in which the bulk of the observations are dispersed within the interval bounded by the smallest and largest values. Secondly, as the number of observations is increased the range generally tends to become larger; therefore, it is not proper to use the ranges to compare the variation in two sets of data unless they contain the same numbers of values. Finally, the range is the least stable of our measures of variation for all but the smallest sample sizes; that is, in repeated samples taken from the same source the ranges will exhibit more variation from sample to sample than will the other measures.

The range differs from most of our statistical measures in that it is a relatively good measure of variation for small numbers of observations, but becomes less and less reliable as the sample size increases. Because it is easy to calculate and is reasonably stable in small samples, it is not uncommonly used in statistical quality control where samples of four or five observations are often sufficient.

In recent years the range and statistics based on the range have found favor with people who are interested in the development of rapid statistical methods for arriving at answers with a minimum of lengthy or involved computations. It also is the basis for other recently developed techniques that are beyond the scope of this book (see reference 3.4).

3.11   THE VARIANCE AND THE STANDARD DEVIATION

Since the disadvantages of the range limit its usefulness, we need to consider other measures of variation. Suppose we have n numbers, X_1, X_2, $X_3, \ldots, X_n$, whose mean is $\overline{X}$. If we were to plot these values and $\overline{X}$ on the X axis as in Figure 3.5 (only five values are shown) and measure the distance of each of the X's from the mean $\overline{X}$, it seems reasonable that the average, or mean, of these distances should provide a measure of variation. These

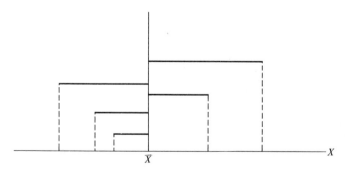

FIGURE 3.5.   *Deviations from the sample mean*

distances, or *deviations from the mean*, are equal to $(X_1 - \bar{X}), (X_2 - \bar{X}), \ldots,$ $(X_n - \bar{X})$, or, in general, $(X_i - \bar{X})$, and their mean is

$$\frac{1}{n} \sum_{i=1}^{n} (X_i - \bar{X})$$

But this quantity is always equal to zero, since the algebraic sum of the deviations of a set of numbers from its mean is always equal to zero. This can be seen as follows:

$$\sum (X_i - \bar{X}) = \sum X_i - n\bar{X}$$

but

$$\bar{X} = \frac{1}{n} \sum X_i \quad \text{or} \quad n\bar{X} = \sum X_i$$

Therefore

$$\sum (X_i - \bar{X}) = \sum X_i - \sum X_i = 0 \tag{3.9}$$

The trouble is that we have used not the distances of the X_i to the mean $\bar{X}$, but the signed distances, and the remedy is to ignore their algebraic signs. We have then the *mean deviation*

$$\frac{1}{n} \sum_{i=1}^{n} |X_i - \bar{X}| \tag{3.10}$$

where $|X_i - \bar{X}|$, the *absolute value* of $X_i - \bar{X}$, is just $X_i - \bar{X}$ with the sign converted to $+$ if it happens to be $-$.

The mean deviation, though it appears to be relatively simple, is not of great interest. It is not particularly easy to calculate, and the absolute values make theoretical developments difficult. There are theoretical reasons why one should use squares instead of absolute values. Suppose we do use the square instead of the absolute value as a measure of deviation. In the squaring process the negative signs will disappear; hence the sum of the squares of the deviations from the mean will always be a positive number greater than zero unless all the observations have the same value. In symbols, the sum of squares of deviations from the mean is

$$\sum_{i=1}^{n} (X_i - \bar{X})^2 \tag{3.11}$$

This quantity, for simplicity, will be referred to as the *sum of squares*. Hereafter, whenever the phrase *sum of squares* appears it should be taken to mean *the sum of squares of deviations from the sample mean*. To avoid ambiguity, if the sum of squares of the observations, or the sum of squares for any other quantities, is meant, the phrase will be qualified accordingly.

It is clear that the sum of squares provides a measure of dispersion. If all the observed values are identical, the sum of squares is equal to zero. If the values tend to be close together the sum of squares will be small, but if they scatter over a wide range the sum of squares will be correspondingly large. To illustrate this characteristic and, incidentally, to show how the sum of squares is calculated according to the definition given as equation (3.11), we use the numbers

$$12, 6, 15, 3, 12, 6, 21, 15, 18, 12$$

Their mean is

$$\overline{X} = \frac{1}{n} \sum X_i = \frac{120}{10} = 12$$

To find the deviations from the mean we subtract $\overline{X} = 12$ from each of the X values. We get

$$0, -6, 3, -9, 0, -6, 9, 3, 6, 0$$

We can use the fact that the sum of the deviations from the mean is equal to zero to check our arithmetic:

$$(3 + 9 + 3 + 6) - (6 + 9 + 6) = 0$$

To complete our calculations we square each of the deviations and sum them:

$$0 + 36 + 9 + 81 + 0 + 36 + 81 + 9 + 36 + 0 = 288$$

The sum of squares for these ten numbers is

$$\sum_{i=1}^{10} (X_i - \overline{X})^2 = 288$$

The calculations are summarized in the following table.

X_i	$X_i - \overline{X}$	$(X_i - \overline{X})^2$
12	0	0
6	−6	36
15	3	9
3	−9	81
12	0	0
6	−6	36
21	9	81
15	3	9
18	6	36
12	0	0
120	0	288

$$n = 10 \qquad \overline{X} = 12$$

In contrast to the preceding example, which displays a fair amount of variation, suppose we have the numbers

$$12, 10, 12, 14, 10, 13, 12, 11, 14, 12$$

We find the sum of squares as before:

X_i	$X_i - \bar{X}$	$(X_i - \bar{X})^2$
12	0	0
10	-2	4
12	0	0
14	2	4
10	-2	4
13	1	1
12	0	0
11	-1	1
14	2	4
12	0	0
120	0	18

$$n = 10 \qquad \bar{X} = 12$$

As could be expected, since the variation in the second set of numbers is less than in the first set, the sum of squares, 18, is considerably smaller than that calculated for the first set. Notice that the mean is the same as in the preceding example; the sum of squares measures spread *about* the mean, whatever the mean may be.

It is obvious that if we have a large number of values, or if the sum of the numbers is not divisible by the sample size n, this procedure for calculating the sum of squares could become rather tedious. Fortunately, there is another method for computing the sum of squares that does not necessitate finding the individual deviations from the mean.

We can rewrite the sum of squares as

$$\sum (X_i - \bar{X})^2 = \sum (X_i^2 - 2\bar{X}X_i + \bar{X}^2)$$

If we now apply Rules 1, 2, and 3 of Section 3.2, we get

$$\sum (X_i - \bar{X})^2 = \sum X_i^2 - 2\bar{X} \sum X_i + n\bar{X}^2$$

But

$$\bar{X} = \frac{1}{n} \sum X_i \quad \text{and} \quad \bar{X}^2 = \frac{1}{n^2} (\sum X_i)^2$$

Therefore

$$\sum (X_i - \bar{X})^2 = \sum X_i^2 - 2\frac{1}{n} (\sum X_i)^2 + \frac{1}{n} (\sum X_i)^2$$

so that

$$\sum (X_i - \bar{X})^2 = \sum X_i^2 - \frac{1}{n} (\sum X_i)^2 \qquad \textbf{(3.12)}$$

The expression on the right-hand side of equation (3.12) provides an alternative procedure for computing a sum of squares that is especially useful when a desk calculator is available. For this reason it is often referred to as the *machine formula* for sums of squares, and it should be used for all but the most simple sets of data. To apply the formula, we obtain the sum of the squares of the observed values as well as their sum, square the sum, divide it by n (the number of observations), and subtract the result from the sum of squares of the observed values.

There is associated with any sum of squared quantities an expression or number known as its *degrees of freedom*, which may be defined as the number of squares minus the number of independent linear restrictions imposed upon the quantities involved. For n numbers there are n squares of deviations from the mean, of which only $n - 1$ are independent; that is, when $n - 1$ of them are specified the nth one is also determined. This follows from the fact that the sum of the deviations from the mean must be zero. The sum of squares of deviations of the n values from their mean has, therefore, $n - 1$ degrees of freedom. We shall make it a practice always to give the degrees of freedom associated with any new sum of squares whenever it first arises.

Although the sum of squares is a measure of variation, it is usually more convenient to use the mean squared deviation or the root mean squared deviation. The mean squared deviation is the *variance*, s^2; it is found by dividing the sum of squares by its degrees of freedom:

$$s^2 = \frac{1}{n - 1} \sum (X_i - \bar{X})^2 \tag{3.13}$$

The variance* is an average value for the squares of the deviations. The reason for dividing by $n - 1$ rather than by n, the number of observations, will be discussed in the section concerned with estimation. When the machine formula is used to obtain the sum of squares, the variance is

$$s^2 = \frac{1}{n - 1} \left[\sum X_i^2 - \frac{1}{n} (\sum X_i)^2 \right] \tag{3.14}$$

The *standard deviation*, or root mean squared deviation, of the numbers in a sample of size n is the square root of the variance; that is,

$$s = \sqrt{s^2} \tag{3.15}$$

The standard deviation s is used partly because its units are those of the original data. If the X_i are measurements in pounds, then $\bar{X}$ has pounds as its unit. The variance s^2, however, being a sum of squares of deviations in pounds, has square pounds as its unit; but its square root s has the pound as its unit again, which is what we want: The spread should be measured in terms of the units involved.

---

*In the literature the sample estimate of variance s^2 is not infrequently defined with the sample size n as the divisor rather than the degrees of freedom $n - 1$, as is done here. The latter definition has the advantage that the sample estimate will be an *unbiased* estimate for the variance of the population. The concept of unbiased estimation will be discussed in Chapter 7.

We use the nine numbers given below to illustrate the procedures for calculating the variance and standard deviation:

$$3, 6, 2, 5, 3, 8, 6, 7, 5$$

Step 1: Find the sum of squares.

$$\sum X_i = 45$$

$$\bar{X} = \frac{1}{n}\sum X_i = \tfrac{45}{9} = 5$$

$X_i - \bar{X}$	-2	1	-3	0	-2	3,	1	2	0	0
$(X_i - \bar{X})^2$	4	1	9	0	4	9	1	4	0	32

$$\sum (X_i - \bar{X})^2 = 32$$

Step 2: To get the variance, divide the sum of squares by its degrees of freedom.

$$s^2 = \frac{1}{n-1}\sum (X_i - \bar{X})^2 = \tfrac{32}{8} = 4$$

Step 3: To obtain the standard deviation take the square root of the variance.

$$s = \sqrt{s^2} = \sqrt{4} = 2$$

If we were to use the machine formula for the sum of squares in Step 1 we would find:

$$\sum X_i = 45$$

$$\sum X_i^2 = 9 + 36 + 4 + 25 + 9 + 64 + 36 + 49 + 25 = 257$$

$$\sum X_i^2 - \frac{(\sum X_i)^2}{n} = 257 - \frac{(45)^2}{9} = 257 - 225 = 32$$

When we want to calculate the variance and standard deviation for data which have been grouped or classified to form a frequency table we follow the three-step procedure outlined above, but the calculation of the sum of squares requires a slight modification. As when computing the mean $\bar{X}$, we proceed as though each value in a given class were equal to the class mark. To find the sum of squares, we calculate the mean for the distribution by the procedure of Section 3.4, and find the deviations of the class marks v_j from the mean. The square of the deviation of a class mark from the mean, $(v_j - \bar{X})^2$, is the amount each value in the class contributes to the sum of squares. If there are f_j items in the jth class, the total contribution of the class is $(v_j - \bar{X})^2 f_j$; therefore, the sum of squares is the sum of the contributions of all of the classes:

$$\sum (v_j - \bar{X})^2 f_j$$

39

and the variance for the grouped data is

$$s^2 = \frac{1}{n-1} \sum (v_j - \bar{X})^2 f_j \tag{3.16}$$

where $n = \sum f_j$ is the total number of observations in the data.

Let us use the numbers in the following frequency distribution to go through a sample calculation. The numbers have been adjusted to simplify the arithmetic.

Class	v_j = Class mark	f_j = Frequency
0– 4	2	30
5– 9	7	51
10–14	12	10
15–19	17	10
		101

The calculations required to obtain the variance and standard deviation for this distribution are displayed in the following table.

v_j	f_j	$v_j f_j$	$v_j - \bar{X}$	$(v_j - \bar{X})^2$	$(v_j - \bar{X})^2 f_j$
2	30	60	−5	25	750
7	51	357	0	0	0
12	10	120	5	25	250
17	10	170	10	100	1000
	101	707			2000

$$\bar{X} = \frac{1}{n} \sum v_j f_j = \tfrac{707}{101} = 7$$

$$s^2 = \frac{1}{n-1} \sum (v_j - \bar{X})^2 f_j = \tfrac{2000}{100} = 20$$

$$s = \sqrt{s^2} = \sqrt{20} = 4.47$$

Note that in the preceding example the deviations of the class marks from the mean do not sum to zero. For grouped data it is the sum of the products of the frequencies times the deviations of the class marks from the mean that is equal to zero.

The machine formula for the sum of squares of grouped data is

$$\sum v_j^2 f_j - \frac{1}{n} (\sum v_j f_j)^2 \tag{3.17}$$

where v_j is the class mark. If we use the machine formula to find the sum of squares for the table just above, the calculations are as follows:

v_j	v_j^2	f_j	$v_j f_j$	$v_j^2 f_j$
2	4	30	60	120
7	49	51	357	2499
12	144	10	120	1440
17	289	10	170	2890
		101	707	6949

$$\sum v_j^2 f_j - \frac{1}{n}(\sum v_j f_j)^2 = 6949 - \frac{(707)^2}{101}$$

$$= 6949 - 4949$$

$$= 2000$$

$$s^2 = \tfrac{2000}{100} = 20$$

$$s = \sqrt{20} = 4.47$$

Because of the information lost in grouping, the variance and standard deviation are, in general, not exact when calculated from the grouped data. They are good approximations, however, and the smaller the class interval, the better the approximation. Neither the mean nor the variance can be calculated when the distribution contains open-ended classes.

3.12   CHANGES OF SCALE (CODING)

Now that we have seen how certain measures of location and of variation are calculated, we consider a principle whose application will, in many instances, lead to a substantial reduction in the amount of arithmetic required to obtain some of these measures. This saving is effected by the application of a *linear transformation* to the original data, grouped or ungrouped. A linear transformation may consist of a translation of the data to a new origin, or it may take the form of an expansion or contraction of the scale of measurement. A translation results when the same constant is added to, or subtracted from, every value in a set of data. An expansion or contraction of the scale of measurement is obtained by multiplying every observed value by the same suitably chosen constant. In most applications the transformation employed will involve both a translation and a change in the measurement scale.

For a set of n numbers, $X_1, X_2, \ldots, X_n$, a simple translation will be effective if these n values are such that the addition to each of the same constant will give us a set of values containing relatively fewer digits than the original numbers. For example, given the numbers

$$381, 386, 383, 389, 393, 384, 386$$

if we subtract 380 from each (add minus 380), we get the new set

$$1, 6, 3, 9, 13, 4, 6$$

and it is obvious that it would be easier to work with the latter. Formally, we have used a transformation whose equation is

$$U_i = X_i - 380$$

where the U_i are the *transformed values*.

Suppose we have the numbers

$$.003, .008, .011, .015, .006, .008, .005$$

Here we are inclined to ignore the decimal point and to work with the integers

$$3, 8, 11, 15, 6, 8, 5$$

In other words, we transform the original numbers by multiplying each by 1000. The corresponding equation is

$$U_i = 1000X_i$$

The transformations used in the preceding examples are both special cases of the general linear transformation

$$U_i = AX_i + B \tag{3.18}$$

where the X_i are the observed values, the U_i are the transformed values, and A and B are constants. The additive constant B may be positive or negative. It may also be zero. In the latter case we would have only an expansion or contraction. The multiplicative constant A may have any value greater than zero. If A is equal to 1 we have a simple translation. Keep in mind that division by A is the same as multiplication by the reciprocal $1/A$.

After a set of raw data has been transformed, we find the mean, variance, and standard deviation of the U's in the usual way, i.e.,

$$\overline{U} = \frac{1}{n} \sum U_i$$

$$s_U^2 = \frac{1}{n-1} \sum (U_i - \overline{U})^2$$

$$s_U = \sqrt{s_U^2}$$

After these measures have been calculated for the transformed values it will be necessary to retransform them, or convert them back, to the original units and origin. To see how this is done we examine the relationships implied by the transformation given as equation (3.18). If we sum both sides of this equation we get

$$\sum U_i = A \sum X_i + nB$$

If we now divide both sides by the sample size n, we have

$$\overline{U} = A\overline{X} + B \qquad (3.19)$$

This can be solved for $\overline{X}$ in terms of $\overline{U}$:

$$\overline{X} = \frac{1}{A}(\overline{U} - B) \qquad (3.20)$$

The relationship between the variances is derived as follows:

$$U_i = AX_i + B$$

$$\overline{U} = A\overline{X} + B$$

$$U_i - \overline{U} = A(X_i - \overline{X})$$

$$(U_i - \overline{U})^2 = A^2(X_i - \overline{X})^2$$

$$\sum (U_i - \overline{U})^2 = A^2 \sum (X_i - \overline{X})^2$$

$$\frac{1}{n-1}\sum (U_i - \overline{U})^2 = \frac{A^2}{n-1}\sum (X_i - \overline{X})^2$$

$$s_U^2 = A^2 s_X^2 \qquad (3.21)$$

Also

$$s_U = A s_X \qquad (3.22)$$

so that

$$s_X^2 = \frac{1}{A^2} s_U^2 \qquad (3.23)$$

and

$$s_X = \frac{1}{A} s_U \qquad (3.24)$$

We see that if every X_i is multiplied by a positive constant A, the mean and standard deviation are multiplied by the same constant and the variance is multiplied by the square of the constant. If a constant B is added to every X_i, it is also added to the mean but has no effect on the variance and standard deviation.

The truth of these formulas can be grasped visually by imagining a city 6000 feet above sea level and four mountains with peaks 1200, 1800, 3600, and 4200 feet above the city. The peaks average

$$\frac{1200 + 1800 + 3600 + 4200}{4} = 2700 \text{ feet}$$

above the city. To find the average of their heights above sea level, we could convert all three to measurements from sea level by adding 6000 and then

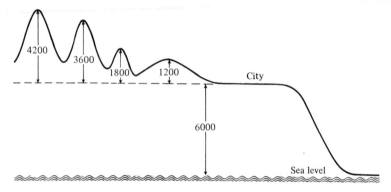

FIGURE 3.6. *Change of scale*

average the results, but we know intuitively that the average height above sea level is 2700 + 6000, or 8700, feet. This is equation (3.19) with A equal to 1 and B equal to 6000.

Similarly, to find the average height above the city in yards instead of feet, we could convert all four heights to yards by multiplying by 1/3 and then averaging, but intuitively we know that the average height above the city in yards is $1/3 \times 2700$, or 900. This is equation (3.19) with A equal to 1/3 and B equal to 0.

Finally, the standard deviation of 1200, 1800, 3600, and 4200 turns out to be 1428.3. And if the mountain heights are spread out by an amount 1428.3 feet, they ought to be spread out an amount $1/3 \times 1428.3$, or 476.1, yards. This is a case of equation (3.22) with A equal to 1/3.

EXAMPLE 1

Find the mean and variance for the seven numbers

$$381, 386, 383, 389, 393, 384, 386$$

Procedure: Let $U_i = X_i - 380$, i.e., $A = 1$, $B = -380$; then we have:

								Sum
U_i	1	6	3	9	13	4	6	42
$U_i - \bar{U}$	-5	0	-3	3	7	-2	0	0
$(U_i - \bar{U})^2$	25	0	9	9	49	4	0	96

$$\bar{U} = \tfrac{42}{7} = 6$$
$$s_U^2 = \tfrac{96}{6} = 16$$
$$\bar{X} = \bar{U} + 380 = 6 + 380 = 386$$
$$s_X^2 = s_U^2 = 16$$

EXAMPLE 2

Find the mean, variance, and standard deviation for the nine numbers

$$2.43, 2.46, 2.42, 2.45, 2.43, 2.48, 2.46, 2.47, 2.45$$

Procedure: The appropriate transformation is $U_i = 100X_i - 240$. Here $A = 100$, $B = -240$.

X_i	$U_i = 100X_i - 240$	$U_i - \bar{U}$	$(U_i - \bar{U})^2$
·2.43	3	-2	4
2.46	6	1	1
2.42	2	-3	9
2.45	5	0	0
2.43	3	-2	4
2.48	8	3	9
2.46	6	1	1
2.47	7	2	4
2.45	5	0	0
	45	0	32

$$\bar{U} = \tfrac{45}{9} = 5$$

$$s_U^2 = \tfrac{32}{8} = 4$$

$$s_U = \sqrt{4} = 2$$

We convert to the original scale as follows:

$$\bar{X} = \frac{\bar{U} + 240}{100} = \frac{5 + 240}{100} = 2.45$$

$$s_X^2 = \frac{1}{(100)^2}\, s_U^2 = \frac{4}{10,000} = .0004$$

$$s_X = \frac{1}{100}\, s_U = \frac{2}{100} = .02$$

Linear transformations may also be used effectively when we calculate the mean and variance for grouped data. Suppose we want these measures for the distribution of earnings of part-time employees discussed in Section 3.4 (see Table 3.1) and reproduced in part below. In order to transform these data we select one of the class marks, designate it by v_o, and subtract it from other class marks. The choice of v_o is arbitrary, but it is usual to select a class mark near the center of the distribution. For our example we use the fourth one, 1200. Since the distribution has equal class intervals, every difference $v_j - v_o$ is a multiple of the class interval 200; therefore as a second step in the transformation we divide each of the differences by 200.

v_j	f_j	$v_j - v_o$	$u_j = \frac{1}{200}(v_j - v_o)$
$ 600	12	− 600	− 3
800	21	− 400	− 2
1000	52	− 200	− 1
1200	70	0	0
1400	68	200	1
1600	36	400	2
1800	16	600	3
2000	11	800	4
2200	9	1000	5
2400	5	1200	6

The mean and variance on the U scale are found in the usual way:

$$\bar{U} = \frac{1}{n} \sum u_j f_j = \frac{177}{300} = .59$$

$$s_U^2 = \frac{1}{n-1} \left[\sum u_j^2 f_j - \frac{1}{n} (\sum u_j f_j)^2 \right]$$

$$s_U^2 = \frac{1}{299}[1181 - \frac{1}{300}(177)^2] = 3.60$$

Since the transformation we used was

$$u_j = \frac{1}{200}(v_j - 1200)$$

the mean on the X scale is

$$\bar{X} = 200\bar{U} + 1200 = 200(.59) + 1200 = \$1318$$

u_j	u_j^2	f_j	$u_j f_j$	$u_j^2 f_j$
− 3	9	12	− 36	108
− 2	4	21	− 42	84
− 1	1	52	− 52	52
0	0	70	0	0
1	1	68	68	68
2	4	36	72	144
3	9	16	48	144
4	16	11	44	176
5	25	9	45	225
6	36	5	30	180
		300	177	1181

The variance and standard deviation are:

$$s_X^2 = (200)^2 s_U^2 = 40,000(3.6) = 144,000$$

$$s_X = 200 s_U = 200\sqrt{3.6} = \$380$$

For a distribution with *equal class intervals*, a transformation similar to that used above may be accomplished simply by setting one class mark equal to zero and numbering the others consecutively, starting at the zero class and counting in both directions. The classes before the zero class will have negative U-values, those after it will have positive U-values. After the desired measures have been calculated on the U scale they are transformed back to the X scale by the following equations.

$$\overline{X} = c\overline{U} + v_o \tag{3.25}$$

$$s_X^2 = c^2 s_U^2 \tag{3.26}$$

$$s_X = c s_U \tag{3.27}$$

where c is the class interval and v_o is the class mark that was taken to be the zero point on the new scale. Transformations of this kind are not particularly useful if the classes are not of equal width.

3.13 INDEX NUMBERS

Index numbers give quantitative descriptions of change over time, usually economic change. Table 3.2 gives for 1965–68 each year's total electric power production for the United States in billions of kilowatt-hours. The ratio of the figure for 1966 to that for 1965 is 1249/1158, or 1.078; multiplication by 100 gives 107.8, the second entry in the second row. We can say that in 1966, production was 107.8% what it was in 1965, or that production was up 7.8%. The other two entries in the row are 113.7 ($100 \times 1317/1158$) and 123.7 ($100 \times 1433/1158$). The 1967 production of power was 13.7% above the 1965 production, and the 1968 production was 23.7% above the 1965 production.

TABLE 3.2.   U.S. Electric Power Production

	Year			
	1965	1966	1967	1968
Electric power produced (billions of kilowatt-hours)	1158	1249	1317	1433
Production index: 1965 base	100.0	107.8	113.7	123.7
Production index: 1967 base	87.9	94.8	100.0	108.8

An index number is a ratio, multiplied by 100 to put it in the form of a percentage. The indices in the second row of Table 3.2 all have for their denominator 1158, the production figure for 1965, which is thus the *base*

47

year and serves as the standard of comparison. If instead we divide the four production figures by 1317, the figure for 1967, we obtain the production indices with 1967 as the base year; these are given in the last row of the table. For example, production in 1966 was 94.8% of what it became in 1967.

An index number series gives a clear picture of trend. The theory and computation of an index number are ordinarily more complicated than are those for the production index above, because an index number ordinarily represents the total combined effect of changes in a number of varying quantities. The best-known index is the U.S. Bureau of Labor Statistics Consumer Price Index, or CPI, usually called the cost-of-living index. The CPI is a statistical measure of changes in prices of goods and services bought by urban wage earners and clerical workers. Its importance lies in part in the fact that union contracts often contain cost-of-living escalation clauses.

TABLE 3.3. Simple Aggregate Price Index

Item		1960 price p_{0i}	1965 price p_{1i}	1970 price p_{2i}
1. Milk (dollars/qt)		$0.26	$0.27	$0.31
2. Steak (dollars/lb)		1.05	1.08	1.17
3. Butter (dollars/lb)		0.75	0.76	0.85
4. Pepper (dollars/lb)		2.50	2.10	2.20
	Total	$4.56	$4.21	$4.53
Price index computed by formulas (3.28)		100.0	92.3	99.3

The prices of some 400 items go into the CPI. To make clear its structure, we shall construct a simple illustrative example involving the four items whose prices are listed in Table 3.3. We take 1960 as the base year, and the problem is to construct a sensible index for 1965 compared with 1960 and for 1970 compared with 1960. The first procedure that comes to mind is simply to add the prices for a year and divide by the total 4.56 for 1960, which gives the indices

$$100 \times \frac{4.56}{4.56} = 100.0 \qquad 100 \times \frac{4.21}{4.56} = 92.3 \qquad 100 \times \frac{4.53}{4.56} = 99.3$$

In other words, if p_{0i}, p_{1i}, and p_{2i} represent the respective prices of item i ($i = 1, 2, 3, 4$) for each of the three years, we compute

$$100 \times \frac{\Sigma_i\, p_{0i}}{\Sigma_i\, p_{0i}} = 100 \qquad 100 \times \frac{\Sigma_i\, p_{1i}}{\Sigma_i\, p_{0i}} \qquad 100 \times \frac{\Sigma_i\, p_{2i}}{\Sigma_i\, p_{0i}} \qquad \textbf{(3.28)}$$

But the indices 92.3 for 1965 and 99.3 for 1970 make it appear that prices have dropped below the 1960 level. A glance at the table shows that although the prices of milk, steak, and butter have risen considerably, this increase is more than offset in our computation by the decrease in the price of pepper, which costs a lot per pound. Since pepper is surely a negligible item in the average budget, we should get a clearer idea of food costs if we throw it out, which leads to new totals and indices:

	1960	*1965*	*1970*
Total (pepper omitted)	$2.06	$2.11	$2.33
Price index	100.0	102.4	113.1

Now the indices reflect an increase in prices. Pepper played a disproportionate role. But perhaps one of the other items plays in a less obvious way a disproportionate role, too.

TABLE 3.4. Price Index With Base-year Quantity Weights (The Laspeyres Index Number)

Item	*1960 quantity* q_{0i}	*1960 cost* $p_{0i}q_{0i}$	*1965 cost* $p_{1i}q_{0i}$	*1970 cost* $p_{2i}q_{0i}$
1. Milk	728 qt	$189.28	$196.56	$225.68
2. Steak	312 lb	327.60	336.96	365.08
3. Butter	55 lb	41.25	41.80	46.75
4. Pepper	0.3 lb	0.75	0.63	0.66
	Total	$558.88	$575.95	$638.17
Price index computed by equation (3.29)		100.0	103.0	114.2

This shows that the prices must somehow be weighted according to their importance. The problem of units also suggests that prices should be weighted. The milk price is given in dollars per quart, but why not use gallons instead? Why is a quart rather than a gallon comparable to a pound, the unit for the other three items? If the milk cost is expressed in dollars per gallon, it becomes four times what it was and exerts proportionally greater influence in the computation given by the formulas (3.28).

Suppose the typical family of four in 1960 purchased the four items in the amounts shown in Table 3.4. The four food items, together with the quantities in which they were purchased, is called a "market basket." It leads to a reasonable and widely used index. For item i, the 1960 price was p_{0i} and the 1960 quantity was q_{0i}; hence, $p_{0i}q_{0i}$ was the total spent on item i in the base year. For example, 728 quarts of milk at $0.26 per quart (Table 3.3) comes to 0.26×728, or $189.28, for the year's expenditure on milk. The remaining figures in the 1960 cost column of Table 3.4 are computed the same way; their sum, $558.88, is the total spent on the market basket in 1960.

Now in 1965 the price for item i was p_{1i}; if the quantity were still q_{0i} as in the base year, the total spent on item i in 1965 would be $p_{1i}q_{0i}$. Thus, 728 quarts of milk at \$.027 per quart comes to \$196.56. The rest of the 1965 column is computed the same way; its sum, \$575.95, is what the 1960 market basket would cost in 1965.

In point of fact, buying patterns change. Nonetheless, we use the 1960 quantities q_{0i} in 1965 also—we hold the market basket constant. If I switch from beer to champagne, my increased expenses are not to be entirely attributed to inflation or the diminished purchasing power of the dollar. To measure that, we must imagine that living standards are constant. The total array of foods which in 1960 cost \$558.88 in 1965 cost \$575.95, and the increase reflects a genuine increase in cost, not an increase in standard of living (which may have taken place also). The ratio 575.95/558.88, or 1.030, an index of 103.0, measures the increase relative to the base year; in 1965 prices were up 3.0% over their 1960 level. The index for 1970 being 114.2, prices then were up 14.2% over their 1960 level.

Notice that pepper now plays a negligible role, as it should. The 1965 pepper expenditure was down 12 cents, but this hardly affects the total picture.

The actual CPI is computed as in our example, although it involves not four food items, but around 400 items concerning food, transportation, medical costs, and so on. The general description of a price index is this: Let the index i refer to the item; i ranges from 1 to 4 in our example and from 1 to about 400 for the real CPI. Let the index n refer to the time period; n ranges over 0, 1, and 2 in our example, but any number of times can be considered and the period could be a month, say, rather than five years. The price of item i in period n is p_{ni} and the quantity is q_{ni}. The amount spent on item i in the base period is $p_{0i}q_{0i}$, for a grand total of $\sum p_{0i}q_{0i}$. If in period n the quantities were q_{0i}, as in the base period, the total for item i would be $p_{ni}q_{0i}$ and the grand total expended would be $\sum p_{ni}q_{0i}$. The index

$$I_{n:0} = 100 \times \frac{\sum_i p_{ni}q_{0i}}{\sum_i p_{0i}q_{0i}} \tag{3.29}$$

measures the change in cost for a fixed buying pattern. This is called the *Laspeyres index number*.

The Laspeyres index has the algebraically equivalent form

$$I_{n:0} = 100 \times \frac{\sum_i p_{0i}q_{0i}(p_{ni}/p_{0i})}{\sum_i p_{0i}q_{0i}}$$

In other words, $I_{n:0}$ is 100 times the weighted sum (see equation (3.6), page 28) of the price ratios p_{ni}/p_{0i} for the various items, the weights being the amounts $p_{0i}q_{0i}$ spent in the base period.

The *Paasche index number* is defined by:

$$P_{n:0} = 100 \times \frac{\sum_i p_{ni}q_{ni}}{\sum_i p_{0i}q_{ni}} = 100 \times \frac{\sum_i p_{0i}q_{ni}(p_{ni}/p_{0i})}{\sum_i p_{0i}q_{ni}}$$

The Laspeyres index measures the relative costs of maintaining base-period standards in the base period and in period n; the Paasche index measures the relative costs of maintaining period-n standards in the base period and in period n. The Laspeyres index is the more convenient to use on a continuing basis, because the weights remain fixed. The CPI is a modified Laspeyres index computed monthly, with the weights revised from time to time to account for changes in buying patterns.

Hosts of indices in some form related to formula (3.29) are computed to measure changes in regional and national retail and wholesale prices, industrial and agricultural production, and so on. The rationale for each is the same as that for the CPI.

PROBLEMS

1. Write out the following summations as sums of the terms involved.

a. $\displaystyle\sum_{i=1}^{5} X_i^3 f_i.$
b. $\displaystyle\sum_{i=1}^{4} a^i Y_i.$
c. $\displaystyle\sum_{i=2}^{5} Y_i^{i+1}(-1)^{i+1}.$

d. $\displaystyle\sum_{i=3}^{9} (Y_i - a^i).$
e. $\displaystyle\sum_{i=1}^{3} Y_i^2 - 3.$
f. $\displaystyle\sum_{i=4}^{7} X_i/Y_i.$

2. Express the following in summation notation.
a. $X_1 Y_1 + X_2 Y_2 + X_3 Y_3 + X_4 Y_4.$
b. $Y_1^2 f_1 + Y_2^2 f_2 + Y_3^2 f_3 + Y_4^2 f_4.$
c. $(Y_1 + Y_2 + Y_3)^2.$
d. $X_1 + X_2 + X_3 - Y_1 - Y_2 - Y_3.$
e. $Y_1 - Y_2^2 + Y_3^3 - Y_4^4 + Y_5^5 - Y_6^6.$

f. $Y - \dfrac{Y^2}{2} + \dfrac{Y^3}{3} - \dfrac{Y^4}{4} + \dfrac{Y^5}{5}.$

3. Given that

$$
\begin{array}{lll}
X_1 = 2 & X_4 = 2 & X_7 = 6 \\
X_2 = 3 & X_5 = 3 & X_8 = 4 \\
X_3 = 4 & X_6 = 5 & X_9 = 7
\end{array}
$$

find:

a. $\displaystyle\sum_{i=1}^{9} X_i.$
b. $\displaystyle\sum_{i=1}^{9} X_i^2.$
c. $\left(\displaystyle\sum_{i=1}^{9} X_i\right)^2.$

d. $\displaystyle\sum_{i=4}^{9} X_i.$
e. $\displaystyle\sum_{i=2}^{5} (X_i - 3)^2.$
f. $\displaystyle\sum_{i=1}^{9} (X_i - 4).$

g. $\displaystyle\sum_{i=1}^{9} X_i - 4.$
h. $\displaystyle\sum_{i=6}^{9} iX_i.$

4. Show that

a. $\displaystyle\sum_{i=1}^{n} (Y_i - c)^2 = \sum_{i=1}^{n} Y_i^2 - 2c \sum_{i=1}^{n} Y_i + nc^2.$

b. $\displaystyle\sum_{i=1}^{n} (Y_i - \bar{Y})^2 = \sum_{i=1}^{n} Y_i^2 - n\bar{Y}^2,$ where $\bar{Y} = \dfrac{1}{n}\sum_{i=1}^{n} Y_i.$

c. $\displaystyle\sum_{i=1}^{n} (Y_i - \bar{Y}) = 0,$ where $\bar{Y} = \dfrac{1}{n}\sum_{i=1}^{n} Y_i.$

5. Show that

a. $\displaystyle\sum_{i=1}^{n} Y_i^2$ is not necessarily equal to $\left(\displaystyle\sum_{i=1}^{n} Y_i\right)^2.$

b. $\displaystyle\sum_{i=1}^{n} X_i Y_i$ is not necessarily equal to $\left(\displaystyle\sum_{i=1}^{n} X_i\right)\left(\displaystyle\sum_{i=1}^{n} Y_i\right).$

6. Given that $\quad X_1 = 6 \qquad X_2 = 5 \qquad X_3 = 1 \qquad X_4 = 4$
$\qquad\qquad\qquad Y_1 = 7 \qquad Y_2 = 4 \qquad Y_3 = 3 \qquad Y_4 = 6$

find:

a. $\displaystyle\sum_{i=1}^{4} X_i Y_i.$

b. $\left(\displaystyle\sum_{i=1}^{4} X_i\right)\left(\displaystyle\sum_{i=1}^{4} Y_i\right).$

c. $\displaystyle\sum_{i=1}^{4} (X_i - Y_i).$

d. $\displaystyle\sum_{i=1}^{4} (X_i - 4)(Y_i - 5).$

e. $\displaystyle\sum_{i=1}^{4} X_i Y_i - \dfrac{1}{4}\left(\displaystyle\sum_{i=1}^{4} X_i\right)\left(\displaystyle\sum_{i=1}^{4} Y_i\right).$

f. $\displaystyle\sum_{i=1}^{4} X_i^2 Y_i.$

7. For each of the following sets of numbers find:
a. The mean. b. The median.
c. The mode or modes. d. The range.
e. The variance. f. The standard deviation.

(i) 2, 5, 9, 11, 13.
(ii) 1, 3, 3, 5, 6, 6.
(iii) 4, 10, 2, 8, 4, 14, 10, 12, 8.
(iv) 3, 6, 2, 5, 3, 8, 6, 7, 5.
(v) −4, 2, −6, 0, −4, 6, 2, 4, 0.
(vi) 13, 19, 11, 17, 13, 23, 19, 21, 17.
(vii) 16, 2, 22, 8, 6, 20, 24, 14.
(viii) −1, 2, −2, 1, −1, 4, 2, 3, 1.

8. For the following yields of corn (grams) obtained from each of thirty hills, find:
a. The mean. b. The median.
c. The range. d. The variance.
e. The standard deviation.

982	1205	258	927	620	1023
395	1406	1012	762	840	960
1056	793	713	736	1582	895
1384	862	1152	1230	1261	624
862	1650	368	358	956	1425

9. For the following empirical spring constants of ten wood beams find:
   a. The mean.
   b. The variance.
   c. The range.
   d. The standard deviation.

.0105	.0193	.0152	.0229	.0244
.0190	.0208	.0279	.0253	.0276

10. The difference in transconductance between the two triodes was measured on each of forty dual-triode electron tubes. The data are given below in micromhos. Find the mean, variance, and standard deviation.

70	480	−50	−100	10
0	190	−150	220	−240
310	−330	440	30	90
−340	360	−180	210	−80
50	−270	−40	−30	20
−40	60	200	−230	−450
−20	−400	80	90	110
−90	−20	60	130	−200

11. The following is the distribution for the number of defective items found in 404 lots of manufactured items. Find the mean, median, mode, variance, and standard deviation of the number defective per lot.

Number of defective items	Number of lots
0	53
1	110
2	82
3	58
4	35
5	20
6	18
7	12
8	9
9	3
10	1
11	2
12	1

12. For the estimated numbers of females in the labor force (1972) as given in problem 12 of Chapter 2 find:
    a. The mean age.
    b. The median age.
    c. The variance.
    d. The standard deviation.

13. Find the mean and median.

Class	Relative frequency
20 but less than 40	.12
40 " " " 60	.28
60 " " " 80	.36
80 " " " 100	.24

14. For each of the following sets of data find:
a. The mean and median without grouping the data.
b. The variance and standard deviation without grouping.
c. The mean, median, and mode after grouping the data.
d. The variance and standard deviation after grouping.

 (i) The forty-eight gains in weight of problem 4 of Chapter 2.
 (ii) The contents of the eighty soil samples of problem 10 of Chapter 2.
 (iii) The differences in cutoff voltages of the forty-eight electron tubes of problem 13 of Chapter 2.
 (iv) The ninety-six determinations of problem 14 of Chapter 2.

15. Three sets of data had means of 15, 20, and 24 based on 30, 35, and 50 observations, respectively. What is the mean if these three sets are combined?

16. Given the following percentages of defective items in eight samples, find the percentage of defective items when the samples are combined into one large sample.

Sample size	Percent defective
50	6.0
20	5.0
35	20.0
150	0.0
100	1.0
75	4.0
40	2.5
200	0.5

17. If the mean for X is equal to 6 and the variance of X is equal to 10, what are the mean and variance of U, where
 a. $U = X + 5$?   **b.** $U = 3X$?   **c.** $U = 3X + 5$?

18. If X has a mean equal to 200 and a standard deviation equal to 10, what are the mean and standard deviation of U, where
 a. $U = X + 20$?   **b.** $U = 4X$?   **c.** $U = 4X + 20$?

19. If $U = 5X + 20$, $\bar{U} = 100$, and $s_U^2 = 40$, what are the mean and variance of X?

20. If $U = 100X - 250$, $\bar{U} = 5$, and $s_U^2 = 400$, find the mean, variance, and standard deviation of X.

21. For each of the following sets of numbers use a linear transformation to find the mean, variance, and standard deviation.
 a. 97, 106, 94, 103, 97, 112, 106, 109, 103.

b. 532, 535, 531, 534, 532, 537, 535, 536, 534.

c. 6876, 6878, 6881, 6880, 6881, 6878.

d. 4.32×10^{-6}, 4.35×10^{-6}, 4.39×10^{-6}, 4.41×10^{-6}, 4.43×10^{-6}.

22. Given the following frequency distribution, use a change of scale to find the mean, variance, and standard deviation.

Class	Frequency
33–37	10
38–42	10
43–47	51
48–52	30

23. Given the following frequency distribution, use á change of scale to find the mean, variance, and standard deviation.

Class	Frequency
16–21	15
22–27	16
28–33	5
34–39	5

24. In an investigation of electronic equipment reliability, a record of the time between equipment malfunctions was kept for nearly two years. Forty pieces of equipment were involved and gave rise to 850 observations on times between malfunctions.

a. Find the median and the mode.

b. Using a change of scale, find the mean, variance, and standard deviation.

Time between malfunctions (*hours*)	Number of observations
$0 \leq X < 100$	20
$100 \leq X < 200$	43
$200 \leq X < 300$	60
$300 \leq X < 400$	75
$400 \leq X < 500$	95
$500 \leq X < 600$	138
$600 \leq X < 700$	240
$700 \leq X < 800$	97
$800 \leq X < 900$	62
$900 \leq X < 1000$	20
Total	850

25. Given the following set of ten measurements of a physical constant, use a linear transformation to find the mean, variance, and standard deviation. Give these measures on both the U scale and the X scale.

2.481×10^{-6}	2.475×10^{-6}
2.478×10^{-6}	2.477×10^{-6}
2.481×10^{-6}	2.480×10^{-6}
2.483×10^{-6}	2.488×10^{-6}
2.485×10^{-6}	2.491×10^{-6}

26. For these retail sales volumes

1968	66,978 millions of dollars
1969	65,810 ” ” ”
1970	68,352 ” ” ”
1971	63,409 ” ” ”

find the sales indices (a) with 1968 as the base year, and (b) with 1969 as the base year.

27. In 1963 the CPI was 106.7; in 1964 it was 108.1. If a worker in 1963 earned $2.54 per hour and in 1964 earned $2.60 per hour, did his buying power increase or decrease?

28. For the following data find the price index with 1965 as the base year.

	1965		1970	
Item	Unit price	Units sold	Unit price	Units sold
A	$ 1.50	350	$ 2.00	600
B	15.00	100	12.50	125
C	7.50	200	10.00	300

29. For the following data, find the retail price index for each year, using 1960 as the base.

Retail Price of Selected Electrical Appliances

	Average unit price			Thousands of units sold
Appliance	1960	1965	1970	1960
A	$295	$305	$308	3650
B	334	340	345	1025
C	250	261	270	1300
D	43	44	47	1275

REFERENCES

3.1 COXTON, FREDERICK E., DUDLEY J. COWDEN, and BEN W. BOLCH. *Practical Business Statistics*, 4th edition. Prentice-Hall, Englewood Cliffs, 1969. Chapters 3 and 4.

3.2 HOEL, PAUL G. *Elementary Statistics*, 3rd edition. John Wiley & Sons, New York, 1971. Chapter 2.

3.3 HUFF, DARRELL. *How to Lie with Statistics*. Norton, New York, 1965. Chapters 5 and 6.

3.4 SNEDECOR, GEORGE W., and WILLIAM G. COCHRAN. *Statistical Methods*, 6th edition. Iowa State University Press, Ames, 1967. Chapter 5.

CHAPTER

4

Elementary Probability

4.1 INTRODUCTION

As pointed out in Chapter 1, the mathematical theory of probability provides a basis for evaluating the reliability of the conclusions we reach and the inferences we make when we apply statistical techniques to the collection, analysis, and interpretation of quantitative data. Since probability plays so important a role in the theory and applications of statistics, we need an acquaintance with the elements of the subject.

In this chapter we consider briefly some of the basic ideas of probability theory. These ideas are illustrated here mostly by examples involving cards and dice. The connections with statistics follow in the remaining chapters.

The most difficult and technical considerations come in Sections 4.4 and 4.5, each of which closes with a summary of the main facts and concepts needed subsequently. The intent of the summaries is to make it possible to use probability ideas after a limited study of them.

4.2 THE MEANING OF PROBABILITY

Imagine a *random experiment* or *observation*; that is, imagine an operation which can result in any one of a definite set of possible outcomes, but which is governed by chance so that the actual outcome cannot be predicted with complete certainty. We have in mind the drawing of a card from a well-shuffled deck, for example, or the rolling of a pair of dice.

If the random experiment consists in drawing a card from an ordinary deck, there are fifty-two possible outcomes—the fifty-two cards in the deck. This set of all possible outcomes or results of the experiment is called the *sample space.** Since thirteen of the fifty-two possible outcomes in the sample space are spades, almost everyone will say that, if the deck was shuffled well, the chance of drawing a spade (the chance that the outcome is a spade) is 13/52. Similarly, almost everyone will say that the chance of drawing an ace is 4/52. This is because the outcomes in the sample space are regarded as being equally likely.

For rolling a pair of dice, the sample space—the set of all thirty-six possible outcomes or results—is exhibited in full in Table 4.1. Here 3–1 denotes the result that the one die shows three dots and the other shows one dot. The outcome 1–3—where the order is reversed—is also listed in the table, because the two dice are to be distinguished from one another. (Perhaps it is best to think of a red die and a green one, even though the dice of an actual pair are made so similar that telling them apart would require very close examination.) If the dice are fair ones (not loaded), everyone expects the thirty-six outcomes to be equally likely. Since the total number of dots showing is 4 for three of the outcomes (namely, for 3–1, 2–2, and 1–3), we expect the probability of rolling a 4 to be 3/36. Since the total showing is 7 for six of the outcomes (namely, for 6–1, 5–2, 4–3, 3–4, 2–5, and 1–6), we expect the probability of rolling a 7 to be 6/36.

TABLE 4.1   Sample Space for Rolling Dice

1–1	1–2	1–3	1–4	1–5	1–6
2–1	2–2	2–3	2–4	2–5	2–6
3–1	3–2	3–3	3–4	3–5	3–6
4–1	4–2	4–3	4–4	4–5	4–6
5–1	5–2	5–3	5–4	5–5	5–6
6–1	6–2	6–3	6–4	6–5	6–6

These examples are instances of the classical conception of probability: There is a definite, finite set of possible outcomes or results or cases (the fifty-two cards, or the thirty-six combinations for the rolled pair of dice); this is the sample space. Within the sample space, there is some smaller set of outcomes (the spades, or the aces, or the dice-pairs that total 4, or the ones that total 7) whose probability we seek; this smaller set is called an *event*, or, variously, a *subset*, and the outcomes or cases making up the event are called the *favorable cases*. The probability of the event is taken to be the ratio of the number of outcomes in the event to the number of outcomes in the

---

*Sometimes it is called the *outcome space*; this is a better term, but *sample space* has become standard.

sample space, that is, the ratio of the number of favorable cases to the total number of cases:

$$\text{Probability} = \frac{\text{Number of favorable cases}}{\text{Total number of cases}} \qquad (4.1)$$

In drawing a card, the probability of the event "ace"—the chance of getting an ace—is 4/52, because the event "ace" comprises four of the fifty-two cases. In rolling dice, the probability of the event "seven"—the chance of rolling a total of 7—is 6/36, because the event "seven" comprises six of the thirty-six cases.

Now formula (4.1) is to be viewed as a *way of computing* a probability and *not* as a *definition* of the probability. Whether or not the computation leads to a result that corresponds with reality depends on the circumstances. The chance of drawing an ace is 4/52 if the deck was well shuffled—but not if a sleight-of-hand expert did the shuffling. The chance of rolling a 7 is 6/36 if the dice are fair—but not if they are loaded. The chance a coin will land heads may be 1/2 (there is one favorable case, heads, out of two possible cases, heads and tails)—but this is not necessarily true if the coin is bent (there even exist coins with heads on both sides). The formula (4.1) leads to the right answer if all the possible cases (all the outcomes in the sample space) are equally likely.

The words "right answer" in this last sentence presuppose the existence of a right answer. Most of us feel that, if a particular pair of dice is rolled, even a loaded pair, there does exist a certain definite probability that the result will be a seven, even though we may be entirely ignorant of the actual numerical value of that probability. This parallels the fact that most of us feel that the sixth moon of Jupiter has a certain definite mass in tons, even though we may be entirely ignorant of the actual numerical value of that mass. And most of us feel that, if a particular coin (perhaps bent or unbalanced in some way) is tossed, there does exist a certain definite probability (perhaps unknown to us) that it will land heads upward.

To give a satisfactory definition of this probability is very difficult, just as it is very difficult to define with precision concepts such as mass and force in physics. As in the case of physical concepts, the fruitful procedure is to worry less about how to define probability and more about how to measure it. To get an idea of the probability that a particular coin will show heads, the obvious procedure is to toss the coin a number of times and check the fraction of times it comes up heads. If 500 tosses yield 255 heads (and 245 tails), the probability of heads must be something like 255/500, or .51.

Experience shows that if a coin is tossed repeatedly, the relative frequency (fraction) of heads tends to stabilize at a definite value, which we take to be the probability of heads. Figure 4.1 shows the results of such an experiment. The horizontal scale in this figure represents the number of tosses of the coin, and the height of the curve over any given point on the horizontal scale represents the relative frequency of heads up to that

59

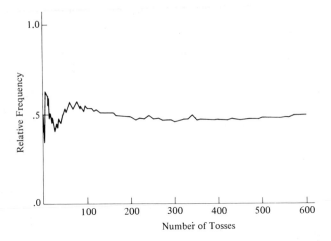

FIGURE 4.1.   *Relative frequencies of heads for a balanced coin*

point. In this experiment the coin was tossed 600 times in all. Since the relative frequency seems to be settling down at a value near 1/2, we can say that the coin is well balanced.

Figure 4.2 shows the same effect for a different coin. Here, the relative frequency is converging to something like .3, and the coin is seen to be unbalanced.

It is typical for events to show this kind of stability. Suppose we repeat many times an experiment, like rolling dice, and keep track of an event, like obtaining a seven. Suppose that at each repetition of the experiment we compute the relative frequency with which the event has occurred

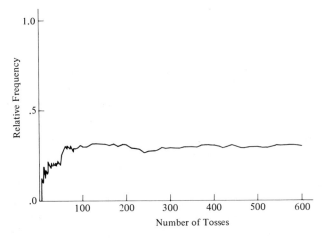

FIGURE 4.2.   *Relative frequencies of heads for an unbalanced coin*

in the sequence of trials up to that point. Quite generally, this relative frequency will stabilize at some limit which we take to be the probability of the event. This probability is to be regarded as a natural characteristic of the experiment and the event itself, just as the mass of the sixth moon of Jupiter is a physical characteristic of that body. (A different conception of probability is briefly treated in Section 4.8.)

Now just as physical quantities like force and mass can often be computed mathematically, so can this probability. The formula applicable in many cases of interest to us is formula (4.1): The probability as given by formula (4.1) will often agree closely with the value at which the relative frequency of the event would stabilize in a long sequence of empirical trials of the experiment. This kind of agreement will exist when the outcomes of the experiment (the elements of the sample space) are equally likely or nearly so, and this in turn will be the case in the presence of an appropriate symmetry: when the coin is balanced, for example, or the dice are uniformly made or the deck is shuffled so that no card has precedence over any other.

Computing a probability by formula (4.1) requires computing the numerator (the number of favorable cases) and the denominator (the total number of cases). In the examples considered thus far, these values were found by actually counting out the cases. This cannot usually be done, however, and we need some mathematical techniques for computing these numbers. Often they can be found by what we shall call the *addition principle* and the *multiplication principle*.

4.3   THE ADDITION PRINCIPLE

If someone has counted the eleven girls in a class and the thirteen boys, he knows without counting the whole class over again that there are twenty-four students altogether. This is because of the addition principle. Two sets of objects are said to be *disjoint* or *mutually exclusive* if there is no object that belongs to both sets.

THE ADDITION PRINCIPLE: *If one set contains a objects and a second set contains b objects, and if the two sets are disjoint, then the two sets taken together contain a + b objects.*

For example, there are 4 aces in an ordinary deck of cards and 4 kings, so there are 4 + 4, or 8, cards that are *either* ace *or* king. It is essential that the two sets in question be disjoint, however: There are 4 aces and 13 spades, but the number of cards that are either ace or spade is not 17 (4 + 13), because the set of aces and the set of spades share a card—the ace of spades. (The correct answer is one less than 17, since exactly one card has been double counted.)

The addition principle extends in an obvious way to three or more sets: Since there are 4 jacks, 4 queens, and 4 kings, there are 4 + 4 + 4, or 12, face cards all told.

We tend to use the addition principle correctly and without reflection. The multiplication principle is more complicated.

4.4 THE MULTIPLICATION PRINCIPLE

A good starting point in coming to a definition of the multiplication principle is the old rhyme,

> As I was going to St. Ives,
> I met a man with seven wives.
> Every wife had seven sacks,
> Every sack had seven cats,
> Every cat had seven kits.
> Kits, cats, sacks, and wives,
> How many were going to St. Ives?

The usual answer is "one": Only "I" was going to St. Ives. According to *The Oxford Dictionary of Nursery Rhymes*, one eighteenth-century authority gives the answer "none," interpreting the question as, "How many Wives, Sacs, Cats, and Kittens went to St. Ives?"

Let us compute the answer that is unacceptable in the nursery: the number of kits, cats, sacks, and wives coming *from* St. Ives. The number of wives is 7. Since each wife has 7 sacks, the total number of sacks is 7 · 7, or 49. Since each of these 49 sacks has 7 cats, the total number of cats is 49 · 7, or 343. Since each of these 343 cats has 7 kits, the total number of kits is 343 · 7, or 2401.

Wives	7
Sacks	49
Cats	343
Kits	2401
Total	2800

The number of kits, cats, sacks, and wives coming from St. Ives is, therefore, 2800. If we include the man as well, the total increases to 2801, a number less round than 2800 and hence more arresting.

The successive multiplications here are instances of what we shall call the multiplication principle—it could well be called the St. Ives principle. It can be used to solve a surprising variety of counting problems.

THE MULTIPLICATION PRINCIPLE: *We are to make two choices, a first-stage choice followed by a second-stage choice:*

(i) *The number of alternatives open to us at the first stage is a.*

(ii) *No matter which alternative we select at the first stage, the number of alternatives open to us at the second stage is b.*

In these circumstances, the number of two-stage alternatives, or simply results, is $a \cdot b$.

EXAMPLE 1

If at the first stage we are to choose one of the St. Ives man's wives, the number of alternatives, a, is 7. If at the second stage we are to choose one of the sacks in the keeping of this wife, then, no matter which wife we happen to have selected at the first stage, the number of alternatives now open to us, b, is 7. According to the principle, the number of sacks is $a \cdot b = 7 \cdot 7$, or 49.

Starting afresh with another task, that of choosing a sack at the first stage and then choosing one of this sack's cats at the second stage, we know from the first computation that the alternatives at the (new) first stage number 49: a is 49. And no matter which sack we select at the first stage, the number of second-stage alternatives b—the number of cats belonging in this sack—is 7. According to the principle, the number of cats is $a \cdot b = 49 \cdot 7$, or 343.

Finally, for choosing a cat and then one of the cat's kits, a is 343 (the number of cats, just derived) and b is 7 (the number of kits per cat), so that there are $a \cdot b = 343 \cdot 7$, or 2401, kits in all. (To show that there are 2800 kits, cats, sacks, and wives *in toto*, we need only apply the addition principle.)

EXAMPLE 2

A host has in his larder beef, trout, and capon. In his wine closet are Burgundy, Claret, Zinfandel, Chablis, Moselle, Riesling, and Champagne. Taste or fashion dictates that with the beef he may serve only Burgundy, Claret, Zinfandel, or Champagne and that with trout or capon he may serve only Chablis, Moselle, Riesling, or Champagne. How many meat–wine combinations (count trout and capon as meat) are available to him?

He first chooses the meat and then the wine. The alternatives at the first stage are beef, trout, and capon; their number, a, is 3. The set of alternatives open to the host at the second stage varies with the selection made at the first stage; the following table lists them.

Choice of meat	*Alternatives at the second stage*			
Beef	Burgundy	Claret	Zinfandel	Champagne
Trout	Chablis	Moselle	Riesling	Champagne
Capon	Chablis	Moselle	Riesling	Champagne

Although the *set* of possible wines varies with the meat chosen, their *number* does not; this number, b, is 4.

By the multiplication principle, the number of meat–wine pairs is $a \cdot b = 3 \cdot 4$, or 12. An alteration of the above table leads to an exhibit of all twelve pairs. With each second-stage alternative, we simply couple the meat dish at the left of its row:

Beef–Burgundy Beef–Claret   Beef–Zinfandel Beef–Champagne
Trout–Chablis Trout–Moselle   Trout–Riesling Trout–Champagne
Capon–Chablis Capon–Moselle   Capon–Riesling Capon–Champagne

This exhibit shows why the multiplication principle works: We all know that to find the number of pebbles in a rectangular array we can multiply the number of rows by the number of pebbles in each row; there is no need to count the pebbles individually.

For a case in which the multiplication principle does not apply, suppose the host finds Riesling and Champagne unacceptable with trout but will serve Chablis with beef:

Choice of meat	*Alternatives at the second stage*				
Beef	Burgundy	Claret	Zinfandel	Champagne	Chablis
Trout	Chablis	Moselle			
Capon	Chablis	Moselle	Riesling	Champagne	

Again a is 3, but the number of alternatives at the second stage is no longer constant. There *is* no b, and the multiplication principle does not apply. While the number of meat–wine pairs can be *counted up* (there are eleven of them), it cannot be *computed*. Of course the answer for the original set of rules, too, could be arrived at by counting up all the possibilities, but the idea is to derive the answer from a general principle that works even when an exhaustive count would be prohibitive.

EXAMPLE 3

A woman in New York may take a plane to Chicago or to St. Louis. From Chicago she may fly on to Seattle, to San Francisco, or to Los Angeles. From St. Louis she may fly on to San Francisco, to Los Angeles, or to San Diego. To how many West Coast cities may she go?

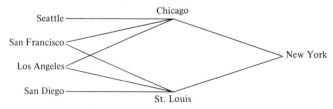

At the first stage she has $a = 2$ alternatives, and at the second she has $b = 3$. By the multiplication principle, the number of destinations is $a \cdot b = 2 \cdot 3$, or 6. This answer is wrong—the number of destinations is only 4. The trouble is not far to seek: The various first-stage selections coupled with the various second-stage selections do not lead to distinct results (destinations).

Thus, to the statement of the multiplication principle we must add this proviso:

Each first-stage alternative coupled with each one of its second-stage successors leads to a distinct result.

This condition holds in Example 1 and in the first part of Example 2, and it also holds in Example 3 if we ask not for the number of *destinations*, but for the number of *routes* to the West Coast.

The multiplication principle also works if we have a sequence of three choices instead of just two. Here the first-stage and second-stage choices are to satisfy conditions (i) and (ii) above, and the third-stage choice must satisfy the analogous condition:

(iii) *No matter which alternative we select at the first stage, and no matter which alternative we select at the second stage, the number of alternatives open to us at the third stage is c.*

In these circumstances, the number of different results (we assume again that different choices lead to different results) is $a \cdot b \cdot c$.

EXAMPLE 4

Suppose the woman in Example 3 may from Seattle or San Francisco fly on to Tokyo or to Hong Kong and may from Los Angeles or San Diego fly on to Hong Kong or to Manila. How many routes to the Orient are available to her? As before, a equals 2 and b equals 3. No matter which West Coast city she is in after the first two legs of the journey (and, in the cases of San Francisco and Los Angeles, no matter whether she got there via Chicago or via St. Louis), she has $c = 2$ third-stage alternatives open to her. By the three-stage multiplication principle, there are $a \cdot b \cdot c = 2 \cdot 3 \cdot 2$, or 12, routes all told.

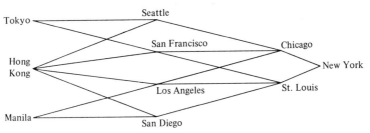

The multiplication principle extends in the obvious way to a sequence of four or more choices.

EXAMPLE 5

In the original St. Ives problem, we found the number of cats by using the two-stage multiplication principle twice. A single application of the three-stage principle with a, b, and c equal to 7 yields the correct answer $a \cdot b \cdot c = 7 \cdot 7 \cdot 7$, or 343, in one operation. And the four-stage principle shows at one stroke that there are $7 \cdot 7 \cdot 7 \cdot 7$, or 2401, kits.

EXAMPLE 6

We turn now to a problem nearer to statistics, though it may not seem so at first, that of counting the number of three-letter "words" that can be made up from the five letters A, B, C, D, and E. The "word" need not make sense (CDA is counted as well as BAD), a letter may be repeated (BDB is counted), and order matters (AED and ADE are counted as different).

We must successively choose letters to fill the three blanks __ __ __. Since in each blank we can use any of the five letters, the three-stage multiplication principle with a, b, and c equal to 5 shows that there are $5 \cdot 5 \cdot 5$, or 125, possible words.

In general, from an "alphabet" of a letters one can make up a^n "words" of length n.

EXAMPLE 7

This time we count the three-letter words that can be made from A, B, C, D, and E when repeats are prohibited (BDB is this time not counted). As before, we must successively choose letters to fill the three blanks __ __ __. Since we may fill the first blank with any of the five letters, the number of first-stage alternatives is $a = 5$:

$$
\begin{array}{l}
\text{A} \ \underline{\quad} \ \underline{\quad} \\
\text{B} \ \underline{\quad} \ \underline{\quad} \\
\text{C} \ \underline{\quad} \ \underline{\quad} \\
\text{D} \ \underline{\quad} \ \underline{\quad} \\
\text{E} \ \underline{\quad} \ \underline{\quad}
\end{array}
$$

If the first blank was filled with A, the second may be filled with B, C, D, or E; if the first blank was filled with B, the second may be filled with A, C, D, or E; and so on.

First-stage choice		Second-stage alternatives			
A__ __		AB__	AC__	AD__	AE__
B__ __		BA__	BC__	BD__	BE__
	etc.				

Thus *b* equals 4 this time; there are always four alternatives at the second stage. Finally, the third blank may be filled with any of the three unused letters; for example, from BC___ we may go on to BCA, BCD, or BCE. So *c* equals 3, and the total number of "words" is thus $a \cdot b \cdot c = 5 \cdot 4 \cdot 3$, or 60. Here is a systematic table of them.

TABLE 4.2. The Sixty Permutations of A, B, C, D, E, Taken Three at a Time

ABC	ABD	ABE	ACB	ACD	ACE	ADB	ADC	ADE	AEB	AEC	AED
BAC	BAD	BAE	BCA	BCD	BCE	BDA	BDC	BDE	BEA	BEC	BED
CAB	CAD	CAE	CBA	CBD	CBE	CDA	CDB	CDE	CEA	CEB	CED
DAB	DAC	DAE	DBA	DBC	DBE	DCA	DCB	DCE	DEA	DEB	DEC
EAB	EAC	EAD	EBA	EBC	EBD	ECA	ECB	ECD	EDA	EDB	EDC

Thus the five letters A, B, C, D, and E can be lined up in $5 \cdot 4 \cdot 3$ ways when taken three at a time. A lining up is called a *permutation*; if we denote the number of permutations of five distinct things taken three at a time by $_5P_3$, what we have shown is that $_5P_3 = 5 \cdot 4 \cdot 3$.

Answers like this are most conveniently expressed by using the *factorial notation*. The symbol *n*!, read *n-factorial*,* is the product of the integers from 1 to *n*:

$$n! = n(n - 1)(n - 2) \cdots 3 \cdot 2 \cdot 1 \tag{4.2}$$

For example,

$$5! = 5 \cdot 4 \cdot 3 \cdot 2 \cdot 1$$

From the definition it is clear that, if *r* is a number between 1 and *n*, then

$$n! = n(n - 1)! = n(n - 1)(n - 2)!$$
$$= n(n - 1)(n - 2) \cdots (n - r + 1)(n - r)! \tag{4.3}$$

and, if we divide both sides of equation (4.3) by $(n - r)!$, we see that

$$\frac{n!}{(n - r)!} = n(n - 1)(n - 2) \cdots (n - r + 1) \tag{4.4}$$

Thus

$$_5P_3 = 5 \cdot 4 \cdot 3 = \frac{5!}{2!}$$

It is convenient to define 0! as 1:

$$0! = 1 \tag{4.5}$$

We can now state the general rule governing permutations or linings up.

---

*This use of the exclamation mark is to be distinguished from the ordinary one. The gravity of mathematical discourse makes confusion unlikely.

PERMUTATIONS: *The number of permutations of n distinct things taken r at a time* $(1 \leq r \leq n)$ *is:*

$$_nP_r = n(n-1)\cdots(n-r+2)(n-r+1) = \frac{n!}{(n-r)!} \qquad (4.6)$$

The argument for the relation (4.6) is the same as for the special case in Example 7. We can think of the *n* objects as distinct symbols or letters with which we are to fill in a succession of *r* blanks, using a different letter in each blank. The set of alternatives at any stage is the set of letters as yet unused, and the numbers of these for the first stage, second stage, third stage, etc., are n, $n-1$, $n-2$, etc. According to the multiplication principle, the number of permutations is the product of these numbers, of which there are *r* (one for each blank). This gives relation (4.6).

If *r* equals *n*, we have a special case. *All n objects are to be lined up,* and we suppress the phrase "taken *n* at a time."

PERMUTATIONS: *The number of permutations of n distinct things is*

$$_nP_n = n! = n(n-1)\cdots 3 \cdot 2 \cdot 1 \qquad (4.7)$$

The number of permutations of the digits 0 through 9 is

$$10! = 3,628,800$$

and the number of permutations of the twenty-six letters of the alphabet is

$$26! = 403,291,461,126,605,635,584,000,000$$

In these examples the answer certainly must be arrived at not by counting out all the cases, but by the application of general principles.

EXAMPLE 8

In Example 7 we found the number of three-letter words that can be made from A, B, C, D, and E with repetitions disallowed. We now ask how many *subsets* of size three can be made up. We still distinguish ABC from ABD, since they contain different letters, but we do not distinguish ABC from ACB, since they differ merely in the order in which the letters come. The letters in the *set* are not lined up at all; we could write them in a jumble:

$$\begin{matrix} & & & & & & & C \\ & C & & & & B & & \\ A & & B & & \text{or} & & & \\ & & & & & & A & \end{matrix}$$

The usual mathematical notation is {A, B, C}.

Such a set, such an unordered selection of three of the five letters, we call a *combination*; it is to be sharply distinguished from a permutation. We want the number of such combinations, the number of combinations of five distinct objects taken three at a time, a number we denote $_5C_3$.

Let us temporarily write x in place of $_5C_3$, the number whose value we seek. Consider this two-stage procedure: At the first stage we choose one of the x combinations. At the second stage we take the three letters chosen (the combination) and line them up in some order. For example, we may choose the combination {A, C, D} and then line up the letters in it in the order DAC. The number of alternatives at the first stage is x. The number of alternatives at the second stage is simply the number of permutations of the three letters chosen at the first stage, and this number we know to be 3!. So $a = x$ and $b = 3!$. But after making these two choices, what we arrive at is some permutation of three of the five letters. Each permutation can arise in exactly one way from such a pair of choices. By the two-stage multiplication principle, the product $a \cdot b$, or $x \cdot 3!$, is the same as the number $_5P_3$ of permutations of five things taken three at a time. Since we already know that $_5P_3$ is equal to 5!/2!, we can conclude that $x \cdot 3!$ equals 5!/2!, and solving for x gives our answer

$$_5C_3 = x = \frac{5!}{3! \, 2!}$$

which comes out to 10.

Here is a list of the ten combinations.

{A, B, C}	{A, D, E}
{A, B, D}	{B, C, D}
{A, B, E}	{B, C, E}
{A, C, D}	{B, D, E}
{A, C, E}	{C, D, E}

Writing out each of these ten combinations in each of its six permuted forms gives the set of sixty permutations in Table 4.2 (perhaps in a different order).

In the argument in the preceding example, we may replace 5 by a general number n, and we may replace 3 by r, where we suppose $r \le n$. From a set of n distinct objects we are to choose a subset of size r. (A set contained in a larger one is called a *subset*.) The number of ways this can be done is called the number of combinations of n things taken r at a time and is denoted by $_nC_r$ or, more commonly, by $\binom{n}{r}$. We can choose a combination in $_nC_r$ ways, and then permute the r objects in the combination in $r!$ ways, arriving at one of the $_nP_r$ permutations. By the two-stage multiplication principle: $_nC_r \times r! = {_nP_r} = n!/(n - r)!$; and we can divide through by $r!$ to get our answer:

COMBINATIONS: *The number of combinations of n distinct objects taken r at a time (the number of subsets of size r) is*

$$\binom{n}{r} = {}_nC_r = \frac{n!}{r!\,(n-r)!} \tag{4.8}$$

Notice that for the case where r is equal to n, the number of combinations is $n!/n!\,0!$, which is 1 by the convention (4.5). This is the right answer: There is but one subset that contains all the n objects. The answer is also 1 for the case where r is equal to 0. This is itself just a convention: There exists exactly one set with nothing in it.

It is sometimes hard to tell whether a problem requires combinations or whether it requires permutations. To answer this question, we ask ourselves whether or not the arrangement or order of the objects is relevant. If we need to take order into account, permutations are called for; if order is irrelevant, combinations are called for. Consider the following two examples:

EXAMPLE 9

Problem: If there are seven horses in a race, in how many ways can three from among them finish first, second, and third?
Analysis: Here we are definitely interested in the order in which the horses cross the finish line; if we have bet on a particular horse to win, we collect nothing if he places or shows. Since order is important, we use permutations; the answer is

$$_7P_3 = \frac{7!}{4!} = 210$$

EXAMPLE 10

Problem: How many five-card hands can be dealt from a 52-card deck?
Analysis: Here order is irrelevant; no player will object if he must rearrange the cards he has been dealt to get a straight flush. Since order is irrelevant, we use combinations; the answer is

$$\binom{52}{5} = \frac{52!}{5!\,47!} = 2{,}598{,}960$$

We have in this section looked into the beginnings of *combinatorial analysis*, the branch of mathematics that deals with counting.

SUMMARY. In addition to the multiplication principle itself, the main combinatorial facts used subsequently are these:

1. The number of permutations or orderings of n distinct things is:

$$_nP_n = n! = n(n-1)\cdots 3\cdot 2\cdot 1$$

2. The number of permutations of n distinct things taken r at a time is:

$$_nP_r = n(n-1)\cdots(n-r+1) = \frac{n!}{(n-r)!}$$

3. The number of combinations of n distinct things taken r at a time (that is, the number of subsets of size r) is:

$$\binom{n}{r} = \frac{n!}{r! \, (n-r)!}$$

4.5 COMPUTING PROBABILITIES

Recall that our probabilities are to be computed by the formula

$$\text{Probability} = \frac{\text{Number of favorable cases}}{\text{Total number of cases}} \qquad (4.9)$$

We can often compute the numerator and denominator by the rules of the last section.

E X A M P L E 1

Problem: What is the probability of a flush (all cards of the same suit) in a five-card hand from an ordinary deck?

Analysis: In the last example of Section 4.4, we saw that the total number of hands (order disregarded) is $\binom{52}{5}$. With thorough shuffling and fair dealing, these outcomes are equally likely; the denominator for formula (4.9) is $\binom{52}{5}$. Now a flush in spades is a combination of some five of the thirteen spades, and so there are $\binom{13}{5}$, or 1287, of them; similarly, there are $\binom{13}{5}$ flushes in each of the other suits. Hence the numerator is $4 \cdot \binom{13}{5}$, and so the probability of a flush is

$$\frac{4 \cdot \binom{13}{5}}{\binom{52}{5}} = \frac{5{,}148}{2{,}598{,}960} = .00198$$

E X A M P L E 2

In Example 7 of the last section, we saw that there are 60 three-letter words (without repeated letters) that can be made of the letters A, B, C, D, and E. If one of the sixty words is chosen at random (all sixty outcomes in the sample space assumed equally likely), what is the probability it starts with either A or E? The denominator is $5 \cdot 4 \cdot 3$. The number of words starting with A is the number of ways of filling the blanks in A __ __ with letters from B, C, D, and E, and this number is $4 \cdot 3$, or 12. This is also the number of words starting with E, so the numerator is $2 \cdot 4 \cdot 3$, and the probability is:

$$\frac{2 \cdot 4 \cdot 3}{5 \cdot 4 \cdot 3} = \frac{2}{5}$$

Many examples can be carried through in the same way; see the problems at the end of the chapter.

We turn now to some general properties of probabilities. We illustrate each one by examples in which the outcomes are equally likely, so that probabilities are given by formula (4.9). Each property also holds, however, even if the outcomes are not equally likely. We denote events by A and B, etc., and we denote their probabilities by $P(A)$ and $P(B)$, etc.

The first property is obvious:

$$0 \le P(A) \le 1 \tag{4.10}$$

The second property has to do with adding probabilities. An example will make clear its meaning and truth.

EXAMPLE 3

For rolling a pair of dice, the sample space consists of the thirty-six outcomes in Table 4.1. If A is the event that the total is 4, we know that A contains three outcomes:

$$A = \{3\text{–}1, 2\text{–}2, 1\text{–}3\}$$

The event B that the total is 3 contains two outcomes:

$$B = \{2\text{–}1, 1\text{–}2\}$$

Now "A or B" stands for the event that the total is *either* 4 *or* 3:

$$A \text{ or } B = \{3\text{–}1, 2\text{–}2, 1\text{–}3, 2\text{–}1, 1\text{–}2\}$$

By three applications of formula (4.9) for computing probabilities,

$$P(A \text{ or } B) = \tfrac{5}{36} = \tfrac{3}{36} + \tfrac{2}{36} = P(A) + P(B)$$

The general rule is this:

ADDITION OF PROBABILITIES: *If the events A and B are disjoint, then*

$$P(A \text{ or } B) = P(A) + P(B) \tag{4.11}$$

As explained in Section 4.3, A and B are disjoint, or mutually exclusive, if, as in the preceding example, they have no outcomes in common. In this case, the number of outcomes in "*A* or *B*" is the number in *A* plus the number in *B*, so equation (4.11) is a consequence of formula (4.9).

Events *A* and *B* may be said to be disjoint *if they cannot both happen at the same time*. Understanding this point will remove a common source of confusion. The sample space represents *a single trial* of the experiment, and *A* and *B* are disjoint if they cannot both occur in one trial. The dice in Example 3 cannot total both 4 and 3 at once; but none of this prevents them from totaling 4 on one trial and 3 on another trial.

Equation (4.11) can be extended to three events: If *A*, *B*, and *C* are disjoint in the sense that no two can happen at once, then

$$P(A \text{ or } B \text{ or } C) = P(A) + P(B) + P(C) \qquad \textbf{(4.12)}$$

The same thing holds for four or more events.

EXAMPLE 4

The events that dice total 2, 4, 6, 8, 10, and 12 have respective probabilities (refer to Table 4.1) 1/36, 3/36, 5/36, 5/36, 3/36, and 1/36. The probability that some one of these events occurs—the probability, that is, of an even-valued total—is therefore

$$\tfrac{1}{36} + \tfrac{3}{36} + \tfrac{5}{36} + \tfrac{5}{36} + \tfrac{3}{36} + \tfrac{1}{36} = \tfrac{18}{36} = \tfrac{1}{2}$$

If *A* and *B* are not disjoint, equation (4.11) does not apply, but there is another formula that does:

$$P(A \text{ or } B) = P(A) + P(B) - P(A \text{ and } B) \qquad \textbf{(4.13)}$$

EXAMPLE 5

A card is drawn at random from an ordinary deck; *A* is the event of drawing a spade, and *B* is the event of drawing a face card. Here "*A* or *B*" is the event of drawing a card that is a spade *or* a face card *or* both—the word "or" does not exclude the possibility that *both* events occur. Of course, "*A* and *B*" is the event that the card is both a spade *and* a face card. The number of outcomes in *A* is 13, the number in *B* is 12, and the number in "*A* and *B*" is 3. By equation (4.13), the probability of drawing a spade or a face card is:

$$P(A \text{ or } B) = \tfrac{13}{52} + \tfrac{12}{52} - \tfrac{3}{52} = \tfrac{22}{52}$$

Each of the two terms $P(A)$ and $P(B)$ on the right in equation (4.13) accounts for the outcomes that are both in *A* and in *B*; subtracting $P(A \text{ and } B)$ compensates for this double counting. Formula (4.13) contains as a special case the rule (4.11) that applies when *A* and *B* are disjoint events: If *A* and *B* are disjoint, then the event "*A* and *B*" cannot happen and hence has probability 0.

The *complement* of an event *A* is the "opposite" event, the one that happens exactly when *A* does not. We denote it by $\bar{A}$.

COMPLEMENTARY EVENTS: *The probabilities of A and $\bar{A}$ are related by:*

$$P(\bar{A}) = 1 - P(A) \qquad (4.14)$$

EXAMPLE 6

In drawing a five-card hand from an ordinary deck, what is the probability that there is more than one suit represented in the hand? It would be complicated to solve this directly, but the probability of the complementary event (a flush) was found in Example 1. The probability we seek is:

$$1 - \frac{5,148}{2,598,960} = .99802$$

CONDITIONAL PROBABILITY: *The conditional probability of an event B given another event A, which we denote P(B | A), is defined by*

$$P(B \mid A) = \frac{P(A \text{ and } B)}{P(A)} \qquad (4.15)$$

This equation represents a definition, not a fact. (If $P(A) = 0$, the conditional probability is not defined.) An example will show that the definition is a sensible one.

EXAMPLE 7

In rolling dice, let A be the event that the total does not exceed 5. The triangle in the accompanying table encloses the outcomes in A, and the probability of A, $P(A)$, is 10/36. Let B be the event that the total is even. We saw in Example 4 that $P(B)$ is 1/2; the eighteen outcomes favoring B are shown in boldface in the table. If you know that A has occurred— that the total is at most 5—what should you take as the probability of B?

1–1	1–2	**1–3**	1–4	**1–5**	1–6
2–1	**2–2**	2–3	**2–4**	2–5	**2–6**
3–1	3–2	**3–3**	3–4	**3–5**	3–6
4–1	**4–2**	4–3	**4–4**	4–5	**4–6**
5–1	5–2	**5–3**	5–4	**5–5**	5–6
6–1	**6–2**	6–3	**6–4**	6–5	**6–6**

For those of us untrained in Zen, it is difficult to imagine rolling the dice and noticing that the total is 5 or less without also noticing whether or not the total is even. An effective way to understand the notion of conditional probability is to imagine that a friend or referee has rolled the dice out of your sight and that he reports to you that the total does not exceed 5 but does not tell what the total is. If you are in receipt of this partial information about the outcome, what should be your probability for B?

To know that the total is 5 or less is to know that the outcome is one of those in the triangle. As far as you are concerned, after the referee's report, the sample space consists of the ten outcomes in the triangle. Four of these, the ones in boldface, correspond to an even total, so your *conditional probability*, given the partial information, should be 4/10.

This is exactly the answer that formula (4.15) gives. The event "*A* and *B*," the event that the total is both even and at most 5, consists of the four boldface outcomes within the triangle, so $P(A \text{ and } B)$ is equal to 4/36; since we know already that $P(A)$ equals 10/36, formula (4.15) gives

$$P(B \mid A) = \frac{\frac{4}{36}}{\frac{10}{36}} = \frac{4}{10}$$

which does check.

The ordinary probability $P(B)$ we sometimes call an *unconditional probability* to distinguish it from the conditional probability $P(B \mid A)$.

EXAMPLE 8

For the experiment of drawing a single card from a deck of fifty-two cards, let A be the event "spade," and let B be the event "face card." Then "*A* and *B*" consists of the three face cards that are also spades, so $P(A \text{ and } B)$ is 3/52. Since $P(A)$ equals 13/52, the definition (4.15) gives

$$P(B \mid A) = \frac{\frac{3}{52}}{\frac{13}{52}} = \frac{3}{13}$$

As before, this makes sense: If the referee draws a card and tells you it is a spade, as far as you are concerned the thirteen spades are now the possible outcomes and, of these, three favor the event "face card." Notice that, since $P(B) = 12/52 = P(B \mid A)$, the conditional and unconditional probabilities happen to coincide in this case, which is not true in Example 7.

Multiplying both sides of formula (4.15) by $P(A)$ gives

$$P(A \text{ and } B) = P(A) \cdot P(B \mid A) \qquad \textbf{(4.16)}$$

Sometimes, as in Examples 7 and 8, we know $P(A)$ and $P(A \text{ and } B)$ in advance and we put them into formula (4.15) to find the value of $P(B \mid A)$. On the other hand, sometimes it is $P(A)$ and $P(B \mid A)$ that we know in advance, and we put them into formula (4.16) to find the value of $P(A \text{ and } B)$:

EXAMPLE 9

The experiment consists of drawing two cards in succession from a deck, without replacing the card after the first drawing. Let A be the event that the first card drawn is a spade, and let B be the event that the second card drawn is a diamond. The chance of A, $P(A)$, is 13/52. Now, if the first card drawn is indeed a spade, then, just prior to the second drawing, the deck consists of fifty-one cards, of which thirteen are diamonds, so the conditional chance of a diamond on the second draw must be 13/51: $P(B \mid A) = 13/51$. By formula (4.16), the chance of a spade and then a diamond is

$$P(A \text{ and } B) = \tfrac{13}{52} \cdot \tfrac{13}{51}$$

(In this example, interpreting $P(B \mid A)$ requires no conceptual referee; there is no difficulty in imagining yourself between the two draws, knowing the first card was a spade but ignorant of what the second will be.)

INDEPENDENCE: *The events A and B are called independent if*

$$P(A \text{ and } B) = P(A) \cdot P(B) \tag{4.17}$$

To see the idea behind this definition, divide both sides of formula (4.17) by $P(A)$, which gives $P(A \text{ and } B)/P(A) = P(B)$. By definition (4.15), then, formula (4.17) is the same thing as

$$P(B \mid A) = P(B) \tag{4.18}$$

In other words, A and B are independent if the conditional probability of B, given A, is the same as the unconditional probability of B.

In Example 7, $P(B)$ is 1/2 and $P(B \mid A)$ is 4/10, so A and B are not independent. Imagine that an adversary offers to bet you on the outcome of the experiment. Each of you is to stake $1.00; if the dice show an even total—if B occurs—you win, and if the total is odd, your adversary wins. Since $P(B)$ equals 1/2, the bet is fair. But suppose the referee rolls the dice and announces to you and your adversary that the total was at most 5—that A occurred—and *then* your adversary offers to bet you as before. Since now your chance of winning is only $P(B \mid A) = 4/10$, you will reject the offer. (The bet is now fair if he puts up $1.50 to your $1.00.) The point is that A influences B: The occurrence of A decreases the chance that B will occur. In this sense, A and B fail to be independent.

In Example 8, on the other hand, $P(B \mid A)$ is equal to $P(B)$. The probability of a face card is 3/13, and this is so even if you know the card is a spade. In this example, A does not influence B: The occurrence of A leaves unaltered the chance that B occurs. In this sense, A and B are independent.

Equation (4.17) defines independence. Dividing it through by $P(A)$ gives equation (4.18), which is perhaps more intuitive as a condition for independence. We could just as well divide through by $P(B)$, which leads from equation (4.17) to:

$$P(A \mid B) = P(A) \tag{4.19}$$

Here the occurrence of B neither increases nor decreases the probability of A. Thus, equations (4.17), (4.18), and (4.19) all mean the same thing, and A has no influence on B if and only if B has no influence on A.

Sometimes we can compute $P(A)$, $P(B)$, and $P(A \text{ and } B)$, and then use equation (4.17) to find out whether or not A and B are independent. Sometimes, on the other hand, we *assume* that A and B are independent; if we know the values of $P(A)$ and $P(B)$, we can then use equation (4.17) to find the value of $P(A \text{ and } B)$. The following example presents such a case:

E X A M P L E 10

The experiment consists in rolling a pair of dice twice in succession. Let A be the event that the first roll gives a 7, and let B be the event that the second roll gives a 4. From our previous computations, we know that A should have probability 6/36 and B should have probability 3/36. Now it is reasonable to assume that A and B are independent: The occurrence of a 7 on the first roll should not, since the dice have no memory, alter the chance of a 4 on the second roll. Under this assumption, the chance of a 7 followed by a 4 is:

$$P(A \text{ and } B) = \tfrac{6}{36} \cdot \tfrac{3}{36} = \tfrac{1}{72}$$

Recall that A and B are disjoint if they cannot both occur *on the same trial* of an experiment. In the same way, independence of A and B refers to a single trial, because A and B themselves refer to the same trial. Thus, A and B are independent if knowing that A has occurred on a particular trial of an experiment does not affect your probability for B on that trial—nothing is said about the occurrence of B on some other trial of the experiment. This is so even in Example 10. There, the experiment consists of rolling the dice *twice in a row*. In other words, the experiment consists in carrying through twice the more modest experiment of rolling the dice once.

The concepts *independent* and *disjoint* (or mutually exclusive) are often confused with one another. They are in fact diametrically opposed: Disjoint events cannot, in general, be independent. Suppose that A and B are disjoint—that they cannot both happen. If you know that A has occurred, then you automatically know that B cannot have occurred, so $P(B \mid A)$ must be 0. Thus $P(B \mid A)$ and $P(B)$ must differ (except in the uninteresting case where $P(B)$ equals 0, in which B is impossible in the first place), so A and B are not independent.

SUMMARY. The main probability facts and definitions needed in what follows are these:

1. If A and B are disjoint (if they cannot both occur at the same time), then
$$P(A \text{ or } B) = P(A) + P(B)$$

2. If A and $\bar{A}$ are complementary (if the occurrence of $\bar{A}$ is the same thing as the nonoccurrence of A), then
$$P(\bar{A}) = 1 - P(A)$$

77

3. The conditional probability of B, given A, is defined by:

$$P(B \mid A) = \frac{P(A \text{ and } B)}{P(A)}$$

This equation is sometimes used in the form

$$P(A \text{ and } B) = P(A) \cdot P(B \mid A)$$

4. The events A and B are defined to be independent (to reflect the idea that the occurrence of one does not alter the probability of occurrence of the other) if

$$P(A \text{ and } B) = P(A) \cdot P(B)$$

This condition is the same as

$$P(B \mid A) = P(B)$$

and the same as

$$P(A \mid B) = P(A)$$

4.6 REPEATED INDEPENDENT TRIALS

Consider repeating an experiment several times over and keeping track of the occurrence of some event.

EXAMPLE 1

To fix ideas, let the experiment be the rolling of a pair of dice, suppose the experiment is repeated three times in a row, and let the event be the rolling of a 7. Let us denote the occurrence of a 7 by S, for success, and the occurrence of anything else by F, for failure ("success" and "failure," like "favorable case," are merely conventional terms). Table 4.3 lists all the possible histories for the three rolls (ignore the list of probabilities for the moment). The sequence SSS indicates that all three rolls resulted in success (a 7); SSF indicates that the first two rolls

TABLE 4.3.   Independent
Trials with $p = 1/6$

Sequence	Probability
SSS	$(\frac{1}{6})^3$
SSF	$(\frac{1}{6})^2(\frac{5}{6})$
SFS	$(\frac{1}{6})^2(\frac{5}{6})$
SFF	$(\frac{1}{6})(\frac{5}{6})^2$
FSS	$(\frac{1}{6})^2(\frac{5}{6})$
FSF	$(\frac{1}{6})(\frac{5}{6})^2$
FFS	$(\frac{1}{6})(\frac{5}{6})^2$
FFF	$(\frac{5}{6})^3$

resulted in success and the last roll resulted in failure (non-seven); and so on. (Example 6 of Section 4.4 shows why there must be 2^3, or 8, possibilities.)

If the dice are rolled three times in a row, what is the probability of obtaining some particular sequence, say SSF? If the dice are fair, the probability of success on any one trial is 1/6, and so the probability of failure is 5/6. We should further assume, as in Example 10 of the last section, that there is independence from trial to trial—that the result on one trial can in no way influence the result on a different trial. Hence, we multiply probabilities. The chance of getting S on the first roll and then S on the second roll and then F on the third roll is (1/6)(1/6)(5/6). The other probabilities in Table 4.3 are computed the same way.

What is the probability of getting exactly one success (and two failures)? There are three ways this can happen: SFF, FSF, and FFS. Each of these sequences has probability $(1/6)(5/6)^2$—one factor of 1/6 for the one S and two factors of 5/6 for the two F's. Thus the probability of getting exactly one success is:

$$P(1) = 3(\tfrac{1}{6})(\tfrac{5}{6})^2 = \tfrac{75}{216} = .347$$

The sequences containing two S's and one F are SSF, SFS, and FSS, and each has probability $(1/6)^2(5/6)$, so the probability of getting exactly two successes is:

$$P(2) = 3(\tfrac{1}{6})^2(\tfrac{5}{6}) = \tfrac{15}{216} = .069$$

Finally, the chance of three successes is the chance of SSS, namely,

$$P(3) = (\tfrac{1}{6})^3 = \tfrac{1}{216} = .005$$

and the chance of no successes is the chance of FFF, namely,

$$P(0) = (\tfrac{5}{6})^3 = \tfrac{125}{216} = .579$$

The general principle is this: We repeat an experiment, singling out an event we call success.

We let p = the probability of success on a single trial,
$1 - p$ = the probability of failure on a single trial,
n = the number of trials,
r = the number of successes.

The probability that S occurs exactly r times (so that F must occur $n - r$ times) is:

$$P(r) = \binom{n}{r} p^r (1 - p)^{n-r} \qquad (4.20)$$

For this formula to be valid, *the trials must be independent.*

The rule (4.20) may be derived in this way: One sequence which contains r S's and $n - r$ F's is:

$$\underbrace{SS \ldots S}_{\substack{r \\ \text{times}}} \underbrace{FF \ldots F}_{\substack{n - r \\ \text{times}}}$$

By independence, the probability of r S's in a row followed by $n - r$ F's in a row is $p^r(1 - p)^{n-r}$. We do not insist that the r S's occur in the *first* r trials; we insist only that exactly r of the trials produce S and $n - r$ of them produce F. The probability of each such sequence is $p^r(1 - p)^{n-r}$. Equation (4.20) follows because the number of such sequences is $\binom{n}{r}$. That is, from the n trials there are $\binom{n}{r}$ ways to choose a combination of r trials in which to put S's, and the other trials must take F's. The arguments in Example 1 are special cases of this one, and the computations agree.

According to the binomial theorem of algebra,

$$(x + y)^n = \sum_{r=0}^{n} \binom{n}{r} x^r y^{n-r}$$

The quantities $\binom{n}{r}$ are therefore called *binomial coefficients*, and the probabilities in equation (4.20) are called *binomial probabilities*. To save the trouble of calculating, the binomial coefficients are tabulated in Table 1 of the Appendix for values of n and r from 0 to 15. Since the binomial coefficients are symmetric, that is, since $\binom{n}{r}$ is equal to $\binom{n}{n-r}$, not all the coefficients are given for the larger values of n.

EXAMPLE 2

For a final example of binomial probabilities, consider the experiment of drawing a card from a deck. Let success S be the drawing of a spade, and suppose we repeat the experiment five times. In this case, $p = 1/4$, $1 - p = 3/4$, and $n = 5$. It is to be emphasized that after each trial the card is returned to the deck (and the deck shuffled). Otherwise there would not be independence from trial to trial; clearly, the occurrence of S on the first trial would decrease the chance of S on the second trial because, on the second drawing, one spade would be missing. The probability that exactly three spades are drawn is:

$$P(3) = \binom{5}{3}\left(\frac{1}{4}\right)^3\left(\frac{3}{4}\right)^2 = \frac{90}{1024} = .0879$$

4.7   FINITE SAMPLING

E X A M P L E   1

As in Example 2 of the preceding section, let us suppose we draw five cards from a deck, but this time suppose we do not after each trial replace the card drawn, and suppose that we ignore the order in which the cards come. In other words, we choose at random a combination of five of the fifty-two cards.

We ask for the probability of getting exactly three spades. Now the sample space consists of the $\binom{52}{5}$ combinations of the fifty-two cards taken five at a time. How many favorable cases are there? To make up a hand containing exactly three spades, we must make two choices. First, we must choose three of the thirteen spades, and there are $\binom{13}{3}$ ways to do this; then we must choose two of the thirty-nine non-spades, and there are $\binom{39}{2}$ ways to do this. By the multiplication principle there are thus $\binom{13}{3} \cdot \binom{39}{2}$ favorable cases, so the probability of exactly three spades is:

$$\frac{\binom{13}{3} \cdot \binom{39}{2}}{\binom{52}{5}} = \frac{2,717}{33,320} = .0815$$

Notice that this probability differs from the probability .0879 at the end of the last section. This difference reflects the effect of not returning the card to the deck after each trial.

The general rule is this: Suppose we have $a + b$ distinct objects divided into two classes, say a class of red ones and a class of blue ones. Suppose there are a red objects and b blue objects. And suppose we take at random a sample of size n and ask for the probability that exactly r of the objects in it are red.

Thus, we let

$a =$ the number of red objects,
$b =$ the number of blue objects,
$a + b =$ the total number of objects,
$n =$ the number of objects drawn,
$r =$ the number of red objects drawn.

81

The probability of getting exactly r red objects (and $n - r$ blue ones) is:

$$\frac{\binom{a}{r}\binom{b}{n-r}}{\binom{a+b}{n}} \tag{4.21}$$

These quantities have the forbidding name of *hypergeometric probabilities.*

In Example 1, there were thirteen red objects (spades) and thirty-nine blue ones (non-spades), so $a = 13$ and $b = 39$. The reasoning underlying formula (4.21) is the same as in the example: The denominator is the total number of combinations of the $a + b$ objects taken n at a time. Among these combinations, the ones that contain exactly r red objects and $n - r$ blue ones are the ones that result from merging some combination of r of the a red objects with some combination of $n - r$ of the b blue objects, and the numerator is the number of pairs of such mergeable combinations.

The formula (4.21) arises in connection with taking a sample from a small population. If instead of drawing a hand from a deck split into spades and non-spades, we draw a sample from, say, a population of voters split into Republicans and Democrats, the mathematics is the same. However, if the population is very large in comparison with the sample (as in most sampling problems), then the mathematics of the preceding section gives an *approximate* description of sampling probabilities. This is because if one element sampled from a very large population is Republican, say, this hardly affects the chance that another element of the sample is Republican. For this reason we shall find the binomial probabilities more useful than the hypergeometric probabilities.

4.8   SUBJECTIVE PROBABILITY AND BAYES' THEOREM*

The probabilities discussed in this chapter have all been *objective* in the sense that we have taken the probability of an event as being a property of the event itself. Statistics is sometimes placed in the framework of a different conception of probability: *subjective*, or *personal*, probability.

Consider the hypothesis that there is life on Mars; let H denote this hypothesis and let $\bar{H}$ denote the opposite hypothesis that Mars supports no life. Certainly, people have varying degrees of belief in H and say things like, "It is fairly likely that there is life on Mars," or "It is improbable that there is life on Mars." Adherents of the theory of subjective probability hold that it is possible to assign to H a probability $P(H)$ which represents numerically the degree of a person's belief in H. The idea is that $P(H)$ will be different for different people, because they have different information about H and

---

*The contents of this section are in no way required for an understanding of the material in subsequent chapters.

assess it in different ways. This conception of probability does not require ideas of repeated trials and the stabilizing of relative frequencies.

Setting aside the problem of how subjective probabilities are to be arrived at in the first place, we shall consider here only a method for modifying them in the light of new information or data.

Suppose a space probe equipped with a life-detection device has landed on Mars and has sent back a message saying that there is indeed life there. This new item of information, call it D (for $data$), will certainly alter our attitude towards the hypothesis H. But we know the device is not fool-proof. Suppose we know from previous laboratory tests of the life-detection device that, if there *is* life on Mars, then the chance, which we denote $P(D \mid H)$, that the device will report the existence of life has numerical value .8. Suppose we also know that, if there is *no* life on Mars, then the chance, which we denote $P(D \mid \overline{H})$, that the device will report the existence of life has numerical value .1.

We are to compute a *new* probability $P(H \mid D)$ of the hypothesis, given the data from the probe. Since personal probabilities are assumed to obey the rules of Section 4.5, we can proceed as follows. By the definition (4.15) of conditional probability, $P(H \mid D)$ is equal to $P(H \text{ and } D)/P(D)$, and applying the formula (4.16) to the numerator gives

$$P(H \mid D) = \frac{P(H) \cdot P(D \mid H)}{P(D)}$$

Now D happens if "H and D" happens *or* if "$\overline{H}$ and D" happens. Therefore, by the addition rule (4.11), $P(D) = P(H \text{ and } D) + P(\overline{H} \text{ and } D)$. Using formula (4.16) on each of these last two terms now gives $P(D) = P(H) \cdot P(D \mid H) + P(\overline{H}) \cdot P(D \mid \overline{H})$. Substituting this for the denominator in the formula displayed above gives the answer:

$$P(H \mid D) = \frac{P(H) \cdot P(D \mid H)}{P(H) \cdot P(D \mid H) + P(\overline{H}) \cdot P(D \mid \overline{H})} \qquad \textbf{(4.22)}$$

This formula constitutes *Bayes' rule* or *Bayes' theorem*. Given the *prior* probability $P(H)$ (and $P(\overline{H}) = 1 - P(H)$) and the respective probabilities $P(D \mid H)$ and $P(D \mid \overline{H})$ of observing the data D if H and $\overline{H}$ hold, we can use Bayes' rule to compute the *posterior* probability $P(H \mid D)$, the personal probability for H after the information in D has been taken into account. In our example, $P(D \mid H) = .8$ and $P(D \mid \overline{H}) = .1$, so the formula gives

$$P(H \mid D) = \frac{.8 \times P(H)}{.8 \times P(H) + .1 \times P(\overline{H})}$$

If $P(H) = .3$, say, so that $P(\overline{H}) = .7$, then $P(H \mid D) = .77$. Notice that $P(H \mid D)$ exceeds $P(H)$ here; observing D increases our personal probability of H because H "explains" D better than $\overline{H}$ does $(P(D \mid H) > P(D \mid \overline{H}))$.

It is sometimes said that Bayes' theorem is controversial. This is only partly true. If probabilities satisfy the rules of Section 4.5, then they must also satisfy equation (4.22). The question that is disputed is whether probabilities can sensibly be assigned to hypotheses in the first place. In this book we shall formulate all statistical concepts within the framework of the objective, or frequency, theory of probability. For a treatment of statistics from the subjective point of view, see reference 4.4.

PROBLEMS

1. List the different possible outcomes when three coins are tossed. How many are there? How many result in two heads? Two or more heads?

2. In Table 4.1, how many outcomes have a total equal to 10? Greater than or equal to 9? Equal to 7 or 11?

3. A coin is tossed and a die is rolled. List the twelve outcomes of this experiment. What is the probability of
   a. Tail and six?
   b. Head and even number?

4. Given three tags numbered 1, 2, and 3, list all possible different arrangements. If they are arranged at random, what is the probability that they are in increasing order? That the number 2 tag is in the middle? That numbers 1 and 2 are next to each other and in increasing order?

5. In a beauty contest with five finalists, in how many ways can a queen, a first runner-up, and a second runner-up be selected?

6. If there are nine starters in a race, in how many different ways can first, second, and third prizes be awarded?

7. Ten tags numbered consecutively from 1 to 10 can in how many ways be arranged so that those numbered 1 and 2 will be adjacent?

8. In how many ways can six people be arranged in a row? In how many ways can they be arranged in a circle if the orientation of the circle is ignored?

9. From the six numbers 1, 2, 3, 4, 5, and 6, how many three-digit numbers can be formed if
   a. A given integer can be used only once?
   b. A given integer can be used any number of times?
   c. The last digit must be even and a given integer may be used only once?

10. How many different license plates are possible if they are to consist of the following, and if not all digits can be 0:
    a. A four-digit number?
    b. A letter followed by a four-digit number?
    c. Two letters followed by a four-digit number?
    d. Two letters and four digits in any order?

11. In how many ways can a committee of three be selected from ten individuals?

12. If, on an examination consisting of twelve questions, a student may omit four, in how many ways can he select the problems he will attempt?

13. How many thirteen-card bridge hands can be dealt from a deck of fifty-two cards?

14. Given twelve areas from which to choose, in how many ways can a student select
    a. A major and minor area?
    b. A major and first and second minors?
    c. A major and two minors if it is not necessary to order the minors?

15. If a group consists of five men and five women, in how many ways can a committee of four be selected if
    a. The committee is to consist of two men and two women?
    b. There are no restrictions on the numbers of men and women on the committee?
    c. There must be at least one man?
    d. There must be at least one of each sex?

16. In how many ways can a group of eight boys and four girls be divided into two groups consisting of four boys and two girls?

17. If five-card hands are dealt from a 52-card deck, how many of them consist of
    a. Two pairs?   b. Full houses?
    c. Straight flushes?   d. Four of a kind?

18. A menu offers a choice of six appetizers, five salads, eight entrees, four kinds of potatoes, seven vegetables, and ten desserts. If a complete meal consists of one of each, in how many ways can one select his dinner?

19. A basic cocktail recipe calls for a jigger of the base (gin, vodka, rum, bourbon, etc.), 1/2 jigger of sour (lemon or lime), and a teaspoon of sweet (sugar, grenadine, cointreau, etc.). If a bar stocks nine bases, two sours, and six sweeteners, how many different cocktails can be mixed? How many rum cocktails can be mixed?

20. An urn contains two white, three black, and five red balls. One ball is selected at random. Find the probability that it is
    a. A red ball.   b. Either black or white.
    c. Not white.

21. A box contains ten red tags numbered from 1 through 10 and ten white tags numbered from 1 through 10. If one tag is selected at random, what is the probability that it is
    a. Red?   b. An even number?
    c. Red and even?   d. Red or even?

22. One card is selected at random from a deck of fifty-two cards. Find the probability that it is
    a. A face card.   b. A spade.
    c. An ace or a king.   d. An ace and a king.
    e. An ace or a face card. f. A heart or a spade or a jack.

23. A and B are independent events: $P(A) = .6$, $P(B) = .8$. What is the probability that both will occur? That neither will occur? That one or the other or both will occur?

24. Two dice are rolled. What is the probability that they show the same number? Different numbers?

25. Poker dice have their six faces labeled with Ace, King, Queen, Jack, Ten, and Nine. If we roll one poker die and select one card at random from a 52-card deck, what is the probability that the uppermost face on the die and the card are the same denomination?

26. Two balls are drawn from an urn containing three white and seven black balls. What is the probability of obtaining two white balls if
   a. The first is replaced before drawing the second?
   b. The first is *not* replaced before drawing the second?

27. In a class of thirty students, ten are girls. Two students are selected at random and without replacement. What is the probability that both are girls?

28. Urn I contains five white and five black balls. Urn II contains seven white and three black. Under which of the following plans is the probability of getting two white balls the greatest?
   a. Draw one ball from each urn.   **b.** Draw two balls from Urn I.
   c. Put all twenty balls in one urn and then draw two.

29. Two cards are selected without replacement from a 52-card deck. Find the probability that
   a. Both are aces.   **b.** Both are of the same suit.
   c. Both are the same denomination.   **d.** They are of different suits.
   e. They are of the same color.

30. Two dice are tossed. What is the probability of two 6's? No 6's? At least one 6?

31. An urn contains two white, three red, and five black balls. A second urn contains one white, six red, and three black balls. One ball is selected at random from each urn. Find the probability that
   a. Both are the same color.   **b.** One is white and one is red.
   c. At least one is red.   **d.** Neither one is black.

32. A coin is tossed twice. What is the probability of two heads? Two heads or two tails?

33. If a fair coin is tossed five times, what is the probability of all heads? All tails? All heads or all tails?

34. If four coins are tossed what is the probability of at least one head and at least one tail?

35. Let A and B be two events such that $P(A) = .3$, $P(B) = .7$, $P(AB) = .1$. Find each of the following:
   a. $P(\bar{A})$ **b.** $P(\bar{B})$
   c. $P(\bar{A} \text{ and } \bar{B})$ **d.** $P(A \text{ and } B)$
   e. $P(A \text{ and } \bar{B})$ **f.** $P(\bar{A} \text{ and } B)$
   g. $P(A \mid B)$ **h.** $P(\bar{B} \mid A)$

36. What is the probability of a bridge hand that consists of the thirteen cards of one suit?

37. What is the probability of a bridge hand that contains no face cards? Consider aces to be face cards.

38. In a bridge game you and your partner hold ten trump between you.
   a. What is the probability that one opponent holds the three missing trump?
   b. You hold the ace and queen. One of the opponents holds the king. Should you finesse or lead the ace; that is, which play has the greater probability of succeeding?

39. A box contains five white tags numbered from 1 to 5, five red tags numbered from 1 to 5, and five green tags numbered from 1 to 5. If two tags are selected at random and without replacement what is the probability that
   a. Both are the same number?

    b. Both are the same color?

    c. They are consecutive numbers but of different colors?

    d. They are consecutive numbers of the same color?

40. With five poker dice (see problem 25), if all five are rolled at the same time what is the probability of

    a. A full house?   **b.** A straight?

    c. One pair?   **d.** Two pair?

    e. Three of a kind?

41. If five-card hands are dealt from a 52-card deck, what is the probability of

    a. One pair?   **b.** Three of a kind?

    c. A straight?   **d.** A flush?

42. A pair of dice are rolled until the first 7 appears. What is the probability that it will occur on the third roll? What is the probability that more than three rolls will be required?

43. If cards are selected one at a time *without replacement* from a 52-card deck, what is the probability that the fourth spade will be obtained on the tenth draw?

44. A spinner for a child's game is arranged so that it may point to any of five numbers with equal probability:

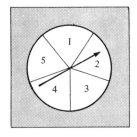

What is the probability of

    a. An even number?

    b. An even number or a number less than 3?

    c. Two 3's in two spins?

    d. One even number and one odd number in two spins?

    e. Four 2's in six spins?

    f. At least one 2 in six spins?

45. Four coins are tossed. What is the probability of

    a. Three heads?   **b.** Two or more heads?

    c. At least one head?

46. Given four independent trials of a random experiment such that the probability of a success on a single trial is 1/3, find the probability of

    a. Three successes.   **b.** No successes.

    c. At least one success.

47. If the probability that any child born is a boy is equal to 1/2 and if sex is independent from child to child, what is the probability that if eight children are born on a given day in a given hospital

    a. All will be boys?   **b.** Two will be boys?

    c. At least one will be a boy?

48. In a triangle taste test, the taster is presented with three samples, two of which are alike, and is asked to pick the odd one by tasting. If a taster has no well-developed sense and can pick the odd one only by chance, what is the probability that in six trials he will make
     a. Five or more correct decisions?   **b.** No correct decisions?
     c. At least one correct decision?

49. A process produces 10% defective items. If we take a sample of three items, what is the probability we will find
     a. No defectives?   **b.** Not more than one defective?

50. A process is considered to be in control if it produces no more than 10% defectives. The process is stopped and checked if a sample of ten contains more than one defective. What is the probability it will be stopped needlessly when it is producing 5% defectives?

51. The World Series terminates when one team wins its fourth game. If the two teams are evenly matched, i.e., if the probability that either team will win any one game is 1/2, what is the probability that the series will terminate at the end of the fourth game? The fifth game? The sixth game? The seventh game?

52. If teams A and B are competing in the World Series and the probability that A wins any one game is .6, find the probability that
     a. A wins in four games.   **b.** B wins in five games.
     c. Six games are required to complete the series.

53. A type of electron tube, A, and its ruggedized version, B, are installed at random in single-tube units. Thirty percent of the tubes are of type B. The probability that type B will fail in the first hundred hours of continuous operation is .1; the probability that type A will fail is .3. If a particular unit fails, what is the probability it had a type A tube installed? A type B? Use Bayes' rule (4.22).

REFERENCES

4.1 FELLER, WILLIAM. *An Introduction to Probability Theory and Its Applications*, 3rd edition, Volume I. John Wiley & Sons, New York, 1968.

4.2 MOSTELLER, FREDERICK, ROBERT E. K. ROURKE, and GEORGE B. THOMAS, JR. *Probability with Statistical Applications*, 2nd edition. Addison-Wesley, Reading, Massachusetts, 1970.

4.3 PARZEN, EMANUEL. *Modern Probability Theory and Its Applications*. John Wiley & Sons, New York, 1960.

4.4 SAVAGE, I. RICHARD. *Statistics: Uncertainty and Behavior*. Houghton Mifflin, Boston, 1968.

5

Populations, Samples, and Distributions

5.1 POPULATIONS

In the broadest meaning of the term, a statistical *population*, or *universe*, is simply a set or collection; the things of which the population is composed are called its *elements*. Sometimes, the population is specified by a complete list of its elements, as when the voting population of a town is explicitly listed on the voting rolls. More commonly, a population is specified by a definition of some kind, or by the singling out of a characteristic common to its elements, as when we speak of the population of 12AX7-type electron tubes produced by a given manufacturer during a given year, the population of patients receiving a certain medical treatment, or the population of infected trees of a species under attack by a particular disease. Such examples extend the original notion of the population of a geographic area.

The populations in the preceding examples are all *finite*. Statistics also involves certain hypothetical *infinite populations*. Consider an experiment to measure a physical quantity, such as the speed of light or the percent copper in a sample of brass. Different executions of the experiment will give different answers, because of the combined effect of small errors that creep in (this being why experiments are customarily carried through a number of times). To analyze the data, the experimenter considers not only the answers he has obtained, but the hypothetical, infinite population of all answers he would obtain if he were to repeat the experiment infinitely often under identical conditions.

The analysis of a manufacturing process often involves an infinite population, the hypothetical population of all the items (all the electron tubes, say) that the process would produce if it were to run indefinitely under constant conditions. Sometimes, random experiments like those in the examples in Chapter 4 are viewed as infinite populations: There is an infinite population of tosses of a coin or rolls of a pair of dice, and to toss the coin or roll the dice is to observe an element of the population.

Often a finite population is so large as to be effectively infinite for the purposes of statistical analysis. An effective way to acquire an initial understanding of what it means for a population to be infinite is to imagine the population to be finite but so very large that removing a number of elements from it has no discernible effect on the composition of the population. That infinite populations are constructs of the human mind does not make them less important in practical affairs.

Ordinarily, a statistical analysis involves only certain aspects of a population—only certain attributes or characteristics of the elements of the population. In a population of voters, we are perhaps concerned only with the voter's party affiliation, and not with his height, blood type, etc. In a population of trees, we may be concerned with height but not age. In a population of electron tubes, we may be concerned only with whether or not the tube is defective according to certain standards.

Since the primary objective of inductive statistics is to make inferences about populations, it is important that the population concerned be carefully specified. To know how the population of property owners in a town feels on some issue is not necessarily to know how the population as a whole feels. And the population appropriate to one method of measuring a physical quantity may be inappropriate to another method.

5.2 SAMPLES

For inquiring into the nature of a population it would be ideal if we could with ease and economy examine each one of its elements, but this is usually out of the question. Sometimes it is impossible because some of the elements are physically inaccessible. In other cases it is uneconomic. Obviously, we will not test every item produced if the test destroys the item. Even when all the elements are available, they may be so numerous that a complete census is not justified; often, for most practical purposes, sufficiently accurate results may be more quickly and inexpensively obtained by examining only a small part of the population. And of course it is in the nature of an infinite population that its elements cannot all be examined.

In most situations, then, we must be content with investigating only a part of the whole population. The part investigated is a *sample*. Samples may be collected or selected in a variety of ways. A *systematic sample* is one selected according to some fixed system—taking every hundredth name from the telephone book, for example, or selecting machined parts from a tray according to some definite pattern. Most statistical techniques presuppose an element of randomness in the sampling, and we shall be concerned almost exclusively with *random samples*.

Consider first a finite population, say of size 50, from which we take a sample, say of size 5. There are $\binom{50}{5}$ such samples, a sample being a subset or combination of size 5 (see Section 4.4). The sample is random if it is selected in such a way that all $\binom{50}{5}$ samples have the same probability of being chosen. (Notice that randomness is really a property of the selection procedure rather than of the particular sample that happens to result.) In general, there are $\binom{N}{n}$ samples of size n in a finite population of size N, and random sampling means choosing one in such a way that all are equally likely to be chosen. Selecting a random sample is a random experiment of the sort discussed in Chapter 4.

Although the concept of a random sample is fairly easy to grasp, there are situations in which it is not clear how to obtain one. If we can list all the elements of a population and number them, we can get a random sample by drawing numbered tags or tickets from a bowl, or we can use a table of random numbers to decide which elements to include in the sample. But if we cannot enumerate the population, these techniques are useless. How, for instance, would we obtain a random sample of oranges from a tree, fish from a river, or trees from a forest? How can a public opinion poller obtain a random sample of people in a city? We shall not go into such questions of sampling technique here (see references 5.1 and 5.3). We assume we have successfully obtained a random sample from the population in which we are interested, and investigate the inferences that can be based on such a sample.

Random sampling as defined above is sometimes called sampling *without replacement*, because an element sampled is not returned to the population before the next element of the sample is drawn. (Compare Example 2 on page 80 with Example 1 on page 81.)

To understand the notion of random sampling from an *infinite* population, consider first a finite population of 100 electron tubes of which 10 are defective and 90 are nondefective. In a random sample of size 1, the chance of getting a defective tube is .1. The chance of getting any one particular tube is .01, but the chance of getting some one of the 10 defective tubes is .1. In a random sample of size 2, the chance that both elements are defective is:

$$\frac{\binom{10}{2}}{\binom{100}{2}} = \frac{10 \cdot \frac{9}{2}}{100 \cdot \frac{99}{2}} = \frac{10}{100} \cdot \frac{9}{99}$$

(This follows by formula (4.21) on page 82 or by a direct analysis.) The factor 10/100 on the right here is .1—which is the chance of a defective in a sample of just 1—and the other factor, 9/99, or .091, is near the same value. The second factor is less than .1 because if one element of the sample is defective then one defective has been "used up," lessening the chance that the other element of the sample is also defective.

Now consider a population of 1000 tubes of which 100 are defective and 900 are nondefective, so that the proportions of defective and non-defective elements are 10% and 90%, just as before. Again we take a sample of size 2. The chance that both are defective is:

$$\frac{\binom{100}{2}}{\binom{1000}{2}} = \frac{100 \cdot \frac{99}{2}}{1000 \cdot \frac{999}{2}} = \frac{100}{1000} \cdot \frac{99}{999}$$

Again the first factor is .1—the proportion of defective tubes, or the chance of a defective in a sample of 1. The other factor, 99/999, or .099, is closer to .1 than 9/99, or .091, was. For the population of 1000, one defective element in the sample affects less than it did for the population of 100 the chance that the other element is also defective. This is to be expected, because one element "uses up" a smaller proportion of the population of 1000 than of the population of 100. Thus, for a finite population of tubes of which 10% are defective, the chance of two defectives in a sample of size 2 is very close to .1 × .1, *if the population is very large*. For random sampling from an infinite population there is exact equality. In this ideal case, drawing one element from the population and putting it in the sample "uses up" a completely negligible proportion of the population.

In general, the elements of a sample from an infinite population are *independent of one another*. Here, independence has the meaning given it in the preceding chapter. The event that one element of the sample has a certain characteristic (like defectiveness) or measurement (like height) is independent of the event that some other element of the sample has a certain characteristic or measurement.

5.3   RANDOM VARIABLES

Many of the random experiments or observations discussed in Chapter 4 have numbers associated in a natural way with the outcomes. In rolling a pair of dice, one can observe the total number of dots; in tossing a coin three times in a row, one can count the number of times heads turns up; in a poker hand, one can count the number of aces. Such a number, determined by a chance mechanism, is called a *random variable*. We denote random variables by X and Y, etc.

Before looking further into this idea, consider a physically determined variable that has no element of randomness. To find the area of a square, you measure the length l of one of its sides and then multiply that length by itself, computing l^2. Now l is a variable; it may be 1.5 feet or 8.3 cubits, depending on the square in question. To keep in mind this element of variability, it helps to regard l as a name for the length of the side *before the side is measured.* Measuring the side of a specific square converts l into a specific number. The variable l is useful for making general statements such as, "The area is l^2."

And now, let X be the total on a pair of dice. The dice may show a total of 7 when actually rolled, in which case X is 7; or they may show 5, in which case X is 5; and so on. Now X is a number whose value depends on the outcome of a random experiment, and the outcome cannot be predicted. To keep in mind this variability and unpredictability, it helps to regard the random variable as a name for the number connected with the outcome of the experiment *before the experiment is performed.* Carrying out the experiment converts the random variable into a specific number.

Selecting a random sample from a population, finite or infinite, is a random experiment, and most random variables of concern to us will arise from sampling. The number of defectives in a sample of electron tubes is a random variable. In a sample of people, their individual heights are all random variables, and so is the average of these heights.

There is a classification of random variables that is based on the set of values the variable can take on. The random variable is *discrete* if there is a definite distance from any possible value of the random variable to the next possible value. The number of defectives in a sample is discrete, the distance between successive possible values being 1. A height measured to the nearest tenth of an inch takes as value one of the numbers ... , 60.0, 60.1, 60.2, ... ; it is discrete because the distance from one possibility to the next is 0.1.

A *continuous* random variable, on the other hand, is assumed able to take any value in an interval. A height measured with complete accuracy can, in principle, take on any positive value, and so is a continuous variable. So can measurements such as weight, temperature, pressure, time, and the like, provided they are measured with complete accuracy. In reality, there is a limit to the precision with which measurements can be made, and continuous random variables are only a useful idealization, just as infinite populations are.

5.4 DISTRIBUTIONS OF RANDOM VARIABLES

The behavior of a discrete random variable can be described by giving the probability with which it takes on each of its values when the experiment is carried out.

EXAMPLE 1

We know from Chapter 4 that the probability of rolling a 7 with a pair of fair dice is $1/6$. Letting X be the discrete random variable that represents the total for the two dice (X is a name for the total "before the dice are rolled"), we can express this fact by writing: $P(X = 7) = 1/6$. Similarly, the probability of rolling a 4 is $3/36$: $P(X = 4) = 3/36$. Here is a table of all the probabilities (they can be determined by counting cases in Table 4.1, page 58):

$$P(X = 2) = \tfrac{1}{36} \qquad P(X = 3) = \tfrac{2}{36}$$
$$P(X = 4) = \tfrac{3}{36} \qquad P(X = 5) = \tfrac{4}{36}$$
$$P(X = 6) = \tfrac{5}{36} \qquad P(X = 7) = \tfrac{6}{36}$$
$$P(X = 8) = \tfrac{5}{36} \qquad P(X = 9) = \tfrac{4}{36}$$
$$P(X = 10) = \tfrac{3}{36} \qquad P(X = 11) = \tfrac{2}{36}$$
$$P(X = 12) = \tfrac{1}{36}$$

This collection of probabilities is called the *distribution* of the discrete random variable X. The distribution can be used to answer any question about X. For instance, the chance of "X is 7 or 11" is:

$$P(X = 7 \text{ or } X = 11) = P(X = 7) + P(X = 11) = \tfrac{6}{36} + \tfrac{2}{36} = \tfrac{2}{9}$$

A pair of dice was rolled 100 times and a record kept of the number of times each possible value for the sum of the faces occurred. Figure 5.1a shows the observed relative frequencies; Figure 5.1b shows the corresponding probabilities. The two figures would agree more closely if the dice had been rolled 1000 times, say. The probabilities represent a theoretical limit toward which the observed relative frequencies should tend as the number of rolls increases beyond bound.

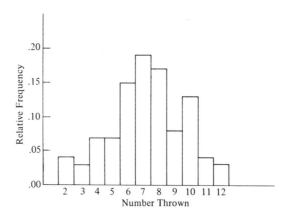

FIGURE 5.1a. *Distribution of the outcomes when a pair of dice was rolled 100 times*

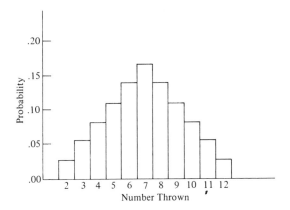

FIGURE 5.1b.   *Theoretical distribution of the outcomes when a pair of dice is rolled*

EXAMPLE 2

Suppose a box contains six white balls and three red ones. If we select four balls at random without replacement (that is, if we take a random sample of size 4), and if we let X be the number of white balls in the sample, then X is a random variable which can take the values 1, 2, 3, and 4 (there must be at least one white ball because we select four balls, and there are only three red ones in the box). The probability of getting r white balls in the sample is given by the formula (4.21) on page 82:

$$P(X = r) = \frac{\binom{6}{r}\binom{3}{4-r}}{\binom{9}{4}} \qquad r = 1, 2, 3, 4$$

The individual probabilities (shown in Figure 5.2) are:

$$P(X = 1) = \tfrac{6}{126} \qquad P(X = 2) = \tfrac{45}{126}$$
$$P(X = 3) = \tfrac{60}{126} \qquad P(X = 4) = \tfrac{15}{126}$$

This set of probabilities is the distribution of X. They sum to 1, and they suffice to answer any question about the probability that X will have a given property. For instance, the probability that X is even is:

$$P(X \text{ is even}) = P(X = 2) + P(X = 4) = \tfrac{60}{126}$$

The probability that X is 3 or more is:

$$P(X \geq 3) = P(X = 3) + P(X = 4) = \tfrac{75}{126}$$

A discrete random variable is described by its distribution—the list of probabilities for its various possible values. This sort of distribution does not work for a continuous random variable, because such a variable takes on

95

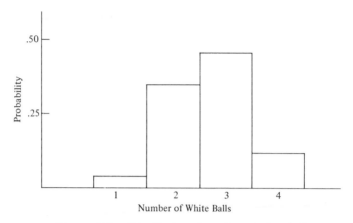

FIGURE 5.2. *Distribution of number of white balls*

any given value with probability *zero*: If X is continuous, then $P(X = 3.1)$ is 0, $P(X = 2.854)$ is 0, etc. This seems paradoxical at first, since X must assume *some* value when the experiment is carried out. But consider a line segment; each point in it has length zero, whereas all the points together give a segment with positive length. In the same way, X has probability 0 of taking on any one given number but has probability 1 of taking on *some* number (some number not specified in advance of the experiment). In consequence, the distribution of a continuous X must be given not by a list of probabilities, but by a *continuous curve*.

EXAMPLE 3

A dart is thrown randomly at a dart board, and the distance X to the center is measured. The behavior of X is described by a curve like that in Figure 5.3. The curve lies entirely above the horizontal axis, and the

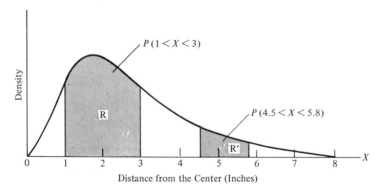

FIGURE 5.3. *Theoretical distribution of the distance from the center*

area under the curve is 1—that is, the area between the curve and the horizontal axis is 1. The probability that, when the experiment is carried out, X will assume a value in a given interval equals the area under the curve and over that interval. The chance that X lies between 1 and 3 is the area of the shaded region R in Figure 5.3; the chance that it lies between 4.5 and 5.8 is the area of the shaded region R'. Notice that, since an individual point has probability 0, $P(4.5 < X < 5.8)$ is the same as $P(4.5 \leq X \leq 5.8)$; it makes no difference whether or not the endpoints of the interval are included.

We have all along interpreted probabilities in terms of limiting relative frequencies, and we can give a similar interpretation to the curve in Figure 5.3 by using the histograms of Chapter 2. If we were to throw the dart at the board 100 times and measure the distance to the center to the nearest inch, using a class interval of one inch, then the histogram would resemble that in Figure 5.4. If we were to throw the dart 1000 times instead of 100, we could use shorter class intervals, say quarter-inch intervals, and more of them, and the histogram would resemble that in Figure 5.5.

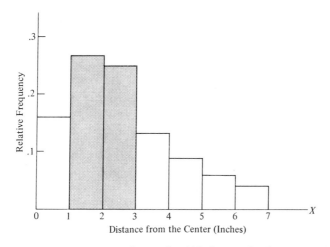

FIGURE 5.4. *Distribution for 100 throws of a dart*

If we continue throwing the dart, using more and more intervals of smaller and smaller length, the histogram will approach the curve in Figure 5.3. In each histogram the area of a bar is proportional to the observed relative frequency in that class, and so an area under the histogram (like the areas of the shaded regions in Figures 5.4 and 5.5) represents an observed relative frequency which converges to a probability (like that represented by the area of the shaded region R in Figure 5.3).

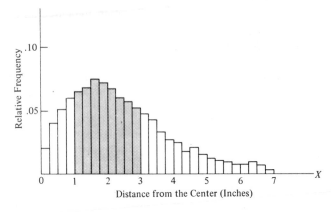

FIGURE 5.5. *Distribution for 1000 throws of a dart*

The distribution of any continuous random variable is specified by a curve like that in Figure 5.3. The curve is called a *frequency curve*, and the area under the curve between two limits on the horizontal scale is the probability that the random variable will take on a value lying between those two limits. The height of the curve over a point on the horizontal scale is called a *probability density*; it has no direct probability meaning, as have the areas under the frequency curve.

If the distribution of a continuous variable is specified by a frequency curve, the question arises as to how the frequency curve is itself specified. This is only rarely done by an actual curve carefully drawn on graph paper. Sometimes, as in the following example, the distribution is specified by a geometric description.

EXAMPLE 4

Suppose X always has value between 0 and 2, and suppose its distribution is given by the straight line in Figure 5.6. By the rule for the area of a triangle, the area under the line is 1. To get the probability that X

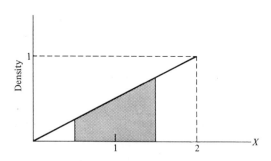

FIGURE 5.6. *A triangular distribution*

lies between 1/2 and 3/2, we compute the area of the shaded trapezoid in the figure. The base of the trapezoid has length 1 and the sides have lengths 1/4 and 3/4, so the area rule for trapezoids gives

$$Similar\ Triangles \qquad 1 \times \frac{\frac{1}{4} + \frac{3}{4}}{2} = \frac{1}{2} \qquad A\ (trap) = \left(\frac{h_1 + h_2}{2}\right) b$$

and this is the probability sought:

$$P(\tfrac{1}{2} \le X \le \tfrac{3}{2}) = \tfrac{1}{2}$$

Usually, distribution curves for continuous random variables are specified by mathematical formulas of greater or lesser complexity (for example, formula (5.13) below), and the relevant probabilities—that is, the relevant areas—are determined by the methods of integral calculus. Such determinations lie outside the scope of this book. For various important frequency curves often encountered in statistical practice, tables of these areas have been constructed. Several such tables are given in the Appendix; they represent the frequency curves we shall need in the succeeding chapters.

5.5 EXPECTED VALUES OF RANDOM VARIABLES

For a discrete random variable X, the expected value of X, denoted $E(X)$, is the weighted mean of the possible values of X, the weights being the probabilities of these values (see formula (3.6) on page 28). Thus

$$E(X) = \sum_r rP(X = r) \tag{5.1}$$

where the sum extends over all possible values r of X. For example, suppose X can assume the values 1, 2, and 3, and suppose X has the distribution in Table 5.1.

TABLE 5.1.

r	1	2	3
$P(X = r)$	.25	.40	.35

Ex

Here

$$E(X) = \sum_{r=1}^{3} rP(X = r) = 1 \times .25 + 2 \times .40 + 3 \times .35 = 2.10$$

The words "expected value" are misleading in that, in this example, 2.10 is not to be expected at all as a value of X, since 1, 2, and 3 are the only possible values. But $E(X)$ is what is to be expected in an *average* sense. The expected value of X is also called the *mean* of X. This mean is similar to the

99

mean for a set of numerical data, treated in Section 3.4, but the two kinds of mean are not to be identified with one another.

Just as the mean for numerical data can be viewed as a center of gravity (see Figure 3.2 on page 27), so can $E(X)$. For the distribution in Table 5.1, imagine weights positioned on a seesaw at each of the possible values of X, each weight being proportional to the probability of the value it represents, as in Figure 5.7; the expected value 2.10 is where a fulcrum will balance the seesaw.

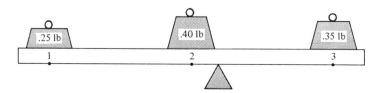

FIGURE 5.7.   *The expected value as a center of gravity: discrete case*

For Examples 1 and 2 of the preceding section, the expected values are, respectively,

$$2 \times \tfrac{1}{36} + 3 \times \tfrac{2}{36} + 4 \times \tfrac{3}{36} + 5 \times \tfrac{4}{36} + 6 \times \tfrac{5}{36} + 7 \times \tfrac{6}{36} + 8 \times \tfrac{5}{36}$$
$$+ 9 \times \tfrac{4}{36} + 10 \times \tfrac{3}{36} + 11 \times \tfrac{2}{36} + 12 \times \tfrac{1}{36} = 7$$

and

$$1 \times \tfrac{6}{126} + 2 \times \tfrac{45}{126} + 3 \times \tfrac{60}{126} + 4 \times \tfrac{15}{126} = \tfrac{8}{3}$$

For a continuous X, as for a discrete one, the mean $E(X)$ represents an average. It is the value X can be expected to have on the average, the actual value on a trial being greater or less than $E(X)$ and distributed in such a way as to balance out at $E(X)$. Just as in the case of the discrete variable, $E(X)$ can be viewed as a center of gravity also in the continuous case. If we were to draw the frequency curve on some stiff material of uniform density, such as plywood or metal, cut it out, and balance it on a knife edge arranged perpendicular to the horizontal scale, the value corresponding to the point of balance would be the expected value. Figure 5.8 illustrates this for the curve of Figure 5.3; compare it with the analogous Figure 3.1 on page 26, which relates to the mean for grouped numerical data.

For the frequency curve in Example 4 of the preceding section, the expected value works out to 4/3. The computation of expected values in the continuous case, requiring as it does the methods of integral calculus, lies outside the scope of this book. It will be possible nonetheless to use the results of such computations for statistical purposes.

Suppose a random variable has expected value $E(X)$ equal to μ. The *variance* of the random variable is defined as

$$\mathrm{Var}(X) = E(X - \mu)^2 \tag{5.2}$$

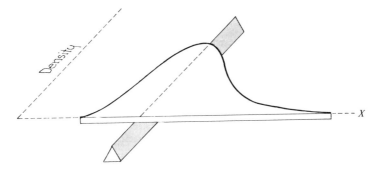

FIGURE 5.8. *The expected value as center of gravity: continuous case*

and this definition applies in both the discrete and continuous cases. Now $(X - \mu)^2$, which is itself a random variable, is always positive, and the more distant X is from μ, the greater is $(X - \mu)^2$. The expected value of $(X - \mu)^2$ measures the amount by which the distribution is spread around the mean μ, much as does the variance for a set of numerical data as defined on page 38.

In all cases, $\mathrm{Var}(X)$ is greater than or equal to 0. In the extreme case in which $\mathrm{Var}(X)$ is equal to 0, the value of X is μ with probability 1, and X is not really random at all.

The *standard deviation* of X is:

$$\text{St Dev}(X) = \sqrt{\mathrm{Var}(X)} = \sqrt{E(X - \mu)^2} \qquad (5.3)$$

For the distribution in Table 5.1, the mean μ was 2.10, and so the variance is

$$.25 \times (1 - 2.1)^2 + .40 \times (2 - 2.1)^2 + .35 \times (3 - 2.1)^2 = .59$$

and the standard deviation is $\sqrt{.59}$, or .768.

The mean is often denoted by μ, the variance by σ^2, and the standard deviation by σ; sometimes μ_X, σ_X^2, and σ_X are used instead, to indicate that the terms refer to computations involving X. Whatever the units of X (feet, degrees, etc.), its mean and standard deviation have these same units, too.

If X is a random variable, discrete or continuous, and if A and B are fixed numbers, then

$$U = AX + B$$

is another random variable. The expected values of these two random variables are related by the equation

$$E(U) = AE(X) + B \qquad (5.4)$$

This is analogous to the change-of-scale formula (3.19) on page 43 and can be understood in the same way—see Figure 3.6 and its accompanying explanation. If X is a random temperature in centigrade degrees, the same temperature in Fahrenheit degrees, U, is $\frac{9}{5}X + 32$; it is only natural that the expected values of U and X should be related by the formula $E(U) = \frac{9}{5}E(X) + 32$.

The variance and standard deviation also obey the rules of Section 3.12:

$$\mathrm{Var}(U) = A^2 \, \mathrm{Var}(X) \tag{5.5}$$

and

$$\mathrm{St\ Dev}(U) = A \cdot \mathrm{St\ Dev}(X) \tag{5.6}$$

for positive A.

Suppose X has mean μ and variance σ^2 (standard deviation σ), and consider the related variable

$$U = \frac{X - \mu}{\sigma} = \frac{1}{\sigma} X - \frac{\mu}{\sigma}$$

According to equation (5.4),

$$E(U) = \frac{1}{\sigma} E(X) - \frac{\mu}{\sigma} = \frac{1}{\sigma} \cdot \mu - \frac{\mu}{\sigma} = 0$$

and according to equation (5.5),

$$\mathrm{Var}(U) = \left(\frac{1}{\sigma}\right)^2 \cdot \mathrm{Var}(X) = \left(\frac{1}{\sigma}\right)^2 \times \sigma^2 = 1$$

Thus

$$E\left(\frac{X - \mu}{\sigma}\right) = 0 \tag{5.7}$$

and

$$\mathrm{Var}\left(\frac{X - \mu}{\sigma}\right) = 1 \tag{5.8}$$

if X has mean μ and standard deviation σ. Subtracting μ from X centers it at 0, and dividing by σ standardizes the variability; $(X - \mu)/\sigma$ is the random variable X *standardized* to have mean 0 and standard deviation 1.

5.6 SETS OF RANDOM VARIABLES

Random variables often come in pairs. This happens whenever there is a *pair* of numbers associated with each of the various outcomes of an experiment. If a man is drawn at random from some population, his height X in inches is one random variable and his weight Y in pounds is another. These random variables are associated with one another because they are associated with one experiment (the drawing of the person from the population); X and Y attach to the same man.

Expected values of sums satisfy the formula

$$E(X + Y) = E(X) + E(Y) \tag{5.9}$$

For example, if X is the income of the husband in a family and Y is the income of the wife, $X + Y$ is the family income (other sources excluded). If in a population of families the average income for husbands is \$9,000 and the average income for wives is \$5,000, certainly the average income for families must be \$14,000. Formula (5.9) expresses the general form of this fact.

In Chapter 4 we gave a definition of independence of events (equation (4.17), page 76), a definition embodying the idea that knowing whether or not one of two events occurred does not in any way help us to guess whether or not the other occurred. There is a similar notion of independence of random variables X and Y; it embodies the idea that knowing the value of X does not in any way help us to guess the value of Y, and vice versa.

For instance, suppose two dice are rolled, one die colored red and one green to keep them straight; let X be the number showing on the red die and let Y be the number showing on the green die. Since there is no interaction between the dice, the value that X takes on when the dice are rolled has no influence on the value Y takes on; X and Y are independent. On the other hand, if X and Y are the height and weight of a man, then X and Y are not independent: If you know that X is very large, then you know that Y is likely to be large also.

The fact that will be of use to us is that, *if X and Y are independent,* then

$$\text{Var}(X + Y) = \text{Var}(X) + \text{Var}(Y) \tag{5.10}$$

Without giving a full derivation of this fact, we can give a partial argument for it by considering a case of dependence. Suppose that X is some random variable (with positive variance), and suppose that Y is its negative: $Y = -X$. Certainly, X and Y are dependent: To know X is to know Y exactly. Now, for every outcome of the experiment, $X + Y$ is equal to 0, so $X + Y$ has no variability at all and $\text{Var}(X + Y)$ is 0. Thus in equation (5.10), the right side, certainly positive, exceeds the left side, which vanishes. Here, equation (5.10) fails because X and Y vary in such a way that in $X + Y$ their variability cancels out. In other cases, their variability reinforces in such a way that the left side of equation (5.10) exceeds the right. But if X and Y are independent, they can interact in no way at all, so this sort of cancelling and reinforcing is impossible and the variances exactly add up in accordance with equation (5.10).

We shall often be concerned with whole sets of random variables. Suppose we have at hand a random sample of size n from some population (say a sample of people), and suppose we have measurements $X_1, X_2, \ldots, X_n$ (say the heights of the people), one measurement for each element of the sample. Choosing a random sample is a random experiment, and each X_i is a number associated with the outcome; thus, $X_1, X_2, \ldots, X_n$ are random variables. The procedures of Chapter 3—the computations of means and variances for sets of data—are usually performed on samples.

The rule (5.9) extends to sets of random variables:

$$E\left(\sum_{i=1}^{n} X_i\right) = \sum_{i=1}^{n} E(X_i) \tag{5.11}$$

If $X_1, X_2, \ldots, X_n$ come from a random sample of size n from an infinite population, then they are independent. As explained in Section 5.2, this is the essential feature of samples from infinite populations. The formula (5.10) can be extended to more than two random variables *if they are independent* of one another:

$$\text{Var}\left(\sum_{i=1}^{n} X_i\right) = \sum_{i=1}^{n} \text{Var}(X_i) \qquad (5.12)$$

5.7 NORMAL DISTRIBUTIONS

A *normal distribution*, or normal frequency curve, is given by the formula

$$\frac{1}{\sqrt{2\pi}\sigma} \exp\left[-\frac{1}{2\sigma^2}(x-\mu)^2\right] \qquad (5.13)$$

What is important for us is not this formula, but the fact that the normal distribution is given by the symmetrical, bell-shaped curve of Figure 5.9. We shall see how to find the areas under the curve by a table in the Appendix.

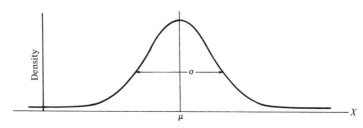

FIGURE 5.9. *A normal curve*

There is a normal distribution for each pair μ and σ^2, where μ is any number and σ^2 is positive. And μ and σ^2 are the mean and variance of the distribution. If we fix μ and let σ^2 vary, we get a family of curves with the same mean but different variances, as shown in Figure 5.10. The lower and more spread out the curve, the greater the variance σ^2. If we fix σ^2 and let μ vary, we get a family of curves with the same shape but different locations along the axis, as shown in Figure 5.11. The further to the right the curve, the greater the mean μ.

Experience has shown that many continuous random variables in diverse fields of application have distributions for which a normal distribution may serve as a mathematical or theoretical model or for which a normal distribution may be used as a good approximation. As we have seen, there

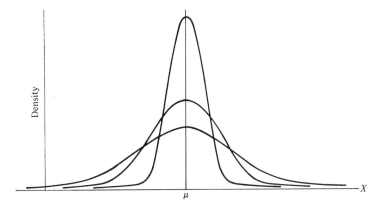

FIGURE 5.10. *Normal distributions with the same mean, different variances*

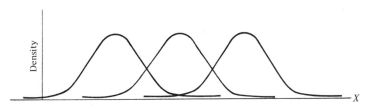

FIGURE 5.11. *Normal distributions with the same variance, different means*

is a normal distribution for each pair μ and σ^2. Although it would be impossible to construct a table for each of them, we can select one, tabulate its areas, and use this table with appropriate conversion formulas to find probabilities for any normally distributed variable. The distribution tabulated in Table II of the Appendix is the *standard normal distribution*, and it is defined as that normal distribution which has *mean 0 and variance 1*.

Let Z be a standard normal variable, that is, a normal variable for which μ is 0 and σ^2 is 1. In the table of areas of the normal curve, Table II, values of Z from .00 to 4.00 are given in the leftmost column. The second column gives the area under the curve *between zero and the given value of Z*. For example, if we want the area between zero and 1.53, we find 1.53 in the left column and read the area .43699 in the second column. Since the standard normal curve is symmetric about zero, the area between $-Z$ and zero is equal to the area between zero and Z; therefore, only positive values of Z are given in the table. Since area is proportional to probability, the total area under the curve is equal to 1.

We can illustrate the use of the table of normal areas by several examples. A rough sketch of the curve together with the area desired is a great help in finding probabilities by means of the table.

105

EXAMPLE 1

Problem: Find the probability that a single random value of Z will be between .53 and 2.42.

Solution: The shaded area in Figure 5.12 is equal to the desired probability. The area given in the table for $Z = 2.42$ is .49224, but this is the area from zero to 2.42. The tabled area for .53 is .20194. Referring to the sketch, we see that the area between .53 and 2.42 is the difference between their tabular values:

$$P(.53 < Z < 2.42) = .49224 - .20194 = .29030$$

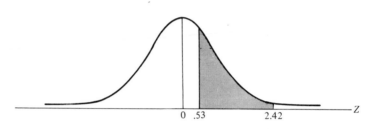

FIGURE 5.12

EXAMPLE 2

Problem: What is the probability that Z will be greater than 1.09?

Solution: The shaded area to the right of $Z = 1.09$ is the probability that Z will be greater than 1.09. In the table the area between zero and 1.09 is .36214. The total area under the curve is equal to 1 so that the area to the right of zero must be .50000; therefore (Figure 5.13),

$$P(Z > 1.09) = .50000 - .36214 = .13786$$

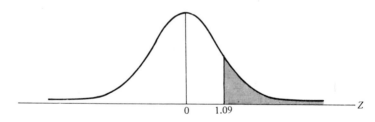

FIGURE 5.13

EXAMPLE 3

The probability that Z will be greater than $-.36$ is the total area to the right of $Z = -.36$ and consists of the area between $-.36$ and zero plus the area under the right-hand half of the curve (Figure 5.14):

$$P(Z > -.36) = .14058 + .50000 = .64058$$

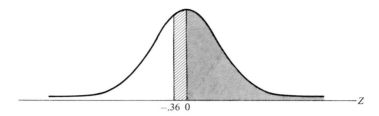

FIGURE 5.14

EXAMPLE 4

The probability that a random value of Z is between -1.00 and 1.96 is found by adding the corresponding areas as indicated by Figure 5.15:

$$P(-1.00 < Z < 1.96) = .34134 + .47500 = .81634$$

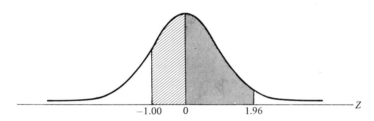

FIGURE 5.15

As a general rule, if a and b are on the *same side of the origin we subtract* the corresponding areas. If they are on *opposite sides we add.*

A slightly different use of the table is required in the following examples.

EXAMPLE 5

Problem: Find a value for Z such that the probability of a larger value is equal to .02500.

Solution: The probability of a larger value is the area to the right of Z. The area between zero and Z must be $.50000 - .02500$, or $.47500$. We read down the area column until we locate .47500, and find the desired value, $Z = 1.96$ (Figure 5.16).

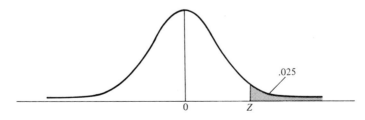

FIGURE 5.16

107

EXAMPLE 6

Problem: Find the value of Z such that the probability of a larger value is .78814.

Solution: Since the area to the right of Z is greater than .50000, we know that Z must be negative and that the area between Z and zero must be .78814 − .50000, or .28814. Reading down the area column, we locate .28814 and find that the corresponding Z is −.80 (Figure 5.17).

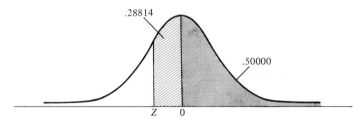

FIGURE 5.17

EXAMPLE 7

Problem: Find the value for b such that $P(-b < Z < b) = .90106$.

Solution: The endpoints $-b$ and b are symmetrically placed; therefore, half the area between them must be between zero and b. In the table we find, opposite the area .45053, the value $Z = 1.65$ (Figure 5.18).

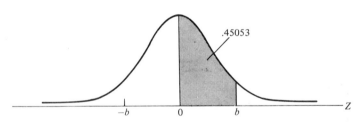

FIGURE 5.18

Now that we have seen how the table of normal areas is used to find probabilities for the standard normal variable, we turn our attention to the general case of the normal variable with mean μ and variance σ^2.

The key to using the standard normal areas for finding probabilities for the general normal variable is to pass to the *standardized* variable. If X is a random variable with mean μ and variance σ^2, then, by equations (5.7) and (5.8) on page 102, the standardized variable

$$Z = \frac{X - \mu}{\sigma} \qquad \text{(5.14)}$$

has mean 0 and variance 1. If X is normally distributed, Z is a *standard normal variable.*

Let X be normal with mean μ and variance σ^2, and suppose we want to find the probability that a randomly selected value for X will be between a and b. We use the standardization formula (5.14) and find that when $X = a$,

$$Z = \frac{a - \mu}{\sigma}$$

and that when $X = b$,

$$Z = \frac{b - \mu}{\sigma}$$

Therefore, whenever X is between a and b, the standard variable Z will be between $(a - \mu)/\sigma$ and $(b - \mu)/\sigma$. We have, then,

$$P(a < X < b) = P\left(\frac{a - \mu}{\sigma} < Z < \frac{b - \mu}{\sigma}\right)$$

Thus we can turn to the tables and find the probability that Z is between $(a - \mu)/\sigma$ and $(b - \mu)/\sigma$.

To illustrate, suppose that a certain type of wooden beam has a mean breaking strength of 1500 pounds and a standard deviation of 100 pounds, and that we want to know the relative frequency of all such beams whose breaking strength is between 1450 and 1600 pounds. The standardization formula becomes

$$Z = \frac{X - 1500}{100}$$

and

$$P(1450 < X < 1600) = P\left(\frac{1450 - 1500}{100} < Z < \frac{1600 - 1500}{100}\right)$$

$$= P(-.50 < Z < 1.00)$$

$$= .19146 + .34134$$

$$= .53280$$

We may conclude that about 53% of the beams have breaking strengths between 1450 and 1600 pounds.

5.8 THE BINOMIAL DISTRIBUTION

In Section 4.6 we discussed repeated independent trials. There is a sequence of trials, each trial results either in success or in failure, and the trials are independent—the outcome on one trial in no way influences the outcome on another trial.

Let $\quad n =$ the number of trials,
$\quad\quad\quad p =$ the probability of success on a single trial,
$\quad\quad 1 - p =$ the probability of failure on a single trial,
$\quad\quad\quad X =$ the number of successes in the n trials.

We saw in Section 4.6 that the probability of exactly r successes is given by

$$P(r) = P(X = r) = \binom{n}{r} p^r (1 - p)^{n-r} \quad\quad r = 0, 1, \ldots, n \quad\quad (5.15)$$

The integers $0, 1, 2, \ldots, n$ are the possible values of the random variable X, and equation (5.15) gives its distribution. By substituting the proper value for r in equation (5.15) we find the probability of this value. We call X a *binomial random variable,* and we call its distribution (5.15) a *binomial distribution.*

Suppose we toss a coin five times. The probability p of a head (success) is $1/2$, and the probability $1 - p$ of a tail (failure) is $1/2$. Hence, the probability of getting exactly r heads in the five tosses is:

$$P(r) = P(X = r) = \binom{5}{r} \left(\frac{1}{2}\right)^r \left(\frac{1}{2}\right)^{5-r} \quad\quad r = 0, 1, 2, 3, 4, 5$$

The probability of exactly three heads is

$$P(3) = \binom{5}{3} \left(\frac{1}{2}\right)^3 \left(\frac{1}{2}\right)^2 = 10 \left(\frac{1}{2}\right)^5 = \frac{10}{32}$$

and the probability of no heads is

$$P(0) = \binom{5}{0} \left(\frac{1}{2}\right)^0 \left(\frac{1}{2}\right)^5 = 1 \cdot 1 \cdot \left(\frac{1}{2}\right)^5 = \frac{1}{32}$$

Calculating the remaining probabilities the same way gives the distribution in Table 5.2. Note that these probabilities add to 1.

TABLE 5.2. Binomial Probability Distribution, $p = 1/2$, $n = 5$

r	0	1	2	3	4	5
$P(r) = P(X = r)$	$\frac{1}{32}$	$\frac{5}{32}$	$\frac{10}{32}$	$\frac{10}{32}$	$\frac{5}{32}$	$\frac{1}{32}$

In practical problems we are usually interested not in the probability that X assumes some individual value, but instead in the probability that X will not exceed a specified value or that X will lie in a given interval. These may be found by adding terms in the distribution. For example, the probability of two or more heads in five tosses is:

$$P(X \geq 2) = \sum_{r=2}^{5} P(r) = P(2) + P(3) + P(4) + P(5) = \frac{26}{32}$$

The probability that the number of heads will be greater than two but less than or equal to four is:

$$P(2 < X \leq 4) = \sum_{r=3}^{4} P(r) = P(3) + P(4) = \tfrac{15}{32}$$

The probability that there will be at least one head is:

$$P(1 \leq X \leq 5) = \sum_{r=1}^{5} P(r) = \tfrac{31}{32}$$

Note that this last probability may more easily be found by using the rule for complementary events (formula (4.14), page 74); that is, the probability of at least one head is:

$$P(X \geq 1) = 1 - P(X = 0) = 1 - \tfrac{1}{32} = \tfrac{31}{32}$$

Notice that for writing probabilities associated with discrete variables it is important to distinguish between *greater than or equal to* ($\geq$) and *greater than* ($>$), and also between *less than or equal to* ($\leq$) and *less than* ($<$). This distinction is unnecessary in the case of a continuous variable, since there the probability of a single specified value is 0.

A *binomial population* is one in which the elements may be split into two classes: male and female, defective and nondefective, inoculated and not inoculated, and the like. The classes may be conventionally labelled *success* and *failure*. Let p represent the proportion of successes in the population and $1 - p$ the proportion of failures. Suppose we take a random sample of size n from the population. The probability that a particular element in the sample turns out to be a success is p, since that is the proportion of successes in the population. If the population is infinite, the sample elements are independent and so the rule (5.15) applies: The probability of exactly r successes in the random sample of n is given by the rule (5.15). Moreover, this rule will be sufficiently accurate for all practical purposes if the population is large compared with the sample size n. In this case the elements in the sample are virtually independent because transferring an element from the population to the sample hardly affects the composition of the population. (If the sample and population were of comparable sizes, the hypergeometric probabilities of page 82 would be called for.)

As an example, suppose an advertising agency claims that of the college students who smoke, 25% smoke brand A. If we obtain a random sample of four students who smoke, and if the claim is true, what is the probability that at least one of them will be found to smoke brand A? Since the population of smoking students is large, the number X of students in the sample who smoke follows the binomial distribution to all intents and purposes. Under the assumption that the claim is true, p is $1/4$, and so

$$P(r) = P(X = r) = \binom{4}{r}\left(\frac{1}{4}\right)^{r}\left(\frac{3}{4}\right)^{4-r} \qquad r = 0, 1, 2, 3, 4$$

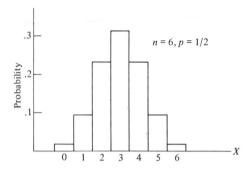

FIGURE 5.19a.   *The binomial distribution with p = 1/2, n = 6*

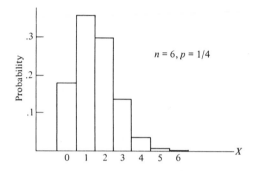

FIGURE 5.19b.   *The binomial distribution with p = 1/4, n = 6*

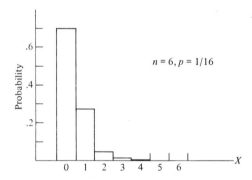

FIGURE 5.19c.   *The binomial distribution with p = 1/16, n = 6*

The probability of our finding at least one smoker of brand A is

$$P(X \geq 1) = 1 - P(0) = 1 - \binom{4}{0}\left(\frac{1}{4}\right)^0 \left(\frac{3}{4}\right)^4 = 1 - \frac{81}{256} = \frac{175}{256}$$

or

$$P(X \geq 1) = P(1) + P(2) + P(3) + P(4) + P(5)$$

$$= \frac{108}{256} + \frac{54}{256} + \frac{12}{256} + \frac{1}{256} = \frac{175}{256}$$

There is a separate binomial distribution for each integer n and each p between 0 and 1. The mean and variance of the binomial distribution can be shown to be

$$\mu = np \qquad (5.16)$$

and

$$\sigma^2 = np(1 - p) \qquad (5.17)$$

The binomial distribution is symmetric if $p = .5$; otherwise, it is skew, the degree of skewness increasing as p moves towards 0 or 1. The probability distribution for $n = 6$ and $p = 1/2, 1/4,$ and $1/16$ are shown graphically in Figures 5.19a, 5.19b, and 5.19c, respectively.

5.9   THE NORMAL APPROXIMATION TO THE BINOMIAL

Since, as the sample size increases, the number of individual binomial probabilities increases and each one involves higher powers of p and $1 - p$, calculating these probabilities becomes tedious for moderate values of n and practically impossible for larger values. Binomial tables have been tabulated for sample sizes up to 100, but if tables are not available or if n exceeds 100, we need an approximation. The most important approximation uses the table areas for the standard normal distribution. The approximation is important not just for computational purposes, but also for a general understanding of the binomial distribution.

It can be shown that, as the sample size (or number of trials) n increases, the binomial distribution becomes very close to a normal distribution with mean np and variance $np(1 - p)$. (As remarked in the preceding section, np and $np(1 - p)$ *are* the mean and variance of the number of successes.) Whenever our sample is sufficiently large, the number X of successes in the sample is approximately normally distributed, and we can use the normal tables to approximate the probabilities in which we are interested.

If X is nearly normal with mean np and variance $np(1 - p)$—that is, with standard deviation $\sqrt{np(1 - p)}$—then the *standardized* binomial variable

$$Z = \frac{X - np}{\sqrt{np(1 - p)}} \qquad (5.18)$$

is approximately a standard normal variable (see equations (5.7) and (5.8), and also equation (5.14)). Therefore, the probability that X will lie between a and b will be approximately the probability that a standard normal variable Z will lie between

$$a' = \frac{a - np}{\sqrt{np(1 - p)}} \qquad \text{and} \qquad b' = \frac{b - np}{\sqrt{np(1 - p)}}$$

Thus,

$$P(a \leq X \leq b) \cong P(a' \leq Z \leq b')$$

where the symbol $\cong$ means *is approximately equal to*.

113

EXAMPLE 1

Suppose we take a sample of 100 from a binomial population in which the proportion p of successes is .36. We ask for the probability that the number X of successes will be between 24 and 42, inclusive. Here the mean, variance, and standard deviation of X are:

$$\mu = np = 100 \times .36 = 36$$
$$\sigma^2 = np(1 - p) = 100 \times .36 \times .64 = 23.04$$
$$\sigma = \sqrt{np(1 - p)} = \sqrt{23.04} = 4.8$$

The standardization formula is:

$$Z = \frac{X - 36}{4.8}$$

Hence (here Z represents a random variable with exactly a standard normal distribution),

$$P(24 \leq X \leq 42) = P\left(\frac{24 - 36}{4.8} \leq \frac{X - 36}{4.8} \leq \frac{42 - 36}{4.8}\right)$$

$$\cong P\left(\frac{24 - 36}{4.8} \leq Z \leq \frac{42 - 36}{4.8}\right)$$

$$= P\left(-\frac{12}{4.8} \leq Z \leq \frac{6}{4.8}\right) = P(-2.5 \leq Z \leq 1.25)$$

From the table for normal areas we get

$$P(-2.5 \leq Z \leq 1.25) = .49379 + .39435 = .88814$$

The exact probability (taken from binomial tables) is .907386. Our approximation, .88814, is accurate to about 2%. Rounding off .88814 to .89, we see that the normal approximation gives

$$P(24 \leq X \leq 42) \cong .89$$

EXAMPLE 2

Suppose again that we take a binomial sample of 100 and again ask for the probability that the number X of successes will be between 24 and 42. This time, however, we suppose the proportion p of successes in the population is .40. Here

$$\mu = np = 100 \times .40 = 40$$
$$\sigma^2 = np(1 - p) = 100 \times .40 \times .60 = 24$$

$$\sigma = \sqrt{np(1 - p)} = \sqrt{24} = 4.9$$

The standardization is

$$Z = \frac{X - 40}{4.9}$$

so

$$P(24 \leq X \leq 42) = P\left(\frac{24 - 40}{4.9} \leq \frac{X - 40}{4.9} \leq \frac{42 - 40}{4.9}\right)$$

$$\cong P\left(-\frac{16}{4.9} \leq Z \leq \frac{2}{4.9}\right) = P(-3.26 \leq Z \leq .41)$$

By the normal table,

$$P(-3.26 \leq Z \leq .41) = .49944 + .15910 = .65854$$

Rounding off gives

$$P(24 \leq X \leq 42) \cong .66$$

EXAMPLE 3
It is also possible to approximate probabilities defined by a single
inequality. Suppose we ask for the probability that the number X of
successes in a sample of 100 is 45 or more. If p is .36, we standardize
by the mean and standard deviation of Example 1:

$$P(X \geq 45) = P\left(\frac{X - 36}{4.8} \geq \frac{45 - 36}{4.8}\right)$$

$\mu = np = 36$

$\sigma = \sqrt{np(1 - p)} = 4.8$

$$\cong P\left(Z \geq \frac{45 - 36}{4.8}\right) = P(Z \geq 1.88)$$

$$= .50000 - .46995 = .03005$$

If p is .40, we use the standardization of Example 2:

$$P(X \geq 45) = P\left(\frac{X - 40}{4.9} \geq \frac{45 - 40}{4.9}\right)$$

$$\cong P\left(Z \geq \frac{45 - 40}{4.9}\right) = P(Z \geq 1.02)$$

$$= .50000 - .34614 = .15386$$

Rounding off to two places in each result, we have

$$P(X \geq 45) \cong .03 \quad \text{if } p = .36$$

and

$$P(X \geq 45) \cong .15 \quad \text{if } p = .40$$

Of course, the larger p is, the more likely we are to get 45 or more
successes.

It is sometimes convenient to work not with the number X of successes in n trials, but instead with the fraction $f = X/n$ of successes. Dividing both the numerator and denominator in formula (5.18) by n gives:

$$Z = \frac{f - p}{\sqrt{p(1 - p)/n}} \qquad (5.19)$$

This ratio thus has approximately a standard normal distribution for large n; it is, in fact, f standardized, because f has mean p and variance $p(1 - p)/n$.

EXAMPLE 4

Suppose n is 100 and p is .36. What is the probability that the fraction f of successes will lie between .24 and .42? Here the mean, variance, and standard deviation of f are:

$$E(f) = p = .36$$
$$\text{Var}(f) = p(1 - p)/n = .36 \times .64/100 = .002304$$
$$\text{St Dev}(f) = \sqrt{p(1 - p)/n} = .048$$

Hence, by formula (5.19), the standardized f is

$$Z = \frac{f - .36}{.048}$$

and

$$P(.24 \leq f \leq .42)$$

$$= P\left(\frac{.24 - .36}{.048} \leq \frac{f - .36}{.048} \leq \frac{.42 - .36}{.048}\right)$$

$$\cong P\left(\frac{.24 - .36}{.048} \leq Z \leq \frac{.42 - .36}{.048}\right) = P(-2.5 \leq Z \leq 1.25)$$

$$= .88814 \cong .89$$

Note that the answer arrived at in Example 4 is the same as the answer to Example 1, because n and p are the same in the two examples and because $.24 \leq f \leq .42$ is the same thing as $24 \leq X \leq 42$. Any given problem can be solved in terms of X or in terms of f; the answer will be the same in either case.

We noted in Example 1 that the normal approximation gave an answer about 2% off from the true answer. This accuracy suffices for many practical purposes. Further accuracy can be achieved by using the *continuity correction*. The exact value of the probability sought in Example 1 is

$$P(24 \leq X \leq 42) = \sum_{r=24}^{42} \binom{100}{r} (.36)^r (.64)^{100-r}$$

It is represented by the combined areas of the bars in Figure 5.20. In Example 1 we approximated this probability by the area under the normal curve (the one for a μ of 36 and a σ of 4.8) between 24 and 42. Examination of the figure shows that we should obtain a better approximation if we find the

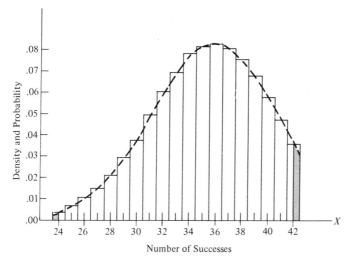

FIGURE 5.20. *Normal approximation to a binomial distribution*

area under the normal curve between 23.5 and 42.5, because this will include the areas of the two shaded regions, omitted in the previous approximation. With this procedure we get:

$$P(24 \leq X \leq 42) = P(23.5 \leq X \leq 42.5)$$

$$= P\left(\frac{23.5 - 36}{4.8} \leq \frac{X - 36}{4.8} \leq \frac{42.5 - 36}{4.8}\right)$$

$$\cong P(-2.60 \leq Z \leq 1.35)$$

$$= .49534 + .41149 = .90683$$

The error in this second approximation is less than 0.1%.

In general, to apply the continuity correction, we subtract $\frac{1}{2}$ from the lower value on the X scale and add $\frac{1}{2}$ to the upper value and then proceed as before. This enables us also to approximate the probability that X will take on a single specified value, as shown in the following example:

EXAMPLE 5

Suppose n is 80 and p is .16. We ask for the chance of exactly twenty successes. In this case

$$\mu = np = 80 \times .16 = 12.8$$
$$\sigma = \sqrt{np(1 - p)} = \sqrt{80 \times .16 \times .84} = 3.279$$

117

Using the continuity correction gives

$$P(X = 20) = P(19.5 \le X \le 20.5)$$

$$= P\left(\frac{19.5 - 12.8}{3.279} \le \frac{X - 12.8}{3.279} \le \frac{20.5 - 12.8}{3.279}\right)$$

$$\cong P(2.04 \le Z \le 2.35) = .49061 - .47932 = .01129$$

The exact probability is .012234.

PROBLEMS

1. Given that X is a random variable with the distribution shown below, find the probability that:
   a. $.5 \le X \le 1$.   b. $X \ge .75$.
   c. $.25 \le X \le .75$.   d. $X \le .1$.

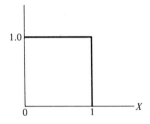

2. If X has the distribution shown below, find
   a. $P(X \ge 2)$.   b. $P(0 \le X \le 3)$.
   c. $P(X \le -1)$.   d. $P(-2 \le X \le 2)$.
   e. $P(X \ge -2)$.

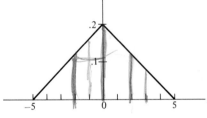

3. If X has the distribution shown below, find
   a. a.   b. $P(X \le 1)$.
   c. $P(X \ge 2)$.   d. $P(1 \le X \le 3)$.
   e. C such that $P(X \le C) = .4$.

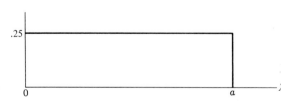

4. Given that X has the distribution shown below, find
   a. θ.
   b. $P(-1 \le X \le 2)$.
   c. $P(X \ge 1.5)$.
   d. C such that $P(-C \le X \le C) = .6$.
   e. C such that $P(X \ge C) = .8$.

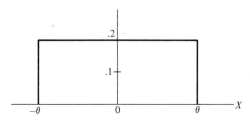

5. Given that X has the probability distribution given in the following table, find the mean μ and the variance σ^2.

r	0	1	2	3	4
$P(X = r)$	$\frac{1}{16}$	$\frac{4}{16}$	$\frac{6}{16}$	$\frac{4}{16}$	$\frac{1}{16}$

6. Given that X has the probability distribution given in the following table, find the mean and variance of X.

r	-1	0	1	2
$P(X = r)$	.1	.2	.3	.4

7. The *hypergeometric distribution* is the appropriate model when samples are selected without replacement from a finite population consisting of two kinds of elements: successes and failures. If the population consists of n successes and m failures, and if we take a sample of size r, the distribution for the number of successes, X, in the sample is given by (see (4.21))

$$P(X = k) = \frac{\binom{n}{k}\binom{m}{r-k}}{\binom{n+m}{r}} \qquad k = 0, 1, 2, \ldots, r$$

   a. Give the distribution for X, the number of red balls in a sample of size 3 taken from an urn which contains three red balls and four white ones.
   b. Work out the probabilities for the values that X can take.
   c. Find the mean number of red balls in samples of size 3, i.e., the mean of X.

8. From a lot of twenty bushings which contains three that are not within the tolerances, a sample of five is selected without replacement.
   a. Give the distribution for the number of defective bushings in the sample.
   b. What is the probability that the sample contains no defectives?
   c. What is the probability there is at least one defective?

9. The distribution for the number X of times a coin must be tossed to obtain the first head is:
$$P(X = r) = (\tfrac{1}{2})^r \qquad r = 1, 2, \ldots$$

Find the probability that:
a. The first head occurs on the third toss.
b. Fewer than five tosses are required.
c. More than three tosses are required.

10. A die is rolled until a 6 appears. If X is the number of rolls required, the probability distribution of X is:

$$P(X = r) = \tfrac{1}{6}(\tfrac{5}{6})^{r-1} \qquad r = 1, 2, 3, \ldots$$

Find
a. $P(X = 2)$.   b. $P(X \le 2)$.
c. $P(X > 2)$.

11. Given that Z is the standard normal variable, use the table of normal areas to find
a. $P(0 \le Z \le 1)$.   .34134   b. $P(Z \ge 1)$.   ?. .5000 - .34134
c. $P(-1 \le Z \le 1)$.   .68268   d. $P(Z \ge -1)$. ?. .5000 + .34134

12. If Z is the standard normal variable, find
a. $P(Z \le .75)$. .27337   b. $P(.25 \le Z \le .75)$. .27337 - .0987)
c. $P(-.25 \le Z \le .75)$. .09871 + .27337   d. $P(Z \le -.25)$. .50000 - .09871

13. Given Z is the standard normal variable, find
a. $P(-1.96 \le Z)$.   b. $P(-1.96 \le Z \le -1.5)$.
c. $P(.38 \le Z \le 1.42)$. .4222 - .14803   d. $P(-.49 \le Z \le 1.05)$.

14. Given Z is the standard normal variable, find
a. $P(Z \le 1.23)$.   b. $P(Z \le -2.12)$.
c. $P(Z \ge 1.17)$.   d. $P(Z \ge -.62)$.
e. $P(-1.56 \le Z \le -.64)$.   f. $P(-.72 \le Z \le 1.89)$.

15. Given Z is the standard normal variable, find C such that:
a. $P(Z \ge C) = .025$.   b. $P(Z \le C) = .02872$.
c. $P(-C \le Z \le C) = .95$.

16. Given that Z is the standard normal variable, find C such that:
a. $P(Z \le C) = .95543$.   b. $P(Z \le C) = .30854$.
c. $P(Z \ge C) = .99981$.   d. $P(Z \ge C) = .03216$.
e. $P(-C \le Z \le C) = .45150$.   f. $P(1 \le Z \le C) = .12193$.

17. Given that X is a normal variable with $\mu = 50$ and $\sigma = 10$, find
a. $P(X \le 65)$. $Z \le 1.5$ .35314   b. $P(X \le 25)$. $Z \le 2.5$ .49379
c. $P(42 \le X \le 62)$. -.8 ≤ Z ≤ 1.2   d. $P(38 \le X \le 47)$. -1.2 ≤ Z ≤ -.3
   .03/88 + .38493   .38493 - .01197

18. Given that X is normal with $\mu = 15$ and $\sigma^2 = 25$, find
a. $P(X \le 20)$.   b. $P(X \le 13)$.
c. $P(10 \le X \le 18)$.   d. $P(19 \le X \le 40)$.

19. Given that X is normal with $\mu = .05$ and $\sigma = .012$, find
a. $P(X \ge .074)$.   b. $P(.071 \le X \le .077)$.

20. Given that X is normal with $\mu = .130$ and $\sigma^2 = .000625$, find
a. $P(X \ge .126)$.   b. $P(.110 \le X \le .165)$.

21. Given that X is normally distributed, find the value of C such that

$$P(\mu - C\sigma \le X \le \mu + C\sigma) = .95.$$

22. If X is normal with $\mu = 50$ and $\sigma^2 = 100$:
a. Find C such that $P(X \le C) = .18406$.

(margin notes, left side:)
$\frac{65-50}{10}$
$\frac{42-50}{10} \le Z \le \frac{62-50}{10}$
$\frac{42-50}{10} \le Z$
$\frac{25-50}{10} = -2.5$
$\frac{47-50}{10}$
$\frac{38-50}{10} \le Z \le$

b. Find two numbers, A and B, that are equidistant from μ and are such that $P(A \le X \le B) = .966$.

23. Given that X is normal, $\sigma = 5$, and $P(X \ge 78.5) = .06681$, find μ.

24. Given that X is normal, $\mu = 19$, and $P(X \le 22.5) = .63683$, find σ^2.

25. If the resistances of carbon resistors of 1200 ohms nominal value are normally distributed with $\mu = 1200$ ohms and $\sigma = 120$ ohms:

a. What proportion of these resistors would have resistances greater than 1000 ohms?

b. What proportion would have resistances that do not differ from the mean by more than 1% of the mean?

c. What proportion do not differ from the mean by more than 5% of the mean?

26. If the service lives of electron tubes in a particular application are normally distributed, and if 92.5% of the tubes have lives greater than 2160 hours while 3.92% have lives greater than 17,040 hours, what are the mean and standard deviation of the service lives?

27. Given the binomial distribution

$$P(X = r) = \binom{5}{r} \left(\frac{1}{3}\right)^r \left(\frac{2}{3}\right)^{5-r} \qquad r = 0, 1, 2, \ldots, 5$$

find:

a. $P(X = 3)$.   **b.** $P(X \ge 4)$.

c. $P(X = 0)$.   **d.** $P(X \ge 1)$.

28. Give the distribution for the number of heads in six tosses of a fair coin. Find the probabilities associated with every possible value of the variable. By finding the appropriate expected values, obtain the mean and variance of the number of heads.

29. In a large orchard 10% of the apples are wormy. If four apples are selected at random, what is the probability that

a. Exactly one will be wormy?

b. None will be wormy?

c. At least one will be wormy?

30. An automatic lathe is said to be out of control and is checked if a sample of five turnings contains any that are defective. If 2% of its output are defective, what is the probability that the lathe will be declared out of control after a given sample is checked? Assume the probability of a defective is the same for every item selected.

31. In a triangle test the probability due to chance alone of a correct decision on a single trial is equal to 1/3. In eighteen trials, what is the probability of fourteen or more correct decisions due to chance alone? Use the normal approximation.

32. In the preceding problem, what is the probability that we are wrong if we conclude a person can do better than by chance alone when he makes ten or more correct decisions?

33. If a fair die is rolled 200 times,

a. What is the probability that a 1 will occur between 30 and 50 times, inclusive?

b. What is the probability a 1 will occur fewer than 20 times?

34. If a process produces 5% defective items, and if we take a sample of one-hundred, what is the probability of fewer than five defectives?

35. If one crosses garden peas having the gene pair (red, white) with peas also having the (red, white) gene pair, one-fourth of the progeny are expected to have white flowers. If sixty-four plants from such a cross are examined, what is the probability that there will be exactly sixteen with white flowers?

36. When a sample is taken without replacement from a finite population, and the sample size is small relative to the size of the population, the binomial distribution with $p = n/(n + m)$ can be used to approximate the hypergeometric probabilities (see problem 7, above). Make use of this approximation to find the probability asked for in part (c) of problem 8. What is the error in the approximation?

37. Another discrete probability distribution of importance is the *Poisson distribution*. It is an appropriate model for the distribution of the number of elements per unit of time or space when the average number of elements per unit is relatively small. Examples of variables which have a Poisson distribution are the number of defects per side of phonograph records, the number of particles or organisms per unit of volume in a dilute solution, and the number of electron tubes requiring replacement in a particular type of electronic equipment per unit of time. The Poisson distribution is also used as an approximation to the binomial when the mean, $\mu = np$, is small. It has the form

$$P(X = r) = \frac{e^{-\theta}\theta^r}{r!} \qquad r = 0, 1, 2, 3, \ldots$$

where θ is the mean, or average value, of X. Values of $e^{-\theta}$ may be found in standard mathematical tables. Tables of Poisson probabilities are also available. Given $\theta = 2$ and $e^{-2} = .135$, find
a. $P(X = 0)$.   b. $P(X = 1)$.
c. $P(X \geq 2)$.

38. If the number of telephone calls passing through a given switchboard has a Poisson distribution with mean θ equal to $3t$ where t is the time in minutes, find the probability of:
a. Two calls in any one minute ($e^{-3} = .050$).
b. Five calls in two minutes ($e^{-6} = .0025$).
c. At least one call in one minute.

39. At a particular location on a river, the number of fish caught per man hour of fishing effort has a Poisson distribution with θ equal to 1.2. If a man fishes there for one hour, what is the probability he will catch exactly two fish? At least one fish? ($e^{-1.2} = .301$.)

40. Use the Poisson distribution to approximate the probability asked for in problem 34. The exact probability is .43598. Which is better in this case, the normal or the Poisson approximation? In general, the Poisson provides the better approximation to cumulative binomial probabilities when the probability, p, is less than about .075.

41. Derive the recursion formula for Poisson probabilities,

$$P(X = r) = \frac{\theta}{r} P(X = r - 1)$$

and use it to obtain $P(X = r)$ when r has values 0, 1, 2, and 3, and θ is 1 and e^{-1} is .368.

REFERENCES

5.1 COCHRAN, W. G. *Sampling Techniques*, 2nd edition. John Wiley & Sons, New York, 1963.

5.2 HOGG, ROBERT V., and ALLEN T. CRAIG. *Introduction to Mathematical Statistics*, 3rd edition. Macmillan, New York, 1970.

5.3 KISH, L. *Survey Sampling*. John Wiley & Sons, New York, 1965.

5.4 PARZEN, EMANUEL. *Modern Probability Theory and Its Applications*. John Wiley & Sons, New York, 1960.

6

Sampling Distributions

6.1 SAMPLING AND INFERENCE

It is in order to discover facts about populations that we draw samples from them. Imagine the voting population of a city split between those who intend to vote for candidate A in a coming election and those who intend to vote for candidate B. An opinion poller trying to predict the outcome of the election draws a random sample of size 100 from the population of voters. If in the population a proportion of .36 favor candidate A (and a proportion .64 favor B), what is the chance that the number of voters in the sample who favor A will be 45 or more? In Example 3 of Section 5.9 we approximated this probability by using the normal distribution (favoring A was there called success). If X is the number of voters in the sample who favor A, then

$$P(X \geq 45) \cong .03 \qquad \text{if } p = .36$$

If a proportion .36 of the voting population favor A, then the chance that $X \geq 45$ is about .03.

It is natural to challenge the relevance of this sort of calculation to the problem of making inferences about the population of voters. Indeed, if the opinion poller actually knew that the proportion in the population favoring A was .36—the assumption underlying the computation—then he would not have gone to the trouble of drawing a sample in the first place. He drew the sample, after all, in order to get some idea what proportion of all the voters do in fact favor A. This proportion is a number p which is unknown to the poller, so why assume that p is .36?

Now the poller makes guesses about p on the basis of X, the number in the sample of 100 who favor A; X will for his sample have some specific value like 72 or 18. Even without benefit of statistical theory, we do know that if X is 72 then the poller should guess that p is somewhere around .72; that p is .36 would be a bad guess. If X is 18 the poller should guess that p is something like .18; that p is .95 would be a bad guess. We know also that the poller could make more accurate guesses about p if the sample size were 1000 instead of 100. But we want to go beyond these initial ideas to a more detailed understanding of how the poller should guess at p and what kind of precision he can hope for.

In the case where X is 72, we regard .36 as a very bad guess for p because if p really *is* only .36 then it is very strange indeed that X should be so large as 72. And this is the relevance of probability computations based on the assumption that p is .36. Our computation showed that if p were .36 then the chance would be only about .03 that X is even as great as 45. A detailed understanding of how the poller ought to guess requires a detailed knowledge of the distribution of X for the case where p equals .36. But of course there is nothing special about .36, and we must also know the distribution of X in the case where p is .40, say. In Example 3 of Section 5.9 we treated this case as well:

$$P(X \geq 45) \cong .15 \qquad \text{if } p = .40$$

It is a virtue of mathematics that, by letting p be general, we can in principle consider all values of p at the same time; that is, we can give a description of the distribution of X for the general p between 0 and 1; formula (5.15), page 110, provides the description. This description we require in general form precisely because the poller does not know the actual value of p in advance.

We draw samples to discover facts about a population, and these facts are usually expressed in terms of numbers called *parameters*. In the discussion above, the parameter was p, the proportion in the voting population who favor A. In general, a parameter is a number describing some aspect of a population. In making inferences about a parameter on the basis of a sample, we usually deal with *statistics*, which are numbers that can be computed from the sample. In the discussion above, the statistic was X, the number of people in the sample of 100 who favor candidate A. The poller is ignorant of the value of the parameter p; once he has drawn his sample, he knows the value of the statistic X and can use it to make inferences (guesses) about p.

Our example is typical. Generally, we are concerned with one or more parameters that help describe a population. We do not know the values of the parameters (and usually never will). We draw a sample and compute one or more statistics on the basis of the sample. We have actual numerical values for the statistics. And we use the statistics to make inferences about the parameters. In order to know how to make these inferences, we must know about the distributions of the statistics.

125

For a further example, consider the average weight μ (in pounds) of the population of trout in Crater Lake. We do not know the value of the parameter μ and we never will. To get an idea of what μ is, we take a sample of trout and compute the average $\bar{X}$ of their weights (as in Chapter 3); the statistic $\bar{X}$ is something we find the actual numerical value of. On the basis of $\bar{X}$ we make inferences about μ. Without statistical theory, we know that $\bar{X}$ somehow estimates μ, but to know just how to make the inferences and how exact they will be, we need to know the distribution of the random variable $\bar{X}$ —we need to know its *sampling distribution.*

6.2 EXPECTED VALUES AND VARIANCES

The mean and variance of a population of numbers are defined as the mean and variance of a single random observation from that population, that is, as $E(X_1)$ and $\text{Var}(X_1)$ for a random sample X_1 of size 1. The population is said to be discrete or continuous according as a single observation X_1 has discrete or continuous distribution. A discrete population may be finite or infinite; a continuous population must be infinite, though it may be approximated by a large but finite population.

Suppose the population has the five elements 2, 4, 6, 8, and 10. In this case the population mean μ is:

$$\mu = \tfrac{1}{5}(2 + 4 + 6 + 8 + 10) = 6$$

Now suppose we take a random sample of size 2 without replacement. There are $\binom{5}{2}$, or 10, different outcomes—different samples of size 2—and each of them has a sample mean $\bar{X}$:

Sample	Sample mean $\bar{X}$
2,4	3
2,6	4
2,8	5
2,10	6
4,6	5
4,8	6
4,10	7
6,8	7
6,10	8
8,10	9

The sample being random, each outcome has probability 1/10. The probability that $\bar{X}$ has the value 5 is the probability of getting the sample 2,8 or the sample 4,6, so $P(\overline{X} = 5) = 2/10$. This and analogous computations give the sampling distribution of $\overline{X}$:

r	3	4	5	6	7	8	9
$P(\overline{X} = r)$	.1	.1	.2	.2	.2	.1	.1

By the definition (5.1), page 99, of the expected value for a discrete random variable,

$$E(\overline{X}) = 3 \times .1 + 4 \times .1 + 5 \times .2 + 6 \times .2 + 7 \times .2$$
$$+ 8 \times .1 + 9 \times .1 = 6$$

The point is that $E(\overline{X})$ coincides with the population mean μ.

This is always so. Let $X_1, X_2, \ldots, X_n$ be a random sample of size n from a population, finite or infinite, discrete or continuous. The sample mean is, as in Chapter 3,

$$\overline{X} = \frac{1}{n} \sum_{i=1}^{n} X_i \qquad (6.1)$$

and always*

$$E(\overline{X}) = \mu \qquad (6.2)$$

This is because of the rules for manipulating expected values: Applying to formula (6.1) the rule (5.4) and then (5.11), we have:

$$E(\overline{X}) = \frac{1}{n} E\left(\sum_{i=1}^{n} X_i \right) = \frac{1}{n} \sum_{i=1}^{n} E(X_i)$$

Since each individual X_i is a single observation from the population, $E(X_i)$ has the same value as μ. Equation (6.2) follows by Rule 3 for summations, page 22.

Equation (6.2) is sometimes expressed as: The mean of the mean is the mean. Each *mean* here has a different meaning, and the statement is short for: The expected value E (first *mean*) of the sample mean $\overline{X}$ (second *mean*) is the population mean μ (third *mean*).

If the population is infinite, so that the elements $X_1, X_2, \ldots, X_n$ in the random sample are *independent*, then we have for the variance of $\overline{X}$ the formula

$$\text{Var}(\overline{X}) = \frac{\sigma^2}{n} \qquad (6.3)$$

where σ^2 is the population variance. The standard deviation is:

$$\text{St Dev}(\overline{X}) = \frac{\sigma}{\sqrt{n}} \qquad (6.4)$$

---

*This and the other numbered formulas in this section will be used constantly in the rest of the book. Although we give derivations of them, the derivations are not needed for the sequel; an understanding of the *meaning* of the formulas will suffice.

To see why formula (6.3) holds for an infinite population, use formula (5.5) and then (5.12); the latter formula is applicable because the X_i are independent:

$$\text{Var}(\bar{X}) = \text{Var}\left(\frac{1}{n}\sum_{i=1}^{n}X_i\right) = \frac{1}{n^2}\text{Var}\left(\sum_{i=1}^{n}X_i\right) = \frac{1}{n^2}\sum_{i=1}^{n}\text{Var}(X_i)$$

But each $\text{Var}(X_i)$ is σ^2, since X_i is a single observation from the population, and so Rule 3 for summations, page 22, yields formula (6.3).

Formulas (6.3) and (6.4) apply only when *the population is infinite*. If the population is finite, formula (6.3) must be replaced by the formula

$$\text{Var}(\bar{X}) = \frac{N-n}{N-1}\cdot\frac{\sigma^2}{n}$$

where N is the size of the population. The factor $(N-n)/(N-1)$ is the *finite population correction factor*. In the example above, the population variance is:

$$\sigma^2 = E(X_1 - 6)^2 = \tfrac{1}{5}(16 + 4 + 0 + 4 + 16) = 8$$

And the variance of $\bar{X}$ is:

$$E(\bar{X} - 6)^2 = 9 \times .1 + 4 \times .1 + 1 \times .2 + 1 \times .2 + 4 \times .1 + 9 \times .1 = 3$$

which agrees with the above formula for $N = 5$ and $n = 2$:

$$3 = \frac{5-2}{5-1}\cdot\frac{8}{2}$$

If the population size N is large in comparison with the sample size n, then the correction factor is nearly 1, so that the formula for $\text{Var}(\bar{X})$ for a finite population is practically the same thing as formula (6.3) in this case.

In addition to the mean and variance of $\bar{X}$, we can find the mean of the sample variance s^2. Recall from Chapter 3 that

$$s^2 = \frac{1}{n-1}\sum_{i=1}^{n}(X_i - \bar{X})^2 \tag{6.5}$$

For a sample from an *infinite* population, we have the formula

$$E(s^2) = \sigma^2 \tag{6.6}$$

For the sake of simplicity, we derive this only for the case where μ is 0. By formula (3.12),

$$\sum(X_i - \bar{X})^2 = \sum X_i^2 - \frac{1}{n}(\sum X_i)^2 = \sum X_i^2 - n\bar{X}^2$$

If $\mu = 0$, so that $E(X_i) = 0$ and $E(\bar{X}) = 0$, then $E(X_i^2) = \sigma^2$ and $E(\bar{X}^2) = \text{Var}(\bar{X}) = \sigma^2/n$; therefore

$$E\left(\sum_{i=1}^{n}(X_i - \bar{X})^2\right) = \sum_{i=1}^{n}\sigma^2 - n\frac{\sigma^2}{n} = (n-1)\sigma^2$$

which gives formula (6.6).

Formula (6.6) concerns the mean of the variance, whereas (6.3) concerns the variance of the mean. To keep these straight, the terms must be expanded: Formula (6.6) concerns the expected value of the sample variance, and (6.3) concerns the variance of the sample mean.

6.3 SAMPLING FROM NORMAL POPULATIONS

Let $\overline{X}$ be the sample mean for an independent sample of size n. As we saw in the last section, if the population mean and variance are μ and σ^2, then $\overline{X}$ has mean μ and variance σ^2/n, and this is true whatever the form of the parent population may be. Suppose now that the population is *normal*. In this case $\overline{X}$ is *normally distributed with mean μ and variance σ^2/n*. This is a fundamental fact about normal populations.

This characteristic is plainly seen in the results of a sampling exercise. Each of 158 statistics students took two random samples of five values each from a population approximately normal with mean 40 and variance 100. Each computed the two means and also the mean of the ten values combined into one sample. Table 6.1 shows the resulting distributions of sample means, and Figures 6.1 and 6.2 show the histograms.

TABLE 6.1. Distributions of the Sample Means in Samples of 5 and 10

Mean	Frequency ($n = 5$)	Frequency ($n = 10$)
25–27	1	1
27–29	1	1
29–31	4	2
31–33	18	0
33–35	18	5
35–37	37	14
37–39	47	36
39–41	60	43
41–43	41	26
43–45	45	19
45–47	27	9
47–49	12	1
49–51	1	1
51–53	4	0
Totals	316	158

The means for these empirical distributions are 40.06 for samples of size 5 and 39.98 for samples of size 10. The variances are 20.95 and 12.64. Even with relatively small numbers of means, the histograms show a tendency toward the symmetrical, bell-shaped normal curve; the means and variances agree well with the theoretical values $\mu = 40$, $\sigma^2/5 = 20$, and $\sigma^2/10 = 10$.

129

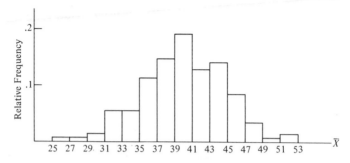

FIGURE 6.1. *Histogram for the means of samples of size 5*

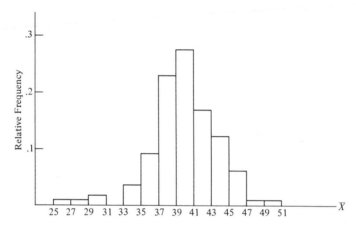

FIGURE 6.2. *Histogram for the means of samples of size 10*

6.4 THE STANDARDIZED SAMPLE MEAN

Since $\overline{X}$ has mean μ and standard deviation $\sigma/\sqrt{n}$, the standardized variable

$$Z = \frac{\overline{X} - \mu}{\sigma/\sqrt{n}} \tag{6.7}$$

has mean 0 and variance 1; see formulas (5.7) and (5.8) on page 102.

If the population is normal, then Z, defined by equation (6.7), is a standard normal variable and we may use the table of normal areas to calculate probabilities for the sample mean.

EXAMPLE 1

Problem: Given a normal distribution with mean 50 and variance 100, find the probability that the mean of a sample of twenty-five observations will differ from the population mean by less than four units.

Solution: We want

$$P(-4 < \overline{X} - \mu < 4)$$

If we divide each member of the inequality by $\sigma/\sqrt{n}$ we have

$$P(-4 < \overline{X} - \mu < 4) = P\left(\frac{-4\sqrt{n}}{\sigma} < \frac{\overline{X} - \mu}{\sigma/\sqrt{n}} < \frac{4\sqrt{n}}{\sigma}\right)$$

$$= P\left(\frac{-4\sqrt{25}}{10} < Z < \frac{4\sqrt{25}}{10}\right)$$

$$= P(-2 < Z < 2)$$

$$= .95450$$

EXAMPLE 2

Problem: For the normal distribution of the preceding example find two values equidistant from the mean such that 90% of the means of all samples of size n of 100 will be contained between them.

Solution: From the table of normal areas we have

$$.90 = P(-1.64 \leq Z \leq 1.64)$$

From equation (6.7),

$$.90 = P\left(-1.64 \leq \frac{\overline{X} - \mu}{\sigma/\sqrt{n}} \leq 1.64\right)$$

Therefore,

$$.90 = P(-1.64 \leq \overline{X} - 50 \leq 1.64)$$

$$= P(-1.64 + 50 \leq \overline{X} \leq 1.64 + 50)$$

$$= P(48.36 \leq \overline{X} \leq 51.64)$$

and the desired numbers are 48.36 and 51.64.

6.5 THE CENTRAL LIMIT THEOREM

The central limit theorem concerns the approximate normality of means of random samples or of sums of random variables; we accordingly state it in two forms.

Suppose $X_1, X_2, \ldots, X_n$ is a sample from an infinite population with mean μ and variance σ^2; the X_i are independent random variables.

FIRST FORM: *If n is large, then*

$$\frac{\overline{X} - \mu}{\sigma/\sqrt{n}} \tag{6.8}$$

has approximately a standard normal distribution, or (what is the same) $\overline{X}$ has approximately a normal distribution with mean μ and standard deviation $\sigma/\sqrt{n}$.

131

We know that whatever the parent population may be, the standardized variable (6.8) has mean 0 and standard deviation 1; and we know that, if the parent population is normal, then variable (6.8) has exactly a standard normal distribution. The remarkable fact is that, even if the parent population is not normal, the standardized mean is approximately normal if n is large. The importance of the theorem lies in the fact that it permits us to use normal theory for inferences about the population mean regardless of the form of the population, provided only that the sample size is large enough.

To prove the central limit theorem requires the full apparatus of mathematical probability. But we can illustrate it by starting with a specific non-normal distribution, a J-shaped exponential distribution with mean μ of 2 and variance σ^2 of 4. Figure 6.3a shows this distribution (solid line) and the normal distribution (dashed line) with the same mean and variance. The two distributions are very dissimilar.

For samples with size n equal to 4 from the exponential population of Figure 6.3a, the sample mean $\overline{X}$ has mean 2 and variance 1. Figure 6.3b shows the exact distribution (solid line) of $\overline{X}$, together with the normal distribution (dashed line) with mean 2 and variance 1. The two curves are rather similar.

Figure 6.3c shows the same pair of curves for a sample size n of 12 (the mean and variance are now 2 and 1/3), and here the agreement is really quite close. These graphs show insufficient detail for the tails of the distribution; the normal approximation is usually better for values near the mean than for values far removed. As appears from this example, however, the sample need not be excessively large before we can feel reasonably safe in using the central limit theorem.

A second version of the central limit theorem concerns the sum $\sum X_i$ of a set $X_1, X_2, \ldots, X_n$ of random variables all having the same distribution with mean μ and variance σ^2.

SECOND FORM: *If n is large, then*

$$\frac{\sum_{i=1}^{n} X_i - n\mu}{\sigma\sqrt{n}} \tag{6.9}$$

has approximately a standard normal distribution, or (what is the same) $\sum X_i$ *has approximately a normal distribution with mean* $n\mu$ *and standard deviation* $\sigma\sqrt{n}$.

This theorem is really the same as the first one, because $\sum X_i$ is $n\overline{X}$, so that the variable (6.9) is just $(n\overline{X} - n\mu)/\sigma\sqrt{n}$, and algebra reduces this to the variable (6.8).

This theorem (together with more general versions of it) is one of the reasons why the normal distribution often arises in nature. If one performs a complicated physical measurement, the measurement error is the sum $\sum X_i$ of many small independent random errors X_i. The height of a plant is

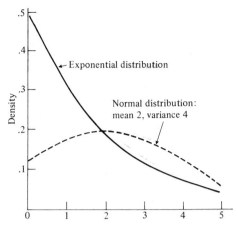

FIGURE 6.3a. *Exponential and normal distributions with $\mu = 2$ and $\sigma^2 = 4$*

FIGURE 6.3b. *Distribution of $\bar{X}$ for samples of 4 and the normal distribution with the same mean and variance*

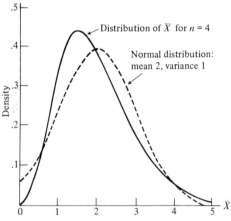

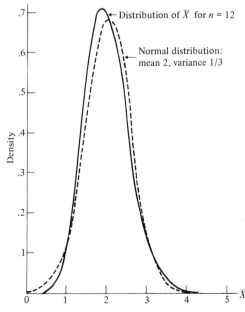

FIGURE 6.3c. *Distribution of $\bar{X}$ for samples of 12 and the normal distribution with the same mean and variance*

133

the sum $\sum X_i$ of many small independent increments X_i. In such cases the normal distribution at least roughly approximates the distribution of the sum.

The normal approximation to the binomial, as treated in Section 5.9, really comes under the central limit theorem. In an infinite (or finite but large) population split into two categories, success and failure, label each element in the success category with a 1 and each element in the failure category with a 0. Now a random sample of size n from the population becomes converted into a set $X_1, X_2, \ldots, X_n$ of independent random variables, each having value either 0 or 1. The number of successes is the number of 1's, and this is $\sum X_i$, so the central limit theorem applies. In this case (see formulas (5.16) and (5.17)), $n\mu = np$ and $\sigma\sqrt{n} = \sqrt{np(1-p)}$. Variable (6.9) is the same thing as the standardized number of successes (see equation (5.18)); it has approximately a standard normal distribution.

PROBLEMS

1. For a sample of size 100 from a normal distribution with mean 10 and variance 16, what are the mean and variance of the sample mean?

2. For a sample of size 64 from a continuous population with mean 50 and standard deviation 20, what are the mean and standard deviation of the sample mean?

3. A certain type of electron tube has a mean transconductance equal to 10,000 μmhos (micromhos). The variance of the transconductances is 3600. If we take samples of twenty-five tubes each and for each sample we find the mean transconductance, between what limits (symmetric with respect to the mean) would 50% of the sample means be expected to lie?

4. If the population of times measured by three-minute egg timers is normally distributed with μ equal to 3 minutes and σ equal to .2 minutes, and if we test samples of twenty-five timers, find the time that would be exceeded by 95% of the sample means.

5. For sampling from a normal distribution with variance σ^2, the distribution of s^2 has mean σ^2 and variance $2\sigma^4/(n-1)$. As the sample size increases, the distribution of s^2 approaches a normal distribution. If we take a sample of size 73 from a normal population with σ^2 equal to 80, what is the approximate probability that s^2 will be greater than 100? Less than 40? Between 50 and 110?

6. Let the numbers 1, 2, 3, 4, 5, and 6 constitute a population. If samples of size 3 are drawn without replacement, there are twenty different possible samples. List these twenty samples and find the mean and median for each of them. Find the mean and variance of the twenty sample means. Do the same for the medians. Which measure, mean or median, shows the smaller variation from sample to sample?

CLASS SAMPLING EXERCISES

A. Each student will draw two different samples of five elements each from the normal population of Table VII of the Appendix. The procedure for drawing a sample is as follows:

1. Select any page in the table of random numbers (Table VI). Drop a pencil point anywhere on the page. Read the nearest four digits. For example, my pencil fell so that the nearest four digits were 0506. I interpret this as meaning I shall start drawing my random numbers in the fifth row and sixth column. I turn to the first page of the random number table and locate the fifth row and sixth column.

2. Copy off five consecutive three-digit numbers reading down. In the example these were:

$$957$$
$$260$$
$$068$$
$$203$$
$$662$$

3. Turn to the list of the population values (Table VII). The random numbers drawn above are the identification numbers for my sample. Opposite the identification number read the observed value. For the example:

Identification number	Observed value
957	5722
260	3358
068	2513
203	3171
662	4419

a. For each sample of 5, find the mean and variance.
b. Combine the two samples into one sample of 10. Find the mean and variance.
c. Construct frequency distributions for the means and variances of all samples of size 5 drawn by the members of the class. Find the means and variances for the distributions and compare them with the population values. Draw the histograms.
d. Do the same for the samples of 10.

B. The individual random digits in the table of random numbers (Table VI) should have a discrete uniform distribution,

$$P(X = r) = \tfrac{1}{10} \qquad r = 0, 1, 2, \ldots, 9$$

For this distribution μ is 4.5, and σ^2 is 8.25.
a. Each student should select five samples of ten random digits each from the table of random numbers.
b. For each sample obtain the mean, $\bar{X}$.
c. Combine the five samples into one sample of size 50 and find the mean.
d. Construct a frequency distribution and draw the histogram for the means of the samples of size 10 drawn by the members of the class. Does it appear that the distribution of sample means is tending towards a normal distribution, as the central limit theorem says it should?
e. Do the same for the samples of size 50.
f. Obtain the mean and variance for the class distribution of the sample

means ($n = 10$). These are estimates of $\mu = 4.5$ and $\text{Var}(\bar{X}) = .825$, respectively.

g. Do the same for the distribution of means of samples of size 50.

REFERENCES

6.1 Hoel, Paul G. *Elementary Statistics,* 3rd edition. John Wiley & Sons, New York, 1971. Chapter 6.

6.2 Hogg, Robert V., and Allen T. Craig. *Introduction to Mathematical Statistics*, 3rd edition. Macmillan, New York, 1970. Chapter 4.

7

Estimation

7.1 INTRODUCTION

A statistician collects data by experiment, sample, or sample survey in the hope of drawing conclusions about the phenomenon under investigation. From his experimental results or sample values he wants to pass to *inferences* about the underlying population. He may use his data for the *estimation* of the values of unknown parameters or for *tests of hypotheses* concerning these values.

In Section 6.1 we discussed an opinion poller who takes a sample from a voting population divided into those who favor candidate A and those who favor B, the unknown parameter being the proportion p who favor A. The poller may estimate p (try to guess its value), or he may test a hypothesis about p—test the hypothesis, say, that $p > 1/2$ (try to guess whether A will win the election). In either case he infers something about p.

This chapter deals with methods of estimation and the principles underlying them. Testing is taken up in Chapter 8.

7.2 ESTIMATION

We have at hand a sample from a population involving an unknown parameter; the problem is to construct a sample quantity that will serve to estimate the unknown parameter. Such a sample quantity we call an *estimator*; the actual numerical value obtained by evaluating an estimator in a given instance is the *estimate*. For example, the sample mean $\overline{X}$ is an estimator for the population mean μ; if for a specific sample the sample mean is 10.31, we say 10.31 is our estimate for μ. Notice that an estimator must be a statistic; it must, of course, depend only on the sample and not on the parameter to be estimated.

Now the sample mean $\overline{X}$ is an estimator for the population mean μ, but then so is the quantity $\overline{X} + 1000$. We will all agree that, as an estimator for μ, $\overline{X}$ is more reasonable than $\overline{X} + 1000$, but why? Because $\overline{X}$, unlike $\overline{X} + 1000$, is equal to μ *on the average*:

$$E(\overline{X}) = \mu \tag{7.1}$$

for all μ (see equation (6.2) on page 127). This is a statement typical of statistical theory. Putting ourselves in the position of the experimenter, we do not know μ (and doubtless never will); given the sample, we do know $\overline{X}$; and *whatever* the unknown μ may be, $\overline{X}$ balances out at μ in the sense that $E(\overline{X})$ is equal to μ.

This discussion leads us to the following definition:

UNBIASED ESTIMATOR: *An estimator $\hat{\theta}$ of a parameter θ is said to be unbiased if it has expected value θ, whatever θ may be, that is if*

$$E(\hat{\theta}) = \theta \tag{7.2}$$

for all θ.

We have seen that $\overline{X}$ has this desirable property. So has the sample variance: If $X_1, X_2, \ldots, X_n$ is an independent sample, then the sample variance

$$s^2 = \frac{1}{n-1} \sum_{i=1}^{n} (X_i - \overline{X})^2 \tag{7.3}$$

is an unbiased estimator of σ^2:

$$E(s^2) = \sigma^2 \tag{7.4}$$

(See equation (6.6), page 128.) Notice that s^2 is a statistic; it does not depend on the unknown μ and σ^2. The point of equation (7.4), the condition for unbiasedness, is not that we can somehow check it for the true values of μ and σ^2—we do not know what these true values are. The point is that equation (7.4) holds *whatever* values μ and σ^2 may happen to have. The same remark applies to any unbiased estimator.

It was exactly in order to make the sample variance unbiased that, in the original definition (3.13) on page 38, we divided by the then-mysterious $n-1$; division by n would have introduced bias. As an estimator of σ, the sample standard deviation

$$s = \sqrt{\frac{1}{n-1} \sum_{i=1}^{n} (X_i - \overline{X})^2} \tag{7.5}$$

is ordinarily used, even though it is somewhat biased.

Returning to the mean, consider a sample $X_1, X_2, \ldots, X_{100}$ of size 100, say. Here $\overline{X}$, or

$$\frac{1}{100} \sum_{i=1}^{100} X_i \tag{7.6}$$

is an unbiased estimator of μ. But if we throw out the last fifty observations, the remaining ones, $X_1, X_2, \ldots, X_{50}$, form a sample of size 50 by themselves, and their mean

$$\frac{1}{50} \sum_{i=1}^{50} X_i \tag{7.7}$$

is another unbiased estimator of μ. Given the full sample of 100, we will all agree that the expression (7.6) is a better estimator of μ than the expression (7.7) is, but why? Each of the two estimators is unbiased, but one feels that (7.6) is stronger than (7.7) because there is somehow more information in it. This idea can be made precise by using variances: The expression (7.6) has variance $\sigma^2/100$ (see equation (6.3), page 127; here σ^2 is the population variance, also unknown to us), whereas the expression (7.7) has the larger variance $\sigma^2/50$. Since variance measures spread, of two unbiased estimators we naturally prefer the one with smaller variance.

The precision of an unbiased estimator $\hat{\theta}$ of a parameter θ is customarily measured by its variance or by its standard deviation:

$$\text{St Dev}(\hat{\theta}) = \sqrt{E(\theta - \hat{\theta})^2}$$

This is sometimes called the *standard error*. For the mean $\overline{X}$ it is $\sigma/\sqrt{n}$; here the spread is very small if n is very large.

A *minimum variance unbiased estimator* is an estimator which, in the first place, is unbiased and which, in the second place, has smaller variance than *any other* unbiased estimator.

7.3 CONFIDENCE INTERVALS FOR NORMAL MEANS: KNOWN VARIANCE

We have seen that the sample mean $\overline{X}$ is an unbiased estimator of the population mean μ. Now if the parent population is *normal*, it is even possible to show that $\overline{X}$ is a minimum variance unbiased estimator of μ. In this sense, we may say that, for a given sample size, $\overline{X}$ is the *best* estimator of μ.

To prove that $\overline{X}$ is best or optimal in the sense of having the smallest possible variance lies outside the purpose of this book (see reference 7.2 for a proof). It is simple and natural to estimate μ by $\overline{X}$, and we do know that $\overline{X}$ is unbiased and has variance σ^2/n—even if we have not proved this variance to be minimal.

This section deals with the problem of estimating the mean μ of a normal population when the variance σ^2 is known. This is a rather artificial

139

circumstance: If one is ignorant of the mean he is usually ignorant of the variance as well. Assuming σ^2 known, however, serves to simplify the reasoning and make clear the principles underlying estimation; it also serves to introduce the more complicated and more realistic case, treated in the next two sections, where σ^2 is unknown.

EXAMPLE 1

Ten patients were given two soporific drugs, A and B. In each case, the patient slept longer under the effect of B than of A, and Table 7.1 shows the amount of the increase in each case.

TABLE 7.1.
Additional Hours Sleep
Gained by Using Drug B
Instead of Drug A

Patient	Increase
1	1.2
2	2.4
3	1.3
4	1.3
5	0.0
6	1.0
7	1.8
8	0.8
9	4.6
10	1.4

$$\bar{X} = 1.58 \text{ hours}$$

Let us assume we know from experience that the increase is normally distributed with some mean μ and that the variance σ^2 is 1.66. The estimator $\bar{X}$ then has a variance $\sigma^2/10$, or .166, and a standard deviation $\sigma/\sqrt{10}$, or .408. Knowing this and the fact that $\bar{X}$ is normally distributed, we can calculate the probability that $\bar{X}$ is within .8, say, of the population mean μ: We do not know μ, but whatever value it may have, the standardized variable $(\bar{X} - \mu)/.408$ has a standard normal distribution and hence (see Figure 7.1)

$$P(\mu - .8 \le \bar{X} \le \mu + .8) = P\left(-\frac{.8}{.408} \le \frac{\bar{X} - \mu}{.408} \le \frac{.8}{.408}\right)$$

$$= P\left(-1.96 \le \frac{\bar{X} - \mu}{.408} \le 1.96\right) = .95$$

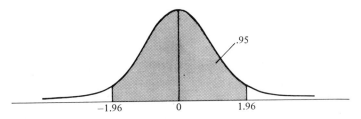

FIGURE 7.1. *Standard normal curve*

Thus the chance is 95% that $\overline{X}$ is off by .8 or less. Since $\mu - .8 \leq \overline{X} \leq \mu + .8$ is the same as $\overline{X} - .8 \leq \mu \leq \overline{X} + .8$ (both being the same as $|\overline{X} - \mu| \leq .8$), we can say that

$$P(\overline{X} - .8 \leq \mu \leq \overline{X} + .8) = .95 \qquad (7.8)$$

whatever μ may be. Now $\overline{X}$ for our data in Table 7.1 has the value 1.58, and it is tempting to replace the $\overline{X}$ in equation (7.8) by 1.58:

$$P(1.58 - .8 \leq \mu \leq 1.58 + .8) = .95. \qquad (7.9)$$

That is, it is tempting to conclude that there is probability .95 that the unknown μ lies between .78 (1.58 − .8) and 2.38 (1.58 + .8). But this would be incorrect: Although μ is unknown to us, it is not a random variable, but a fixed number. Thus .78 $\leq \mu \leq$ 2.38 is simply either true or false; the probability on the left in equation (7.9) is accordingly either 1 or 0—and we do not know which, since we do not know μ.

Although equation (7.9) is wrong as it stands, the idea lying behind it can be made sense of by means of *confidence intervals*. The first thing to understand is the source of the error in passing from equation (7.8) to equation (7.9). Consider a related but simpler case. Let Y be the total obtained in rolling a pair of fair dice. As we know from Chapter 4, the chance of rolling a 7 is 1/6: $P(Y = 7) = 1/6$. Suppose we actually roll the dice and obtain a total of 3; if in the equation $P(Y = 7) = 1/6$ we replace Y by 3, we get $P(3 = 7) = 1/6$, which is nonsense (the probability of $3 = 7$ is 0, not 1/6). Or suppose we happen to roll a 7; if in the equation $P(Y = 7) = 1/6$ we replace Y by 7, we get $P(7 = 7) = 1/6$, again nonsense (the probability of $7 = 7$ is 1, not 1/6).* In passing from equation (7.8), which is true, to equation (7.9), which is false, we have made the same error, that of replacing inside a probability statement the random variable $\overline{X}$ by the specific value 1.58 that it happened to assume when the experiment was carried out.

---

*It is perhaps illuminating to observe also that in the expected value $E(Y)$ the random variable Y cannot be replaced by a numerical value. In fact this expected value is 7: $E(Y) = 7$. If we roll a 3, substitution yields the equation $E(3) = 7$, nonsense once more. The illegitimacy of these substitutions becomes clearer if we keep in mind that Y is a name for the total number of dots "before the dice are rolled."

141

For Example 1 above,

$$L = \overline{X} - .8 \quad \text{and} \quad R = \overline{X} + .8$$

are 95% *confidence limits* for μ, and the interval bounded by L and R is a 95% *confidence interval* for μ. Now L and R are random variables, and the interval they determine is a random interval. What is the chance that the confidence limits surround μ, or that the confidence interval includes μ?

Now $L \leq \mu \leq R$ if $\overline{X} - .8 \leq \mu \leq \overline{X} + .8$, and this is the same as $|\overline{X} - \mu| \leq .8$ or $-.8 \leq \overline{X} - \mu \leq .8$. Since $(\overline{X} - \mu)/.408$ has a standard normal distribution, whatever μ may be,

$$P(L \leq \mu \leq R) = P(-.8 \leq \overline{X} - \mu \leq .8)$$

$$= P\left(-\frac{.8}{.408} \leq \frac{\overline{X} - \mu}{.408} \leq \frac{.8}{.408}\right)$$

$$= P\left(-1.96 \leq \frac{\overline{X} - \mu}{.408} \leq 1.96\right) = .95$$

Thus the terms $L = \overline{X} - .8$ and $R = \overline{X} + .8$ have the property that the probability of $L \leq \mu \leq R$ is *always* .95, no matter *what* value the unknown μ may happen to have.

Since the limits L and R have a 95% chance of enclosing the true μ between them, whatever μ may be, they are called 95% confidence limits. For the data in Table 7.1, L is .78 and R is 2.38, and we say we are 95% confident that $.78 \leq \mu \leq 2.38$. This is not to be interpreted as saying μ is random and has a 95% chance of lying between .78 and 2.38; it is really only a rephrasing of equation (7.8). The confidence we have in the limits .78 and 2.38 really derives from our confidence in the *statistical procedure* that gave rise to them.* The procedure gives random variables L and R that have a 95% chance of enclosing the true μ; whether their specific values .78 and 2.38 actually enclose μ we have no way of knowing.

To construct confidence intervals for the general case, we need some auxiliary concepts. If Z is a standard normal variable, the quantity Z_{ξ}, defined by the relationship

$$P(Z > Z_{\xi}) = \xi$$

(see Figure 7.2), is the *upper percentage point* of the standard normal distribution corresponding to a probability of ξ. It is the point on the Z scale such that the probability of a *larger* value is equal to ξ. The upper 2.5% point for the standard normal distribution is denoted by $Z_{.025}$ and is the value on the Z scale such that the area to the *right* of it is .025. By the table of normal areas, Table II, we find that $Z_{.025}$ is equal to 1.96.

---

*This accords with at least one everyday use of the word "confidence": What confidence a layman has in a physician's advice very likely derives from what confidence he has in the physician.

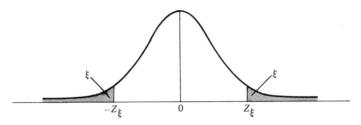

FIGURE 7.2. *Standard normal curve*

Because of the symmetry of the standard normal distribution, its lower percentage points are equal in absolute value to the corresponding upper ones but are negative. Thus $-Z_\xi$ is the point on the Z scale such that the probability of a *smaller* value is ξ—the area to the *left* of $-Z_\xi$ is ξ. There is probability .025 that a standard normal variable is less than $-Z_{.025}$, or -1.96. In terms of percentage points, we have, by definition,

$$P(-Z_{\alpha/2} \leq Z \leq Z_{\alpha/2}) = 1 - \alpha \tag{7.10}$$

Note that we use the $\tfrac{1}{2}\alpha$ percentage points in order to have $100(1 - \alpha)\%$ of the area between them; each tail has area $\tfrac{1}{2}\alpha$ so the two together have area α.

Now consider a normal population with unknown mean μ and known variance σ^2. Since the standardized variable $(\overline{X} - \mu)/(\sigma/\sqrt{n})$ has the standard normal distribution, it follows that

$$P\left(-Z_{\alpha/2} \leq \frac{\overline{X} - \mu}{\sigma/\sqrt{n}} \leq Z_{\alpha/2}\right) = 1 - \alpha \tag{7.11}$$

Since multiplication by a positive number leaves inequalities undisturbed, the probability in equation (7.11) is the probability that

$$-Z_{\alpha/2}\frac{\sigma}{\sqrt{n}} \leq \overline{X} - \mu \leq Z_{\alpha/2}\frac{\sigma}{\sqrt{n}}$$

Now these two inequalities are together the same thing as

$$|\overline{X} - \mu| \leq Z_{\alpha/2}\frac{\sigma}{\sqrt{n}}$$

and hence they are the same thing as

$$-Z_{\alpha/2}\frac{\sigma}{\sqrt{n}} \leq \mu - \overline{X} \leq Z_{\alpha/2}\frac{\sigma}{\sqrt{n}}$$

Adding $\overline{X}$ to all three members of this last expression gives

$$P\left(\overline{X} - Z_{\alpha/2}\frac{\sigma}{\sqrt{n}} \leq \mu \leq \overline{X} + Z_{\alpha/2}\frac{\sigma}{\sqrt{n}}\right) = 1 - \alpha \tag{7.12}$$

143

The equations (7.11) and (7.12) are the same thing because of the algebraic rules for manipulating inequalities. The $100(1 - \alpha)\%$ confidence interval is the interval bounded by the confidence limits

$$L = \bar{X} - Z_{\alpha/2} \frac{\sigma}{\sqrt{n}} \quad \text{and} \quad R = \bar{X} + Z_{\alpha/2} \frac{\sigma}{\sqrt{n}} \quad \text{(7.13)}$$

By equation (7.12), there is probability $1 - \alpha$ that the confidence interval will contain the unknown μ, whatever μ may be.

In Example 1,

$$1 - \alpha = .95 \qquad \alpha = .05 \qquad \frac{\alpha}{2} = .025 \qquad Z_{.025} = 1.96$$

Since $\sigma = \sqrt{1.66}$ and $n = 10$, and since the data give $\bar{X} = 1.58$,

$$L = \bar{X} - 1.96 \frac{\sqrt{1.66}}{\sqrt{10}} = 1.58 - .8 = .78$$

and

$$R = \bar{X} + 1.96 \frac{\sqrt{1.66}}{\sqrt{10}} = 1.58 + .8 = 2.38$$

EXAMPLE 2

Problem: For a sample of 25 from a normal distribution with known variance σ^2 of 100, the sample mean $\bar{X}$ was found to be 15. We are to calculate 90% confidence limits.

Solution: Here,

$$1 - \alpha = .90 \qquad \alpha = .10 \qquad \frac{\alpha}{2} = .05 \qquad Z_{.05} = 1.645$$

By computation,

$$L = 15 - 1.645 \frac{10}{\sqrt{25}} = 15 - 3.29 = 11.71$$

$$R = 15 + 1.645 \frac{10}{\sqrt{25}} = 15 + 3.29 = 18.29$$

We are 90% confident that μ lies between 11.71 and 18.29, in that the procedure itself will 90% of the time give limits that enclose μ.

EXAMPLE 3

Problem: For the data of Example 2 we are to calculate 95% confidence limits.

Solution: Here $Z_{\alpha/2}$ is 1.96, as in Example 1, and so

$$L = 15 - 1.96 \frac{10}{\sqrt{25}} = 15 - 3.92 = 11.08$$

$$R = 15 + 1.96 \frac{10}{\sqrt{25}} = 15 + 3.92 = 18.92$$

The length of the 95% confidence interval is 2 × 3.92, or 7.84; the length of the 90% confidence interval (Example 2) is 2 × 3.29, or 6.58. The 90% confidence interval is better in that it is shorter; it apparently gives greater precision. But of course we have less confidence in it (90% as opposed to 95%). Confidence has been traded for precision, and neither interval is really better than the other.

7.4   THE t-DISTRIBUTION

The interval estimates of the last section, where σ^2 was assumed known, were based on the fact that, in normal sampling, the standardized mean

$$\frac{\overline{X} - \mu}{\sigma/\sqrt{n}} \tag{7.14}$$

has a distribution that does not depend on μ and σ^2, namely, the standard normal distribution. In trying to construct a confidence interval for the case of unknown variance, we are lead to ask what happens if in the expression (7.14) we merely replace σ by its estimator s, the sample standard deviation. We then have the statistic

$$t = \frac{\overline{X} - \mu}{s/\sqrt{n}} \tag{7.15}$$

and happily it turns out that this statistic has a distribution that does not depend on μ and σ^2 (although it does depend on n).

The expression (7.15) is the first of a number of t-statistics we shall encounter. The t-distributions form a family of distributions dependent on a parameter, the degrees of freedom. For the t-variable (7.15) the degrees of freedom are $n - 1$, where n is the sample size. In general, the degrees of freedom for a t-statistic are the degrees of freedom associated with the sum of squares used to obtain an estimate of a variance.

The t-distribution is a symmetric distribution with mean zero. Its graph is similar to that of the standard normal distribution, as Figure 7.3 shows. There is more area in the tails of the t-distribution, and the standard normal distribution is higher in the middle. The larger the number of degrees of freedom, the more closely the t-distribution resembles the standard normal. As the number of degrees of freedom increases without limit, the t-distribution approaches the standard normal distribution, and it is convenient to regard the standard normal distribution as a t-distribution with an infinite number of degrees of freedom.

Table III of the Appendix gives percentage points of the t-distribution: points on the t scale such that the probability of a larger t is equal to a specified value. The percentage point t_ξ is defined as that point at which

$$P(t > t_\xi) = \xi$$

145

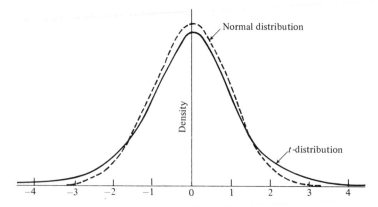

FIGURE 7.3. *The t-distribution with 5 degrees of freedom and the standard normal distribution*

Since the distribution is symmetric about zero, only positive t-values are tabulated. The lower ξ percentage point is $-t_\xi$, because

$$P(t < -t_\xi) = P(t > t_\xi) = \xi$$

In general, we denote a percentage point for t by $t_{\xi,v}$, where ξ is the probability level and v is the degrees of freedom.

To find a percentage point in Table III, we locate the row of the table that corresponds to the given degrees of freedom v and then take the value in that row that is also in the column headed by the given probability level ξ. For example, $t_{.01,15}$ is the .01 percentage point of t with 15 degrees of freedom. Using Table III, we find that it is equal to 2.602: If 15 is the degrees of freedom for t, then $P(t > 2.602) = .01$. The bottom line of the table corresponds to an infinite number of degrees of freedom, that is, to the standard normal distribution. Thus, the .05 percentage point for the standard normal, $Z_{.05}$, is $t_{.05,\infty} = 1.645$, and the .025 percentage point, $Z_{.025}$, is $t_{.025,\infty} = 1.96$.

7.5 CONFIDENCE INTERVALS FOR NORMAL MEANS: UNKNOWN VARIANCE

By the definition of percentage points,

$$P(-t_{\alpha/2,v} \leq t \leq t_{\alpha/2,v}) = 1 - \alpha$$

if t has a t-distribution with v degrees of freedom. The fact underlying the construction of confidence intervals in the case where σ^2 is unknown is that the statistic (7.15) has a t-distribution with $n - 1$ degrees of freedom, where n is the sample size and the population is assumed normal. Therefore,

$$P\left(-t_{\alpha/2,n-1} \leq \frac{\bar{X} - \mu}{s/\sqrt{n}} \leq t_{\alpha/2,n-1}\right) = 1 - \alpha \qquad (7.16)$$

If we multiply each member of the expression within the parentheses by $s/\sqrt{n}$, subtract $\overline{X}$ from each, and then multiply through by -1, we arrive at

$$P\left(\overline{X} - t_{\alpha/2,n-1}\frac{s}{\sqrt{n}} \leq \mu \leq \overline{X} + t_{\alpha/2,n-1}\frac{s}{\sqrt{n}}\right) = 1 - \alpha \qquad (7.17)$$

On the basis of equation (7.17), we define the $100(1 - \alpha)\%$ confidence interval as the interval bounded by the limits

$$L = \overline{X} - t_{\alpha/2,n-1}\frac{s}{\sqrt{n}} \qquad \text{and} \qquad R = \overline{X} + t_{\alpha/2,n-1}\frac{s}{\sqrt{n}} \qquad (7.18)$$

The point is that, where the confidence limits (7.13) involve the population standard deviation σ, assumed known in Section 7.3 but not here, the confidence limits (7.18) instead involve the sample standard deviation s, an estimate of σ. Thus these limits can be computed from the sample alone; we need not know σ. By equation (7.17) the probability that the confidence interval includes μ—the probability that the confidence limits L and R surround μ—is just $1 - \alpha$. The interpretation of these limits is just as for those in Section 7.3.

EXAMPLE 1

Let us return to the data of Example 1 in Section 7.3, but this time without the unrealistic assumption that we know the population variance. The sample variance s^2 for the data in Table 7.1 is 1.513, so the sample standard deviation s is $\sqrt{1.513}$, or 1.30, and $s/\sqrt{n}$ is $s/\sqrt{10}$, or .389. The degrees of freedom $n - 1$ is 9. If we are to compute 95% confidence limits ($\alpha = .05$, $\alpha/2 = .025$), the appropriate percentage point is $t_{.025,9}$, or 2.262. Since $\overline{X}$ is equal to 1.58, the 95% confidence limits are

$$L = \overline{X} - 2.262\frac{s}{\sqrt{10}} = 1.58 - 2.262 \times .389 = 1.58 - .88 = .70$$

and

$$R = \overline{X} + 2.262\frac{s}{\sqrt{10}} = 1.58 + 2.262 \times .389 = 1.58 + .88 = 2.46$$

We are 95% confident that μ lies between .70 and 2.46, in the sense that the random variables L and R (which for our data take values .70 and 2.46) have probability .95 of enclosing μ between them, whatever μ may be.*

---

*The t-distribution was discovered in 1908 by W. S. Gosset, who wrote under the name "Student." The data in the example are his; see reference 7.1.

7.6 SAMPLE SIZE

For the case of a known population variance σ^2, the confidence interval given by the limits (7.13) has width

$$w = 2Z_{\alpha/2} \frac{\sigma}{\sqrt{n}} \tag{7.19}$$

If σ^2 is unknown, so that we must use the limits (7.18), the confidence interval has width

$$w = 2t_{\alpha/2, n-1} \frac{s}{\sqrt{n}} \tag{7.20}$$

Commonly we should like to know, in advance of sampling, how large a sample is required to estimate the mean with specified precision, as measured by the confidence level together with the width of the confidence interval.

EXAMPLE 1

Problem: Suppose we know σ^2, so that equation (7.19) applies, and suppose we know in fact that σ^2 is equal to 100. Suppose further that we want a 95% confidence interval of width 5; in other words, we want a 95% chance that our estimate $\overline{X}$ will be within 2.5 of the true μ. What sample size is required?
Solution: We have

$$w = 5 \qquad \sigma = 10 \qquad Z_{.025} = 1.96$$

and so by equation (7.19)

$$5 = 2 \times 1.96 \frac{10}{\sqrt{n}}$$

Thus $\sqrt{n}$ must be 7.8, so n must be 60.8—or actually 61.

EXAMPLE 2

If we have σ^2 equal to 100 as before, and still want a w of 5 but require a 99% confidence interval, then

$$w = 5 \qquad \sigma = 10 \qquad Z_{.005} = 2.576$$

so equation (7.19) gives

$$5 = 2 \times 2.576 \frac{10}{\sqrt{n}}$$

This time $\sqrt{n}$ is 10.3, so n must be 106. *For a fixed width, greater confidence requires larger sample size.*

EXAMPLE 3

Problem: Suppose σ^2 is 100 and we want a 95% confidence interval, as in Example 1, but suppose we require a w of 3.

Solution: Here

$$w = 3 \qquad \sigma = 10 \qquad Z_{.025} = 1.96$$

so

$$3 = 2 \times 1.96 \frac{10}{\sqrt{n}}$$

which implies that $\sqrt{n}$ is 13.1; n must be 172. *For a fixed level of confidence, attaining a smaller width w requires a larger sample.*

If the variance is not known, equation (7.20) applies. In this case, the width w depends on the sample itself because of the factor s, and the situation is more complicated. To find the n needed for a given precision requires some advance notion of the size of σ, either from past experience or from a preliminary sample. Using equation (7.19) in place of equation (7.20) will give a very rough idea of what n must be. See reference 7.4.

7.7   ESTIMATING BINOMIAL p

In Section 5.8 we defined a binomial population as a population whose elements are classified as belonging to one of two classes conventionally labelled success and failure. We represent the proportion of the population that belongs to the first class by p and the proportion that belongs to the second class by $1 - p$. In general, p is unknown and the problem is to estimate it.

Suppose we have at hand an independent sample of size n; let X be the number of successes in the sample, and let f (equal to X/n) be the proportion of successes. As stated in Section 5.8, X has mean np and variance $np(1 - p)$, and f has mean, variance, and standard deviation

$$E(f) = p$$
$$\text{Var}(f) = p(1 - p)/n$$
$$\text{St Dev}(f) = \sqrt{p(1 - p)/n}$$

The first equation shows that f is an unbiased estimator of p. The second gives the variance of this estimator. Its value, of course, cannot be found without knowledge of the value of the parameter p to be estimated. However, this variance is largest (for fixed n) when p is $1/2$, so that

$$\text{Var}(f) \le \frac{1}{4n}$$

This gives a conservative idea of the variance. Or we can get an idea of the variance by replacing p by its estimator f: The variance is approximated by $f(1 - f)/n$.

149

We now turn our attention to the problem of finding interval estimates for the proportion p. The calculation of "exact" confidence intervals based on the binomial probabilities is complex; therefore, tables and graphs of these intervals have been constructed for various confidence probabilities. Table IV of the Appendix gives the 95% confidence intervals for p for a number of sample sizes from 10 to 1000. If our sample size is one of those tabled and is less than 100, we find the number observed in the leftmost column and then move horizontally into the column corresponding to our sample size. The two numbers we find there are the endpoints of the interval and may be expressed as either percentages or relative frequencies. For example, suppose I take a sample of thirty students and find that eight of them do not smoke. In the column for $n = 30$ I find the figures 12 and 46 opposite the observed number 8. I may then state that, on the basis of this sample, I am 95% confident that the percentage of nonsmoking students is between 12% and 46%. Alternatively, the confidence interval for the relative frequency of nonsmoking students is .12 to .46.

For sample sizes greater than or equal to 100, we use the column for observed relative frequency rather than that for the observed number of successes. If n is 250 and X is 75, then the observed fraction is 75/250, or .3. We locate .3 in the Fraction Observed column, and in the column for values of n equal to 250 we find the corresponding pair of values to be 24 and 36. This means our 95% confidence interval for p is from .24 to .36.

If the observed fraction f is greater than .50 we use $1 - f$ and subtract each limit from 100. For example, out of 1000 heads of families questioned it was found that 930 owned one or more television receivers. The observed fraction, .93, is greater than .50. We subtract .93 from 1.00 to get .07. The corresponding figures in the column for $n = 1000$ are 6 and 9. We subtract these from 100 to get 94 and 91, respectively. The 95% confidence interval for the percentage of families that own TV sets is 91% to 94%.

Interpolation may be used in this table and is straightforward for the three largest sample sizes. For example, if n is 500 and X is 150, then the observed fraction f is 150/500, or .30. For $n = 250$ the confidence limits would be .24 and .36. For $n = 1000$ the limits would be .27 and .33. The proportion we want is

$$\frac{500 - 250}{1000 - 250} = \frac{250}{750} = \frac{1}{3}$$

Therefore, the lower limit is

$$.24 + \tfrac{1}{3}(.27 - .24) = .25$$

and the upper limit is

$$.36 + \tfrac{1}{3}(.33 - .36) = .35$$

For values of n from 10 to 50, inclusive, the interpolation is not quite as simple, for we must calculate for each sample size the observed number that corresponds to a given observed fraction. Let n be 25 and X be 15. Then f is 15/25, or .60. For $n = 20$ the observed number corresponding to $f = .60$ is 20(.60), or 12, and the confidence limits are .36 and .81. For $n = 30$ the value of X used to enter the table is 30(.60), or 18, and the confidence limits are .40 and .77. Since our sample size, 25, is midway between $n = 20$ and $n = 30$, our confidence limits are

$$.36 + \tfrac{1}{2}(.40 - .36) = .38$$

and

$$.81 + \tfrac{1}{2}(.77 - .81) = .79$$

The confidence limits in Table IV are based on exact binomial probabilities. Another approach is required if we have no tables or want a confidence level not tabulated. The normal approximation to the binomial provides a method of finding approximate confidence limits for large sample sizes. A knowledge of the method is of practical importance and also deepens our understanding of binomial estimation.

As stated in Section 5.9, the standardized fraction of successes

$$\frac{f - p}{\sqrt{p(1 - p)/n}} \qquad (7.21)$$

has for large n approximately a standard normal distribution; see equation (5.19), page 116, and the example following it. If in the expression (7.21) we replace each p in the denominator by its estimator f, we get a ratio

$$\frac{f - p}{\sqrt{f(1 - f)/n}} \qquad (7.22)$$

which turns out also to have approximately a normal distribution for large n.

By the definition of the percentage points $Z_{\alpha/2}$ for the standard normal distribution, we therefore have the approximate equation

$$P\left(-Z_{\alpha/2} \leq \frac{f - p}{\sqrt{f(1 - f)/n}} \leq Z_{\alpha/2}\right) \cong 1 - \alpha \qquad (7.23)$$

If we operate on the inequalities here just as we did in constructing the confidence intervals in Sections 7.3 and 7.5, we arrive at

$$P\left(f - Z_{\alpha/2}\sqrt{\frac{f(1 - f)}{n}} \leq p \leq f + Z_{\alpha/2}\sqrt{\frac{f(1 - f)}{n}}\right) \cong 1 - \alpha$$

Therefore, the random variables

$$L = f - Z_{\alpha/2}\sqrt{\frac{f(1 - f)}{n}} \quad \text{and} \quad R = f + Z_{\alpha/2}\sqrt{\frac{f(1 - f)}{n}}$$

have approximate probability $1 - \alpha$ of containing between them the true value of p, whatever it may be; they therefore can be used as approximate $100(1 - \alpha)\%$ confidence limits if n is large.

151

TABLE 4#

EXAMPLE 1

Problem: In a town, a sample of 100 voters contained 64 persons who favored a bond issue. Between what limits can we be 95% confident that the proportion of voters in the community who favor the issue is contained?

Solution: Here,

$$n = 100 \qquad X = 64 \qquad f = .64 \qquad Z_{.025} = 1.96$$

Hence

$$\sqrt{\frac{f(1 - f)}{n}} = \sqrt{\frac{.64 \times .36}{100}} = .048$$

and

$$L = .64 - 1.96 \times .048 = .64 - .094 = .546$$

$$R = .64 + 1.96 \times .048 = .64 + .094 = .734$$

We are 95% confident the true proportion is covered by the interval from .55 to .73. The 95% confidence limits from Table IV are .54 and .73; the normal approximation is quite accurate.

PROBLEMS

1. For the following results from samples from normal populations, what are the best estimates for the mean, the variance, the variance of the mean, the standard deviation, and the standard deviation of the mean?
    a. $n = 9, \sum X_i = 36, \sum (X_i - \bar{X})^2 = 288.$
    b. $n = 16, \sum X_i = 64, \sum (X_i - \bar{X})^2 = 180.$
    c. $n = 9, \sum X_i = 450, \sum (X_i - \bar{X})^2 = 32.$
    d. $n = 25, \sum X_i = 500, \sum X_i^2 = 12,400.$
    e. $n = 16, \sum X_i = 320, \sum X_i^2 = 6640.$

2. For each of the following samples from normal populations find the best estimates for $\mu, \sigma^2, \sigma, \text{Var}(\bar{X})$, and St Dev($\bar{X}$).
    a. 6, 15, 3, 12, 6, 21, 15, 18, 12.
    b. 4, 10, 2, 8, 4, 14, 10, 12, 8.
    c. 2, 5, 9, 11, 13.
    d. 1, 3, 3, 5, 6, 6.
    e. $-4, 2, -6, 0, -4, 6, 2, 4, 0.$
    f. 6676, 6678, 6681, 6680, 6681, 6678.

3. Given the following results from random samples from binomial populations, find the best estimates for p, the variance and standard deviation of X, and the variance and standard deviation of the observed fraction, f.
    a. $n = 25, X = 5.$　　　　　　　　b. $n = 64, X = 32.$
    c. $n = 400, X = 144.$　　　　　　d. $n = 100, X = 64.$

4. In a sample of 100 small castings, 98 were not defective. What are the best estimates for (a) the proportion of nondefectives in the lot from which the sample was taken, and (b) the standard deviation of the estimator?

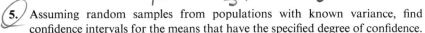

IF σ is Know use z if σ is know use t

5. Assuming random samples from populations with known variance, find confidence intervals for the means that have the specified degree of confidence.
   a. $n = 9$, $\bar{X} = 20$, $\sigma^2 = 9$, confidence $= 95\%$.

   use z
   b. $n = 16$, $\bar{X} = 52$, $\sigma^2 = 64$, confidence $= 99\%$.
   c. $n = 25$, $\bar{X} = 120$, $\sigma^2 = 400$, confidence $= 90\%$.

6. Assuming samples from normal populations with known variance find:
   a. The degree of confidence used if $n = 16$, $\sigma = 8$, and the total width of a confidence interval for the mean is 3.29 units.
   b. The sample size when $\sigma^2 = 100$ and the 95% confidence interval for the mean is from 17.2 to 22.8.
   c. The known variance when $n = 100$ and the 98% confidence interval for the mean is 23.26 units in width.

7. Find the value of t such that
   a. The probability of a larger value is .005 when ν (degrees of freedom) is equal to 27.
   b. The probability of a smaller value is .975 when $\nu = 14$.
   c. The probability of a larger value, sign ignored, is .90 when $\nu = 40$.

8. For random samples from normal populations the quantity

$$t = \frac{\bar{X} - \mu}{s/\sqrt{n}}$$

has a t-distribution with $n - 1$ degrees of freedom. In each of the following find the indicated quantity:
   a. $n = 25$, $\bar{X} - \mu = 3$, $s = 2$. Find t.
   b. $t = 2$, $n = 16$, $\bar{X} - \mu = 8$. Find s^2.
   c. $n = 25$, $s = 20$, probability of a larger t is .05. Find $\bar{X} - \mu$.
   d. $n = 16$, $\bar{X} - \mu = 10$, probability of a smaller t is .90. Find s.

9. Assuming unknown variances, find 95% confidence intervals for the means based on the sample results given in problem 1 above.

10. Assuming unknown variances, and using the data given in problem 2 above, find
   a. 95% confidence intervals for the means for parts a and b.
   b. 99% confidence intervals for the means for parts c, d, and e.
   c. 98% confidence intervals for part f.

11. Sensitivity tests were made on twenty randomly selected tubes of a given type. The mean was 3.2 microvolts and the estimated variance was .20. Find a 95% confidence interval for the mean sensitivity of this type of tube.

12. A sample of nine plots had a mean yield of 100 grams and an estimated standard deviation equal to 15 grams. Find a 98% confidence interval for the mean yield.

13. Nine samples of a solution were analyzed for copper concentration in grams per liter, giving $\bar{X} = 9.50$ and $s^2 = .0064$. Find a 95% confidence interval for the true unknown concentration.

14. An important physical constant is the ratio, e/m, of the charge of the electron to its mass. From a cathode ray tube, the following experimental values for e/m were obtained. The dimensions are emu per gram.

153

1.7604×10^7	1.7638×10^7	1.7609×10^7
1.7563×10^7	1.7556×10^7	1.7582×10^7
1.7525×10^7	1.7663×10^7	1.7624×10^7
1.7620×10^7	1.7605×10^7	1.7621×10^7

a. From these data, what inferences can we make in terms of point estimates?
b. Find the 99% confidence interval for e/m.

15. Twenty children were given a standard IQ test. They were then given a special course designed to increase IQ, and were tested again at the end of the course. The differences between first and second scores had a mean equal to 4. The estimated variance was 25. Find a 99% confidence interval for the mean difference.

16. A certain stimulus was tested for its effect on blood pressure. Twenty men had their blood pressure measured before and after the stimulus. The results are given below. Find a 99% confidence interval for the mean change in blood pressure.

$$8, 7, 1, 9, -8, -3, 1, 2, -8, 2, 3, 8, 1, 7, -5, -4, 0, 7, -1, 5$$

17. In an attempt to determine the wavelength of a spectral line, the following values were obtained. Find a 98% confidence interval for the true wavelength.

$$5892, 5900, 5885, 5890, 5895, 5893$$

18. Use the data of problem 8, Chapter 3, to find a 95% confidence interval for the mean yield of corn per hill.

19. Use the data of problem 9, Chapter 3, to find a 99% confidence interval for the mean spring constant of this type of wood beam.

20. Use the data of problem 10, Chapter 3, to find a 90% confidence interval for the mean difference in transconductance.

21. Find a 95% confidence interval for the mean based on the following distribution. Here, $n = 60$.

Class	Relative frequency
10 but less than 20	.10
20 " " " 30	.30
30 " " " 40	.40
40 " " " 50	.20

22. Use the data of problem 24, Chapter 3, to find a 99% confidence interval for the mean time between malfunctions for all equipment of this type.

23. The mean weight gain of fifteen swine fed a given ration during a thirty-day period was forty pounds. The standard deviation was 4. Find a 95% confidence interval for the true mean thirty-day gain under this ration.

24. A sample of twenty-four blooms taken from a particular strain of roses had an average width of four inches with a standard deviation of $\frac{1}{2}$. Find a 98% confidence interval for the mean width of the blooms of this rose.

25. The following distribution is that for the lengths of mayfly larvae. Find a 95% confidence interval for the mean length.

X: Length (mm)	Number of larvae
$11 \le X < 15$	2
$15 \le X < 17$	4
$17 \le X < 19$	7
$19 \le X < 21$	9
$21 \le X < 23$	6
$23 \le X < 25$	15
$25 \le X < 27$	12
$27 \le X < 29$	5
$29 \le X < 33$	4

26. The following are determinations of ascorbic acid content of randomly selected turnip plant leaves. One leaf was taken from each of sixteen randomly selected plants. Find 95% confidence limits for the mean content. What statement can you make on the basis of this interval? Why may you make this statement?

$$9.35 \quad 8.65 \quad 11.68 \quad 12.77 \quad 8.81 \quad 9.52 \quad 12.61 \quad 9.87$$
$$8.68 \quad 9.82 \quad 10.29 \quad 10.99 \quad 10.76 \quad 10.55 \quad 10.43 \quad 12.04$$

27. Use the table of binomial confidence intervals to find 95% confidence intervals for p when:

a. $n = 10$, $X = 7$. **b.** $n = 50$, $X = 0$.
c. $n = 100$, $X = 23$. **d.** $n = 100$, $X = 64$.
e. $n = 250$, $X = 150$. **f.** $n = 1000$, $X = 50$.

28. Use the table of binomial confidence intervals to find 95% confidence intervals for p when:

a. $n = 15$, $X = 12$. **b.** $n = 30$, $X = 30$.
c. $n = 100$, $X = 87$. **d.** $n = 250$, $X = 125$.
e. $n = 1000$, $X = 120$. **f.** $n = 250$, $X = 200$.

29. Use interpolation in the table of binomial confidence intervals to find 95% confidence intervals for p in each of the following situations:

a. $n = 40$, $X = 28$. **b.** $n = 60$, $X = 6$.
c. $n = 750$, $X = 375$. **d.** $n = 175$, $X = 35$.

30. Use interpolation in the table of binomial confidence intervals to find 95% confidence intervals for p when:

a. $n = 500$, $X = 125$. **b.** $n = 150$, $X = 115$.
c. $n = 12$, $X = 6$. **d.** $n = 25$, $X = 15$.

31. In a certain lake, a sample of 1000 fish was obtained by use of nets. It was found that 290 were members of the bass family. Give a 95% confidence interval for the percentage of bass among fish in the lake.

32. In a sample of 100 farm operators, 64 were also the owners of the farm. Find a 95% confidence interval for the proportion of operators who are also owners. Use the normal approximation to the binomial.

155

33. If 10% of a sample of 400 items were found to be defective, what is the 99% confidence interval for the proportion defective in the lot from which the sample was taken? Use the normal approximation to the binomial.

34. In a sample of 100 high-pressure castings, 20 were found to have chill folds resulting from improper heating of the mold. Find the 99% confidence interval for the true percent of all castings which have chill folds.

35. One fourth of 300 persons interviewed were opposed to a certain program. Calculate a 99% confidence interval for the fraction of the population who are in opposition to the program. Use the normal approximation.

36. Using a sample of 100 items, I found that a 95% confidence interval for the population mean had limits 10 and 30. Out of 200 additional samples of the same size, only 65% had means that fell within my limits, 10 to 30. Was I not right in expecting about 95% of these sample means to lie in this interval? Explain.

37. If a normal population has a known standard deviation σ of .75, how large a sample must be taken in order that the total width of the 95% confidence interval for the population mean will not be greater than .8?

38. If X is a normal variable with known variance equal to 625, how large a sample must we take to be 99% confident that the sample mean will not differ from the true mean by more than five units?

39. If a normal population is known to have σ equal to 5, how large a sample should we take in order to be 95% confident that the sample mean will not differ from the population mean by more than one unit?

40. Suppose the diameter of ball bearings made by a given process are known to be normally distributed with a known standard deviation σ of .5. How large a sample must we take to be 95% confident that our estimate for the mean will not differ from the true mean diameter by more than .01?

41. The maximum value that can be attained by the variance of the sample fraction, f, is $1/4n$; hence, the maximum width of a $100(1 - \alpha)\%$ confidence interval for p, using the normal approximation, is $Z_{\alpha/2}/\sqrt{n}$. How large a sample should we take from a binomial population in order to be about 95% confident that the sample fraction will not differ from p more than .02?

42. Using the maximum standard deviation of f (see problem 41 above) find the sample size such that we can be about 99% confident that f will not differ from p by more than .05.

CLASS SAMPLING EXERCISE

Each student should select three random samples of size $n = 5$ from the normal distribution, Table VII of the Appendix, in the manner described in the Class Sampling Exercise A following the problems for Chapter 6.

For each of the samples find a 95% confidence interval for the mean, μ.

List all of the intervals obtained by the members of the class. What percentage of them contain μ?

REFERENCES

7.1 FISHER, R. A. *Statistical Methods for Research Workers*, 13th edition. Hafner, New York, 1963.

7.2 HOGG, ROBERT V., and ALLEN T. CRAIG. *Introduction to Mathematical Statistics*, 3rd edition. Macmillan, New York, 1970. Chapters 6, 7, and 8.

7.3 MOSTELLER, FREDERICK, ROBERT E. K. ROURKE, and GEORGE B. THOMAS, JR. *Probability with Statistical Applications*, 2nd edition. Addison-Wesley, Reading, 1970. Chapter 12.

7.4 SNEDECOR, GEORGE W., and WILLIAM G. COCHRAN. *Statistical Methods*, 6th edition. Iowa State University Press, Ames, 1967. Chapters 1, 2, and 3.

make 95% C.I. for

μ (a)

μ (b)   compare

#3 a.) $n = 9$ $\Sigma X_i = 36$ $\Sigma(X_i - \bar{X})^2 = 288$

b.) $n = 100$ $\Sigma X_i = 405$ $\Sigma(X_i - \bar{X})^2 = 3465$

approx C.I for p based on normal approx to binomial $(np > 5, n(1-p) > 5)$

95% C.I. $f \pm 1.96\sqrt{\dfrac{f(1-f)}{n}}$

for any other % C.I.

$(100)(1-\alpha)\%$ $f \pm Z_{\alpha/2}\sqrt{\dfrac{f(1-f)}{n}}$

8

Tests of Hypotheses

8.1   INTRODUCTION

Turning from estimation to the theory of testing hypotheses, let us consider an example that exhibits in concrete form the problems that arise in the general case.

A "triangle test" provides one way of checking whether a candidate for a food technician's evaluation panel can distinguish subtle differences in taste. In a single trial of this test the subject is presented with three food samples, two of which are alike, and is asked to select the odd one. Except for the taste difference, the samples are as similar as possible, and the order of presentation is random. In the absence of any ability at all to distinguish tastes, the subject has a one-third chance of correctly distinguishing the odd food sample, and the question is whether he can do better than that.

To check the subject's ability, we present him with a series of triangle tests, and the order of presentation is randomized within each trial to eliminate any consistent bias and to make the trials independent of one another. Let p be the probability that the subject correctly identifies the odd food sample in a single trial. Then $p > 1/3$ if the subject has an ability in taste discrimination, and $p = 1/3$ if he has none. (Since it is hard to see how he could do worse than chance, we rule out the possibility $p < 1/3$ on a priori grounds.)

To place the problem in a standard framework, we label these two hypotheses:

Null hypothesis H_0: $p = 1/3$
Alternative hypothesis H_a: $p > 1/3$

We confront the problem of testing the null hypothesis H_0 against the alternative H_a. The hypotheses H_0 and H_a together make up what we call the *model*; we assume a priori that either H_0 is true or else H_a is true.

If we make n trials with the subject, and if X is the number of correct identifications he makes, then X has the binomial distribution with parameters n and p:

$$P(X = r) = \binom{n}{r} p^r (1 - p)^{n-r} \qquad r = 0, 1, 2, \ldots, n \qquad (8.1)$$

We want to use the statistic X to decide whether or not the alternative hypothesis H_a is more reasonable or plausible than the null hypothesis H_0— that is, whether or not the subject has ability. And we want to set up in advance of experimentation a rule for making the decision; we want to set up a statistical procedure in the form of a *test*. This parallels what we do in constructing confidence intervals, for a given problem settling on confidence limits $\overline{X} \pm 2.262(s/\sqrt{n})$, say, in advance of sampling, and letting the sample give to these limits actual numerical values. In the present problem we want to set up a *rejection region* or *critical region*, a set R of X-values that will lead us to reject H_0 and prefer H_a to H_0. If the experiment gives to X a numerical value lying in R, we reject H_0; otherwise, we do not.

To illustrate, suppose that n is 10. Consider two rejection regions:

$$R_5 = \{5, 6, 7, 8, 9, 10\}$$

and

$$R_7 = \{7, 8, 9, 10\}$$

If we use R_5, the rule or test is: If $X \geq 5$, reject H_0 and accept H_a (decide that the subject has ability); if $X < 5$, accept H_0 (decide that the subject has no ability). If we use R_7, the rule is: If $X \geq 7$, reject H_0 and accept H_a; if $X < 7$, accept H_0. (Of course, we could use some cutoff point other than 5 or 7.)

Each of these two rules makes sense: We decide in favor of the hypothesis H_a that $p > 1/3$ when X is large. It is contrary to common sense to use a rule that says to decide in favor of H_a in case $X \leq 3$, for example, or a rule that says to decide in favor of H_a in case X is even. But of the sensible regions R_5 and R_7, which is better? Applying a test may lead to the wrong conclusion. There are in fact two kinds of error possible, called Type I and Type II errors:

> *Type I error:* We reject H_0 but H_0 is true
> *Type II error:* We accept H_0 but H_0 is false

We assess the strength of a test or rejection region by the probabilities of these two kinds of error:

$$\alpha = P(\text{reject } H_0 \mid H_0 \text{ is true}) = P(\text{Type I error})$$
$$\beta = P(\text{accept } H_0 \mid H_0 \text{ is false}) = P(\text{Type II error})$$

159

Naturally we want α and β to be small. The probability α of a Type I error is also called the *size* of the test or the *level of significance*. And $1 - \beta$ is called the *power*.

small

LARGE

True	Conclusion	
situation	H_0 is true	H_0 is false
H_0 is true	No error; Probability $= 1 - \alpha$	Type I error; Probability $=$ size $= \alpha$
H_0 is false	Type II error; Probability $= \beta$	No error; Probability $=$ power $= 1 - \beta$

For the rejection region R_5, a Type I error occurs when the subject has no skill but scores five or more successful identifications just by luck. The chance of this is:

$$\alpha \text{ for } R_5 = P(X \geq 5) = \sum_{r=5}^{10} \binom{10}{r} \left(\frac{1}{3}\right)^r \left(\frac{2}{3}\right)^{10-r} = .213$$

For the rejection region R_7, the chance of a Type I error is:

$$\alpha \text{ for } R_7 = P(X \geq 7) = \sum_{r=7}^{10} \binom{10}{r} \left(\frac{1}{3}\right)^r \left(\frac{2}{3}\right)^{10-r} = .020$$

Now $P(X \geq 7)$ is smaller than $P(X \geq 5)$. As far as Type I error is concerned, then, R_7 is a *better* rejection region than R_5.

But what about β, the chance of a Type II error? If H_0 is false, so that $p > 1/3$, then β depends on which alternative value of p we check. We should write β_p to indicate this dependence on p. Let us check for a p of .65. For the region R_5,

$$\beta_{.65} \text{ for } R_5 = P(X < 5) = \sum_{r=0}^{4} \binom{10}{r} (.65)^r (.35)^{10-r} = .095$$

This time we use .65 as the value for p and .35 as a value for $1 - p$ in the binomial formula because we are computing the chance that we will erroneously accept the null hypothesis that the subject is devoid of skill when in fact he can guess right 65% of the time. For R_7,

$$\beta_{.65} \text{ for } R_7 = P(X < 7) = \sum_{r=0}^{6} \binom{10}{r} (.65)^r (.35)^{10-r} = .486$$

Now $P(X < 7)$ is greater than $P(X < 5)$. As far as Type II error is concerned, R_7 is a *worse* rejection region than R_5.

We can summarize our computations in a table:

	α	$\beta_{.65}$
R_5	.213	.095
R_7	.020	.486

Most Important

The α column makes us prefer R_7, but the β column makes us prefer R_5. This is inevitable: ~~As α goes down, β goes up~~, and vice versa. If we refuse to allow a Type I error at all, so that α is 0, we must always accept H_0, whatever X may be (so the rejection region R is empty); but then if H_0 should be false, we always make an error of Type II, so that β is 1. Or if we demand that β equal 0, we must always reject H_0, whatever X may be (so the rejection region R is $\{0, 1, 2, \ldots, 10\}$); in this case, if H_0 is true we always make an error of Type I, so that α is 1. It is impossible to arrange that both α and β are equal to 0. For whatever consolation it may be, it is equally impossible to arrange that both α and β are equal to 1.

The procedure in a court of law affords an illuminating parallel. Let the null hypothesis be that the defendant is innocent and let the alternative hypothesis be that he is guilty. To condemn an innocent man is to commit a Type I error; to acquit a guilty man is to commit a Type II error. The rules that govern a trial are loosely analogous to a statistical procedure—to a statistical test or a rejection region. Any rule that decreases the chance α of a Type I error (a rule, say, that the defendant need not testify against himself) necessarily increases the chance β of a Type II error. And any rule that decreases the chance β of a Type II error (a rule allowing a split jury to convict, say) necessarily increases the chance α of a Type I error. It is impossible to arrange that both α and β are equal to 0. But it is equally impossible to arrange that both α and β are 1 (the contrary appearance of legal reality notwithstanding).

To return to our taste experiment, since the probability of a Type II error depends on which particular p (exceeding 1/3) obtains, a complete understanding of the test requires a graph of β_p. Such a graph is called the *operating characteristic curve*, or OC curve. The OC curve for our experiment is shown in Figure 8.1.

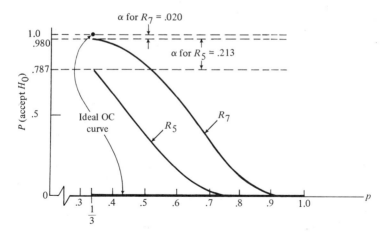

FIGURE 8.1. *OC curves: the probability of accepting H_0: $p = \frac{1}{3}$ as a function of p for $n = 10$ trials and for rejection regions $R_5 = \{5, 6, 7, 8, 9, 10\}$ and $R_7 = \{7, 8, 9, 10\}$*

(Sometimes, $1 - \beta_p$ is graphed instead of β_p; this graph is called the *power curve* for the test. Of course, the OC curve and the power curve are merely different representations of the same information.)

In Figure 8.1, the height of the OC curve labelled R_5 over a point p on the horizontal scale is the probability

$$\beta_p \text{ for } R_5 = P(X < 5) = \sum_{r=0}^{4} \binom{10}{r} p^r (1 - p)^{10-r}$$

of accepting H_0 when the rejection region R_5 is used and p is the actual chance that the subject can correctly identify the odd food sample on a single trial. If $p > 1/3$, this height is β_p, the probability of a Type II error—the probability of incorrectly accepting H_0. If $p = 1/3$ (the left end of the graph), this height is $1 - \alpha$, the probability of correctly accepting H_0. Notice that the curve drops off to the right: Naturally, the more skill the subject has—that is, the greater p is—the less likely the test or experiment is to indicate that he has no skill. Similar remarks apply to the OC curve labelled R_7.

Will the OC curves for our experiment help us to determine the best rejection region? The ideal OC curve would have height 1 at $p = 1/3$ and would immediately jump down to 0 for $p > 1/3$, as indicated in Figure 8.1. But no corresponding rejection region exists. At the left end, the R_7 curve is nearer this ideal than the R_5 curve is; everywhere to the right of this, the R_5 curve is nearer this ideal than the R_7 curve is. That the R_7 curve lies above the R_5 curve *at the left end* makes us prefer R_7 to R_5; that the R_7 curve lies above the R_5 curve *everywhere else* makes us prefer R_5 to R_7. Neither region is better than the other. The rejection region R_7 is optimal in this sense: R_7 has an α of .02, and among rejection regions (for sample size n of 10) with an α this small, R_7 has the smallest β-values. And R_5 is optimal as well: R_5 has an α of .213, and among rejection regions with an α of this size, R_5 has the smallest β-values. This supports our commonsense feeling that all rational rejection regions must have the form

$$\{r, r + 1, \ldots, 10\}$$

For a proof and further theoretical considerations, see reference 8.2.

To get an OC curve nearer the ideal shown in Figure 8.1, we must increase n. In addition to increased accuracy, this means, of course, increased effort, time, and money. Figure 8.2 repeats the upper OC curve from Figure 8.1 ($n = 10$ and $R = \{7, 8, 9, 10\}$). The middle curve is the OC curve for an n of 50 and an R equal to $\{24, 25, \ldots, 50\}$; the bottom one is the OC curve for an $n = 200$ and an R equal to $\{82, 83, \ldots, 200\}$. In the case where n is 50 and the case where n is 200 (curves (b) and (c), respectively, in Figure 8.2), the cutoff point of the rejection region was chosen to make α equal to .02 again. The higher n is, the more rapidly the curve drops from $1 - \alpha$, or .98, towards the horizontal scale.

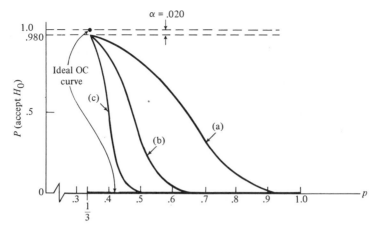

FIGURE 8.2. *OC curves: the probability of accepting H_0: $p = \frac{1}{3}$ as a function of p for* (a) $n = 10$ *trials and $R = \{7, 8, 9, 10\}$,* (b) $n = 50$ *trials and $R = \{24, 25, \ldots, 50\}$, and* (c) $n = 200$ *trials and $R = \{82, 83, \ldots, 200\}$*

In the sequel we shall encounter many testing problems. They share certain features with the example above, and their analysis can conveniently be set out in a standard sequence of steps.

1. Formulate the null hypothesis H_0 in statistical terms.
2. Formulate the alternative hypothesis H_a in statistical terms.
3. Set the level of significance α and the sample size n.
4. Select the appropriate statistic and the rejection region R.
5. Collect the data and calculate the statistic.
6. If the calculated statistic falls in the rejection region R, reject H_0 in favor of H_a; if the calculated statistic falls outside R, do not reject H_0.

Each of these steps calls for comment:

Step 1. The null hypothesis must be stated in statistical terms. It would not suffice in our example merely to hypothesize that the subject cannot distinguish subtle differences in taste; we need the specific binomial model, together with the identification of $p = 1/3$ as representing absence of skill.

Step 2. The alternative hypothesis is essential to the problem. Suppose that, in order to check alleged ESP powers in a subject, we present him at each of a series of trials with three cards—one diamond and two spades—presented face down and in random order. He is to pick out the diamond. The form is that of the triangle test, and H_0: $p = 1/3$ again represents the null hypothesis of no ability. Should the alternative hypothesis again be H_a: $p > 1/3$? Although that would seem to represent positive ESP prowess, it is sometimes claimed that certain subjects have ESP power but disbelieve in its existence and hence, subconsciously and perversely, change from a

163

right answer to a wrong one. Since p is less than 1/3 for such a subject, the alternative hypothesis should include the cases $p < 1/3$ as well as the cases $p > 1/3$; we should take $H_a: p \neq 1/3$. In the taste experiment, an excessively large X leads us to reject H_0 in favor of H_a; in the present case, an excessively small X should also lead us to reject H_0 in favor of H_a. (In 3000 ESP trials, 1900 correct guesses, which is 900 over the 1000 to be expected at chance, would be terrifying—but so would 100 correct guesses, which is 900 under expectation.) Since the form of the alternative hypothesis affects the form of the appropriate test, the alternative hypothesis must correctly represent the problem at hand.

Step 3. The test procedures for the three OC curves in Figure 8.2 all correspond to an α level of 2%. The greater the effort expended in sampling —that is, the greater n is—the better (smaller) are the corresponding β-values.

Step 4. In the taste experiment, the statistic is the number X of successes and the rejection region has the commonsense form $\{r, r + 1, \ldots, n\}$. In all our testing problems, common sense will dictate the proper form of the rejection region; choosing the exact region (choosing the actual value of r in our example) requires knowing the distribution of the statistic (the binomial distribution, in our example).

Step 5. The sampling procedure must accord with the model, the binomial model in our example.

Step 6. The hypotheses H_0 and H_a are not treated in a symmetric fashion. Suppose our test corresponds to the middle OC curve in Figure 8.2: $n = 50$ and $R = \{24, 25, \ldots, 50\}$. If p is 1/3, then $P(X \geq 24)$, or α, is small—namely, .02; thus H_0 does not well "explain" an observed X of 24 or more, and so we reject H_0 if $X \geq 24$. But if $X < 24$ can we confidently accept H_0? Since $P(X < 24)$, or $1 - \alpha$, is equal to .98 if $p = 1/3$, H_0 *does* well explain an observed X of less than 24. But since the OC curve falls off continuously, $P(X < 24)$ is almost .98 for p-values just a little greater than 1/3 (for example, $P(X < 24) = .97$ if $p = .34$), and these p-values also well explain an observed X that is less than 24. In the event that $X < 24$, then, we do not confidently accept H_0 because we cannot confidently reject "all" of H_a. We can reject the values of p far exceeding 1/3 but not those barely exceeding 1/3. Hence the lack of symmetry between H_0 and H_a. We control α by choosing a rejection region that gives a prescribed value for α. The β-values are not completely under our control; they are small for large p but nearly $1 - \alpha$ for p near 1/3. A larger sample has the desirable effect of making the OC curve drop away more rapidly.

Since it becomes awkward continually to speak of not rejecting H_0, we shall in examples speak of accepting H_0, despite the fact that H_0 and H_a do not enter into the testing problem in a symmetric way.

Sometimes, tests of hypotheses are viewed as *tests of significance*. For the taste experiment with an n of 50, an X of 24 or more is said to be *significant at the 2% level*, because if H_0 is true—if $p = 1/3$—then $P(X \geq 24)$ is equal to .02. An X of 24 or more is significant evidence against H_0. But

$P(X \leq 10)$ is under .02 also; is an X of 10 or less significant at the 2% level? Not if the alternative is $p > 1/3$: $X \leq 10$ is unusual if $p = 1/3$, but it is even more unusual if $p > 1/3$. If the alternative is $p \neq 1/3$ (as in the ESP example), then $X \leq 10$ is significant (significant evidence against H_0): $X \leq 10$ is unusual if $p = 1/3$ but not if p is near 0. This emphasizes once more the importance of the alternative in significance testing.

In what follows we shall construct a number of tests of hypotheses. In each case we must actually construct the rejection region R, and these constructions will clarify the general principles set out above. Tests of hypotheses are used extensively in research, though not necessarily in rigid accord with the theory. The theoretical framework, however, makes it possible to understand what test is appropriate to what problem and what the strength of the test will be.

8.2 HYPOTHESES ON A NORMAL MEAN

Consider the null hypothesis that a normal population has a specified mean μ_0, the variance σ^2 being unknown. Under the null hypothesis $H_0: \mu = \mu_0$, the statistic

$$t = \frac{\overline{X} - \mu_0}{s/\sqrt{n}} \tag{8.2}$$

has a t-distribution with $n - 1$ degrees of freedom (see Section 7.4), which can be made the basis of a test.

Suppose first that the alternative hypothesis is $H_a: \mu > \mu_0$. It is intuitively clear that we ought to reject H_0 in favor of H_a when $\overline{X}$ is too large—in fact, when $\overline{X}$ exceeds μ_0 by too much. Since the t-statistic (8.2) increases when $\overline{X}$ increases, we can just as well reject H_0 when t is excessively large. How large? Recall that the upper α percentage point $t_{\alpha, n-1}$ is defined so that $P(t > t_{\alpha, n-1})$ is equal to α. Therefore, if we adopt the rule of rejecting H_0 when t exceeds $t_{\alpha, n-1}$, then the chance of rejecting H_0 when it is true is just α. The testing problem and the rule are

$$\begin{cases} H_0: \mu = \mu_0 \\ H_a: \mu > \mu_0 \\ R: t > t_{\alpha, n-1} \end{cases} \tag{8.3}$$

The rejection region is specified by the inequality $t > t_{\alpha, n-1}$. If we substitute the ratio in equation (8.2) for t here, multiply by $s/\sqrt{n}$, and then add μ_0, the inequality becomes $\overline{X} > \mu_0 + t_{\alpha, n-1}(s/\sqrt{n})$. Thus we reject the null hypothesis $\mu = \mu_0$ when $\overline{X}$ exceeds μ_0 by too much, $t_{\alpha, n-1}(s/\sqrt{n})$ providing the proper measure of "too much."

If μ is equal to μ_0, the distribution of the ratio (8.2) corresponds to the density curve (a) in Figure 8.3. If instead μ is equal to μ_1, say, where $\mu_1 > \mu_0$, then the ratio (8.2) has the density curve (b); it has the same shape

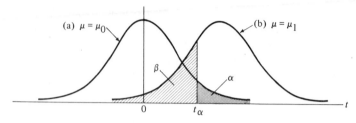

FIGURE 8.3. *Distributions corresponding to* $H_0: \mu = \mu_0$ *and* $H_a: \mu = \mu_1$

as (a) but is displaced to the right, its mean being $\mu_1 - \mu_0$ instead of 0. The cutoff point $t_{\alpha,n-1}$ is where the area of the right tail of curve (a) equals the level α of the test; the area of the left tail of curve (b) is the probability β of a Type II error if the mean μ is really μ_1.

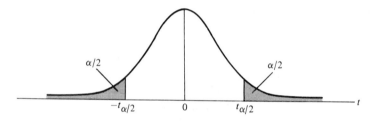

FIGURE 8.4. *A two-tailed critical region on the t-distribution*

Similarly, if the alternative is $\mu < \mu_0$, the sensible thing is to reject $\mu = \mu_0$ when t is small:

$$\begin{cases} H_0: \mu = \mu_0 \\ H_a: \mu < \mu_0 \\ R: \ t < -t_{\alpha,n-1} \end{cases} \qquad (8.4)$$

Notice again that $t < -t_{\alpha,n-1}$ has probability α if μ does equal μ_0; and notice that $t < -t_{\alpha,n-1}$ is the same thing as $\bar{X} < \mu_0 - t_{\alpha,n-1}(s/\sqrt{n})$.

The alternative hypotheses in (8.3) and (8.4) are one-sided, and so are the corresponding rejection regions. A two-sided alternative, including both possibilities $\mu > \mu_0$ and $\mu < \mu_0$, calls for a two-sided rejection region:

$$\begin{cases} H_0: \mu = \mu_0 \\ H_a: \mu \neq \mu_0 \\ R: \ t > t_{\alpha/2,n-1} \qquad \text{or} \qquad t < -t_{\alpha/2,n-1} \end{cases} \qquad (8.5)$$

The cutoff points are $\frac{1}{2}\alpha$ percentage points, since the test is two-tailed; as Figure 8.4 indicates, the total area of the two tails taken together is α. The rejection rule can be restated as $|\bar{X} - \mu_0| > t_{\alpha/2,n-1}$. We reject H_0 if $\bar{X}$ is excessively far from μ_0 in either direction.

EXAMPLE 1

Problem: A manufacturer of small electric motors asserts that on the average they will not draw more than .8 amperes under normal load conditions. A sample of sixteen of the motors was tested and it was found that the mean current was .96 amperes with a standard deviation of .32 amperes. Are we justified in rejecting the manufacturer's assertion?

Solution: Here the null hypothesis that the assertion is correct is $H_0: \mu = .8$. If we are willing to take a risk of 1 in 20 of rejecting his assertion if it is true, we set α at .05. Since we want to reject his assertion only if the evidence indicates that the mean current consumption (the population value) is greater than .8, we have a one-sided alternative $H_a: \mu > .8$. Under the assumption of normality, we use a *t*-statistic with 15 degrees of freedom and a one-tailed test; the cutoff point is $t_{.05,15}$, or 1.753:

$$\begin{cases} H_0: \mu = .8 \\ H_a: \mu > .8 \\ R: t > 1.753 \end{cases}$$

For our data the calculated *t* is:

$$t = \frac{\overline{X} - \mu_0}{s/\sqrt{n}} = \frac{.96 - .80}{.34/4} = 2.00$$

Since this exceeds 1.753, we reject the null hypothesis and conclude that the mean current consumption is greater than .8 amperes.

EXAMPLE 2

Problem: In an attempt to determine whether or not special training will increase IQ, twenty-five children are given a standard IQ test. The children are then given a course designed to increase their IQ scores and are tested once more at the end of the course. The differences between the second and first scores are recorded; the mean difference for the twenty-five children is found to be 3 points, and the sample standard deviation is 9 points. Has the training increased IQ?

Solution: The null hypothesis that the training has no effect is that the population mean of increases is $\mu = 0$. We will reject H_0 only if we think the mean increase is positive, so the alternative is $H_a: \mu > 0$. We need a one-tailed test, and if we set α at .05 the cutoff point is $t_{.05,24}$, or 1.711:

HAS NO effect

HAS effect

$$\begin{cases} H_0: \mu = 0 \\ H_a: \mu > 0 \\ R: t > 1.711 \end{cases} \quad \text{from Table III}$$

The calculated *t* is:

$$t = \frac{\overline{X} - 0}{s/\sqrt{25}} = \frac{3 - 0}{9/5} = 1.667$$

167

The data favor the null hypothesis that the training is without effect.

EXAMPLE 3

Problem: Last year's retail sales records show the average monthly expenditure per person for a certain food product was $5.50. We should like to know whether there has been any significant change in this average during the first quarter of this year.

Analysis: To make a comparison, we sample thirty families and find that the mean expenditure is $5.10 with a standard deviation of $.90. Here the null hypothesis of no change is $H_0: \mu = 5.50$. The two-sided alternative, $H_a: \mu \neq 5.50$, represents a change in either direction, up or down. Therefore, we want a two-tailed test; if α is set at .01, the cutoff is the $\frac{1}{2}\alpha$, or .005, percentage point for 29 degrees of freedom: $t_{.005,29}$ is 2.756. Hence

$$\begin{cases} H_0: \mu = 5.50 \\ H_a: \mu \neq 5.50 \\ R: t > 2.756 \qquad \text{or} \qquad t < -2.756 \end{cases}$$

Since

$$t = \frac{\bar{X} - 5.50}{s/\sqrt{30}} = \frac{5.1 - 5.50}{.9/\sqrt{30}} = -2.434$$

the data indicate no change in the amount spent.

In each of our three examples we observe these features:

1. The null hypothesis always contains the equality statement, and the alternative hypothesis is determined by the question implicit in the statement of the problem.
2. The calculated statistic is based on the difference between the observed mean $\bar{X}$ and the mean μ_0 under the null hypothesis. Since the difference between them is meaningful only in relation to the amount of variation in the data, the statistic is the ratio of the difference to its estimated standard deviation.
3. When the difference between $\bar{X}$ and μ_0 is large enough that the calculated t-value falls into one of the tails of the t-distribution (the appropriate tail or tails are determined by the alternative hypotheses), we reject the null hypothesis because the probability of such a t-value, given that the null hypothesis is true, is too small to be attributed to normal sampling variation.

Whenever we use the t-distribution for calculating confidence intervals or for testing hypotheses, we are assuming that the data are a random sample from a normal population. The first assumption, randomness, is necessary if we want to make probability statements about the results we obtain; therefore it cannot be relaxed.

The second assumption, normality, is not too strong and may be relaxed. Because of the central limit theorem, we may say that even though the population has a distribution that is not normal the t-statistic may be used and the probabilities will not be greatly affected, provided we have a sufficiently large sample. The size sample which may be considered sufficiently large depends upon how much the population concerned departs from normality.

8.3 HYPOTHESES ON A BINOMIAL p

If we take a sample from a binomial population with the intention of using the information it contains to test the hypothesis that p has a specified value p_0, we can use an exact test or an approximate test. To use the exact test we must have tables of the binomial probabilities or be willing to compute them. Ordinarily, then, we use an approximate test based on the central limit theorem.

Under the null hypothesis $H_0: p = p_0$, the ratio

$$Z = \frac{X - np_0}{\sqrt{np_0(1 - p_0)}} \tag{8.6}$$

has approximately a standard normal distribution, where X is the number of successes in the sample (see Section 5.9). The denominator in the ratio (8.6) is the standard deviation of X; we know its value under the null hypothesis, and there is no need to estimate it from the sample.

Testing H_0 is like testing for a normal mean when there are infinitely many degrees of freedom—that is, with the normal distribution in place of the t-distribution. The rejection region will be one-tailed or two-tailed depending on whether the alternative hypothesis is one-sided or two-sided.

Dividing numerator and denominator in the ratio (8.6) by the sample size n gives

$$Z = \frac{X - np_0}{\sqrt{np_0(1 - p_0)}} = \frac{f - p_0}{\sqrt{p_0(1 - p_0)/n}} \tag{8.7}$$

where f is X/n, the fraction of successes in the sample. Clearly, the test may be performed either with X or with f, as convenience dictates. We must, however, be sure to use the right standard deviation in the denominator.

EXAMPLE 1

Problem: In a sample of 400 bushings there were 12 whose internal diameters were not within the tolerances. Is this sufficient evidence for concluding that the manufacturing process is turning out more than 2% defective bushings? Let α be .05.

Solution: The null hypothesis that the process is in control is $H_0: p \le .02$.

169

The alternative hypothesis that it is out of control is $H_a: p > .02$. The upper .05 percentage point $Z_{.05}$ for the standard normal distribution is 1.645. We should reject larger Z-values, since a one-sided test calls for a one-sided rejection region:

$$\begin{cases} H_0: p \le .02 \\ H_a: p > .02 \\ R: \dfrac{X - 400 \times .02}{\sqrt{400 \times .02 \times .98}} > 1.645 \end{cases}$$

Our data give

$$\frac{X - 400 \times .02}{\sqrt{400 \times .02 \times .98}} = \frac{12 - 8}{2.8} = 1.429$$

The data favor the hypothesis that the process is in control; 12 defective bushings out of 400 is not excessively large.

EXAMPLE 2

Problem: To check whether a pair of dice are balanced, we want to test the null hypothesis that the chance of rolling a 7 is 1/6, as the computations in Chapter 4 predict.

Analysis: The alternative to $p = 1/6$ we take to be $p \ne 1/6$, since we are interested in discovering deviations in either direction. If α is .05, the cutoff points are $\pm Z_{.025}$, or ± 1.96, on a two-tailed test. Suppose that n is 500:

$$\begin{cases} H_0: p = \tfrac{1}{6} \\ H_a: p \ne \tfrac{1}{6} \\ R: \dfrac{f - \tfrac{1}{6}}{\sqrt{\tfrac{1}{6} \times \tfrac{5}{6}/500}} > 1.96 \text{ or } < -1.96 \end{cases}$$

If in 500 rolls we get 7 a total of 66 times, then

$$\frac{f - \tfrac{1}{6}}{\sqrt{\tfrac{1}{6} \times \tfrac{5}{6}/500}} = \frac{\tfrac{66}{500} - \tfrac{1}{6}}{\sqrt{\tfrac{1}{6} \times \tfrac{5}{6}/500}} = -2.10$$

The statistic falls into the lower tail of the critical region, so we reject the null hypothesis.

8.4 A CONNECTION BETWEEN TESTING AND ESTIMATION

There is a connection between testing and interval estimation which illuminates both:

Given a level-α test, we can construct a level-α confidence interval by collecting together all the null hypotheses not rejected by the test.

For example, in a two-sided, level-α t-test of $\mu = \mu_0$, the condition for *not* rejecting the null hypothesis (see (8.5)) is:

$$-t_{\alpha/2,n-1} < t = \frac{\overline{X} - \mu_0}{s/\sqrt{n}} < t_{\alpha/2,n-1} \tag{8.8}$$

By the usual algebraic manipulations, this pair of inequalities is the same as:

$$\overline{X} - t_{\alpha/2,n-1} \frac{s}{\sqrt{n}} < \mu_0 < \overline{X} + t_{\alpha/2,n-1} \frac{s}{\sqrt{n}} \tag{8.9}$$

But the extreme terms here are the level-α confidence limits for a normal mean with variance unknown; see formula (7.18) in Section 7.5. The confidence interval consists exactly of those μ_0 having the property that the test does not reject the null hypothesis $H_0: \mu = \mu_0$. The point is that the conditions (8.8) and (8.9) are equivalent and each has probability $1 - \alpha$ if the mean is μ_0; condition (8.8) ensures that the test has probability α of a Type I error, and condition (8.9) ensures that the confidence interval has probability $1 - \alpha$ of covering the true mean.

The principle works equally well the other way around:

Given level-α confidence limits, we can construct a level-α test by the rule of rejecting the null hypothesis if it falls outside the confidence limits.

As an illustration, consider estimating a normal mean when the variance σ^2 is known. The level-α confidence limits (see formula (7.13) in Section 7.3) are:

$$L = \overline{X} - Z_{\alpha/2} \frac{\sigma}{\sqrt{n}} \quad \text{and} \quad R = \overline{X} + Z_{\alpha/2} \frac{\sigma}{\sqrt{n}} \tag{8.10}$$

Now μ_0 lies outside these limits if

$$\mu_0 < \overline{X} - Z_{\alpha/2} \frac{\sigma}{\sqrt{n}} \quad \text{or} \quad \mu_0 > \overline{X} + Z_{\alpha/2} \frac{\sigma}{\sqrt{n}}$$

and this is equivalent to

$$Z_{\alpha/2} < \frac{\overline{X} - \mu_0}{\sigma/\sqrt{n}} \quad \text{or} \quad -Z_{\alpha/2} > \frac{\overline{X} - \mu_0}{\sigma/\sqrt{n}}$$

Thus, if we know the variance σ^2 and want a two-sided, level-α test of the null hypothesis $H_0: \mu = \mu_0$, the rule is to reject if

$$\left| \frac{\overline{X} - \mu_0}{\sigma/\sqrt{n}} \right| > Z_{\alpha/2} \tag{8.11}$$

This is a new test.

Keeping in mind this parallel between interval estimation and testing will help to unify the concepts and techniques of the subsequent chapters, particularly when we note that our tests and estimates have been based on just a few statistics. First is the standardized mean

$$Z = \frac{\overline{X} - \mu}{\sigma/\sqrt{n}} \tag{8.12}$$

From this we construct the confidence limits of formula (8.10) and the test in condition (8.11), appropriate when σ is known. If σ is unknown, we replace it in the denominator in the ratio (8.12) by its natural estimate s. This gives the t-statistic

$$t = \frac{\overline{X} - \mu}{s/\sqrt{n}} \tag{8.13}$$

and the tests and confidence intervals appropriate when σ is unknown.

We have also used the standardized number of successes and the fraction of successes in binomial trials:

$$\frac{X - np}{\sqrt{np(1 - p)}} = \frac{f - p}{\sqrt{p(1 - p)/n}} \tag{8.14}$$

By using the approximate normality of this statistic, we can test for a particular value of p. If we replace p in the denominator by its natural estimator f, we get the statistic

$$\frac{f - p}{\sqrt{f(1 - f)/n}} \tag{8.15}$$

also approximately normally distributed. It is from this statistic that we construct confidence intervals for p.

In the chapters that follow we shall encounter further statistics that arise from standardizing some random variable by its mean and standard deviation and then replacing the standard deviation by its natural estimate. A standard notation will help in this connection. The standard deviation of a statistic Y we denote σ_Y; an estimate of this standard deviation we denote s_Y. Thus, the standard deviation of $\overline{X}$ is $\sigma_{\overline{X}}$, equal to $\sigma/\sqrt{n}$, of which the estimate $s_{\overline{X}}$ is $s/\sqrt{n}$. The number X of successes in binomial trials has standard deviation σ_X, equal to $\sqrt{np(1 - p)}$, and the estimate s_X of this is $\sqrt{nf(1 - f)}$. Finally, the fraction f of successes has standard deviation σ_f, equal to $\sqrt{p(1 - p)/n}$, and the estimate s_f of this is $\sqrt{f(1 - f)/n}$.

PROBLEMS

1. A box contains four marbles, some of which are white. The others are black. To test the hypothesis that there are two of each color we select two *without* replacement and conclude that there are not two of each if both marbles selected are of the same color.

a. What is the probability we will come to the wrong conclusion if, in fact, there are two of each color in the box?

b. Suppose that there is but one white marble in the box. What is the probability that we will falsely conclude that there are two white and two black?

2. Assume the same situation as in problem 1, but assume that a sample of two is selected *with* replacement. Let θ be the number of white marbles in the box. We reject H_0: $\theta = 2$ if both balls are the same color.
   a. What is the probability of a Type I error?
   b. Find the probability of Type II error for each possible value of θ.

3. A pinochle deck consists of forty-eight cards, eight each of the denominations A, K, Q, J, 10, and 9. You are given a deck of forty-eight cards and told that it is either a pinochle deck or a bridge deck with the 2's removed. You select two cards without replacement and on the basis of these are to decide whether or not it is a pinochle deck. If one or both of them is less than a 9, you know it is the bridge deck. If the two cards are identical, two kings of hearts for example, you know it is the pinochle deck. Suppose you get two cards with denominations greater than or equal to a 9 and not identical. You state that it is the pinochle deck. What is the probability you are wrong?

4. In the situation described in problem 3 you take four cards *with* replacement and will reject the hypothesis that you are sampling from the bridge deck with the 2's removed if all four of them are greater than or equal to a 9. What is the probability you will be wrong?

5. Given each of the following sets of values, test the indicated hypothesis.
   a. $n = 25$, $\bar{X} = 28$, $s = 3$, H_0: $\mu = 20$, H_a: $\mu \neq 20$, $\alpha = .05$.
   b. $n = 25$, $\bar{X} = 50$, $s^2 = 100$, H_0: $\mu \geq 55$, H_a: $\mu < 55$, $\alpha = .01$.
   c. $n = 9$, $\bar{X} = 329.3$, $s^2 = 9$, H_0: $\mu \leq 327$, H_a: $\mu > 327$, $\alpha = .025$.

6. For each of the following test the indicated hypothesis.
   a. $n = 16$, $\bar{X} = 1550$, $s^2 = 12$, H_0: $\mu = 1500$, H_a: $\mu \neq 1500$, $\alpha = .01$.
   b. $n = 9$, $\bar{X} = 10.1$, $s^2 = .81$, H_0: $\mu \geq 12$, H_a: $\mu < 12$, $\alpha = .005$.
   c. $n = 49$, $\bar{X} = 19$, $s = 1$, H_0: $\mu \leq 18$, H_a: $\mu > 18$, $\alpha = .05$.

7. Sensitivity tests were made on twelve randomly selected tubes of a given type. The mean was 2.5 microvolts and the estimated variance was .48. Would we conclude that the mean sensitivity of tubes of this type in the given circuit is greater than 2.0 microvolts? Let $\alpha = .01$.

8. The estimated variance based on four measurements of a spring tension was .25 grams. The mean was 26 grams. Test the hypothesis that the true value is 25 grams. Use a 5% level.

9. With a random sample from a normal population with n equal to 8, and $\bar{X}$ equal to 62, and given that the variance of the population is known to be equal to 2, is it reasonable to suppose that μ equals 60? Let $\alpha = .10$.

10. A population has a variance σ^2 of 100. A sample of 25 from this population had a mean equal to 17 and an estimated standard deviation equal to 16. Can we conclude that the mean is less than 25? Let $\alpha = .05$.

11. A sample for which n was 25 had a mean equal to 33 and an estimated variance equal to 100. At the 1% level would we have reason to doubt the claim that the mean is not greater than 27?

12. Given the following information, test the stated hypothesis at the given level.
    a. $n = 9$, $\bar{X} = 76$, $\sum (X_i - \bar{X})^2 = 32$, $H_0 \colon \mu = 75$, $H_a \colon \mu \neq 75$, $\alpha = .10$.
    b. $n = 25$, $\sum X_i = 500$, $\sum X_i^2 = 12{,}400$, $H_0 \colon \mu \leq 17$, $H_a \colon \mu > 17$, $\alpha = .10$.

13. Nine rafters were tested for breaking load, giving a mean breaking strength of 1500 pounds and an estimated variance equal to 14,400. At the 5% level of significance would we have reason to doubt that the mean breaking load of rafters of this type is at least 1600 pounds?

14. Suppose that a sample of fifteen rulers from a given supplier have an average length of 12.04 inches and that the estimated standard deviation of the mean is .015 inches. If α is .02, can we conclude that the average length of rulers produced by this supplier is 12 inches?

15. Twelve rats fed a given ration showed an average gain in weight of 145 grams. The estimated standard deviation of the mean was 2.3 grams. At the 2.5% level can we conclude that the mean gain under this ration is not less than 150 grams?

16. It is known that mean time between malfunctions for a certain type of electronic equipment that uses electron tubes is 500 hours. It is claimed that a completely transistorized model will, on the average, operate at least three times as long without malfunctioning. A number of the latter are put into service and give rise to 61 malfunctions with a mean waiting time equal to 1350 hours. The estimated standard deviation is 720 hours. At the 5% level, is the claim justified?

17. The following are the logarithms of direct microscopic counts on ten samples of raw skim milk. Can we accept the hypothesis that the mean log DMC is not greater than 6.00? Use a 5% level of significance, i.e., let $\alpha = .05$.

6.97	6.83	6.56	6.15	6.99
7.08	6.11	5.95	6.54	6.30

18. The drained weights in ounces for a sample of fifteen cans of fruit are given below. At the 1% level of significance, test the hypothesis that on the average a twelve-ounce drained weight standard is being maintained.

12.1	12.1	12.3	12.0	12.1
12.4	12.2	12.4	12.1	11.9
11.9	11.8	11.9	12.3	11.8

19. The following are the times in seconds that it took the sand in a sample of timers to run through. At the 1% level can we conclude that the mean for timers of this type is not equal to the nominal three minutes?

170	192	204	181	208	193
179	215	174	183	182	165

20. Use the data given in problem 13, Chapter 2, to test the hypothesis that the mean difference in cutoff voltage for the type of tube concerned is equal to zero. Let $\alpha = .05$.

21. In a sample of 400 seeds, 346 of them germinated. At the 2.5% level would we reject the claim that 90% or more will germinate? *"Claim" = Ho*

22. In a sample of 64 die castings we found 8 with defects. On the basis of this sample have we any reason to believe that more than 10% of all such castings would show defects? Use a 5% level of significance. *reason to believe ., , Ha*

23. In a sample of 144 voters it was found that 90 were in favor of a bond issue. Test the hypothesis that opinion is equally divided on this issue. Let $\alpha = .01$.

24. On 384 out of 600 randomly selected farms it was discovered that the farm operator was also the owner. Is there reason to believe that *more* than 60% of the operators are also owners?

REFERENCES

8.1 HOEL, PAUL G. *Elementary Statistics*, 3rd edition. John Wiley & Sons, New York, 1971. Chapter 8.

8.2 HOGG, ROBERT V., and ALLEN T. CRAIG. *Introduction to Mathematical Statistics*, 3rd edition. Macmillan, New York, 1970. Chapter 9.

8.3 MOSTELLER, FREDERICK, ROBERT E. K. ROURKE, and GEORGE B. THOMAS, JR. *Probability with Statistical Applications*, 2nd edition. Addison-Wesley, Reading, Massachusetts, 1970. Chapter 9.

8.4 SNEDECOR, GEORGE W., and WILLIAM G. COCHRAN. *Statistical Methods*, 6th edition. Iowa State University Press, Ames, 1967. Chapters 1, 2, and 3.

9

Two-sample Techniques and Paired Comparisons

9.1   INTRODUCTION

We have looked at some of the inferences that are possible when we have a single random sample from a normal population, and, also, when our random sample is assumed to have been taken from a binomial population. We now consider some of the inferences that may be made when we have two independent random samples, one from each of two populations. We examine some of the methods used when the data are continuous, and then turn our attention to inferences based on samples from two binomial populations.

9.2   SAMPLES FROM TWO NORMAL POPULATIONS

Let $X_{11}, X_{12}, \ldots, X_{1n_1}$ represent the observed values in a sample of size n_1 taken from a normal population with mean μ_1 and variance σ^2, and let $X_{21}, X_{22}, \ldots, X_{2n_2}$ be the observations in a sample of size n_2 taken from a second normal population with mean μ_2 and variance σ^2 (the same σ^2 as for the first population). When we have two samples, an observation X_{ij} has two subscripts; the first denotes the sample, and the second designates the particular element within the sample. Thus X_{24} is the fourth value in the second sample.

Careful study of the two-sample situation outlined in the preceding paragraph reveals three basic assumptions:

1. Independent random samples.
2. Normal populations.
3. Common variance for both populations.

The methods to be presented here are valid only if these assumptions are satisfied. However, we later consider briefly the consequences of relaxing these assumptions.

It is interesting to note that data that satisfy our three assumptions and that fit exactly into the framework of the two-sample situations may be obtained as the result of an experiment for comparing the effects of two treatments. In statistical usage, *treatments* are any procedures, methods, or stimuli whose effects we want to estimate and compare. Treatments in one situation might represent different machines, but in another they could be different operators; they could be different chemicals, or different rates of application of one chemical; and so on.

Suppose that we want to compare the effects of two treatments when they are applied to similar experimental material. We can divide the experimental material into a number of *experimental units* and then assign a treatment to each experimental unit at random by tossing a coin or by using a table of random numbers. We usually impose the minor restriction on our randomization that each treatment is applied to the same number of experimental units. The purposes of randomization will be discussed in Chapter 12.

After the treatments are applied, we obtain an objective measure of the effect of a given treatment from each unit to which the treatment was applied, so that we have a set of values that may be classified into two groups according to the treatments which produced them. If we assume (1) that the responses of all experimental units to which a particular treatment could be applied have a normal distribution, (2) that the variance among the experimental units treated alike is the same for both treatments, and (3) that the responses constitute random samples from the distributions of all such responses, then our three assumptions are satisfied and the methods appropriate to the two-sample situation may be used to estimate the difference between the effects of the treatments and to test the hypothesis that there is no difference in their effects.

Simple experimental designs of this sort are of the class known as *completely randomized* designs. These will be covered in more detail in Chapter 12.

After the data have been obtained, either by selecting the samples or by performing an experiment, the information they contain may be summarized in tabular form, as shown in Table 9.1. The pooled sum of squares, pooled SS, is obtained by adding together the sums of squares for

TABLE 9.1. Summary Table for Two Samples from Continuous Populations

Sample	Size	df	Mean	Sum of squares
1	n_1	$n_1 - 1$	$\bar{X}_1$	$\sum (X_{1j} - \bar{X}_1)^2$
2	n_2	$n_2 - 1$	$\bar{X}_2$	$\sum (X_{2j} - \bar{X}_2)^2$
Totals	$n_1 + n_2$	$n_1 + n_2 - 2$		Pooled SS

the individual samples in the last column of the table. In practical problems these sums of squares would ordinarily be obtained by means of the machine formulas:

$$\sum (X_{1j} - \bar{X}_1)^2 = \sum X_{1j}^2 - \frac{(\sum X_{1j})^2}{n_1}$$

$$\sum (X_{2j} - \bar{X}_2)^2 = \sum X_{2j}^2 - \frac{(\sum X_{2j})^2}{n_2}$$

After the information contained in the data has been summarized in the table, we turn our attention to the estimation of the parameters of interest. As one might suppose, the best unbiased estimators for the population means μ_1 and μ_2 are the respective sample means $\bar{X}_1$ and $\bar{X}_2$, and the best unbiased estimator for the difference between the means, $\delta = \mu_1 - \mu_2$, is the difference between the sample means, $d = \bar{X}_1 - \bar{X}_2$. The latter statistic is of particular interest because two populations are involved, and our primary concern is making inferences about the difference between the means. In experimental situations, the difference between the means is also the difference between the effects of the two treatments.

Since the variance is assumed to be the same for both populations, we could obtain an unbiased estimate for σ^2 from each sample, but the best unbiased estimate is obtained by pooling the information contained in both samples to get the pooled estimate of variance:

$$s^2 = \frac{\text{Pooled SS}}{\text{Pooled df}} = \frac{\sum (X_{1j} - \bar{X}_1)^2 + \sum (X_{2j} - \bar{X}_2)^2}{n_1 + n_2 - 2} \tag{9.1}$$

It is easy to show that this pooled estimate of variance is the weighted mean of the individual sample estimates, where the weights are the degrees of freedom, that is,

$$s^2 = \frac{(n_1 - 1)s_1^2 + (n_2 - 1)s_2^2}{n_1 + n_2 - 2} \tag{9.2}$$

where $s_1^2 = \dfrac{\sum (X_{1j} - \bar{X}_1)^2}{n_1 - 1}$

$s_2^2 = \dfrac{\sum (X_{2j} - \bar{X}_2)^2}{n_2 - 1}$

To find confidence intervals for, or test hypotheses about, the means, we must first find estimates for the variances and standard deviations of the estimators. As is always the case, the variances of the means are estimated by dividing the estimate for the population variance by the appropriate sample size, i.e.,

$$s_{\bar{X}_1}^2 = \frac{s^2}{n_1}$$

$$s_{\bar{X}_2}^2 = \frac{s^2}{n_2} .$$

(9.3)

where s^2 is our *pooled* variance estimator as defined in equation (9.1). The estimated standard deviations of the sample means are the corresponding square roots.

According to equation (5.10), page 103, if X and Y are independent random variables, then their variances add: $\text{Var}(X + Y) = \text{Var}(X) + \text{Var}(Y)$. Now the distribution curve for $-Y$ is the mirror image of that for Y, so their measures of spread are the same: $\text{Var}(-Y) = \text{Var}(Y)$. Hence $X - Y$, or $X + (-Y)$, has for its variance the sum $\text{Var}(X) + \text{Var}(-Y) = \text{Var}(X) + \text{Var}(Y)$. Thus we have the formula:

$$\text{Var}(X - Y) = \text{Var}(X) + \text{Var}(Y)$$

(One might at first expect a minus on the right, but that could even give a negative variance.)

Since $\bar{X}_1$ and $\bar{X}_2$ are the means of independent random samples, they are independent of one another. Under the assumption of common variance, they have variances σ^2/n_1 and σ^2/n_2, respectively; therefore, the variance of their difference $d = \bar{X}_1 - \bar{X}_2$ is:

$$\sigma_d^2 = \frac{\sigma^2}{n_1} + \frac{\sigma^2}{n_2}$$

(9.4)

The *estimated* variance of $\bar{X}_1 - \bar{X}_2$ is

$$s_d^2 = s^2 \left(\frac{1}{n_1} + \frac{1}{n_2} \right)$$

(9.5)

where s^2 is the pooled estimate of the common variance σ^2. If the sample sizes are equal (if $n_1 = n_2 = n$), the estimated variance of d, equation (9.5), reduces to:

$$s_d^2 = \frac{2s^2}{n}$$

(9.6)

EXAMPLE 1

To compare the durabilities of two paints for highway use, 12 four-inch lines of each paint were laid down across a heavily traveled road. The order was decided at random. After a period of time, reflectometer

179

readings were obtained for each line (the higher the readings the greater the reflectivity). The data are as follows:

Paint A	12.5	11.7	9.9	9.6	10.3	9.6
	9.4	11.3	8.7	11.5	10.6	9.7
Paint B	9.4	11.6	9.7	10.4	6.9	7.3
	8.4	7.2	7.0	8.2	12.7	9.2

For these sets of data we find

Paint A	Paint B
$\sum X_{1j} = 124.8$	$\sum X_{2j} = 108.0$
$\bar{X}_1 = 10.4$	$\bar{X}_2 = 9.0$
$\sum X_{1j}^2 = 1312.00$	$\sum X_{2j}^2 = 1010.64$
$(1/n_1)(\sum X_{1j})^2 = 1297.92$	$(1/n_2)(\sum X_{2j})^2 = 972.00$
$\sum (X_{1j} - \bar{X}_1)^2 = 14.08$	$\sum (X_{2j} - \bar{X}_2)^2 = 38.64$

The summary table is:

Paint	n	df	Mean	Sum of squares
A	12	11	10.4	14.08
B	12	11	9.0	38.64
Sums	24	22		52.72

Hence

$$d = \bar{X}_1 - \bar{X}_2 = 1.40$$

The pooled estimate of variance is

$$s^2 = \frac{52.72}{22} = 2.40$$

the estimated variance of the difference between the means is

$$s_d^2 = s^2\left(\frac{1}{n} + \frac{1}{n}\right) = 2.40(\tfrac{2}{12}) = 0.40$$

and the estimated standard deviation of d is

$$s_d = \sqrt{0.40} = 0.63$$

9.3 CONFIDENCE INTERVALS FOR $\mu_1 - \mu_2$ AND μ_i

It is assumed that the populations from which our data were obtained have normal distributions; therefore, the sample means and the difference between them will be normally distributed. Furthermore, $d = \bar{X}_1 - \bar{X}_2$ is an unbiased estimator for $\mu_1 - \mu_2$, and s_d^2, equation (9.5), is an unbiased estimator for the variance of d. Furthermore,

$$t = \frac{d - \delta}{s_d} = \frac{(\overline{X}_1 - \overline{X}_2) - (\mu_1 - \mu_2)}{s\sqrt{\dfrac{1}{n_1} + \dfrac{1}{n_2}}}$$

(9.7)

*[handwritten: $H_0 : \mu_1 = \mu_2$
1.) $H_a : \mu_1 \neq \mu_2$
2.) $H_a : \mu_1 > \mu_2$
3.) $H_a : \mu_1 < \mu_2$
not used for anything this is to justify used to justify C.I.]*

has a *t*-distribution with $n_1 + n_2 - 2$ degrees of freedom and a confidence interval for δ is that interval between

$$L = d - t_{(\alpha/2), n_1 + n_2 - 2} s_d$$

and

(9.8)

$$R = d + t_{(\alpha/2), n_1 + n_2 - 2} s_d$$

As always, the degrees of freedom for t are those associated with the sum of squares used in finding our unbiased estimate of σ^2.

For the numerical example of Section 9.2, the 95% confidence interval for the difference between the mean reflectivity of the two paints is the interval between

$$L = 1.40 - (2.074)(.63) = .09$$

and

$$R = 1.40 + (2.074)(.63) = 2.71$$

*[handwritten: IF $n_1 = n_2$
$Sp^2 = \dfrac{S_1^2 + S_2^2}{2}$]*

We can be 95% confident that the difference between the actual means is between .09 and 2.71.

Note that this confidence interval is for $\delta = \mu_1 - \mu_2$. If we wanted the interval for $\mu_2 - \mu_1$, the estimator would be $\overline{X}_2 - \overline{X}_1$, or -1.40, and the confidence limits would be -2.71 and $-.09$ (the variance of $\overline{X}_2 - \overline{X}_1$ is the same as the variance of $\overline{X}_1 - \overline{X}_2$).

We find a confidence interval for the means of either or both of the populations exactly as we found a confidence interval for the mean of a normal population in Section 7.5, except that the pooled estimate of variance is used to calculate the standard deviation of $\overline{X}_i$ (where i is 1 or 2), rather than the separate estimate of variance that could be obtained from the data in the *i*th sample. The *t*-statistic,

$$t = \frac{\overline{X}_i - \mu_i}{s_{\overline{X}_i}}$$

(9.9)

will, therefore, have the pooled degrees of freedom $n_1 + n_2 - 2$, and the confidence limits for μ_i are:

$$L = \overline{X}_i - t_{(\alpha/2), n_1 + n_2 - 2} s_{\overline{X}_i}$$

and

(9.10)

$$R = \overline{X}_i + t_{(\alpha/2), n_1 + n_2 - 2} s_{\overline{X}_i}$$

181

For the example, 99% confidence limits for the mean reflectivity of paint B are

$$L = 9 - (2.819)\sqrt{\frac{2.40}{12}} = 7.74$$

and

$$R = 9 + (2.819)\sqrt{\frac{2.40}{12}} = 10.26$$

where $2.819 = t_{.005,22}$.

9.4 TESTING THE HYPOTHESIS $\mu_1 = \mu_2$

To test the hypothesis that the difference between the means is equal to a given value, δ_0, we again rely on the quantity defined in equation (9.7), for under the hypothesis $H_0: \mu_1 - \mu_2 = \delta_0$, the statistic

$$t = \frac{\overline{X}_1 - \overline{X}_2 - \delta_0}{s_{\overline{X}_1 - \overline{X}_2}} \tag{9.11}$$

has a t-distribution with $n_1 + n_2 - 2$ degrees of freedom. The test is a simple t-test.

A hypothesis of particular interest in the two-sample case, or in the case of comparing two treatments in a completely randomized experiment, is the one that states that there is no difference between the means: $H_0: \mu_1' = \mu_2$. Under this hypothesis, δ_0 is 0 and the test statistic as given in equation (9.11) reduces to

$$t = \frac{\overline{X}_1 - \overline{X}_2}{s_{\overline{X}_1 - \overline{X}_2}} \tag{9.12}$$

Here, as with other t-tests, the critical region depends upon the alternative hypothesis. If it states simply that the means are not equal ($H_a: \mu_1 \neq \mu_2$), we use the two-tailed critical region $|t| \geq t_{(\alpha/2),n_1+n_2-2}$. If the alternative is one-sided, i.e., $H_a: \mu_1 > \mu_2$ or $H_a: \mu_1 < \mu_2$, we use the one-tailed critical regions $t > t_{\alpha,n_1+n_2-2}$ or $t < -t_{\alpha,n_1+n_2-2}$.

For a one-tailed test, there is often some doubt as to which tail should be used. This difficulty is resolved if we always write our t, equation (9.12), and the alternative hypothesis in such a way that the subscripts are in the same order. If the alternative is $H_a: \mu_2 > \mu_1$, and if we write the numerator of our t-statistic as $\overline{X}_2 - \overline{X}_1$, then the inequality in H_a is an arrowhead pointing to the right and we use the upper tail. If the alternative hypothesis is written as $H_a: \mu_1 < \mu_2$, we would use $\overline{X}_1 - \overline{X}_2$, and the inequality sign then points to the left, showing that we use the lower tail for the critical region.

The determination of the proper tail to use can also be seen this way: For the testing problem

$$\begin{cases} H_0: \mu_1 = \mu_2 \\ H_a: \mu_1 > \mu_2 \end{cases}$$

we ought to reject H_0 in favor of H_a if $\overline{X}_1$ (which estimates μ_1) is greater than $\overline{X}_2$ (which estimates μ_2) by an excessive amount. Since this happens exactly when $\overline{X}_1 - \overline{X}_2$ is greater than 0 by an excessive amount, we reject H_0 if the value of the statistic (9.12) is greater than $t_{\alpha, n_1 + n_2 - 2}$. Similarly, for the problem

$$\begin{cases} H_0: \mu_1 = \mu_2 \\ H_a: \mu_1 < \mu_2 \end{cases}$$

we should prefer H_a to H_0 if $\overline{X}_1$ is greatly less than $\overline{X}_2$, or if $\overline{X}_1 - \overline{X}_2$ is greatly less than 0, so we reject H_0 if the value of the statistic (9.12) is less than $-t_{\alpha, n_1 + n_2 - 2}$.

EXAMPLE 1

Problem: For the following summary table for a two-sample situation, is there any reason to believe that the mean of the first population is less than that of the second? Let $\alpha = .05$.

Sample	n	df	$\overline{X}$	$\sum (X_i - \overline{X})^2$
1	15	14	21	1224
2	9	8	29	756
		22		1980

$$s^2 = \tfrac{1980}{22} = 90 \qquad s_d^2 = 90(\tfrac{1}{15} + \tfrac{1}{9}) = 16$$

Solution: The hypothesis is $H_0: \mu_1 = \mu_2$. The alternative hypothesis is $H_a: \mu_2 > \mu_1$; therefore, we calculate

$$t = \frac{\overline{X}_2 - \overline{X}_1}{s_d} = \frac{29 - 21}{4} = 2$$

The critical region is $t > t_{.05,22} = 1.717$. The calculated t is greater than the tabular value; therefore, we reject the hypothesis and conclude that $\mu_2 > \mu_1$.

EXAMPLE 2

To test the hypothesis that in the example of Section 9.2 the two paints are equal in reflectivity we test the hypothesis $H_0: \mu_1 = \mu_2$ against the alternative $H_a: \mu_1 \neq \mu_2$. The t-statistic is

$$t = \frac{\overline{X}_1 - \overline{X}_2}{s_d} = \frac{1.40}{.63} = 2.222$$

183

The critical region for α of .05 is $|t| \geq t_{.025,22} = 2.074$. Our calculated t falls into the upper tail of the critical region; therefore, we reject the null hypothesis and conclude that the means are not equal.

9.5   WHICH ASSUMPTIONS CAN BE RELAXED?

In Section 9.2 we stated three assumptions under which the methods of Sections 9.3 and 9.4 are valid. Let us now reconsider those assumptions and see which, if any, can be relaxed. The first, randomness, must be satisfied if we are to make probability statements in connection with our inferences.

As is frequently the case, the second assumption, normality, is not a strong assumption, for, because of the central limit theorem, if the samples are sufficiently large, even large departures from normality will not affect the probabilities to any great extent.

The third assumption, common or homogeneous variance, cannot be relaxed. If the population variances are not the same, a significant result for the t-test may be due to the different variances and not to different means. If this assumption is not satisfied there is no exact test of the hypothesis $H_0: \mu_1 - \mu_2 = \delta_0$; however, there are several approximate tests available. See reference 9.4.

9.6   PAIRED COMPARISONS

In the completely randomized experiment for comparing two treatments, the treatments are randomized over, or randomly assigned to, the whole set of experimental units, that is, a random device is used to determine which of the two treatments is applied to any given experimental unit. It is usual to restrict the randomization to the extent that each treatment is applied to the same number of units. As we have seen, the data from this type of experiment can be analyzed by using the two-sample techniques. These are also called the method of group comparisons.

For this type of experiment the efficiency and the precision of estimation are inversely proportional to the *pooled* estimate of variance, s^2; the smaller the variance, the greater the precision. To increase the precision of an experiment, with a fixed amount of experimental material, we have to alter the design of the experiment in order to reduce the unexplained variation in the data as measured by s^2. Since s^2 is based on the variation among experimental units treated alike, either we must reduce this variation by using more homogeneous experimental material, or we must eliminate some of this variation by using a priori information about the responses of the experimental units. It is the latter approach we now consider.

If the experimental units occur in pairs or can be grouped into pairs in such a way that the variation in the responses between the members of any pair is less than the variation between members of different pairs, we can improve the efficiency of our experiment by randomizing the two treatments over the two members of each pair. We restrict our randomization so that each treatment is applied to one member of each pair; hence, we obtain a separate estimate of the difference between the treatment effects from each pair, and the variation between, or among, the pairs is not included in our estimate of the variance. If the variation among the pairs of units is large relative to the variation within the pairs, the variance will be smaller than if a completely randomized design were used.

For example, suppose we want to compare the efficiencies of two different barnacle-resistant paints and there are ten ships available. We could randomly assign the two paints to five ships each and then, after a suitable length of time, obtain a measure of the weight of barnacles clinging to each ship. Since the variance would be based on the variation among ships painted alike we could expect it to be large because the ships would very likely be sailing in different waters for different periods of time.

On the other hand, where the port side of a hull goes, the starboard goes also; therefore, we would probably have a much more precise experiment if we were to paint one side of each hull with one paint, and the other side with the second paint, tossing a coin to decide which side gets which paint. Each ship would then provide a measure of the difference in effectiveness of the two paints, and the variation due to other factors, such as time at sea and the parts of the world where the ships sailed, would be eliminated from our estimate of variance.

These same considerations lead to the use of identical twins or of littermates in animal experiments, and to grouping experimental units into pairs according to some factor such as age, weight, chemical composition, environment, etc. If the pairing is successful, much of the variation due to the factor on which it is based is eliminated from the estimate of variance and the eff iency of the experiment is increased accordingly. The paired experiment is the simplest example of a class of experimental designs known as the *randomized complete block* designs.

The analysis of paired comparisons reduces to the single-sample techniques of Chapters 7 and 8. The data for a paired comparison may be represented as follows:

| | Treatment | | |
Pair	1	2	Difference
1	Y_{11}	Y_{12}	X_1
2	Y_{21}	Y_{22}	X_2
3	Y_{31}	Y_{32}	X_3
$\vdots$			
n	Y_{n1}	Y_{n2}	X_n

In this table a single observation is denoted by Y_{ij}, where the first subscript corresponds to the pair, the second to the treatment. For example, Y_{32} is the response of that member of the *third* pair that had the *second* treatment applied to it.

The assumptions are the same as for the group comparisons: independent random observations, normal populations of responses, and common within-treatment variance.

To estimate the mean difference and to test hypotheses about the difference between the treatment effects, we use the differences between the members of each pair,

$$X_i = Y_{i1} - Y_{i2} \tag{9.13}$$

and treat these as a random sample from the population of differences. We then have

$$\overline{X} = \frac{1}{n} \sum X_i \tag{9.14}$$

and

$$s_X^2 = \frac{1}{n-1} \sum (X_i - \overline{X})^2 \tag{9.15}$$

as unbiased estimates for μ_X, the mean difference, and for σ_X^2, the variance of the differences, respectively.

The variance of the mean difference $\overline{X}$ is estimated unbiasedly by

$$s_{\overline{X}}^2 = \frac{s_X^2}{n} \tag{9.16}$$

Since the differences, X_i, constitute a single random sample from a normal population, the appropriate methods for finding confidence intervals and for testing hypotheses have already been considered in Chapters 7 and 8. Thus $100(1 - \alpha)\%$ confidence limits for μ_X are given by

$$\begin{aligned} L &= \overline{X} - t_{(\alpha/2),n-1} s_{\overline{X}} \\ R &= \overline{X} + t_{(\alpha/2),n-1} s_{\overline{X}} \end{aligned} \tag{9.17}$$

and the test of the hypothesis $H_0: \mu_X = \mu_0$ is the single-sample *t*-test with $n - 1$ degrees of freedom based on the statistic

$$t = \frac{\overline{X} - \mu_0}{s_{\overline{X}}} \tag{9.18}$$

The test of the hypothesis of no difference in the effects of the two treatments is the special case $H_0: \mu_X = 0$.

EXAMPLE 1

In order to determine whether or not a particular heat treatment is effective in reducing the number of bacteria in skim milk, counts were made before and after treatment on twelve samples of skim milk, with the following results. The data are in the form of log DMC, the logarithms of direct microscopic counts.

<table>
<tr><td colspan="4" style="text-align:center">*log DMC*</td></tr>
<tr><td>*Sample*</td><td>*Before treatment*</td><td>*After treatment*</td><td>*Difference* $X_i = Y_{i1} - Y_{i2}$</td></tr>
<tr><td>1</td><td>6.98</td><td>6.95</td><td>.03</td></tr>
<tr><td>2</td><td>7.08</td><td>6.94</td><td>.14</td></tr>
<tr><td>3</td><td>8.34</td><td>7.17</td><td>1.17</td></tr>
<tr><td>4</td><td>5.30</td><td>5.15</td><td>.15</td></tr>
<tr><td>5</td><td>6.26</td><td>6.28</td><td>-.02</td></tr>
<tr><td>6</td><td>6.77</td><td>6.81</td><td>-.04</td></tr>
<tr><td>7</td><td>7.03</td><td>6.59</td><td>.44</td></tr>
<tr><td>8</td><td>5.56</td><td>5.34</td><td>.22</td></tr>
<tr><td>9</td><td>5.97</td><td>5.98</td><td>-.01</td></tr>
<tr><td>10</td><td>6.64</td><td>6.51</td><td>.13</td></tr>
<tr><td>11</td><td>7.03</td><td>6.84</td><td>.19</td></tr>
<tr><td>12</td><td>7.69</td><td>6.99</td><td>.70</td></tr>
<tr><td></td><td></td><td></td><td>3.10</td></tr>
</table>

For these data:

$$\sum X_i = 3.10 \qquad \overline{X} = .258$$

$$\sum X_i^2 = 2.1856 \qquad (\sum X_i)^2/n = .8008$$

$$\sum (X_i - \overline{X})^2 = 2.1856 - .8008 = 1.3848$$

$$s_X^2 = \frac{1.3848}{11} = .12589$$

$$s_{\overline{X}}^2 = \frac{.12589}{12} = .0105$$

$$s_{\overline{X}} = .102$$

For the hypothesis of no effect, $H_0: \mu_X = 0$, against $H_a: \mu_X > 0$,

$$t = \frac{.258}{.102} = 2.53$$

From the tables, $t_{.05,11}$ equals 1.796; therefore, we reject the null hypothesis at the 5% level and conclude that the heat treatment has reduced the number of bacteria.

9.7 GROUPS VERSUS PAIRS

Paired comparisons can give greater precision of estimation than group comparisons, but only if the pairing is effective. To be effective the pairs must be such that the variation among the pairs is greater than the variation between the units within the pairs. The degrees of freedom for the t-test based on paired comparisons are equal to $n - 1$ compared with $2(n - 1)$ for the group comparison based on the same number of experimental units, and since degrees of freedom are like money in the bank they should not be invested unless a suitable return can be expected.

With pairing, then, as compared with grouping, we lose $n - 1$ degrees of freedom. But if the variance is reduced enough to more than compensate for their loss, then a gain in efficiency is achieved. If, however, the experimental material is nearly homogeneous, we have no justification for pairing, because the variation among pairs will be but little greater (if at all) than that within the pairs. We would squander degrees of freedom without getting a sufficient reduction in the variance.

For data from experiments involving two treatments, it is important that the proper method of analysis be employed. If the data are from a paired experiment and if we ignore the pairing and use the group analysis of Sections 9.3 and 9.4, the estimate of variance is inflated by the variation among pairs and will be too large. A difference between the treatment effects that is actually significant might not be detected because of the inflated variance estimate.

To illustrate what can happen when the two-sample techniques are used to analyze paired data, we use the example of Section 9.6 concerning the reduction due to a heat treatment of the number of bacteria in skim milk. The summary table is as follows:

		n	df	$\bar{Y}$	Sum of squares
Before		12	11	6.721	7.2219
After		12	11	6.463	4.7750
	Sums	24	22		11.9969

Here

$$s^2 = \frac{11.9969}{22} = .5453$$

$$s_d^2 = \frac{2(.5453)}{12} = .0909$$

$$s_d = .301$$

For the hypothesis that $\mu_X = 0$,

$$t = \frac{\bar{Y}_1 - \bar{Y}_2}{s_d} = \frac{.258}{.301} = .857$$

which is not significant.

Using this analysis we would conclude that the treatment had no effect. Notice that the standard deviation of the difference between the means is almost three times as large as when these paired data were analyzed by the proper techniques.

Just as we have run into trouble using group techniques to analyze paired data, we are also in trouble if the data from a group experiment are paired. Random pairing would result in a loss of degrees of freedom and, at the same time, the variance estimate could be either larger or smaller than it should be and could lead to the wrong conclusion.

Suppose we were to systematically pair the results of a completely randomized experiment by ranking both sets of responses from high to low and then pairing the largest of each group, the next largest, and so on. Such a procedure would generally result in a variance estimate that is much smaller than it should be, and, therefore, in *t*-values that are too large. We might well detect a difference that does not exist.

The design of the study dictates the method of analysis that should be used.

9.8 TWO SAMPLES FROM BINOMIAL POPULATIONS

We now suppose that we have two independent random samples, one of size n_1 from a binomial distribution with a proportion of successes equal to p_1, the other of size n_2 from a binomial population with proportion of successes equal to p_2. We let X_1 and X_2 be the observed number of successes in first and second samples, respectively.

Our primary objectives will be the estimation of the difference $p_1 - p_2$, and the testing of the hypothesis that $p_1 = p_2$. To achieve these objectives we make use of the normal approximation to the binomial.

The proportion p_i is estimated unbiasedly by the corresponding sample fraction, f_i, that is, X_i/n_i, and the difference $p_1 - p_2$ is estimated unbiasedly by $f_1 - f_2$. The variance of f_i is estimated by

$$s_{f_i}^2 = \frac{f_i(1 - f_i)}{n_i} \tag{9.19}$$

Since f_1 and f_2 are independent, the variance of their difference, $f_1 - f_2$, is the sum of their variances and is estimated by

$$s_{f_1 - f_2}^2 = \frac{f_1(1 - f_1)}{n_1} + \frac{f_2(1 - f_2)}{n_2} \tag{9.20}$$

For large n_1 and n_2, $f_1 - f_2$ is approximately normally distributed, so that

$$\frac{(f_1 - f_2) - (p_1 - p_2)}{\sqrt{\dfrac{p_1(1 - p_1)}{n_1} + \dfrac{p_2(1 - p_2)}{n_2}}} \tag{9.21}$$

189

has approximately a standard normal distribution. If we replace the p_i in the denominator by their estimates f_i, we obtain

$$\frac{(f_1 - f_2) - (p_1 - p_2)}{\sqrt{\dfrac{f_1(1 - f_1)}{n_1} + \dfrac{f_2(1 - f_2)}{n_2}}}$$

and this too has approximately a standard normal distribution. This leads to the approximate confidence limits

$$L = f_1 - f_2 - t_{(\alpha/2),\infty} \sqrt{\frac{f_1(1 - f_1)}{n_1} + \frac{f_2(1 - f_2)}{n_2}}$$

and (9.22)

$$R = f_1 - f_2 + t_{(\alpha/2),\infty} \sqrt{\frac{f_1(1 - f_1)}{n_1} + \frac{f_2(1 - f_2)}{n_2}}$$

To test the hypothesis $H_0 : p_1 = p_2$, that the proportions of successes in the two populations are the same, we use a test based on the standard normal distribution. The hypothesis states that the proportions are equal to each other, but does not specify the common value; therefore, we must estimate the variance of the difference under the assumption that the proportions are the same.

If $p_1 = p_2 = p$, both f_1 and f_2 are unbiased estimates for p, but the best estimate will be obtained by pooling the two samples into one sample of size $n_1 + n_2$ with the pooled number of successes $X_1 + X_2$. The observed fraction for the combined samples,

$$f = \frac{X_1 + X_2}{n_1 + n_2}$$

(9.23)

is our best estimate for the common value of p.

If $p_1 = p_2$, the estimated variance of $f_1 - f_2$ is

$$\frac{f(1 - f)}{n_1} + \frac{f(1 - f)}{n_2}$$

or

$$f(1 - f)\left(\frac{1}{n_1} + \frac{1}{n_2}\right)$$

(9.24)

Under the null hypothesis, the quantity

$$z = \frac{f_1 - f_2}{\sqrt{f(1 - f)\left(\dfrac{1}{n_1} + \dfrac{1}{n_2}\right)}}$$

(9.25)

has approximately a standard normal distribution if n_1 and n_2 are large. This, then, provides a basis for an approximate test procedure. Once again, we have a t-test with infinite degrees of freedom.

EXAMPLE 1

Problem: Two different methods of manufacture, casting and die forging, were used to make parts for an appliance. In service tests of 100 of each type it was found that 10 castings failed during the test, but only 3 forged parts failed. Find 95% confidence limits for the difference between the proportions of the cast and forged parts that would fail under similar conditions.

Solution: Here

$$f_1 = \tfrac{10}{100} = .10$$

$$f_2 = \tfrac{3}{100} = .03$$

$$s_{f_1}^2 = \frac{.10(.90)}{100}$$

$$s_{f_2}^2 = \frac{.03(.97)}{100}$$

$$s_{f_1-f_2}^2 = \tfrac{1}{100}[.10(.90) + .03(.97)] = .001191$$

$$s_{f_1-f_2} = \sqrt{.001191} = .0345$$

From the *t*-table, $t_{.025,\infty}$ is found to be 1.96, and approximate confidence limits for $p_1 - p_2$ are given by

$$L = f_1 - f_2 - t_{.025,\infty}s_{f_1-f_2} = .07 - 1.96(.0345) \doteq .002$$

and

$$R = f_1 - f_2 + t_{.025,\infty}s_{f_1-f_2} = .07 + 1.96(.0345) = .138$$

We are approximately 95% confident that the difference between the proportions of failures is between .00 and .14.

[handwritten margin notes:]
$H_a\colon p_1 > p_2)$ Reject H_0 if $z > z_\alpha$
$H_a\colon p_1 < p_2\}$ Reject H_0 if $z < -z_\alpha$
$H_a\colon p_1 \neq p_2\}$ Reject H_0 if $z > z_{\alpha/2}$ if $z < -z_{\alpha/2}$

[handwritten:] Completely Random

EXAMPLE 2

Problem: In order to test the effectiveness of a vaccine, 150 experimental animals were given the vaccine and 150 were not. All 300 animals were then infected with the disease. Among those vaccinated 10 died as a result of the disease. Among the control group there were 30 deaths. Can we conclude that the vaccine is effective in reducing the mortality rate? Let $\alpha = .05$. *[handwritten: H_0: vaccine no effect]*

Solution: Here we want to test the hypothesis $H_0\colon p_1 = p_2$ against $H_a\colon p_1 > p_2$, where p_1 is the proportion of deaths among the control animals and p_2 is the proportion of deaths among the animals given the vaccine. *[handwritten: H_a: has some effect]*

[handwritten: $R\colon H_0$ if $f_1 > f_2$ by enough]

$$f_1 = \tfrac{30}{150} = .200$$

$$f_2 = \tfrac{10}{150} = .067$$

$$f = \frac{X_1 + X_2}{n_1 + n_2} = \frac{30 + 10}{300} = \frac{40}{300}$$

$$s_{f_1-f_2}^2 = \tfrac{40}{300}(\tfrac{260}{300})(\tfrac{1}{150} + \tfrac{1}{150}) = .001541$$

$$s_{f_1-f_2} = .0392$$

Our calculated t is

$$t = \frac{f_1 - f_2}{s_{f_1 - f_2}} = \frac{.133}{.0392} = 3.40$$

Since the critical region is $t > t_{.05,\infty} = 1.645$, we reject the null hypothesis and conclude that the vaccine is effective in reducing the mortality rate.

A second approximation for testing the hypothesis that $p_1 = p_2$ will be presented in Chapter 10.

PROBLEMS

1. Two samples, one from each of two normal populations having the same variance, gave the following results.
   a. What are the best estimates for μ_1, $\mu_2 - \mu_1$, σ^2, $\sigma_{\bar{X}_1}^2$, and σ_d^2?
   b. Find 95% confidence intervals for μ_1 and $\mu_2 - \mu_1$.

Sample	n	$\bar{X}_i$	$\sum (X_{ij} - \bar{X}_i)^2$
1	11	150	5600
2	11	120	5400

2. Given the following summary table, and assuming common variance,
   a. Find the best estimates for $\mu_1 - \mu_2$, σ^2, $\sigma_{\bar{X}_2}^2$, and σ_d^2.
   b. Find 99% confidence intervals for μ_2 and $\mu_1 - \mu_2$.

Sample	n	$\bar{X}_i$	$\sum (X_{ij} - \bar{X}_i)^2$
1	6	30	300
2	4	20	180

3. In an experiment designed to compare the mean service lives of two types of tires it was found that the difference between the means was 2250 miles, and that the pooled estimate of variance was equal to 625,000. There were twenty tires of each type. Find a 95% confidence interval for the difference between the mean lives of these types of tires.

4. Fifteen of each of two types of fabricated wood beams were tested for breaking load with the following results. Find a 98% confidence interval for the difference between the mean breaking loads.

Type	n	$\bar{X}_i$	$\sum (X_{ij} - \bar{X}_i)^2$
I	15	1560	48,000
II	15	1600	36,000

5. Tests were made on the drag resistance of two types of anchors for small craft. Ten trials were made with each type. The means were 31,750 pounds and 27,000 pounds for types I and II, respectively, and the corresponding estimated standard deviations were 6350 pounds and 3050 pounds. Find a 99% confidence interval for the difference in drag resistance. Would this interval lead you to conclude that there is a real difference?

6. Given the following summary table,
   a. Find 90% confidence intervals for μ_1, μ_2, and $\mu_2 - \mu_1$.
   b. Would the confidence interval for $\mu_2 - \mu_1$ lead you to conclude that the means are different? Why?

Sample	n	$\bar{X}_i$	$\sum (X_{ij} - \bar{X}_i)^2$
1	9	52	68
2	16	55	24

7. Samples from two normal populations with the same variance gave the following results. Find a 95% confidence interval for $\mu_1 - \mu_2$. Find 98% confidence intervals for μ_1 and μ_2.

Sample	n	$\bar{X}$	s
1	9	96	24
2	16	80	24

8. Given the following summary table, find a 95% confidence interval for $\mu_2 - \mu_1$.

Sample	n	$\bar{X}_i$	$\sum (X_{ij} - \bar{X}_i)^2$
1	15	25	55
2	12	20	45

9. Independent random samples from two normal populations with common variance gave the following results. At the 5% level of significance, can we conclude that the mean of the first population is greater than that of the second?

Sample	n	$\bar{X}_i$	$\sum (X_{ij} - \bar{X}_i)^2$
1	15	35.2	35
2	12	34.0	25

10. Independent random samples from two normal populations with common variance gave the following results. Can we conclude that $\mu_2 - \mu_1 = 4$? Let $\alpha = .01$.

Sample	n	$\bar{X}_i$	$\sum (X_{ij} - \bar{X}_i)^2$
1	10	68	82
2	40	70	302

11. Independent random samples from two normal populations with common variance gave the following results. Would we be justified in concluding that the mean of the first population was less than that of the second? Let $\alpha = .05$.

Sample	n	$\bar{X}_i$	$\sum (X_{ij} - \bar{X}_i)^2$
1	10	25	250
2	15	30	302

12. Independent random samples from normal populations with the same variance gave the following results. Can we conclude that the population means are not equal? Let $\alpha = .01$.

Sample	n	Mean	Sum of squares
1	10	17	116
2	6	21	94

13. Independent random samples from normal populations with the same variance gave the following results. Can we conclude that the difference between the means, $\mu_1 - \mu_2$, is less than 5? Let $\alpha = .025$.

Sample	n	Mean	Sum of squares
1	15	22	1224
2	9	25	756

$\sum (x_i - \bar{x}_i)^2$

14. Independent random samples from normal populations with the same variance gave the following results. Test the hypothesis that $\mu_2 - \mu_1 = 10$ at the 2% level of significance.

Sample	n	Mean	Sum of squares
1	12	62.3	264
2	20	77.1	636

15. Independent random samples from normal populations with the same variance gave the following results. Test the hypothesis that μ_2 is equal to 54.2. Let $\alpha = .02$.

Sample	n	Mean	Sum of squares
1	16	51	1830
2	9	65	1482

16. Given the following data for two samples from normal populations with the same variance,
a. Test the hypothesis that μ_1 is greater than or equal to 70. Let $\alpha = .01$.
b. Test the hypothesis that μ_2 is less than or equal to 53. Let $\alpha = .025$.
c. Test the hypothesis that $\mu_1 = \mu_2$. Let $\alpha = .10$.

Sample	n	Mean	Sum of squares
1.	16	63.5	1480
2	15	58.4	1420

17. The following are yields in bushels per acre for two oat varieties. Each was tried on eight plots. Can we conclude that the yields are the same for the two varieties, A and B?

A	71.2	72.6	47.8	76.9	42.5	49.6	62.8	48.2
B	56.6	60.7	45.4	73.0	42.8	65.2	41.7	57.3

18. The following are percentages of fat found in samples of two types of meat. Do the meats have different fat contents?

Meat A	30	26	30	19	25	37	27	38	26	31
Meat B	40	34	28	29	26	36	28	37	35	42

19. To test the effect of controlled grazing versus continuous grazing, sixteen steers were treated each way for a period of time. The gains in weight in pounds for each animal are given below. Can we conclude there is a difference in the mean gain for the two procedures?

Controlled grazing		Continuous grazing	
130	73	44	110
120	56	62	38
61	65	77	66
111	71	58	120
93	109	88	81
56	122	101	54
25	85	42	31
123	131	57	11

20. Two different acids were tested for their effects on the yield of a dye. Eight runs were made with each type. The following yields were obtained. Test the hypothesis that there is no difference in their effects.

Acid 1	Acid 2
134.5	142.0
135.0	150.0
141.5	151.5
143.5	152.0
146.0	152.5
135.0	134.5
134.5	138.5
144.0	146.0

21. Ten pairs of brothers made the following scores on a test. Do these results indicate that in general the older of two brothers will make a higher score?

Brother	Pair									
	1	2	3	4	5	6	7	8	9	10
Older	86	79	67	92	65	75	61	77	91	68
Younger	80	81	60	87	71	72	56	75	93	67

22. To generate some data for illustrating the differences between grouped and paired comparisons, ten egg timers were timed in two positions: vertical, and at 20 degrees from vertical. The values in seconds are shown below.
   a. Treat the data as two groups and calculate the t for testing the hypothesis that the mean time is the same in both positions.
   b. Use paired comparison methods to find the value of t for testing the same hypothesis. Note that when differences among timers are eliminated from the variance, as is the case with paired comparisons, the t-value is larger.
   c. What conclusions would be reached in these two analyses?

	Timer									
	1	2	3	4	5	6	7	8	9	10
Vertical	170	191	205	181	210	192	183	205	185	216
Tipped	160	197	175	181	163	172	177	185	183	177

23. To compare the average weight gains of pigs fed two different rations, nine pairs of pigs were used. The pigs within each pair were littermates, the rations were assigned at random to the two animals within each pair, and they were individually housed and fed. The gains, in pounds, after thirty days are given below.
   a. Test the hypothesis that the mean gains are the same against the alternative that feed A produces a larger grain.
   b. Find a 98% confidence interval for the difference between the average gains.

Ration	Litter									Sum
	1	2	3	4	5	6	7	8	9	
A	60	38	39	49	49	62	53	42	58	450
B	53	39	29	41	47	50	56	47	52	414

Xred   7   −1   10   8   2   12   −7   −5   6

24. Two different methods were used to determine the percent fat content in different samples of meat. Both methods were used on portions of the same meat sample. Do the following data give reason to believe that one method gives higher readings, on the average? Find a 90% confidence interval for the mean difference.

Meat sample	Method I	Method II	Meat sample	Method I	Method II
1	23.1	22.7	9	38.4	38.1
2	23.2	23.6	10	23.5	23.8
3	26.5	27.1	11	22.2	22.5
4	26.6	27.4	12	24.7	24.4
5	27.1	27.4	13	45.1	43.5
6	48.3	46.8	14	27.6	27.0
7	40.5	40.4	15	25.0	24.9
8	25.0	24.9	16	36.7	35.2

25. To investigate the effect on a pulse column of changing the frequency of the pulse, two frequencies were tried with various combinations of amplitude and other factors. When other factors were fixed, the frequency was changed from f_1 to f_2, or from f_2 to f_1, the order being randomized. The following measures of column efficiency were obtained. Does frequency of pulse have an effect on efficiency? Find a 99% confidence interval for the difference.

Run	f_1	f_2	Run	f_1	f_2
1	3.96	4.61	8	7.35	8.12
2	6.13	6.33	9	4.13	4.75
3	8.21	7.38	10	6.37	6.43
4	6.05	6.87	11	7.08	7.38
5	5.21	6.62	12	7.56	6.45
6	5.25	6.82	13	6.24	6.16
7	6.32	6.87	14	8.05	8.14

26. Analyze the data of problem 24 by the method of group comparisons. Do you reach the same conclusions? How much wider is the confidence interval?

27. In a sample of 100 from one binomial population there were 28 successes. A sample of 200 from a second binomial population contained 92 successes.
 a. Find estimates for p_1, p_2, and $p_2 - p_1$.
 b. Estimate the standard deviation of $f_2 - f_1$.
 c. Find a 95% confidence interval for $p_2 - p_1$.
 d. Test the hypothesis that $p_2 = p_1$. Let $\alpha = .01$.

28. Samples of 200 were taken from each of two binomial populations. They contained 104 and 96 successes, respectively.
 a. Find the estimated standard deviation of $p_1 - p_2$.
 b. Find a 98% confidence interval for $p_1 - p_2$.
 c. Test the hypothesis that $p_1 = p_2$. Let $\alpha = .05$.

29. A sample of 500 people were classified as being "athletic" or "non-athletic." Among 300 classified as "athletic" it was found that 48 regularly eat a certain breakfast food. Among the 200 "non-athletic" persons there were 52 who regularly use the product.
 a. Find a 99% confidence interval for the difference in the proportions that use the product. *(Part b follows)*

b. Test the hypothesis there is no difference. Let $\alpha = .10$.

30. In a sample of 50 turnings from an automatic lathe, 5 were found to be outside specifications. The cutting bits were then changed and the machine restarted. A new sample of 50 contained 3 defective turnings.

   a. Find a 95% confidence interval for the decrease in the proportion defective after changing bits.

   b. Can we conclude that the proportion defective has been reduced?

31. A random sample of 900 persons included 433 females and 467 males. Of the males, 8 were found to be color-blind, while only 1 of the females was color-blind. From these data, can we conclude that the proportion that are color-blind is smaller for females than for males?

32. If, during the five-year period 1961–1965, 300 out of 1000 juveniles committed to training schools were girls, and if over the last five years 540 out of 2000 were girls, can we conclude that the proportion of girls among those committed has decreased from the 1961–1965 period?

33. Two different alloys were used in the manufacture of parts for an appliance. One hundred samples of each were subjected to shock testing. Defects developed in 18 of those made from alloy I and in 26 of those made from alloy II. Can we conclude that those made of alloy I stand up to shock better than those made of alloy II?

REFERENCES

9.1 CROXTON, FREDERICK E., DUDLEY J. COWDEN, and BEN W. BOLCH. *Practical Business Statistics*, 4th edition. Prentice-Hall, New York, 1969. Chapters 11 and 12.

9.2 LI, JEROME C. R. *Statistical Inference*, I. Edwards Brothers, Ann Arbor, 1964. Chapters 10, 11, and 21.

9.3 OSTLE, BERNARD. *Statistics in Research*, 2nd edition. Iowa State University Press, Ames, 1963. Chapter 7.

9.4 SNEDECOR, GEORGE W., and WILLIAM G. COCHRAN. *Statistical Methods*, 6th edition. Iowa State University Press, Ames, 1967. Chapter 4.

10

Approximate Tests: Multinomial Data

10.1 THE MULTINOMIAL DISTRIBUTION

In earlier chapters we discussed the binomial distribution in some detail (Section 5.8); recall that it is the appropriate model when we are sampling from a population in which the elements belong to either one of two classes, and the sample is taken in such a manner that the probability of obtaining an element from a given class remains constant—that is, is not affected by the sampling process. We now consider the more general case where the elements of the population are classified as belonging to one of k classes, where $k \geq 2$. We refer to such a population as a *multinomial* population, and, if the proportions of the elements belonging to each class are not changed by the selection of the sample, the appropriate model is the *multinomial distribution*.

The multinomial distribution is the *joint* distribution for the random variables $Y_1, Y_2, \ldots, Y_k$, the numbers of elements in a sample of size n that belong to each of the k classes of the population, Y_i being the number that belong to the ith class. The corresponding sample fractions Y_i/n we denote by f_i. These quantities satisfy the conditions

$$\sum_{i=1}^{k} Y_i = n \qquad (10.1)$$

$$\sum_{i=1}^{k} f_i = 1 \qquad (10.2)$$

The parameters of the multinomial distribution are the sample size n and the proportions $p_1, p_2, \ldots, p_k$ of the elements in the population that belong to each of the k classes, p_i being the proportion that belong to the ith class. Since the k classes contain all of the elements,

$$\sum_{i=1}^{k} p_i = 1 \qquad (10.3)$$

As one might expect, each p_i is estimated unbiasedly by the corresponding sample fraction

$$f_i = \frac{Y_i}{n}$$

10.2 AN HYPOTHESIS ABOUT THE MULTINOMIAL PARAMETERS

The basic hypothesis to be considered here is that the proportions belonging to the k classes are equal to a set of specified values; thus, $H_0 : p_i = p_{i0}$, where $i = 1, 2, \ldots, k$. An exact test for this hypothesis would be difficult to apply, particularly for large sample sizes; therefore, it is usually tested by a procedure involving approximations.

If the hypothesis is true, the mean, or *expected*, number of elements of the ith class in a sample of size n is:

$$E_i = np_{i0}$$

The *observed* number in the ith class is Y_i. If we calculate for each class the quantity

$$\frac{(Y_i - E_i)^2}{E_i}$$

we have the squared difference between the observed and expected numbers in that class relative to its expected number. The sum of these quantities over all classes, denoted by χ^2 (chi-square),

$$\chi^2 = \frac{(Y_1 - E_1)^2}{E_1} + \frac{(Y_2 - E_2)^2}{E_2} + \cdots + \frac{(Y_k - E_k)^2}{E_k}$$

or simply

$$\chi^2 = \sum_{i=1}^{k} \frac{(Y_i - E_i)^2}{E_i} \qquad (10.4)$$

is a measure of the lack of agreement between the data and the hypothesis. The idea is that, if the null hypothesis is true, then the observed frequencies

$$Y_1, Y_2, \ldots, Y_k$$

ought not deviate too much from their respective expected values

$$E_1, E_2, \ldots, E_k$$

The chi-square statistic gathers together the discrepancy between Y_i and E_i for all the values of i. To test the null hypothesis, we ask whether statistic (10.4) has a larger value than can reasonably be accounted for by the workings of chance.

It can be shown that for sufficiently large sample sizes the distribution of the statistic (10.4) can be approximated by a chi-square distribution with $k - 1$ degrees of freedom. Note that the degrees of freedom are equal to one less than the number of *classes* and are not related to the size of the sample.

The χ^2-distribution, or *chi-square distribution*, is a continuous distribution ordinarily derived as the sampling distribution of a sum of squares of independent standard normal variables. It is a skewed distribution such that only non-negative values of the variable χ^2 are possible, and it depends upon a single parameter, the degrees of freedom. The χ^2-distributions for degrees of freedom equal to 1, 4, and 10 are shown in Figure 10.1. It can be seen that the skewness decreases as the degrees of freedom increase. In fact, it can be shown that as the degrees of freedom increase without limit, the χ^2-distribution approaches a normal distribution.

Percentage points of the χ^2-distributions are given in Table V of the Appendix and are defined by

$$P(\chi_v^2 \geq \chi_{\alpha,v}^2) = \alpha$$

—that is, $\chi_{\alpha,v}^2$ is that value for the chi-square distribution with v degrees of freedom such that the area to the *right*, the probability of a *larger* value, is equal to α. For example, the upper 5% point $\chi_{.05,20}^2$ for χ^2 with 20 degrees of freedom is 31.41.

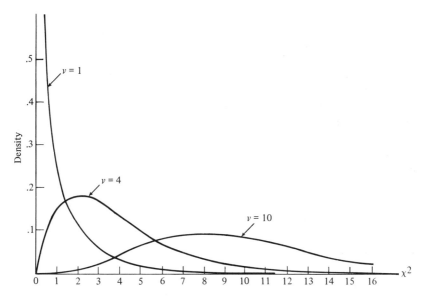

FIGURE 10.1. *Chi-square distributions with 1, 4, and 10 degrees of freedom*

To test the hypothesis H_0 that $p_i = p_{i0}$ for all i, we calculate the multinomial chi-square sum (10.4) and compare the calculated value with the percentage points of the χ^2-distribution with $k - 1$ degrees of freedom. Since good agreement between the observed and expected numbers would result in a small χ^2-value and perfect agreement would give for χ^2 a value of 0, we are justified in rejecting the hypothesis only when χ^2 is large; hence, this test is always a one-tailed test on the upper tail of the χ^2-distribution. The critical region is $\chi^2 \geq \chi^2_{\alpha, k-1}$.

EXAMPLE 1

Problem: A geneticist postulates that in the progeny of a certain dihybrid cross the four phenotypes should be present in the ratio $9:3:3:1$. Examination of 800 members of the progeny generation results in the observed numbers 439, 168, 133, and 60 for the four phenotypes. Are these numbers in agreement with the hypothesized ratio? Let $\alpha = .05$.
Solution: The hypothesis is $H_0: p_1 = \frac{9}{16}, p_2 = \frac{3}{16}, p_3 = \frac{3}{16}, p_4 = \frac{1}{16}$. The calculations may be conveniently arranged in tabular form as follows:

	Phenotype			
	1	2	3	4
Y_i	439	168	133	60
$E_i = np_{i0}$	450	150	150	50
$Y_i - E_i$	-11	18	-17	10
$(Y_i - E_i)^2$	121	324	289	100

$$\chi^2 = \tfrac{121}{450} + \tfrac{324}{150} + \tfrac{289}{150} + \tfrac{100}{50} = 6.36$$

From the table, $\chi^2_{.05(3)}$ is found to be 7.81; therefore, since the calculated value is the smaller, we have no reason to reject the hypothesis. We conclude that the results are in agreement with the expected ratio.

In the above example we may be interested in testing the hypothesis that some, but not all, of the proportions are equal to specified values. For instance, we might be interested in testing that the proportions in the first two phenotypes are $\frac{9}{16}$ and $\frac{3}{16}$, respectively, regardless of the proportions in the last two. In such cases the number of classes is reduced to conform with the hypothesis by combining the unspecified classes into one. For the genetic example they would be: first phenotype, second phenotype, other phenotypes. If we are interested in only one class, the problem falls into the framework of the binomial test, for we would have two classes: the class of interest and the class consisting of "all other classes."

10.3 BINOMIAL DATA

In Section 8.3, we studied tests concerning the proportion p in a binomial population. The two-sided test considered there is a special instance of the chi-square test for the case where k is 2. It is instructive to trace the connection.

We relabel the success category in the population as class 1 and the failure category as class 2 ($k = 2$). If p_0 is the proportion of successes in the population, then class 1 has proportion $p_{10} = p_0$ and class 2 has proportion $p_{20} = 1 - p_0$. And now the null hypothesis

$$H_0: p_1 = p_0 \quad \text{and} \quad p_2 = 1 - p_0$$

is exactly the same thing as the null hypothesis

$$H_0: p = p_0$$

considered in Section 8.3.

If X is the number of successes in a sample of size n, then the number Y_1 of observations falling in class 1 is X and the number Y_2 of observations falling in class 2 is $n - X$. Now the chi-square sum (10.4) for testing H_0 is

$$
\chi^2 = \frac{(Y_1 - np_{10})^2}{np_{10}} + \frac{(Y_2 - np_{20})^2}{np_{20}}
$$

$$
= \frac{(X - np_0)^2}{np_0} + \frac{((n - X) - n(1 - p_0))^2}{n(1 - p_0)} \tag{10.5}
$$

But algebra reduces this expression to

$$
\chi^2 = \left[\frac{X - np_0}{\sqrt{np_0(1 - p_0)}} \right]^2 \tag{10.6}
$$

which is the square of the statistic (8.7) used to test the hypothesis $p = p_0$.

EXAMPLE 1

Problem: At one time the sex ratio in a small eastern city was known to be 8 to 1 in favor of the males (there were eight women for every man). Suppose that in a recent survey we found that a random sample of 450 contained 68 men. Would we be justified in concluding that the ratio had changed?

Solution: If the ratio is 8 to 1, one out of every nine persons is a male; therefore, if the ratio has not changed, the proportion p of males is $1/9$. We test the hypothesis $H_0: p = 1/9$ against the two-sided alternative, $H_a: p \neq 1/9$ at the 1% level of significance. Let X be the number of men in the sample; then

$$Y_1 = X = 68$$
$$Y_2 = n - X = 450 - 68 = 382$$
$$E_1 = \tfrac{1}{9}(450) = 50$$
$$E_2 = \tfrac{8}{9}(450) = 400$$
$$\chi^2 = \frac{(68 - 50)^2}{50} + \frac{(382 - 400)^2}{400} = 7.29$$

203

From Table V of the Appendix, $\chi^2_{.01(1)}$ is found to be 6.63. The calculated χ^2 is greater than the tabular value; therefore, we reject the null hypothesis and conclude that the ratio has changed.

In this calculation we have used equation (10.5). Using equation (10.6) instead gives

$$\chi^2 = \left[\frac{68 - 450 \times \frac{1}{9}}{\sqrt{450 \times \frac{1}{9} \times \frac{8}{9}}} \right]^2 = 2.7^2 = 7.29$$

which checks. The value 2.7 that is to be squared here is the value of the statistic (8.7) used in Section 8.3 for a two-sided test of $H_0: p = p_0$. At the 1% level, we are to reject if the statistic has absolute value exceeding $Z_{.005}$, or 2.576; this is true of our value 2.7, so again we reject. The two procedures necessarily lead to the same conclusion because 6.63, the cutoff point for the chi-square test, is 2.576^2.

Since it is true in general that $\chi^2_{\alpha,1}$ is equal to $Z^2_{\alpha/2}$, a chi-square test based on equation (10.5) is always the same as the two-sided test of Section 8.3.

10.4   A TEST FOR GOODNESS OF FIT

In the tests of hypotheses of the preceding chapters, we assumed that we knew the form of the distribution and we tested for the values of parameters. For example, we *assumed* the population was normal and tested the hypothesis $\mu = \mu_0$. But what if we want to check on the assumption of normality itself? The multinomial chi-square *goodness-of-fit* test can be applied.

For an example, suppose we want to test at the 1% level the hypothesis that the 106 cranial measurements of Table 2.3 come from some normal population. If we combine the first four categories and the last three, the data reduce to Table 10.1. Now we must check whether these observed

TABLE 10.1.   Distribution of Widths in Millimeters of 106 Crania

Class	Measurement	$Y_i = Number$ of observations
1	Less than 135.5	10
2	135.5 to 139.5	21
3	139.5 to 143.5	41
4	143.5 to 147.5	19
5	More than 147.5	15
		$n = 106$

frequencies Y_i agree well with a normal distribution having *some* mean and standard deviation—a mean and standard deviation unspecified in advance. Our first step is to estimate the mean and standard deviation from the sample by $\overline{X}$ and s, which turn out to be

$$\overline{X} = 141.77 \qquad \text{and} \qquad s = 5.41$$

The next step is to compute what probability a normally distributed random variable X with mean 141.77 and standard deviation 5.41 has of falling in each of the five classes represented in Table 10.1. To do this we standardize the class boundaries:

$$(135.5 - 141.77)/5.41 = -1.16$$
$$(139.5 - 141.77)/5.41 = -.42$$
$$(143.5 - 141.77)/5.41 = .32$$
$$(147.5 - 141.77)/5.41 = 1.06$$

The probability that such an X falls in class 2, for example, is the probability that the standardized variable $(X - 141.77)/5.41$ falls between the first two of these figures, namely -1.16 and $-.42$; by Table II in the Appendix this probability is $.37698 - .16276$, or $.21422$. Thus we obtain the probabilities (rounded off) shown in Figure 10.2.

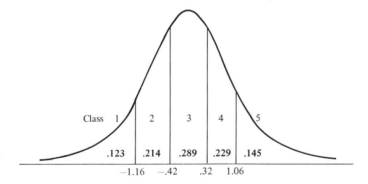

FIGURE 10.2. *Areas for the standard normal curve*

And now we chi-square the observed frequencies in Table 10.1 against these probabilities. Since the probability of class 2 is .214 and the total number of observations is 106, we expect on the average $106 \times .214$, or 22.68, observations to fall in class 2. Table 10.2 shows the remaining calculations.

The number of degrees of freedom in this example is 2. If we had not had to estimate the mean and standard deviation from the sample (by $\overline{X}$ and s), the degrees of freedom would have been (as in Section 10.2) one less than the number of categories: $k - 1$, or 4. But the rule is that we must subtract one additional degree of freedom for each parameter estimated. We have

TABLE 10.2. Calculation of the χ^2 Goodness-of-Fit Test for the Data of Table 10.1

Class	Probability	E_i	Y_i	$Y_i - E_i$	$(Y_i - E_i)^2/E_i$
1	.123	13.04	10	-3.04	.71
2	.214	22.68	21	-1.68	.12
3	.289	30.63	41	10.37	3.51
4	.229	24.27	19	-5.27	1.14
5	.145	15.38	15	$-.38$	.01
Totals	1.000	106.00	106	0.00	$\chi^2 = 5.49$

estimated two parameters, the mean and the standard deviation, so our degrees of freedom are $4 - 2$, or 2. We are to test at the 1% level the hypothesis that the data in Table 10.1 fit a normal curve. The 1% point on a chi-square distribution with 2 degrees of freedom is $\chi^2_{.01,2}$, or 9.21. Our value, 5.49, is less than this; the data do fit well with a normal distribution.

The multinomial chi-square may be used to test the goodness of fit of data with other distributions as well. We need only remember that each expected number should be at least 5, so that the chi-square statistic closely follows the chi-square distribution, and that we lose one degree of freedom for every parameter estimated from the sample.

10.5 CONTINGENCY TABLES

Many sets of enumeration data are such that they may be grouped according to two or more criteria of classification, and it is often the case that we should like to know whether or not these various criteria are independent of one another. For instance, we might like to know whether color preference is independent of sex. In this case we could take a sample of people, record their sex and their favorite color, and classify their responses by sex and by color.

If the data are to be classified according to two criteria, the only case we treat here, the classes based on one of them may be represented by the rows in a two-way table, the classes based on the other by the columns. A cell of the table is formed by the intersection of a row and column. We may then count the numbers of elements in the sample that belong to each cell of the table. The general two-way table with r rows and c columns is presented in Table 10.3. The notation used in Table 10.3 is as follows:

Y_{ij} = number observed to belong to the ith row and jth column. Note that the first subscript denotes the row, the second the column.

R_i = total observed number in the ith row; found by adding across the row.

C_j = total observed number in the jth column; found by adding
down the column.

n = the sample size = $\sum R_i = \sum C_j$.

TABLE 10.3.   The $r \times c$ Contingency Table

Rows	Columns 1	2	3	$\cdots$	c	Row totals
1	Y_{11}	Y_{12}	Y_{13}		Y_{1c}	R_1
2	Y_{21}	Y_{22}	Y_{23}		Y_{2c}	R_2
3	Y_{31}	Y_{32}	Y_{33}		Y_{3c}	R_3
$\vdots$						
r	Y_{r1}	Y_{r2}	Y_{r3}		Y_{rc}	R_r
Column totals	C_1	C_2	C_3		C_c	n

To test the hypothesis that rows and columns represent independent classifications, we compute an expected number E_{ij} for each cell and use the multinomial chi-square. By *independence* we mean that the proportion of each row total that belongs in the jth column is the same for all rows (or that the proportion of each column total that belongs in the ith row is the same for all columns). This is expressed mathematically by saying that the probability that a random element will belong in the (i,j)th cell is equal to the product of the probability that it belongs to the ith row times the probability that it belongs to the jth column. Symbolically, our hypothesis is $H_0: p_{ij} = p_{i.} p_{.j}; i = 1, 2, \ldots, r; j = 1, 2, \ldots, c,$

where p_{ij} = probability of ith row *and* jth column,
$p_{i.}$ = probability of ith row ignoring columns,
$p_{.j}$ = probability of jth column ignoring rows.

The marginal probability $p_{i.}$ is estimated by the observed fraction in the ith row, R_i/n, and $p_{.j}$ by the observed fraction in the jth column, C_j/n. Under the hypothesis of independence, the value of p_{ij}, or of $p_{i.} p_{.j}$, is estimated by the product of these estimates $R_i C_j / n^2$; therefore, the expected number is the sample size n multiplied by the estimated probability:

$$E_{ij} = \frac{R_i C_j}{n} \tag{10.7}$$

We can now find the expected number for each cell in the table.

To perform the test we find the contribution of each cell to the multinomial chi-square. The contribution of the (i, j)th cell is

$$\frac{(Y_{ij} - E_{ij})^2}{E_{ij}}$$

207

There are a total of $r \times c$ such contributions, and the calculated χ^2 is their sum:

$$\chi^2 = \sum_{i,j} \frac{(Y_{ij} - E_{ij})^2}{E_{ij}} \tag{10.8}$$

This chi-square has $(r - 1)(c - 1)$ degrees of freedom, the number of rows less one, multiplied by the number of columns less one.

If the calculated χ^2 exceeds the tabular value for probability α, we reject the hypothesis and conclude that rows and columns do not represent independent classifications; if the calculated χ^2 does not exceed the tabular value, we accept the hypothesis.

EXAMPLE 1

The following simple example will serve to illustrate the procedure:

| | Columns | | | | Row |
Rows	1	2	3	4	totals
1	36	16	14	34	100
2	64	34	20	82	200
3	50	50	16	84	200
Column totals	150	100	50	200	500

The expected numbers are:

$$E_{11} = \frac{(150)(100)}{500} = 30 \qquad E_{12} = \frac{(100)(100)}{500} = 20$$

$$E_{13} = \frac{(50)(100)}{500} = 10 \qquad E_{14} = \frac{(200)(100)}{500} = 40$$

$$E_{21} = \frac{(150)(200)}{500} = 60 \qquad E_{22} = \frac{(100)(200)}{500} = 40$$

$$E_{23} = \frac{(50)(200)}{500} = 20 \qquad E_{24} = \frac{(200)(200)}{500} = 80$$

$$E_{31} = \frac{(150)(200)}{500} = 60 \qquad E_{32} = \frac{(100)(200)}{500} = 40$$

$$E_{33} = \frac{(50)(200)}{500} = 20 \qquad E_{34} = \frac{(200)(200)}{500} = 80$$

The calculated χ^2 has $(4 - 1)(3 - 1)$, or 6, degrees of freedom and is equal to 13.29:

$$\chi^2 = \frac{(36 - 30)^2}{30} + \frac{(16 - 20)^2}{20} + \frac{(14 - 10)^2}{10} + \frac{(34 - 40)^2}{40}$$

$$+ \frac{(64 - 60)^2}{60} + \frac{(34 - 40)^2}{40} + \frac{(20 - 20)^2}{20} + \frac{(82 - 80)^2}{80}$$

$$+ \frac{(50 - 60)^2}{60} + \frac{(50 - 40)^2}{40} + \frac{(16 - 20)^2}{20} + \frac{(84 - 80)^2}{80}$$

$$= 13.29$$

The tabular value for the case where α is .05 and there are 6 degrees of freedom is $\chi^2_{.05(6)}$, or 12.6. Our calculated value is greater than 12.6; therefore, at the .05 level of significance, we reject the hypothesis that rows and columns are independent.

The simplest contingency table, the 2 × 2, can be used to test the hypothesis that two binomial populations have the same relative frequency of successes. Let p_1 be the proportion in the first population and p_2 the proportion in the second. Using the information contained in two random samples, one from each population, we can test the hypothesis $H_0 : p_1 = p_2$.

The results of the two samples may be summarized in a two-way table as follows:

Sample	Successes	Failures	Sizes
1	Y_1	$n_1 - Y_1$	n_1
2	Y_2	$n_2 - Y_2$	n_2
Totals	$Y_1 + Y_2$	$n_1 + n_2 - Y_1 - Y_2$	$n_1 + n_2$

In the preceding table, n_1 and n_2 are the two sample sizes, and Y_1 and Y_2 are the observed number of successes in the first and second samples, respectively.

If we test the hypothesis that the rows and columns of this table are independent we are, in fact, testing the hypothesis that the proportions of successes and failures are independent of the population. This could be true only if $p_1 = p_2$. The calculated χ^2 for the 2 × 2 table will, of course, have one degree of freedom.

EXAMPLE 2

Problem: In order to test the effectiveness of a vaccine, 120 experimental animals were given the vaccine and 180 were not. All 300 animals were then infected with the disease. Among those vaccinated, 6 died as a result of the disease. Among the control group, there were 18 deaths. Can we conclude that the vaccine changes the mortality rate?

Solution: Here

$$n_1 = 120 \qquad n_2 = 180$$
$$Y_1 = 6 \qquad Y_2 = 18$$
$$n_1 - Y_1 = 114 \qquad n_2 - Y_2 = 162$$

and the two-way table is:

	Died	Lived	Totals
Not vaccinated	18	162	180
Vaccinated	6	114	120
Totals	24	276	300

The expected numbers are:

$$E_{11} = \frac{(24)(180)}{300} = 14.4 \qquad E_{12} = \frac{(276)(180)}{300} = 165.6$$

$$E_{21} = \frac{(24)(120)}{300} = 9.6 \qquad E_{22} = \frac{(276)(120)}{300} = 110.4$$

The calculated χ^2 is

$$\chi^2 = \frac{(18 - 14.4)^2}{14.4} + \frac{(162 - 165.6)^2}{165.6} + \frac{(6 - 9.6)^2}{9.6}$$

$$+ \frac{(114 - 110.4)^2}{110.4}$$

$$= 2.45$$

Since the calculated value is less than the tabular value for $\chi^2_{.05(1)}$, which is 3.84, we have no reason, at the .05 level of significance, to reject the hypothesis of independence—no reason to believe that the mortality rates for the two groups are different.

As an interesting sidelight, the preceding example illustrates the dangers of the uncritical acceptance of numerical facts. If, on the basis of the data of Example 2, it were reported that, compared to the control group, only one-third as many of the vaccinated animals died, this would be a factual statement. However, before accepting the conclusion implicit in this statement one should look for additional information. Not only are the actual numbers of deaths in each group important. It is also necessary that the sample sizes be taken into account, since the observed numbers are meaningful only in relation to the size of the experiment.

Suppose that the number of animals in each group had been equal to 20 but that the number of deaths, 6 and 18, remained the same. In this case the calculated chi-square would be equal to 15, and the hypothesis $H_0: p_1 = p_2$ would be rejected. There is, however, no significant difference in the mortality rates when 6 out of 120 is compared with 18 out of 180.

PROBLEMS

1. The following grades were given to a class of 100 students. The expected numbers are those corresponding to the "curve." Can we conclude that the instructor used the curve?

	Grade				
	A	B	C	D	F
Given	10	30	40	16	4
Expected	7	24	38	24	7

2. A jar contains a large number of colored beads. It is supposed that the colors red, yellow, green, and blue are in the proportions $8:7:3:2$. A sample of 400 contains 180 red, 120 yellow, 40 green, and 60 blue beads.
   a. Estimate the proportion of each color in the jar.
   b. Test the hypothesis that one tenth of the beads are blue. Let $\alpha = .01$.
   c. Test the hypothesis that the proportions are $8:7:3:2$. Let $\alpha = .005$.

3. If a sample of 300 peak electrical loads for rural consumers should be distributed among three periods as follows:

2:00 AM–10:00 AM	10:00 AM–6:00 PM	6:00 PM–2:00 AM
84	96	120.

   a. Estimate the proportions of peak loads that occur in each period.
   b. Test the hypothesis that the loads are uniformly distributed among the periods. Let $\alpha = .05$.
   c. Test the hypothesis that one third of the peak loads occur in the 2:00 AM–10:00 AM period. Let $\alpha = .01$.

4. The probabilities for the various outcomes when a pair of dice are tossed are given below with the frequencies observed when a pair of dice were tossed 1800 times.
   a. What is the estimated probability of throwing a 7 with these dice? Of throwing a 12?
   b. At the 1% level of significance are the observed frequencies in agreement with the theoretical values?

	r										
	2	3	4	5	6	7	8	9	10	11	12
$P(X = r)$	$\frac{1}{36}$	$\frac{2}{36}$	$\frac{3}{36}$	$\frac{4}{36}$	$\frac{5}{36}$	$\frac{6}{36}$	$\frac{5}{36}$	$\frac{4}{36}$	$\frac{3}{36}$	$\frac{2}{36}$	$\frac{1}{36}$
Frequency	40	108	175	184	225	330	223	228	128	87	72

5. Someone gave me an interesting pair of dice. I rolled them thirty-six times and obtained the following outcomes. Lacking further information, would you conclude it is a fair pair of dice? Let $\alpha = .01$.

Outcome	2	3	4	5	6	7	8	9	10	11	12
Frequency	0	0	4	1	4	0	5	10	9	3	0

6. One can obtain a pair of dice such that one die will produce only a 1, 5, or 6 with probability of 1/3 for each; and the other die will produce a 3, 4, or 5 with equal probability. Given the results of the thirty-six rolls of a pair of dice tabled in the preceding problem, would you conclude that the dice that produced those results were of the type just described?

7. Suppose that A and O blood types are inherited in a manner such that AO by AO matings should produce offspring of which 75% test A and 25% test O. If a random sample of 200 children from such matings results in 144 who test A and 56 who test O, would we reject the postulated inheritance mechanism?

8. A polling agency reported that in a sample of 156 persons 71 were Democrats, 62 were Republicans, and 23 were independent or belonged to other parties. From these results can it be concluded that the major parties are equally strong in this area?

9. A sampling of shorthorn breeders resulted in the following numbers of red, roan, and white shorthorn cattle. Are these numbers consistent with the hypothesized ratio $1 : 2 : 1$?

Breeder	Red	Roan	White
1	11	11	7
2	8	17	6
3	25	48	23
4	12	19	6
5	10	22	8
6	15	26	40

10. Four samples were taken from the output of a machine during one day. From the following results would we conclude that, on the average, the machine was turning out 5% defective items?

Sample	Defectives	Non-defectives
1	2	98
2	16	84
3	10	90
4	1	99

11. A random sample of 200 drivers contained 62 who had been involved in one or more accidents. Would we reject the hypothesis that the proportion of accident-free drivers is equal to .75?

12. Lacking a table of random numbers, I decided to use the last digits in a set of five-place tables of logarithms. The number of times each integer occurred in a sample of size n of 50 is given below. I would expect each integer to occur, on the average, equally often. Are the observed frequencies in agreement with this expectation?

Integer	0	1	2	3	4	5	6	7	8	9
Frequency of occurrence	3	5	2	4	6	5	6	3	9	7

13. The following is the distribution for the number of defective items found in 150 lots of a manufactured item. We want to test the hypothesis that X, the

X = Number defective	Observed frequency	Expected frequency (rounded)
0	23	20
1	39	41
2	43	41
3	23	27
4	10	14
5	7 ⎫	⎫
6	4 ⎬ 12	⎬ 7
7	1 ⎭	⎭

number of defectives, has a Poisson distribution, and we proceed as follows.
1. The mean $\bar{X}$ is 2. This estimates the parameter θ for the Poisson distribution:

$$f(r) = P(X = r) = \frac{e^{-\theta}\theta^r}{r!} \qquad r = 0, 1, 2, \ldots$$

2. Obtain the probabilities for each value of X from tables of Poisson probabilities, or use the recursion formula,

$$f(r) = \frac{\theta}{r} f(r - 1)$$

For example: $f(0) = e^{-\theta} = e^{-2} = .135$, so

$$\begin{aligned}
f(1) &= 2(.135) = .270, \\
f(2) &= \tfrac{2}{2}(.270) = .270, \\
f(3) &= \tfrac{2}{3}(.270) = .180, \\
f(4) &= \tfrac{2}{4}(.180) = .090,
\end{aligned}$$

etc.

3. The expected number corresponding to a given value of r is $nf(r)$.
4. We combine the last four observed and expected numbers in order that no expected number will be less than 5. Calculate χ^2. The degrees of freedom are equal to 4 since we had to estimate θ.

14. Using the procedure outlined in the preceding problem, test the hypothesis that the data displayed below have a Poisson distribution.

X	0	1	2	3	4	5
Frequency	27	40	18	12	5	1

15. The following is the distribution for the number of westbound cars arriving at a particular intersection in sixty-second intervals. Can it be concluded that a Poisson distribution provides a suitable model? See problem 13.

Number of cars	0	1	2	3	4	5	6	7	8	9	10
Observed frequency	8	23	39	53	36	30	15	7	5	3	1

16. Given the following distribution, test the hypothesis that the data came from a normal distribution.

Class	Observed frequency
$25 \leq X < 50$	15
$50 \leq X < 75$	25
$75 \leq X < 100$	30
$100 \leq X < 125$	20
$125 \leq X < 150$	10

17. Given the following distribution for the yields, in grams, obtained from 100 hills of corn, test that a normal distribution is an appropriate model.

Yield (grams)	Number of hills
$100 \leq X < 300$	3
$300 \leq X < 500$	7
$500 \leq X < 700$	15
$700 \leq X < 900$	26
$900 \leq X < 1100$	22
$1100 \leq X < 1300$	13
$1300 \leq X < 1500$	9
$1500 \leq X < 1700$	5

18. Given the distribution of problem 12, Chapter 2, test for normality.

19. Test the hypothesis that the lengths of mayfly larvae given in problem 25, Chapter 7, are normally distributed.

20. Test the hypothesis that the weight gains of the forty-eight steers given in problem 4, Chapter 2, are normally distributed.

21. Does a normal distribution provide a good fit to the differences in cutoff voltages given in problem 13, Chapter 2?

22. Apply a goodness-of-fit test to the nitrogen contents given in problem 10, Chapter 2. Can we conclude they are normally distributed?

23. Questionnaires were mailed to graduates with degrees in statistics from Iowa State University. The numbers who returned the questionnaires are shown below. Test the hypothesis that the proportion who did not return the questionnaire is independent of the level of degree earned. Let $\alpha = .05$.

	B.S.	M.S.	Ph.D.
Returned	47	42	46
Did not return	13	13	8

24. Do the following data give us reason to believe that the fouling of boat bottoms can be reduced by the use of an anti-fouling paint? Let $\alpha = .01$.

	Paint	
	Anti-fouling	Standard
No fouling	37	15
Some fouling	53	50
Much fouling	10	35

25. Two chemical treatments were applied to random samples of seeds. After treatment, germination tests were conducted, with the following results. Do these data indicate that the chemicals differ in their effects on germination?

Chemical treatment	Number of seeds	Percent germination
A	150	80
B	125	88

26. Two independent polls were taken to investigate public opinion with regard to a proposed recreational facility. One was conducted by a polling agency, the other by a local newspaper. Are the two polls homogeneous with respect to division of opinion? Let $\alpha = .025$.

	Polling agency	Newspaper
Favor	52.5%	47.5%
Oppose	35.0%	37.5%
Undecided	12.5%	15.0%
Sample size	240	200

27. A sample of the employees of an industrial organization were asked to indicate a preference for one of three pension plans. Is there reason to believe that their preferences are dependent upon job classification?

	Plan 1	Plan 2	Plan 3
Supervisors	9	13	20
Clerical	39	50	19
Labor	52	57	41

28. Students in several high schools were asked how they feel about going to college. Students from large schools were matched with those from small schools on the basis of intelligence, sex, and socioeconomic level. Four hundred matched pairs resulted. The responses were:

A: I plan to go to college.
B: I would go, but cannot afford it.
C: I do not plan to go.

Using the results given below, test the hypothesis that there is no relationship between the responses of matched students from large and small schools.

Small school	Large school		
	A	B	C
A	60	40	0
B	50	30	20
C	80	70	50

29. Random samples of male students and female students listened to recordings of readings by a male and a female reader and were asked to rate the readings as very effective, moderately effective, or ineffective. The numbers of each sex who rated the readings in the three categories are given below. The same selection was read by both readers. Test the hypothesis that there is no difference in the responses due to sex of the listener. Sum over sex of reader to get totals.

Reader	Male		Female	
Listener	Male	Female	Male	Female
Ineffective	10	10	5	10
Moderately effective	60	15	25	40
Very effective	30	10	15	50

30. Given the data of problem 29, test the hypothesis that the male and female reader are equally effective. Sum over sex of listener.

31. Using the data of problem 29, test the hypothesis that there is no interaction between sex of listener and sex of reader, i.e., there is no tendency for listeners of one sex to rate higher or lower depending on the sex of the reader. Sum ratings where listener and reader are of the same sex, and where they are of opposite sexes.

32. Two temperatures, T_1 and T_2, and two curing times, C_1 and C_2, were applied in combination to equal numbers of glued joints between pieces of wood. The joints were then tested for tensile strength. The following data are the numbers of sample joints whose tensile strengths exceeded and did not exceed a prescribed standard.

a. Does time of curing affect strength?
b. Does temperature affect strength?
c. Is there an interaction between time and temperature, i.e., is the effect of temperature at the second time different from that at the first time? *Hint:* Compare $T_1C_1 + T_2C_2$ with $T_1C_2 + T_2C_1$.

Temperature	T_1		T_2	
Time	C_1	C_2	C_1	C_2
Failed	25	15	20	5
Passed	25	35	30	45

REFERENCES

10.1 GUTTMAN, IRWIN, and SAMUEL S. WILKS. *Introductory Engineering Statistics.* John Wiley & Sons, New York, 1965. Chapter 12.

10.2 HOEL, PAUL G. *Elementary Statistics,* 3rd edition. John Wiley & Sons, New York, 1971. Chapter 11.

10.3 SNEDECOR, GEORGE W., and WILLIAM G. COCHRAN. *Statistical Methods,* 6th edition. Iowa State University Press, Ames, 1967, Chapter 9.

11

Regression and Correlation

11.1 SIMPLE LINEAR REGRESSION

In most of our statistical procedures so far, we have been concerned with a single observation made on each element of the sample, that is, with a sample of values for a single variable X. We now consider the case where two measurements are made on each element of the sample: where the sample consists of pairs of values, one for each of the two variables X and Y. For example, consider the heights and weights of individuals. If we take a sample of individuals, from each obtain his height and weight, and then let the height be represented by X and the weight by Y, we obtain from the ith person the pair of numbers (X_i, Y_i). If there are n persons in the sample we have a sample of size n which consists of the n number pairs

$$(X_1, Y_1), (X_2, Y_2), \ldots, (X_n, Y_n)$$

Our object is to study the relationship between the variables X and Y. One way to study this relationship is by means of regression.

To use a regression analysis we must know or assume the functional form of the relationship between the variables. This is expressed in the form of a mathematical function in which Y, the dependent variable, is set equal to some expression which depends only on X, the independent variable, and on certain constants or parameters. Assuming that there is a functional relationship does not imply that there is a cause-and-effect relationship. In a given situation we may arrive at the desired functional form by either of two methods: (1) from analytical or theoretical considerations, or (2) by studying scatter diagrams like those of Figure 11.1.

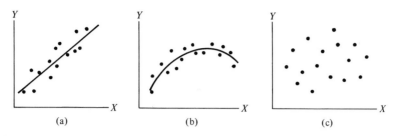

FIGURE 11.1. *Scatter diagrams that suggest* (a) *a linear relationship,* (b) *a curvilinear relationship, and* (c) *no relationship*

A scatter diagram is obtained by plotting the pairs of values of X and Y as points in a plane, where Y is measured along the vertical axis and X along the horizontal axis. After the points have been plotted, observation of the diagram may reveal a pattern to the points that indicates what functional form may be used for the purposes of the analysis. We shall be concerned here with the case in which the points appear to lie along a straight line, or in which theoretical considerations lead us to conclude that the relationship is linear.

Because of sampling variation, the observed values or points will not all lie on the line but will be scattered to some degree about the line. We assume that for each X there is a distribution for Y and that our observed Y-values corresponding to a given X are a random sample from that distribution. The regression curve or line is the curve or line that joins the *means* of the distributions corresponding to all possible values of X. Under these assumptions the relationship we want to estimate is

$$\mu_{Y|X} = A + BX \qquad (11.1)$$

—that is, the mean of Y for a fixed X is equal to $A + BX$, where the constants A and B are the intercept and slope, respectively. The intercept is the value of the mean of Y when X is equal to zero. The slope is the rate of change of $\mu_{Y|X}$ with X, the change in the mean of Y for a unit change in X. Our problem is to use the information in a sample of size n to estimate these constants or parameters.*

A randomly selected Y is represented by

$$Y_i = A + BX_i + e_i \qquad (11.2)$$

where e_i is the random deviation of the observed Y from the mean $A + BX_i$. The population regression equation, equation (11.1), is estimated by the prediction equation

$$\hat{Y} = a + bX \qquad (11.3)$$

---

*In simple linear regression, α and β are usually used to denote the intercept and slope, respectively. Here these symbols have been used for the probabilities of Type I and Type II errors; to avoid confusion, we use A and B for the regression parameters.

where $\hat{Y}$, a, and b are estimators for $\mu_{Y|X}$, A, and B, respectively. To obtain these estimators we use the *method of least squares*. This method will give the best unbiased estimators for A and B if the following assumptions are satisfied:

1. The X-values are known, that is, nonrandom.
2. For each value of X, Y is normally and independently distributed with mean $\mu_{Y|X}$ equal to $A + BX$ and variance $\sigma^2_{Y|X}$, where A, B, and $\sigma^2_{Y|X}$ are unknown parameters.
3. For each X the variance of Y given X is the same; that is, $\sigma^2_{Y|X} = \sigma^2$ for all X.

Although the second assumption includes normality, this is not required by the least squares theory. It is included here because we want to make inferences based on our estimates and for these we shall use normal theory.

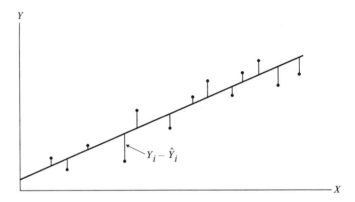

FIGURE 11.2. *Sample points and estimated regression line*

The principle of least squares is illustrated in Figure 11.2. For every observed Y_i there is a corresponding predicted value $\hat{Y}_i$, equal to $a + bX_i$, given by equation (11.3). The deviation of the observed Y from the predicted Y is $Y_i - \hat{Y}_i$, equal to $Y_i - a - bX_i$. The sum of squares of these deviations from the fitted line is

$$\sum (Y_i - \hat{Y}_i)^2 = \sum (Y_i - a - bX_i)^2 \tag{11.4}$$

where the estimators, a and b, are the functions of the sample values that make this sum of squares a minimum. These least squares estimators are:

$$b = \frac{\sum (X_i - \overline{X})(Y_i - \overline{Y})}{\sum (X_i - \overline{X})^2} = \frac{\sum xy}{\sum x^2} \tag{11.5}$$

and

$$a = \overline{Y} - b\overline{X} \tag{11.6}$$

We shall not derive these estimates here; see reference 11.4 for a derivation not requiring calculus. Notice, however, that equation (11.6) implies that the regression line goes through the center of gravity of the points (X_i, Y_i). It can be shown that a and b are unbiased estimates of A and B.

In this chapter we make extensive use of the notation introduced in the rightmost member of equation (11.5). That is, we represent the deviation of an observed value from its mean by the corresponding lowercase letter, thus:

$$x_i = X_i - \bar{X} \quad \text{and} \quad y_i = Y_i - \bar{Y} \tag{11.7}$$

In this notation the sums of squares and crossproducts become:

$$\sum (X_i - \bar{X})^2 = \sum x^2$$
$$\sum (Y_i - \bar{Y})^2 = \sum y^2$$
$$\sum (X_i - \bar{X})(Y_i - \bar{Y}) = \sum xy$$

After we have found numerical values for the estimators a and b given by equations (11.5) and (11.6), we substitute them into the prediction equation $\hat{Y} = a + bX$. There is no other line that could be fitted to the observed points for which the sum of squares of vertical deviations from the line would be smaller.

The machine formulas for the sums of squares and crossproducts are:

$$\sum x^2 = \sum X_i^2 - \frac{(\sum X_i)^2}{n}$$

$$\sum y^2 = \sum Y_i^2 - \frac{(\sum Y_i)^2}{n}$$

$$\sum xy = \sum X_i Y_i - \frac{(\sum X_i)(\sum Y_i)}{n}$$

EXAMPLE 1

The calculations outlined above for obtaining a linear regression equation are illustrated by the following numerical example.

	X	Y	x	y	x^2	xy	y^2
	2	1	-3	-6	9	18	36
	3	3	-2	-4	4	8	16
	4	5	-1	-2	1	2	4
	5	8	0	1	0	0	1
	6	9	1	2	1	2	4
	7	11	2	4	4	8	16
	8	12	3	5	9	15	25
Sums	35	49			28	53	102

$$\bar{X} = 35/7 = 5 \qquad \bar{Y} = 49/7 = 7$$
$$b = 53/28 = 1.89 \qquad a = 7 - 1.89(5) = -2.45$$

The regression equation is:

$$\hat{Y} = -2.45 + 1.89X$$

11.2 PARTITIONING THE SUM OF SQUARES

For a single variable Y, the variation in Y is measured by the sum of squares, all of which can be considered as being due to random or unexplained variation; hence, the estimated variance of Y is based on the total sum of squares. In the regression situation, however, some of the observed variation among the sample Y's is associated with the relationship between Y and X. Figure 11.3 shows one observed point (X_i, Y_i) and the point on

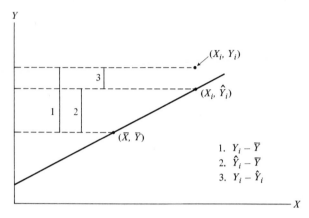

FIGURE 11.3. *Subdivision of* $Y_i - \bar{Y}$

the fitted line whose coordinates are the means $(\bar{X}, \bar{Y})$. We see that the deviation $Y_i - \bar{Y}$ from the mean is the sum of the deviation of Y_i from the corresponding predicted value $\hat{Y}_i$ and the deviation of $\hat{Y}_i$ from $\bar{Y}$; that is,

$$(Y_i - \bar{Y}) = (Y_i - \hat{Y}_i) + (\hat{Y}_i - \bar{Y}) \tag{11.8}$$

The second element, the deviation of $\hat{Y}_i$ from $\bar{Y}$, is associated with the relationship between Y and X, so that this much of the deviation of Y_i from the mean may be said to be accounted for by, or due to, the regression of Y on X. If we square and add both sides of equation (11.8) we find that, since

$$\sum (Y_i - \hat{Y}_i)(\hat{Y}_i - \bar{Y}) = 0$$

we have

$$\sum (Y_i - \bar{Y})^2 = \sum (Y_i - \hat{Y}_i)^2 + \sum (\hat{Y}_i - \bar{Y})^2 \tag{11.9}$$

We have partitioned the total sum of squares for Y into two parts; one part, $\sum (\hat{Y}_i - \bar{Y})^2$, is associated with the regression; the remainder, $\sum (Y_i - \hat{Y}_i)^2$, with the random or unexplained variation in the data. These quantities may be found more simply by using the following formulas:

$$\sum (\hat{Y}_i - \bar{Y})^2 = b \sum xy$$
$$\sum (Y_i - \hat{Y}_i)^2 = \sum y^2 - b \sum xy \tag{11.10}$$

The partitioning we have discussed is conveniently summarized in Table 11.1. We note that the sum of squares for regression has 1 degree of freedom, the sum of squares of deviations has $n - 2$ degrees of freedom, and the total sum of squares has, as usual, $n - 1$ degrees of freedom. The degrees of freedom, as well as the sum of squares, are partitioned.

TABLE 11.1. Partitioned Sum of Squares in Regression

Source of variation	Degrees of freedom	Sum of squares
Due to regression	1	$b \sum xy$
Deviations from regression	$n - 2$	$\sum y^2 - b \sum xy$
Totals	$n - 1$	$\sum y^2$

For the numerical example of Section 11.1, the total variation of the Y's about their mean $\overline{Y}$ is measured by the total sum of squares with degrees of freedom equal to $n - 1$, or 6:

$$\sum y^2 = 102.00$$

The portion of this variation that is accounted for by the linear relation between the variables is the sum of squares with 1 degree of freedom associated with, or due to, regression:

$$b \sum xy = (1.89)(53) = 100.17$$

The remaining unexplained, or random, variation is the variation of the observed Y's about the estimated line. It is measured by the sum of squares of deviations about the regression line. This sum of squares has $n - 2$, or 5, degrees of freedom and is found by subtraction,

$$\sum y^2 - b \sum xy = 102.00 - 100.17 = 1.83$$

The summary table is as follows:

Source	df	Sum of squares
Due to regression	1	100.17
Deviations from regression	5	1.83
Totals	6	102.00

11.3 VARIANCE ESTIMATES

In Section 11.1 we looked at the estimators for the parameters A and B obtained by the method of least squares, but before we can use these estimators to make further inferences about the linear relationship between

Y and X we must obtain estimators for the variance σ^2, and for the variances of the sampling distributions of a and b.

The variance of Y given X, assumed to be the same for all X, is estimated unbiasedly by the mean squared deviation about the regression line, that is, by

$$s_{Y.X}^2 = \frac{1}{n-2} \sum (Y_i - \hat{Y}_i)^2$$

or

$$s_{Y.X}^2 = \frac{1}{n-2} \left[\sum y^2 - b \sum xy \right] \tag{11.11}$$

where the subscripts $Y.X$ indicate that this is the estimator for the variance of Y when we have the regression of Y on X.

The estimated variance of the sample regression coefficient b is the estimate of variance, $s_{Y.X}^2$, divided by the sum of squares for X,

$$s_b^2 = \frac{s_{Y.X}^2}{\sum x^2} \tag{11.12}$$

The estimated variance of the estimator a for the intercept is more complicated:

$$s_a^2 = s_{Y.X}^2 \left(\frac{1}{n} + \frac{\bar{X}^2}{\sum x^2} \right) \tag{11.13}$$

For the numerical example of Section 11.1 we had $n = 7$, $\bar{X} = 5$, $\sum x^2 = 28$, $\sum y^2 = 102$, $\sum xy = 53$, $b = 1.89$, and $a = -2.45$; therefore,

$$s_{Y.X}^2 = \frac{1}{n-2} \left[\sum y^2 - b \sum xy \right] = \tfrac{1}{5}[102 - (1.89)(53)] = \frac{1.83}{5} = .366$$

$$s_b^2 = \frac{s_{Y.X}^2}{\sum x^2} = \frac{.366}{28} = .013$$

$$s_a^2 = s_{Y.X}^2 \left[\frac{1}{n} + \frac{\bar{X}^2}{\sum x^2} \right] = .366[\tfrac{1}{7} + \tfrac{25}{28}] = .379$$

11.4   INFERENCES ABOUT *A* AND *B*

Thus far we have not had to make any assumptions about the form of the distribution of Y given X since the method of least squares will yield the best linear unbiased estimators for A and B if the X's are known values and the Y's are independently distributed with common variance. Now, however, we want to make inferences about A and B on the basis of the estimators a and b; therefore, we must make some distributional assumption.

If we assume that the Y's are normally distributed, it follows that our estimators are normally distributed (they are linear functions of the

Y's, and a linear function of normal variables is normally distributed; recall that the X_i are nonrandom) and that we may base our confidence intervals and tests of hypotheses on the t-distribution. As usual, it can be shown that, even if the distribution of the Y's is not normal, the probabilities based on the t-distribution will be very good approximations if the sample is sufficiently large. Under the normality assumptions, the ratios

$$\frac{b - B}{s_b} \quad \text{and} \quad \frac{a - A}{s_a}$$

have t-distributions, both with $n - 2$ degrees of freedom because the estimates s_b and s_a are based on the sum of squares of deviations from regression that has $n - 2$ degrees of freedom.

From the relationship

$$t = \frac{b - B}{s_b} \qquad (11.14)$$

it is apparent that confidence intervals for B will have the form common to all those we have calculated when the estimator is normally distributed, that is,

$$L = b - t_{\alpha/2,(n-2)}s_b$$
$$R = b + t_{\alpha/2,(n-2)}s_b \qquad (11.15)$$

For the worked example of Section 11.1, the 95% confidence interval for B is

$$L = 1.89 - (2.571)(.114) = 1.60$$

$$R = 1.89 + (2.571)(.114) = 2.18$$

We are 95% confident that the true slope B is contained within the interval 1.60 to 2.18.

Similarly, since

$$t = \frac{a - A}{s_a} \qquad (11.16)$$

the confidence limits for the true intercept A are given by

$$L = a - t_{\alpha/2,(n-2)}s_a$$
$$R = a + t_{\alpha/2,(n-2)}s_a \qquad (11.17)$$

For our example the 99% limits for A are

$$L = -2.45 - (4.032)(.615) = -4.93$$

$$R = -2.45 + (4.032)(.615) = .03$$

We are 99% confident that the intercept, the mean of Y given that X equals zero, is covered by the interval from -4.93 to $.03$.

Equations (11.14) and (11.16) also serve as bases for tests of hypotheses concerning the parameters A and B. Under the null hypothesis that the slope is equal to a given value B_0, that is, $H_0: B = B_0$, the quantity

$$t = \frac{b - B_0}{s_b} \qquad \textbf{(11.18)}$$

has a t-distribution with $n - 2$ degrees of freedom. A common hypothesis is that B equals 0. We want to know whether or not there is a linear association between the variables, for if there is not there is nothing to be gained by using the X's, as they would contribute nothing to the analysis of the Y's. Under this hypothesis, $H_0: B = 0$, we have

$$t = \frac{b}{s_b} \qquad \textbf{(11.19)}$$

We must remember, however, that this quantity is distributed as t only when B is 0. In this situation the alternative hypothesis is usually that B is not equal to zero. There are, of course, situations in which one is interested only in knowing whether or not there is a positive slope (or a negative slope). In these circumstances we would use single-sided alternatives.

To test the hypothesis $H_0: B = 0$ for the numerical example, we calculate the value of t, as follows:

$$t = \frac{b}{s_b} = \frac{1.89}{.114} = 16.58$$

In the t-table we find that $t_{.005(5)}$ equals 4.032; therefore, since the calculated t is greater than the tabular value, we reject the hypothesis that B is 0 at the 1% level of significance. We conclude there is an underlying linear relationship.

The test of the hypothesis that the intercept A is equal to a specified value A_0 is also an ordinary t-test. Under $H_0: A = A_0$, the function

$$t = \frac{a - A_0}{s_a} \qquad \textbf{(11.20)}$$

also has a t-distribution with $n - 2$ degrees of freedom. Here, again, the hypothesis that A is equal to zero is of special interest, for if this is so the population regression line passes through the origin; that is, the mean of Y given that X equals zero is equal to zero. For the example, if we test $H_0: A = 0$, we get

$$t = \frac{a}{s_a} = \frac{-2.45}{.615} = -3.98$$

At the 5% level of significance we would reject the hypothesis and conclude that A is not zero, since $t_{.025(5)}$ is 2.571.

11.5   THE COEFFICIENT OF DETERMINATION

An informative measure is obtained if we look at the fraction of the total variation in Y that is accounted for by the association between Y and X. If we take the ratio of the sum of squares associated with the regression to the total sum of squares for Y, we have

$$r^2 = \frac{\sum (\hat{Y}_i - \overline{Y})^2}{\sum (Y_i - \overline{Y})^2} = \frac{b \sum xy}{\sum y^2} \tag{11.21}$$

This is called the *coefficient of determination*.

It is obvious that r^2 must always be between zero and one, inclusive, for the sum of squares in the numerator can never be less than zero nor greater than the total sum of squares. If all the points are close to the line, the value of r^2 will be close to 1; but as the scatter of the points becomes greater, r^2 will become smaller. For this reason it is a useful measure of the strength of the relationship.

Since r^2 is the fraction of the total variation in Y that is accounted for by the regression, $1 - r^2$ must be the fraction of the variation in Y that is unaccounted for: the fraction associated with the errors of prediction. The latter quantity is sometimes called the *coefficient of alienation*.

The sums of squares may be expressed in terms of r^2 as shown in the following table.

Source	df	Sum of squares
Due to regression	1	$r^2 \sum y^2$
Deviations from regression	$n - 2$	$(1 - r^2) \sum y^2$
Totals	$n - 1$	$\sum y^2$

11.6   SOME USES OF REGRESSION

In addition to the use of a regression analysis to estimate the parameters of the functional relationship between two variables and to test hypotheses concerning these parameters, there are several other applications that are of great importance in practical problems. We briefly consider three of them.

Having fitted a regression and having obtained the prediction equation, we are in a position where, given a value for X, we can predict with some degree of confidence the corresponding mean of Y. We can also predict what a single observed value of Y would be for a given X, but with less confidence. The point estimate for either the mean or a single value is

$$\hat{Y}_0 = a + bX_0 \tag{11.22}$$

where $\hat{Y}_0$ is the predicted value corresponding to the given value X_0.

227

We can find a confidence interval for $\mu_{Y|X_0}$, which by (11.1) is $A + BX_0$, that is, the mean of Y given X_0, by the formula

$$L = \hat{Y}_0 - t_{\alpha/2,(n-2)} s_{\hat{Y}_0}$$
$$R = \hat{Y}_0 + t_{\alpha/2,(n-2)} s_{\hat{Y}_0}$$

(11.23)

The estimated standard deviation of $\hat{Y}_0$ is

$$s_{\hat{Y}_0} = s_{Y.X} \sqrt{\frac{1}{n} + \frac{(X_0 - \bar{X})^2}{\sum x^2}}$$

(11.24)

From the form of $s_{\hat{Y}_0}$ we see that the estimated standard deviation for a predicted mean value depends upon X_0. The farther X_0 gets from the mean of X, the greater will be the standard deviation. As a result, the confidence interval will become wider as the given X is farther displaced from the mean. If we were to calculate a confidence interval for $\mu_{Y|X}$ for every X, the end-points of these intervals would lie on the two branches of a hyperbola, as shown in Figure 11.4. This indicates that we have more confidence near the center than at the extremes of the range of our X-values. It also reflects the fact that we can interpolate—make predictions for values within the range of the X used to estimate the relationship—with more confidence and greater safety than if we try to extrapolate and make predictions for values outside the range of X in our sample. In addition, it may well be that within the range used for estimating the regression equation, the true relationship can be approximated reasonably well by a straight line, but that outside that region the true relationship breaks away sharply from the regression equation.

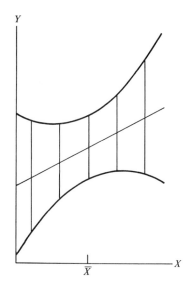

FIGURE 11.4.   *Confidence intervals for the mean of Y given X*

A prediction interval for a *single* value of Y, given that X equals X_0, is found in the same way as a confidence interval for the corresponding mean, but since the variance must include the variance of a single observed Y, the standard deviation is larger:

$$s_{Y_0} = s_{Y.X} \sqrt{1 + \frac{1}{n} + \frac{(X_0 - \overline{X})^2}{\sum x^2}} \tag{11.25}$$

The prediction interval is

$$\hat{Y}_0 \mp t_{\alpha/2, (n-2)} s_{Y_0} \tag{11.26}$$

Here again, because of the dependence on $X_0 - \overline{X}$, the interval will be wider the farther X_0 departs from $\overline{X}$.

Another common use of regression is for statistical control of a variable that cannot be controlled otherwise, or which we do not care to control for practical reasons. Instead, we merely record values of X at the same time as we observe Y and then adjust all the Y's to a common X. Suppose we want to record the time required by electric heating elements to raise the temperature of a measured amount of water a specified number of degrees, and suppose that the line voltage is variable. Certainly, if the voltage is low it will take longer to heat the water than if the voltage is high. We want to eliminate the effect of the varying voltage. We find the cost of voltage-regulating equipment excessive, but we can afford a voltmeter. We now take our readings on the time but also record the voltage during the period of observation. If we let the time be Y and the voltage be X, we fit a regression of Y on X. After this has been done we adjust each Y to the mean of X according to the formula

$$\text{adj } Y_i = Y_i - b(X_i - \overline{X}) \tag{11.27}$$

Figure 11.5 shows two Y's and their adjusted values. The effect of the adjustment given by equation (11.27) is to translate the point (X_i, Y_i) parallel to the regression line to a new origin at $\overline{X}$. The adjusted Y's have a common X and may be compared since the effects of differences among the X's have been removed. Adjustments of this type are useful in a wide variety of applications.

Sometimes, after fitting a regression of Y on X and then observing values of Y, we want to estimate the value of X that produced the observed Y. This is a discrimination problem, or a problem of classification. In biological assays we fit a curve for response against dose of a drug. After the curve has been obtained we observe a response and want to estimate the dose that produced it. This is an important application of regression techniques, but the formulas are too complex to be given here. The interested reader may consult reference 11.5.

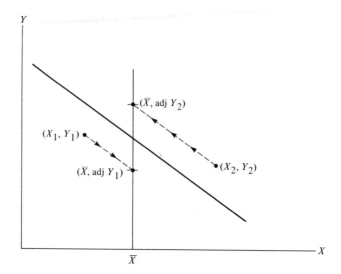

FIGURE 11.5. *Two points before and after adjustment*

11.7 CORRELATION

In the preceding sections of this chapter we have been concerned with the use of regression techniques to estimate the parameters of an assumed linear relation between X and the mean of Y given X. We assumed that the values of X were known and allowed them to be selected and controlled by the experimenter; that is, we did not assume that X was a random variable.

We now consider methods that are appropriate when it is assumed that X and Y are both random variables and have a joint distribution. We want to make inferences about the degree of linear relationship between them without estimating the regression line.

One of the parameters of the joint distribution of X and Y is the *product moment correlation coefficient* (or simply the *correlation coefficient*) ρ. The correlation coefficient ρ is a measure of the *linear* covariation of the variables; that is, it measures the degree of *linear* association between them. It is a dimensionless quantity that may take any value between -1 and 1, inclusive. If ρ is either -1 or 1 the variables have a perfect linear relationship in that all of the points in a sample lie exactly on a line. If ρ is near -1 or 1 there is a high degree of linear association.

A *positive correlation* means that as one variable increases, the other increases. A *negative correlation* means that as one variable increases, the other decreases. Heights and weights of humans are positively correlated, but the age of a car and its trade-in value are negatively correlated. If ρ is equal to zero, we say the variables are *uncorrelated* and that there is no linear association between them. Bear in mind that ρ measures only linear relationship. The variables may be perfectly correlated in a curvilinear relationship and ρ could still equal zero.

In a correlation analysis our problem is to make inferences about ρ. Given a sample of size n, $(X_1, Y_1), (X_2, Y_2), \ldots, (X_n, Y_n)$, we use the *sample correlation coefficient*, r, as an estimator for ρ:

$$r = \frac{\sum xy}{\sqrt{\sum x^2 \sum y^2}} \tag{11.28}$$

Regression techniques and correlation methods are closely related, for r is the square root of the coefficient of determination. It is primarily in interpretation that the differences lie. In correlation, r is an estimator for the population correlation coefficient ρ. In regression, if X is not a random variable there is no correlation, and r^2 is simply a measure of closeness of fit.

It is worthy of note that the estimated correlation coefficient is unaffected by linear transformations. If we let U be $AY + B$ and let V be $CX + D$, the correlation coefficient r_{UV} for U and V is equal to that for X and Y, r_{XY}. This can be shown by substituting for U and V in terms of X and Y in the equation

$$r_{UV} = \frac{\sum (U_i - \bar{U})(V_i - \bar{V})}{\sqrt{\sum (U_i - \bar{U})^2 \sum (V_i - \bar{V})^2}}$$

as follows:

$$r_{UV} = \frac{\sum (AY_i + B - A\bar{Y} - B)(CX_i + D - C\bar{X} - D)}{\sqrt{\sum (AY_i + B - A\bar{Y} - B)^2 \sum (CX_i + D - C\bar{X} - D)^2}}$$

$$= \frac{AC \sum (Y_i - \bar{Y})(X_i - \bar{X})}{\sqrt{A^2 C^2 \sum (Y_i - \bar{Y})^2 \sum (X_i - \bar{X})^2}}$$

$$= \frac{AC \sum xy}{|AC|\sqrt{\sum x^2 \sum y^2}} = \pm r_{XY}$$

The sign before r_{XY} depends upon the signs of A and C.

When we want to make inferences about the population correlation coefficient ρ, we usually assume that the variables X and Y have a joint normal distribution; but even with the assumption of normality, if ρ is not equal to zero the sampling distribution of r is complicated and not at all easy to use. For this reason, tables and graphs have been made for finding confidence intervals for ρ. See reference 11.1 or 11.6.

We may also make use of a normal approximation. R. A. Fisher has shown that, if X and Y are jointly normally distributed, the quantity

$$z = \tfrac{1}{2} \log_e \frac{1 + r}{1 - r} \tag{11.29}$$

is approximately normally distributed with mean

$$\mu_z = \tfrac{1}{2} \log_e \frac{1 + \rho}{1 - \rho} \tag{11.30}$$

and variance

$$\sigma_z^2 = \frac{1}{n - 3} \tag{11.31}$$

This approximation holds fairly well for sample sizes greater than 50. Closer approximations, some of which hold reasonably well for values of n as low as 11, may be found in reference 11.3.

To use this approximation to find a confidence interval for ρ we transform the sample correlation coefficient r to the corresponding z-value by equation (11.29), or by means of Table VIII of the Appendix, which is much easier. We then find the confidence interval for μ_z:

$$L = z - t_{\alpha/2(\infty)} \frac{1}{\sqrt{n - 3}}$$
$$R = z + t_{\alpha/2(\infty)} \frac{1}{\sqrt{n - 3}} \tag{11.32}$$

These limits are then transformed via Table VIII to limits for ρ.

For example, suppose that in a sample of size 52 we find $r = .61$. From Table VIII the corresponding z is equal to .71, and the 95% confidence limits for μ_z are

$$L = .71 - 1.96 \left(\frac{1}{\sqrt{49}} \right) = .43$$

and

$$R = .71 + 1.96 \left(\frac{1}{\sqrt{49}} \right) = .99$$

Referring again to the table, we find that the corresponding limits for ρ are .4053 and .7574, respectively. We may say that these are approximate 95% confidence limits for the unknown population correlation coefficient.

The z-transformation may also be used to test the hypothesis that ρ is equal to a specified value ρ_0, for under this hypothesis

$$t = \frac{z - \mu_{z0}}{\sigma_z} \tag{11.33}$$

has approximately a standard normal distribution (the t-distribution with infinite degrees of freedom).

Suppose we want to test the hypothesis $H_0: \rho = .6$ against the alternative hypothesis $H_a: \rho \neq .6$, and that $n = 103$, $r = .5$. Using the conversion table we find

$$z = \tfrac{1}{2} \log_e \frac{1 + .5}{1 - .5} = .55$$

$$\mu_{z0} = \tfrac{1}{2} \log_e \frac{1 + .6}{1 - .6} = .69$$

The calculated value of the test statistic is

$$t = \frac{.55 - .69}{\frac{1}{10}} = -1.4$$

From the t-table, $t_{.025(\infty)}$ is found to be 1.96; therefore, we accept the hypothesis $H_0: \rho = .6$. Our level of significance is approximately 5%.

If we want to test the hypothesis that the variables are not linearly related, that is, that ρ is 0, we may use an ordinary t-test, for when ρ is 0,

$$t = r \sqrt{\frac{n - 2}{1 - r^2}} \tag{11.34}$$

has the t-distribution with $n - 2$ degrees of freedom. To test $H_0: \rho = 0$ we merely evaluate t by equation (11.34) and compare it with the tabular t-value for the given probability of Type I error.

11.8   CORRELATION AND CAUSE

It has been said, and with justification, that among all of the measures treated in this book, the correlation coefficient is the most subject to misinterpretation. One of the main reasons for this is the frequently false assumption that because two variables are related, a change in one causes a change in the other. If one has a point to prove, it is extremely easy to succumb to this fallacy and to use a perfectly respectable correlation coefficient to "prove" a cause-and-effect relationship that may not exist.

It has been shown that there is a negative correlation between smoking and grades. If one objects to smoking he seizes upon this fact as objective evidence that smoking is harmful, that smoking causes low grades. This may be true, but one could also argue that low grades result in increased nervous tension, which, in turn, causes the individual to smoke more. It could also be true that smoking and low grades are not directly related to each other, but are correlated because both are related to some other factor, such as involvement in extracurricular or social activities.

This last suggestion illustrates another danger in interpretation of the results of a correlation analysis. Frequently, two variables may appear to be highly correlated when, in fact, they are not directly associated with each other but are both highly correlated with a third variable.

Because of sampling variation we can get a significant correlation when the variables are not related, but we are aware of this possibility and control the probability of this kind of error by selecting our level of significance. It is the unwarranted cause-and-effect assumption and the spurious correlation we must beware of.

PROBLEMS

1. Given the following pairs of values,
   a. Find the regression equation, $\hat{Y} = a + bX$.
   b. Find the predicted value of Y given $X = 5$.

X	2	4	6	8	10
Y	3	1	7	5	9

2. Given the following pairs of values,
   a. Find the equation for the regression of Y on X.
   b. Find the predicted value of Y given $X = 6$.

X	1	5	9	13	17
Y	7	6	9	8	10

3. Given the following pairs of values,
   a. Find the equation for the regression of Y on X.
   b. Find the predicted value of Y given $X = 8$.

X	0	1	2	3	4	5	6
Y	1	2	3	5	8	11	12

4. Given the following pairs of values,
   a. Find the regression equation $\hat{Y} = a + bX$.
   b. Find the predicted value of Y given $X = -3$.

X	-3	-2	-1	0	1	2	3
Y	36	33	24	15	9	6	3

5. Find the equation for the regression of Y on X.

X	12	13	14	15	16	17	18
Y	-8	-6	-4	0	6	12	14

6. Find the equation for the regression of Y on X.

X	-10	-6	-2	2	6	10	14	16	20	23
Y	-8	-5	-4	-3	0	4	7	8	11	10

7. In a regression problem: $n = 30$, $\sum X_i = 15$, $\sum Y_i = 30$, $\sum x_i y_i = -30$, $\sum x_i^2 = 10$, and $\sum y_i^2 = 160$.
   a. Find the regression line, $\hat{Y} = a + bX$.
   b. Estimate the variance, $\sigma_{Y \cdot X}^2$.
   c. Test $H_0: B = 0$ against $H_a: B \neq 0$, $\alpha = .05$.

8. In a regression analysis: $n = 18$, $\bar{X} = 6$, $\bar{Y} = 20$, $\sum x_i^2 = 100$, $\sum y_i^2 = 400$, and $\sum x_i y_i = -120$.
   a. Find the equation for the regression of Y on X.
   b. Find the estimated variance.
   c. Test the hypothesis $B = 0$ at the 1% level of significance.
   d. Find and interpret the coefficient of determination, r^2.

9. In a regression analysis: $n = 25$, $\sum X_i = 75$, $\sum Y_i = 50$, $\sum X_i^2 = 625$, $\sum X_i Y_i = 30$, and $\sum Y_i^2 = 228$.
   a. Find the regression equation.
   b. Find $s_{Y \cdot X}^2$, s_a^2, and s_b^2.
   c. Test that $B = 0$. Let $\alpha = .01$.
   d. Find a 95% confidence interval for A.

10. In a regression analysis: $n = 38$, $\bar{Y} = 20$, $\bar{X} = 7$, $\sum y_i^2 = 900$, $\sum x_i^2 = 60$, and $\sum x_i y_i = 180$.
    a. Find the regression equation.
    b. Test the hypothesis that $A = 0$. Let $\alpha = .02$.
    c. Find a 90% confidence interval for B.
    d. What fraction of the variation in Y is accounted for by the relationship?

11. In a regression problem $r = .6$ and $\sum y_i^2 = 400$. What is the sum of squares associated with the regression? With deviations from regression? Given that $n = 27$, what is the estimated variance?

12. Complete the following table and find $s_{Y \cdot X}^2$ and r^2.

Source	df	Sum of squares
Due to regression		
Deviations from regression		600
Totals	25	800

13. In a regression problem: $n = 17$, $\sum x_i^2 = 200$, $b = 2.35$, and $s^2 = 50$. Test the hypothesis that $B = 1$. Let $\alpha = .01$.

14. In a regression problem, $n = 18$, $\sum x_i^2 = 144$, $b = 3.1$, and the estimated variance is 36. Can we conclude that $B > 2$? Let $\alpha = .025$. Find a 95% confidence interval for B.

15. Given that $a = -2$, $n = 16$, $\bar{X} = 6$, $s_{Y \cdot X}^2 = 12.8$, and $\sum x_i^2 = 144$, find a 95% confidence interval for A.

235

16. Given that $a = 4$, $n = 10$, $\bar{X} = 2$, $s_{Y.X}^2 = 32.5$, and $\sum x_i^2 = 90$, test the hypothesis that $A = 10$. Let $\alpha = .05$.

17. Given that $n = 11$, $\bar{Y} = 20$, $\bar{X} = 4$, $\sum x_i^2 = 64$, $\sum x_i y_i = 256$, and $\sum y_i^2 = 1600$,
   a. Find the regression equation.
   b. Find the predicted value for Y given that $X = 6$.
   c. Find a 95% confidence interval for the mean of Y given that $X = 6$.
   d. Find a 95% prediction interval for a single value of Y given $X = 6$.

18. Given that $n = 41$, $\bar{Y} = 10$, $\bar{X} = 12$, $\sum x_i^2 = 400$, $\sum x_i y_i = 100$, and $\sum y_i^2 = 64$,
   a. Find the predicted value of Y given $X = 8$.
   b. Find a 99% confidence interval for the mean of Y given $X = 8$.
   c. Find a 99% prediction interval for a single observation on Y given $X = 8$.

19. A sample of thirty-two graduates with B.S. degrees in statistics reported their starting salaries in their first professional positions. The estimated average annual starting salary by year is given by

$$\hat{Y} = 7130 + 195(X - 1960)$$

   a. How do you interpret the various components of this equation?
   b. What is the estimated annual starting salary for 1978?

20. In the equation $\hat{Y} = a + bX$, where X is pounds and Y is dollars, what units are associated with a? With b? With r^2?

21. The following are the average incomes per acre, Y, produced by a commercial system for taking game animals over a ten-year period.
   a. Estimate the relationship between income per acre and time in years.
   b. Find a 99% confidence interval for B.
   c. What fraction of the variation in income is accounted for by the relationship?

Year	1956	1957	1958	1959	1960	1961	1962	1963	1964	1965
Income per acre	.51	.59	.64	.74	.78	.89	1.01	1.07	1.10	1.18

22. Various known amounts, X, of a compound were chromatographed and the peak area, Y, determined, giving the following results. The peak area has been multiplied by a suitable scale factor.
   a. Estimate the relationship between peak area and volume injected.
   b. Find a 95% confidence interval for the slope of the line.
   c. Test the hypothesis that the line passes through the origin.
   d. To estimate the slope of a line through the origin we use

$$b = \frac{\sum XY}{\sum X^2}$$

   i.e., the uncorrected sums of squares and crossproducts. Find the regression equation $\hat{Y} = bX$ which assumes $A = 0$.

Peak area	Amount injected (cc)	Peak area	Amount injected (cc)
13	.1	62	.4
25	.2	105	.7
27	.2	88	.6
46	.3	63	.4
18	.1	77	.5
31	.2	109	.7
46	.3	117	.8
57	.4	35	.2
75	.5	98	.6
87	.6	121	.8

23. In an experiment to determine the effect of the length of heat treatment time on the resistivity of a type of wire, five samples of wire were treated at each of four times. The observations are resistance per unit volume of the wire. Note that there are twenty observations, each value of X occurring with five different Y's.

X = Time (hours)	2	4	6	8
	21.3	23.2	25.5	25.9
	21.7	23.4	23.6	25.2
Y = Resistance	21.4	23.3	24.7	27.6
	22.1	23.7	26.0	27.1
	20.7	23.0	24.3	26.3

a. Find the regression equation.
b. Test the hypothesis that $B = 1.0$.
c. What fraction of the variation in Y is accounted for by time?
d. Estimate the mean resistance given that $X = 5$.
e. Find a 95% confidence interval for the mean resistance given $X = 5$.

24. The following data are the ultimate loads resulting from tests of joints made with different sizes of common nails.

Nail size	30d	50d	60d
	11.03	11.97	13.69
	10.64	13.63	14.82
Ultimate load	10.48	13.56	15.23
	10.02	15.20	15.45
	10.31	14.84	16.28

a. Find the equation for the regression of ultimate load on nail size.
b. Find a 98% confidence interval for the slope of the line.
c. Is b significantly different from zero?
d. Find a 95% confidence interval for the average ultimate load of joints of this type made with 30d nails.

25. The following data are observations on the horsepower of an engine at 1800 rpm as a function of the viscosity of the oil.

hp	Viscosity	hp	Viscosity
16.8	45	18.1	54
18.1	59	19.2	63
18.5	66	16.9	48
17.0	47	18.6	55
18.8	61	21.0	67
19.7	68	16.4	44
17.5	49	17.7	56
19.0	57	18.2	62
20.2	67	16.7	50
16.3	43	20.8	70

a. Plot the points on graph paper. Let X be viscosity and Y be horsepower.
b. Find and plot the point $(\bar{X}, \bar{Y})$.
c. Find a and b and, hence, the regression equation $\hat{Y} = a + bX$. Draw this line on the graph.
d. Find the deviation of each Y from the corresponding $\hat{Y}$. Square and sum these deviations.
e. Find the sum of squares for deviations from regression by the formula

$$\sum (Y_i - \hat{Y}_i)^2 = \sum y_i^2 - b \sum x_i y_i$$

How do you account for the difference between this figure and that obtained in part **d**?
f. Construct a summary table showing the partitioning of the sum of squares and degrees of freedom.
g. Find the estimated variance $s_{Y\cdot X}^2$ and the variance and standard deviation of b.
h. Find the 95% confidence interval for B.
i. Test the hypothesis that $B = 0$.
j. What is the best estimate for the mean horsepower if the viscosity of an oil is 50? What is the standard deviation of this estimate?
k. Find a 99% confidence interval for the mean horsepower, given the viscosity is 60.

26. The following are the heights of dominant trees, age in years, and measures of available water for sixteen plantings of a commercially important tree.
a. Find the equation for the regression of height on age.
b. Find $s_{Y\cdot X}^2$, s_b^2, and s_a^2.
c. Find a 90% confidence interval for the growth rate.
d. Find the equation for the regression of height on available water.
e. Is the regression of height on available water significant, i.e., is B significantly different from zero?
f. Which variable, age or available water, is the better predictor of height? (*Hint:* Compare the coefficients of determination.)

Height (ft)	Age	Available water	Height (ft)	Age	Available water
33.0	13	.90	20.0	9	.98
34.1	12	.92	23.1	10	1.90
21.0	9	.89	38.1	17	.88
29.5	13	.59	46.6	17	.77
35.4	12	1.24	21.1	8	.78
25.3	10	.57	38.9	15	.94
21.4	8	.77	38.7	14	.70
47.7	16	.91	40.0	15	.99

27. To see if a linear relationship exists between the size of boulders in a stream and the distance from a source, samples of boulders were measured every half-mile downstream beginning at one mile.
   a. Fit the regression of size on distance.
   b. Find a 98% confidence interval for B.
   c. Find a 95% confidence interval for the mean size at a distance of two miles.
   d. Find and interpret the coefficient of determination.

Distance downstream (miles)	Average size (inches)
1.0	41.3
1.5	34.0
2.0	32.5
2.5	35.2
3.0	28.8
3.5	25.6
4.0	30.1
4.5	25.7
5.0	22.6
5.5	20.3
6.0	18.8
6.5	17.1

28. The following table shows the total yearly marketing bill, and farm value for domestic farm food products bought by civilians, for the years 1955–1965, in the United States.
   a. Find the equation for the regression of total marketing bill on year.
   b. Find the equation for the regression of farm value on year.
   c. Find 95% prediction intervals for the total marketing bill, and the farm value for 1970.

Year	Total marketing bill (billion dollars)	Farm value (billion dollars)
1955	32.0	18.3
1956	33.7	18.7
1957	35.2	19.5
1958	36.8	20.8
1959	39.2	20.0
1960	41.0	20.9
1961	41.9	21.0
1962	43.2	21.7
1963	45.3	21.6
1964	47.3	22.5
1965	48.2	24.5

Source: U.S. Department of Agriculture, Economic Research Service.

29. Given the following sets of quantities, find the sample correlation coefficient. Test the hypothesis that $\rho = 0$. Let $\alpha = .05$.
   a. $n = 11, \sum y^2 = 400, \sum xy = 400, \sum x^2 = 625$.
   b. $n = 18, \sum y^2 = 100, \sum xy = 36, \sum x^2 = 36$.

30. Given the following information, find the sample correlation coefficient. Test the hypothesis that $\rho = 0$. Let $\alpha = .01$.
   a. $n = 29, \sum y^2 = 64, \sum xy = 40, \sum x^2 = 100$.
   b. $n = 18, \sum y^2 = 25, \sum xy = 54, \sum x^2 = 144$.

31. Find the sample correlation coefficient and test $H_0: \rho = 0$ for the data of
   a. Problem 8.   b. Problem 17.

32. Find the sample correlation coefficient and test $H_0: \rho = 0$ for the data of
   a. Problem 9.   b. Problem 18.

33. Determinations were made of the amount (ppm) of a soluble compound present at two different depths in a number of soils.
   a. Estimate the correlation between the amounts present at the two depths.
   b. Is there a significant correlation?

12 Inches	20 Inches	12 Inches	20 Inches
24	20	66	84
84	103	31	30
13	16	43	62
13	20	19	26
48	86	7	21
61	36	50	73
112	53	72	83

34. Using the data of problem 28, estimate the correlation between total marketing bill and farm value of domestic farm food products. Is this correlation coefficient significantly different from zero?

35. Find a 95% confidence interval for ρ when:
   a. $n = 28, r = .50.$ **b.** $n = 67, r = -.75.$
   c. $n = 103, r = .84.$

36. Find 99% confidence intervals for ρ when:
   a. $n = 128, r = .14.$ **b.** $n = 19, r = -.30.$
   c. $n = 75, r = .92.$

37. Given that $n = 128$ and $r = .64$, test the hypothesis that $\rho = .9$. Let $\alpha = .01$.

38. Given that $n = 60$ and $r = .42$, test the hypothesis that $\rho \geq .6$. Let $\alpha = .05$.

39. Using the data of problem 33, test the hypothesis that $\rho = .5$ at the 1% level of significance.

40. The following is a twelve-year record for three variables.
   a. Find the correlation coefficient for beer production and expenditures for services. Is this correlation significant?
   b. Find the estimated correlation between beer production and personal income. Is this significant?
   c. Find the estimated correlation between personal income and expenditures for services. Test $H_0: \rho = 0$.
   d. Find 95% confidence intervals for all three correlation coefficients.

Per capita expenditure for services	Per capita personal income	Beer produced per person (gallons)
$365	$ 792	1.10
388	825	1.09
409	868	1.14
436	910	1.15
450	975	1.18
468	1013	1.21
482	1048	1.20
501	1062	1.24
525	1118	1.25
556	1165	1.28
589	1221	1.32
615	1273	1.30

REFERENCES

11.1 DAVID, F. N. *Tables of the Correlation Coefficient.* Cambridge University Press, Cambridge, 1954.

11.2 HUFF, DARRELL. *How to Lie with Statistics.* Norton, New York, 1965. Chapter 8.

11.3 KENDALL, M. G., and A. STUART. *The Advanced Theory of Statistics*, 2nd edition. Griffin, London, 1964.

11.4 MOSTELLER, FREDERICK, ROBERT E. K. ROURKE, and GEORGE B. THOMAS, JR. *Probability with Statistical Applications*, 2nd edition. Addison-Wesley, Reading, Massachusetts, 1970. Chapter 11.

11.5   OSTLE, BERNARD. *Statistics in Research*, 2nd edition. Iowa State University Press, Ames, 1963. Chapters 8 and 9.

11.6   RICHMOND, SAMUEL B. *Statistical Analysis*, 2nd edition. Ronald Press, New York, 1964. Chapter 19.

11.7   SNEDECOR, GEORGE W., and WILLIAM G. COCHRAN. *Statistical Methods*, 6th edition. Iowa State University Press, Ames, 1967. Chapters 6 and 7.

12

Analysis of Variance

12.1 INTRODUCTION

In Chapter 9 we looked at some methods for analyzing and interpreting the results of two simple kinds of experiment for comparing the effect of two treatments. The two-sample techniques are applicable when the experiment is a completely randomized design for two treatments, and the method of paired comparisons is appropriate when the two treatments are randomized *within* each of n pairs of similar experimental units. We now extend these methods to the general case of k samples, or k treatments, in a completely randomized experiment, and the randomized complete block experiment—the k-treatment analog of the paired comparisons. It is here that we will become acquainted with one of the most powerful statistical tools, the *analysis of variance*.

The analysis of variance is an arithmetic device for partitioning the total variation in a set of data according to the various sources of variation that are present. It results in a summary table similar to Table 11.1, which is, in fact, the analysis-of-variance table for simple linear regression; and it provides a convenient form for summarizing and presenting the information contained in a set of data. Furthermore, study of the complete analysis-of-variance table for a set of experimental or sample survey data will show us whether or not valid tests of certain hypotheses exist, and, if so, how the tests should be performed.

12.2 THE ROLE OF RANDOMIZATION

When we perform an experiment designed to compare the effects of several treatments, our estimates for these treatment effects may be biased because of known or unknown factors that influence the results and that may favor some treatments more than others. The elimination of the bias due to these factors is the primary purpose of randomization.

Suppose we have four chemicals and want to study their effects as additives on the breaking strength of a ceramic. We divide the slip (clay) into portions that will be cast into cylinders, and then randomly assign each additive to an equal number of portions. Randomization at this point guards against nonhomogeneity of the slip. After the cylinders have been cast they are placed on racks and fired in a kiln that is large enough that all our cylinders can be fired simultaneously. We should randomize the positions of the cylinders within the kiln, for not all positions will be subject to the same temperature and the temperature at which our cylinders are fired will probably affect their breaking strength. If it should happen that all cylinders containing one additive are subjected to greater heat during firing than those containing the others, the differences among the mean breaking strengths will estimate the differences in the effects of the additives *plus* the effects of the temperatures. If, however, we randomize the positions of the cylinders within the kiln, each cylinder has an equal chance of being fired under the more favorable temperatures and our estimates will be unbiased. One may argue that any specific randomization may result in an arrangement which favors one or another of the additives. This is true, but it is also allowed for in the procedures we use for testing hypotheses and finding confidence intervals. Furthermore, proper randomization will ensure that our assumption of independent observations is satisfied and will permit us to use the mathematics of probability to attach measures of reliability to the inferences we make on the basis of our experimental results.

12.3 THE COMPLETELY RANDOMIZED DESIGN

In Section 9.2 we took a brief look at some of the concepts associated with the completely randomized experiment for comparing the effects of two treatments. We now extend these ideas to the case of k treatments, each of which is assigned at random to n experimental units. The randomization is carried out separately for each of kn experimental units; that is, for each unit we select at random a number from 1 to k to decide which treatment should be applied to that experimental unit. We generally restrict the randomization so that each treatment is applied to the same number of experimental units. Any experiment in which no restrictions, except for the minor one of equal numbers of units per treatment, are imposed on the randomization is said to have a *completely randomized design*. The experimental units are those elements or groups of elements to which the treatments are assigned at random; hence, every experimental unit has an equal chance of receiving any one of the treatments and the experimental units are independent.

After the experiment has been conducted, we have a set of data consisting of the kn responses of the experimental units, classified into k groups according to the treatments that were applied. We assume (1) that the observed values in any one group constitute a random sample of all possible responses under that treatment of all experimental units, (2) that the variation among units treated alike is the same for all treatments, and (3) that the responses are normally distributed. These assumptions are equivalent to assuming that we have k independent random samples from k normal populations that have common variance.

12.4   THE MODEL

When our data consist of k independent random samples of size n, the individual observed values are subject to a single criterion of classification, the sample or treatment to which they belong. Two subscripts will therefore be sufficient to identify completely any observed value; hence we represent an observation by X_{ij}, where the first subscript, i, denotes the sample, and the second, j, the individual observation within the sample. For example, X_{23} is the third observed value in the second sample.

For data of the type considered here, we assume the mathematical model

$$X_{ij} = \mu + \tau_i + e_{ij} \qquad i = 1, 2, \ldots, k, \quad j = 1, 2, \ldots, n \qquad (12.1)$$

which states that any observed value X_{ij} is equal to the overall mean μ for all the populations, plus the deviation τ_i of the ith population mean μ_i from the overall mean, plus a random deviation e_{ij} from the mean of the ith population. In other words, if μ_i is the mean of the ith population, then

$$\mu = \frac{1}{k} \sum \mu_i \qquad (12.2)$$

$$\tau_i = \mu_i - \mu \qquad (12.3)$$

and

$$e_{ij} = X_{ij} - \mu_i = X_{ij} - \mu - \tau_i \qquad (12.4)$$

The τ_i are known as the *group effects*, or *treatment effects*.

For this model, equation (12.1), we shall assume that:

1. μ is an unknown parameter.
2. The τ_i are unknown constants or parameters.
3. The e_{ij} are normally and independently distributed with mean zero and variance σ^2.

245

The second assumption is appropriate in cases where the populations from which the samples are obtained constitute the whole set of populations in which we are interested. In cases where the populations from which the samples are drawn are themselves a sample of the populations that might be employed, the τ_i are assumed to be random variables which are normally and independently distributed with mean zero and variance σ_τ^2. In the first case we say we have a *fixed model*, in the latter a *random model*.

In the analyses of variance that we consider here, the only effect of assuming the random model instead of the fixed model lies in the interpretation of the results; the calculations and tests of hypotheses are not affected.

12.5 CONSTRUCTING THE ANALYSIS-OF-VARIANCE TABLE

Consider the set of data represented symbolically in Table 12.1. We have k groups or samples, each consisting of n observed values. In the table, a group total is represented by $X_{i.}$, where the dot replacing the subscript j shows that we have summed over j, that we have added within the group. The overall sum for the whole set is denoted by $X_{..}$, the dots showing that we have summed over both i and j; that is, we have added within the groups and then over the groups. We write $\overline{X}_{i.}$ and $\overline{X}_{..}$ for the corresponding means. We have, then,

$$X_{i.} = \sum_{j=1}^{n} X_{ij} \qquad \overline{X}_{i.} = \frac{X_{i.}}{n}$$

$$X_{..} = \sum_{i=1}^{k} X_{i.} = \sum_{i=1}^{k} \sum_{j=1}^{n} X_{ij} \qquad \qquad \textbf{(12.5)}$$

$$\overline{X}_{..} = \frac{X_{..}}{kn}$$

TABLE 12.1. k Groups, Each of Size n

	Group					
	1	*2*	*3*	. . .	*k*	
	X_{11}	X_{21}	X_{31}		X_{k1}	
	X_{12}	X_{22}	X_{32}		X_{k2}	
	X_{13}	X_{23}	X_{33}		X_{k3}	
	$\vdots$	$\vdots$	$\vdots$		$\vdots$	
	X_{1n}	X_{2n}	X_{3n}		X_{kn}	
Sum	$X_{1.}$	$X_{2.}$	$X_{3.}$		$X_{k.}$	$X_{..}$
Mean	$\overline{X}_{1.}$	$\overline{X}_{2.}$	$\overline{X}_{3.}$		$\overline{X}_{k.}$	$\overline{X}_{..}$

To construct the corresponding analysis-of-variance table, we must first consider what sources of variation are present and how the total variation is to be partitioned according to these sources. The total variation in the data is measured by the total sum of squares of deviations from the overall mean. One source of variation, the differences among the group means, is measured by the sum of squares of the deviation of the group means from the overall mean. The only remaining variation is that among the observations within the groups, the variation of the individual values about their group means. This we measure by the pooled sum of squares of deviations of the individual observations from the group means.

Consider the total sum of squares

$$\sum_i \sum_j (X_{ij} - \bar{X}_{..})^2$$

If we add and subtract the mean of the ith group within the parentheses we have

$$\sum_i \sum_j (X_{ij} - \bar{X}_{i.} + \bar{X}_{i.} - \bar{X}_{..})^2$$

If we now square the quantity contained within the parentheses we get

$$\sum_i \sum_j (X_{ij} - \bar{X}_{i.} + \bar{X}_{i.} - \bar{X}_{..})^2$$
$$= \sum_i \sum_j (X_{ij} - \bar{X}_{i.})^2 + 2 \sum_i \sum_j (X_{ij} - \bar{X}_{i.})(\bar{X}_{i.} - \bar{X}_{..})$$
$$+ \sum_i \sum_j (\bar{X}_{i.} - \bar{X}_{..})^2$$

The middle term on the right-hand side is zero, since it can be written as

$$2 \sum_i \left[(\bar{X}_{i.} - \bar{X}_{..}) \sum_j (X_{ij} - \bar{X}_{i.}) \right]$$

And since $\sum_j (X_{ij} - \bar{X}_{i.})$ is zero for all i (the sum of the deviations of a set of values about their arithmetic mean is equal to zero) it follows that the total sum of squares can be written

$$\sum_i \sum_j (X_{ij} - \bar{X}_{..})^2 = \sum_i \sum_j (X_{ij} - \bar{X}_{i.})^2 + n \sum_i (\bar{X}_{i.} - \bar{X}_{..})^2$$

$$(12.6)$$

The first term of the right-hand member of equation (12.6) is the pooled sum of squares of deviations of the observations within the groups from the group means. Within each group there are n values and among these n values there are $n - 1$ degrees of freedom. Since there are k such groups, the pooled sum of squares within groups will have $k(n - 1)$ degrees of freedom.

The second term in the right-hand member of equation (12.6) is the sum of squares of deviations of the group means from the overall mean. It is multiplied by n to put it on a per-observation basis. This is a sum of squares of deviations for k quantities, and will therefore have $k - 1$ degrees of freedom.

The analysis-of-variance table corresponding to the identity, equation (12.6), for the partitioning of the sum of squares for Table 12.1 is shown in Table 12.2.

The mean squares of Table 12.2 are the sums of squares divided by their degrees of freedom.

TABLE 12.2.   Analysis of Variance for the Data of Table 12.1

Source of variation	Degrees of freedom	Sum of squares	Mean square
Among groups	$k - 1$	$n \sum_i (\bar{X}_{i.} - \bar{X}_{..})^2$	$\dfrac{n}{k - 1} \sum_i (\bar{X}_{i.} - \bar{X}_{..})^2$
Within groups	$k(n - 1)$	$\sum_i \sum_j (X_{ij} - \bar{X}_{i.})^2$	$\dfrac{1}{k(n - 1)} \sum_i \sum_j (X_{ij} - \bar{X}_{i.})^2$
Totals	$kn - 1$	$\sum_i \sum_j (X_{ij} - \bar{X}_{..})^2$	

In the analysis of variance, Table 12.2, the sources of variation are written in general terms as *among groups* and *within groups*. If our data were the results of a completely randomized experiment for k treatments, each applied to n experimental units, the sources of variation would be *among treatments*, and *among experimental units treated alike*. These are usually shortened to Treatments and Error as shown in Table 12.3.

TABLE 12.3.   Partitioning of the Degrees of Freedom for a Completely Randomized Experiment with k Treatments and n Experimental Units per Treatment

Source	df
Treatments	$k - 1$
Error	$k(n - 1)$
Total	$kn - 1$

The sums of squares are given in Table 12.2 in terms of deviations from the means. Ordinarily they would be computed by the following machine formulas.

FORMULA 1: *Total sum of squares:*

$$\sum_i \sum_j (X_{ij} - \bar{X}_{..})^2 = \sum_i \sum_j X_{ij}^2 - \frac{X_{..}^2}{kn} \qquad \text{(12.7)}$$

FORMULA 2: *Among-groups sum of squares:*

$$n \sum_i (\bar{X}_{i.} - \bar{X}_{..})^2 = \frac{1}{n} \sum_i X_{i.}^2 - \frac{X_{..}^2}{kn} \qquad \text{(12.8)}$$

FORMULA 3: *Within-groups sum of squares (total sum of squares minus among-groups sum of squares):*

$$\sum_i \sum_j X_{ij}^2 - \frac{1}{n} \sum_i X_{i.}^2 \qquad \text{(12.9)}$$

The square of the sum divided by the total number of observed values,

$$\frac{X_{..}^2}{kn}$$

is called the *correction term*.

12.6   A NUMERICAL EXAMPLE

To illustrate the analysis-of-variance calculations outlined in Section 12.5, we apply the procedures to the data of Table 12.4, which have been adjusted to simplify the arithmetic.

EXAMPLE 1

TABLE 12.4.   Numerical Example: 4 Groups of Size 3

	Group				
	1	*2*	*3*	*4*	
	10	11	13	18	
	9	16	8	23	
	5	9	9	25	
Sum	24	36	30	66	156
Mean	8	12	10	22	13

As the first step in constructing the analysis of variance we find the totals and means, as shown in Table 12.4. We then find the sums of squares as follows.

Step 1: The total sum of squares is:

$$\sum_i \sum_j (X_{ij} - \bar{X}_{..})^2 = (10 - 13)^2 + (9 - 13)^2 + (5 - 13)^2$$
$$+ (11 - 13)^2 + \cdots + (25 - 13)^2$$
$$= 428$$

Step 2: The among-groups sum of squares is:

$$n \sum_i (\bar{X}_{i.} - \bar{X}_{..})^2 = 3[(8 - 13)^2 + (12 - 13)^2 + (10 - 13)^2$$
$$+ (22 - 13)^2]$$
$$= 3(116)$$
$$= 348$$

Step 3: The within-groups sum of squares is most easily obtained as the difference between the total sum of squares and the among-groups sum of squares:

$$\sum_i \sum_j (X_{ij} - \bar{X}_{i.})^2 = 428 - 348 = 80$$

We verify this figure by direct calculation:

$$\sum_j (X_{1j} - \bar{X}_{1.})^2 = (10 - 8)^2 + (9 - 8)^2 + (5 - 8)^2 = 14$$

$$\sum_j (X_{2j} - \bar{X}_{2.})^2 = (11 - 12)^2 + (16 - 12)^2 + (9 - 12)^2 = 26$$

$$\sum_j (X_{3j} - \bar{X}_{3.})^2 = (13 - 10)^2 + (8 - 10)^2 + (9 - 10)^2 = 14$$

$$\sum_j (X_{4j} - \bar{X}_{4.})^2 = (18 - 22)^2 + (23 - 22)^2 + (25 - 22)^2 = 26$$

Therefore, the pooled sum of squares within groups is:

$$\sum_i \sum_j (X_{ij} - \bar{X}_{i.})^2 = 14 + 26 + 14 + 26 = 80$$

The analysis-of-variance table for these data follows:

Source	df	SS	MS
Among groups	3	348	116
Within groups	8	80	10
Totals	11	428	

The reader should verify that the use of the machine formulas, equations (12.7), (12.8), and (12.9), will result in the same values for the sum of squares.

The use of the machine formulas will, in general, simplify the calculations.

12.7 ESTIMATION OF EFFECTS

Given the data of Table 12.1 and the analysis of variance, Table 12.2, we may make the following inferences concerning the populations from which our data were obtained.

1. The overall mean $\overline{X}_{..}$ is our best unbiased estimator for μ.
2. The group mean $\overline{X}_{i.}$ is our best unbiased estimator for the population mean $\mu_{i.}$.
3. The difference between two group effects is estimated unbiasedly by the difference between the group means, i.e.,

$$E(\overline{X}_{i.} - \overline{X}_{m.}) = \mu_i - \mu_m$$

$$= (\mu + \tau_i) - (\mu + \tau_m)$$

$$= \tau_i - \tau_m$$

4. The within-groups mean square is our best unbiased estimator for the common variance σ^2.

If we want to find confidence intervals for the means, or for differences among the means, we must first estimate the standard deviations for the corresponding estimators. The estimated variance for a group or treatment mean, *as always*, is our estimate for σ^2 divided by the number of observed values that were averaged to obtain the mean; therefore,

$$s_{\overline{X}_{i.}}^2 = \frac{s^2}{n} \tag{12.10}$$

where s^2 is the within-groups, or error, mean square. The estimated standard deviation of $\overline{X}_{i.}$ is

$$s_{\overline{X}_{i.}} = \sqrt{\frac{s^2}{n}}$$

The estimated variance of the difference between two means is the sum of their variances,

$$s_{\overline{X}_{i.} - \overline{X}_{m.}}^2 = \frac{s^2}{n} + \frac{s^2}{n} = \frac{2s^2}{n} \tag{12.11}$$

251

The corresponding standard deviation is

$$s_{\overline{X}_{i.} - \overline{X}_m.} = \sqrt{\frac{2s^2}{n}}$$

Since we assume that the random errors, the e_{ij} in our model, equation (12.1), are normally distributed, the group means will be normally distributed. This means that the quantity

$$t = \frac{\overline{X}_{i.} - \mu_i}{s_{\overline{X}_{i.}}} \tag{12.12}$$

has a *t*-distribution with $k(n - 1)$ degrees of freedom. Notice that the degrees of freedom are those associated with our estimate of variance, the within-groups mean square. It follows that a $100(1 - \alpha)\%$ confidence interval for the group mean is

$$L = \overline{X}_{i.} - t_{\alpha/2} s_{\overline{X}_{i.}}$$
$$R = \overline{X}_{i.} + t_{\alpha/2} s_{\overline{X}_{i.}} \tag{12.13}$$

Similarly, under our assumptions the difference between two group means is normally distributed; hence

$$\frac{\overline{X}_{i.} - \overline{X}_m. - \mu_i + \mu_m}{s_{\overline{X}_{i.} - \overline{X}_m.}} \tag{12.14}$$

has a *t*-distribution with $k(n - 1)$ degrees of freedom. A confidence interval for the difference between two group effects is given by

$$L = \overline{X}_{i.} - \overline{X}_m. - t_{\alpha/2} s_{\overline{X}_{i.} - \overline{X}_m.}$$
$$R = \overline{X}_{i.} - \overline{X}_m. + t_{\alpha/2} s_{\overline{X}_{i.} - \overline{X}_m.} \tag{12.15}$$

In connection with confidence intervals in this context, a word of caution is necessary. If we calculated a 95% confidence interval for the difference between two group means on the basis of a randomly selected pair of groups, or upon a pair of groups specified in advance of collection of the data, our confidence level will be equal to .95. If, however, we look at the data and then select the groups, our confidence level will not, in general, be equal to .95 and may, in fact, be much smaller. For k groups, there are a total of $k(k - 1)/2$ pairs of means. If we were to find a 95% confidence interval for every pair, the *average* confidence level would be .95, but for any individual interval its value would depend upon the relative positions of the members of the pair when the means are ranked.

In recent years much has been done to develop procedures for making all possible comparisons among the means through the use of confidence intervals, or by means of *t*-tests. A discussion of these procedures will be found in references 12.2 and 12.5.

12.8 THE HYPOTHESIS OF EQUAL MEANS

Given the results of an experiment in which each of k treatments is applied to n experimental units, we construct an analysis-of-variance table that may be summarized as follows:

Source	df	MS	EMS
Treatments	$k - 1$	T	$\sigma^2 + n\kappa_\tau^2$
Error	$k(n - 1)$	E	σ^2
Total	$kn - 1$		

T and E are the mean squares for treatments and error, respectively.

A new feature is the column headed EMS, where EMS stands for *expected mean square*. The entries in this column of the table are the expected values of the corresponding mean squares, those functions of the parameters that are estimated unbiasedly by the experimental mean squares.

The error mean square (within-group mean square), E, has an expected value equal to σ^2, and is, therefore, an unbiased estimator for the common variance. The treatment mean square, T, when we assume the fixed model is appropriate (see Section 12.4), estimates

$$\sigma^2 + n\kappa_\tau^2 \qquad (12.16)$$

where κ_τ^2 is the mean squared deviation among the treatment effects, that is,

$$\kappa_\tau^2 = \frac{1}{k - 1} \sum_i \tau_i^2 \qquad (12.17)$$

If we assume a random model, that is, if the k treatments are considered to be a random sample of size k from an infinite population of possible treatments, then the τ_i are random variables with variance σ_τ^2, and the expected mean square among groups becomes

$$\sigma^2 + n\sigma_\tau^2 \qquad (12.18)$$

Having partitioned the variation in our experimental data in an analysis-of-variance table, we turn our attention to testing the hypothesis that there are no differences among the treatment effects—that the mean response to each treatment is the same for all treatments. This hypothesis is:

$$H_0 : \tau_i = 0 \qquad i = 1, 2, \ldots, k \qquad (12.19)$$

since the τ_i are the deviations of the treatment means from the overall mean, and are therefore all equal to zero if the μ_i are all the same.

The alternative hypothesis is that not all of the τ_i are equal to zero.

The expected mean square for treatments is $\sigma^2 + n\kappa_\tau^2$, where κ_τ^2, equation (12.17), is a function of the sum of squares of the τ_i with the property that if all the τ_i are equal to zero then κ_τ^2 vanishes; hence, under the hypothesis of equal treatment means, both mean squares have the same expected value, σ^2. If the data are assumed to consist of independent random samples from normal populations, and if the hypothesis is true, it can be shown that the ratio of the mean squares, T/E, has an F-distribution with $k - 1$ and $k(n - 1)$ degrees of freedom.

The F-distributions constitute a two-parameter family of distributions whose parameters are the degrees of freedom, v_1, for the numerator mean square; and the degrees of freedom, v_2, for the denominator mean square. The upper percentage points for F are given in Table IX of the Appendix and are defined by

$$P(F_{v_1, v_2} \geq F_{\alpha, v_1, v_2}) = \alpha \tag{12.20}$$

Only the upper points are given because it is a characteristic of the F-distributions that the lower percentage points may be obtained as reciprocals of the upper ones:

$$F_{1-\alpha, v_1, v_2} = \frac{1}{F_{\alpha, v_2, v_1}} \tag{12.21}$$

Under the null hypothesis H_0 that τ_i is 0 for all i, the ratio of the *expected* mean squares for treatments and error is $\sigma^2/\sigma^2 = 1$, but if the hypothesis is not true the ratio is

$$\frac{\sigma^2 + n\kappa_\tau^2}{\sigma^2}$$

Since κ_τ^2 is based on the sum of squares of the τ_i, it will always be greater than zero when not all of the τ_i are equal to zero. Therefore, we would reject the null hypothesis of equal treatment effects only for large values of the ratio; hence, the critical region is

$$\frac{T}{E} \geq F_{\alpha, k-1, k(n-1)} \tag{12.22}$$

For purposes of illustration, let us test the hypothesis that the four groups in Table 12.4 are from populations having the same mean. In the analysis of variance for these data we found:

Source	df	MS
Among groups	3	116
Within groups	8	10

The ratio of the mean squares is

$$F = \frac{T}{E} = \frac{116}{10} = 11.6$$

From the F-table, $F_{.01,3,8}$ is found to be 7.591. Since the calculated value 11.6 exceeds the tabular value, we reject the null hypothesis at the 1% level of significance and conclude that the population means are different.

The F-test tells us whether or not we may conclude that the means are different. It does not tell us where the differences are. The procedures for locating these differences are discussed in references 12.2, 12.4, and 12.5.

If we assume the random model, for which the among-groups mean square has expected value $\sigma^2 + n\sigma_\tau^2$, the test of the hypothesis that σ_τ^2 is equal to 0 is identical with the preceding test of equal group means. For the random model we are generally more interested in estimating σ_τ^2 than in testing this hypothesis. The estimation of σ_τ^2 will be discussed in a later section.

12.9   THE EFFECTS OF UNEQUAL GROUP SIZES

In our discussion of the analysis of variance we have thus far assumed that we have the same number n of observed values in each group or sample. We will now look at some effects of unequal group sizes on the analysis-of-variance table, on the calculations required to complete the table, and on the inferences we may make.

Let n_i be the number of elements in the ith group; that is, we have n_1 observations in the first group, n_2 in the second, and so on. The total number of observed values $N_.$ is then the sum of the numbers in the k groups:

$$N_. = \sum_{i=1}^{k} n_i \tag{12.23}$$

The analysis-of-variance table for k groups of unequal size is shown in Table 12.5.

TABLE 12.5.   Analysis-of-Variance Table for Unequal-Size Groups

Source	df	SS	MS	EMS
Among groups	$k - 1$	$\sum_i n_i(\bar{X}_{i.} - \bar{X}_{..})^2$	G	$\sigma^2 + \dfrac{1}{k-1}\sum_i n_i\tau_i^2$
Within groups	$\sum_i (n_i - 1)$	$\sum_i \sum_j (X_{ij} - \bar{X}_{i.})^2$	W	σ^2
Totals	$N_. - 1$	$\sum_i \sum_j (X_{ij} - \bar{X}_{..})^2$		

Study of this table reveals the following:

1. Among the k groups there are $k - 1$ degrees of freedom, regardless of the sample sizes.

2. In the among-groups sum of squares, each squared deviation of a group mean from the overall mean is multiplied by the corresponding n_i *before* summation.

3. There are $n_i - 1$ degrees of freedom among the n_i elements of the ith group, and the pooled degrees of freedom within groups is the sum $\sum_i (n_i - 1)$. This may be written as $N_. - k$.

4. The total degrees of freedom are, as usual, one less than the total number of observations.

5. In the expected mean square for among groups, the second term differs from $n\kappa_\tau^2$ in that the products $n_i\tau_i^2$ are summed, rather than just the τ_i^2.

In finding the sums of squares by the machine formulas, the only major difference is in the among-groups sum of squares:

$$\sum_i \frac{X_{i.}^2}{n_i} - \frac{X_{..}^2}{N_.} \tag{12.24}$$

The difference is that in the first term the order of operation is opposite from that in the equal-number formula (12.8). Here we divide the square of each group total by the size of the group and then add, whereas with equal numbers we obtain the sum of squares of the group totals, and then divide by n.

The total sum of squares is found in the usual way, and the within-groups sum of squares is the difference between the total sum of squares and the among-groups sum of squares.

Let G denote the among-groups mean square and W the within-group mean square. Under the hypothesis of equal group means, the hypothesis H_0 that τ_i is 0 for all i, both mean squares are estimates of σ^2 and their ratio G/W has an F-distribution with $k - 1$ and $\sum (n_i - 1)$ degrees of freedom; hence the test of this hypothesis is performed in the same way as with groups of equal size.

The variances of the group means will be different from one another, because each mean is the average of different numbers of observed values. For the mean of the ith group

$$s_{\bar{X}_{i.}}^2 = \frac{s^2}{n_i} \tag{12.25}$$

where s^2 is the within-group mean square W. For two group means, the estimated variance of their difference is:

$$s_{\bar{X}_{i.} - \bar{X}_m.}^2 = s^2 \left(\frac{1}{n_i} + \frac{1}{n_m} \right) \tag{12.26}$$

If, in the unequal-number case, we assume the random model, the among-groups expected mean square becomes

$$\sigma^2 + n_0\sigma_\tau^2 \tag{12.27}$$

where

$$n_0 = \frac{1}{k - 1} \left[N_. - \frac{\sum n_i^2}{N_.} \right] \tag{12.28}$$

is a sort of average number of observations per group. In the simple analysis of variance under consideration, this quantity has no effect on the F-test for equal group means, and would require calculation only if we want to obtain an estimate for σ_τ^2.

We illustrate the calculations required for the analysis of variance with unequal numbers by the following simple example. We use the machine formulas for the sums of squares.

EXAMPLE 1

	Group		
	1	*2*	*3*
	10	6	14
	8	9	13
	5	8	10
	12	13	17
	14		16
	11		
Sum	60	36	70	166
Mean	10	9	14	11.1
	$n_1 = 6$	$n_2 = 4$	$n_3 = 5$	$N_. = \sum_i n_i = 15$

The total sum of squares is:

$$\sum_i \sum_j X_{ij}^2 - \frac{X_{..}^2}{N_.} = (10)^2 + (8)^2 + (5)^2 + \cdots + (16)^2 - \frac{(166)^2}{15}$$
$$= 2010 - 1837.07 = 172.93$$

The among-groups sum of squares is:

$$\sum_i \frac{X_{i.}^2}{n_i} - \frac{X_{..}^2}{N_.} = \frac{(60)^2}{6} + \frac{(36)^2}{4} + \frac{(70)^2}{5} - \frac{(166)^2}{15}$$
$$= 600 + 324 + 980 - 1837.07$$
$$= 1904 - 1837.07 = 66.93$$

The within-groups sum of squares is the total sum of squares minus the group sum of squares:

$$172.93 - 66.93 = 106$$

The analysis-of-variance table is as follows:

Source	df	SS	MS
Among groups	2	66.93	33.47
Within groups	12	106.00	8.83
Totals	14	172.93	

To test the hypothesis of equal group means, $H_0: \tau_i = 0$ for all i, the sample F-value is

$$F = \frac{33.47}{8.83} = 3.79$$

From the F-table, $F_{.05,2,12}$ is found to be 3.8853; therefore, we cannot reject the hypothesis of equal means at the 5% level of significance.

The variances for the sample means are:

$$s_{\bar{X}_1.}^2 = \frac{8.83}{6} = 1.47 \qquad s_{\bar{X}_2.}^2 = \frac{8.83}{4} = 2.21 \qquad s_{\bar{X}_3.}^2 = \frac{8.83}{5} = 1.77$$

If we assume the random model, then

$$n_0 = \tfrac{1}{2}[15 - \tfrac{77}{15}] = 4.94$$

and the expected mean square for among groups becomes $\sigma^2 + 4.94\sigma_\tau^2$.

12.10   PRINCIPLES OF DESIGN

For the completely randomized experiment, the pooled estimate of variance—the within-treatment mean square—is an estimate of *experimental error*. Experimental error is defined as the variation among experimental units treated alike. It is clear that in order to have an estimate of experimental error we must have at least two experimental units assigned to each treatment; otherwise, we would not have units treated alike and, hence, we would have no degrees of freedom or estimate for error.

In designing experiments it is important that the experimental unit be carefully specified. It is defined as the element or group of elements over which the treatments are randomized. For a given experiment, every experimental unit has an *equal* chance of receiving any one of the treatments and is *independent* of every other experimental unit.

Consider the following situation. In order to compare the effects of k different rations on the gains in weight of pigs, we conduct a feeding experiment in which n out of a total of kn animals are randomly assigned to each of k pens. After they are placed in the pens, we use some random device to decide which pen gets which ration. At the completion of the experiment we have n weight gains for the n animals fed on each of the rations, but we do not have an estimate of experimental error because there was only one experimental unit, the pen, for each ration. The pen is the unit over which the treatments were randomized; the animal in the pen is a unit of observation but *not* the experimental unit. We have no estimate for the experimental error variance, and therefore no valid test of the hypothesis of equal ration means.

We can correct this situation in either of two ways: (1) We can put each animal in a separate pen, so that each is individually fed, and randomize the treatments over the animals; or (2) we can have two or more pens that receive each ration. The second suggestion is a compromise that may be necessary if our facilities will not permit each animal to be individually fed.

We say that an experiment is *replicated*, or repeated, when there is more than one experimental unit per treatment. If, in a completely randomized experiment, we have n experimental units per treatment, we can say that we have n replicates. The reasons for *replication* are:

1. To obtain an estimate of experimental error.
2. Through increased replication, to obtain an increasingly more precise estimate of error.
3. Through increased replication, to increase the precision with which we estimate a treatment mean.

Increasing the amount of replication *will not* reduce the experimental error, since the variance, σ^2, is a function of the experimental design and not of the number of experimental units per treatment.

The precision of an experiment is inversely proportional to the variance of the difference between two treatment means, that is, to

$$\sigma^2_{\bar{X}_1 - \bar{X}_2} = \frac{2\sigma^2}{n} \tag{12.29}$$

provided we have equal replication of each treatment.

For our purposes we may think of efficiency as being inversely proportional to the experimental error variance, and the relative efficiency of two different experimental designs as being the inverse ratio of their experimental error variances. If one design has an error variance equal to 10 and a second has error variance equal to 5, the first requires twice as many experimental units per treatment as the second in order to have the same precision as measured by the variance of the difference between two treatment means as given by equation (12.29). We say that the second design is twice as efficient as the first.

To increase precision and efficiency, then, we must reduce the variance of the difference between two means, $2\sigma^2/n$. If we increase the amount of replication we achieve a gain in precision but not in efficiency. To get a gain in efficiency we must increase the precision without increasing the size of the experiment. This can be done by selecting an experimental design that will result in a smaller value of σ^2, the experimental error variance.

Among the ways in which experimental error can be reduced, one of the most effective makes use of the "blocking" principle. We use prior information about the experimental units to group them into *blocks*, or sets, of units such that under uniform treatment the variation in the responses among the units within a block will be less than the variation among blocks. As for the paired comparisons of Section 9.6, if the blocking is effective, and if the blocks are large enough that each of our treatments occurs at least once in each block, estimates for a comparison among the treatment effects are

259

obtained from each block, and the estimate of experimental error is independent of the variation among the blocks.

Since the degrees of freedom for our estimate of error will be reduced, as compared with the corresponding completely randomized design, by the degrees of freedom for differences among the blocks, blocks should be used only when there is a sound basis for blocking. We are reluctant to give up degrees of freedom, because the power and sensitivity of our tests of hypotheses become greater as we add degrees of freedom for error. The more degrees of freedom, the greater the probability of detecting a given difference between two treatment effects. Therefore, we are willing to give up degrees of freedom only if there is a net gain in efficiency—only if the experimental error is reduced enough to make up for the loss. This reduction will not occur if the blocking is not effective. The interested reader should consult one or more of references 12.1, 12.3, 12.4, and 12.5.

12.11   THE RANDOMIZED COMPLETE BLOCK DESIGN

Given kn experimental units that can be grouped into n blocks of k units each in such a way that the responses of the units within a block may be expected to be relatively homogeneous as compared to those of units taken from *different* blocks, we may use a *randomized complete block* design for an experiment involving k treatments. The treatments are randomized within each block, the randomization being carried out separately for each block. With k treatments in blocks of size k (k experimental units per block), each treatment occurs once, and only once, in each block. This constitutes the completeness. The paired comparisons of Chapter 9 are randomized complete block experiments with blocks of size two.

The model associated with the randomized block designs is

$$X_{ij} = \mu + \beta_i + \tau_j + e_{ij} \tag{12.30}$$

$$i = 1, 2, \ldots, n \qquad j = 1, 2, \ldots, k$$

where μ is the overall mean; β_i is the effect of the ith block (the deviation of the block mean from the overall mean); τ_j is the effect of the jth treatment; and e_{ij} is the deviation of the observed value, X_{ij}, from its expected value.

We assume that μ, β_i, and τ_j are unknown parameters and that the e_{ij} are normally and independently distributed with mean zero and common variance σ^2.

The observed values may be displayed in a two-way table, as shown in Table 12.6, since they are subject to two criteria of classification, blocks and treatments.

Notice that a treatment total is represented by $X_{.j}$. We have summed over the blocks and, therefore, the subscript i, which designates the block, is replaced by a dot.

TABLE 12.6.   Observed Values from a Randomized Block Experiment

Block	Treatment					Block totals
	1	2	3	$\cdots$	k	
1	X_{11}	X_{12}	X_{13}		X_{1k}	$X_{1.}$
2	X_{21}	X_{22}	X_{23}		X_{2k}	$X_{2.}$
3	X_{31}	X_{32}	X_{33}		X_{3k}	$X_{3.}$
$\vdots$						
n	X_{n1}	X_{n2}	X_{n3}		X_{nk}	$X_{n.}$
Treatment totals	$X_{.1}$	$X_{.2}$	$X_{.3}$		$X_{.k}$	$X_{..}$

The total variation among the kn observed values is measured by the total sum of squares, the sum of squares of the deviations of the X_{ij} from the experiment mean, $\bar{X}_{..}$:

$$\sum_i \sum_j (X_{ij} - \bar{X}_{..})^2 = \sum_i \sum_j X_{ij}^2 - \frac{X_{..}^2}{kn} \qquad (12.31)$$

Algebraic manipulation leads to the identity

$$\sum_i \sum_j (X_{ij} - \bar{X}_{..})^2 = \sum_i \sum_j (X_{ij} - \bar{X}_{i.} - \bar{X}_{.j} + \bar{X}_{..})^2$$
$$+ k \sum_i (\bar{X}_{i.} - \bar{X}_{..})^2$$
$$+ n \sum_j (\bar{X}_{.j} - \bar{X}_{..})^2 \qquad (12.32)$$

which shows us that the total variation is partitioned into *three* parts: (1) the sum of squares of deviations of the responses from the *estimated* expected values, $\bar{X}_{i.} + \bar{X}_{.j} - \bar{X}_{..}$, (2) the sum of squares due to differences among the blocks, and (3) the sum of squares associated with differences among the treatments. This partition is conveniently displayed in the analysis of variance, Table 12.7. In the table "Blocks" stands for *among* blocks, and "Treatments" for *among* treatments.

TABLE 12.7.   Analysis of Variance for a Randomized Complete Block Experiment

Source	df	SS	MS	EMS
Blocks	$n - 1$	$k \sum_i (\bar{X}_{i.} - \bar{X}_{..})^2$	B	$\sigma^2 + k\kappa_\beta^2$
Treatments	$k - 1$	$n \sum_j (\bar{X}_{.j} - \bar{X}_{..})^2$	T	$\sigma^2 + n\kappa_\tau^2$
Error	$(k - 1)(n - 1)$	$\sum_i \sum_j (X_{ij} - \bar{X}_{i.} - \bar{X}_{.j} + \bar{X}_{..})^2$	E	σ^2
Totals	$kn - 1$	$\sum_i \sum_j (X_{ij} - \bar{X}_{..})^2$		

To calculate the sums of squares we use the machine formulas:

FORMULA 1: *Block sum of squares:*

$$\frac{1}{k} \sum_i X_{i.}^2 - \frac{X_{..}^2}{kn} \tag{12.33}$$

FORMULA 2: *Treatment sum of squares:*

$$\frac{1}{n} \sum_j X_{.j}^2 - \frac{X_{..}^2}{kn} \tag{12.34}$$

The error sum of squares is found by subtraction.

FORMULA 3: *The error sum of squares is equal to the total sum of squares, minus the block sum of squares, minus the treatment sum of squares.* **(12.35)**

The treatment effects are estimated by $\overline{X}_{.j} - \overline{X}_{..}$, and the difference between two treatment effects by the difference between the treatment means, $\overline{X}_{.j} - \overline{X}_{.m}$.

The error mean square E is our unbiased estimate for σ^2, the error variance; therefore, the variance of a treatment mean is estimated by

$$s_{\overline{X}_{.j}}^2 = \frac{s^2}{n} = \frac{E}{n} \tag{12.36}$$

and the variance of $\overline{X}_{.j} - \overline{X}_{.m}$ is estimated by

$$s_{\overline{X}_{.j} - \overline{X}_{.m}}^2 = \frac{2E}{n} \tag{12.37}$$

Under the hypothesis of equal treatment effects, the hypothesis H_0 that τ_j is 0 for all j, the treatment mean square T is also an estimate for σ^2; hence, the ratio

$$F_{k-1,(k-1)(n-1)} = \frac{T}{E} \tag{12.38}$$

has an F-distribution with $k - 1$ and $(k - 1)(n - 1)$ degrees of freedom.

Because of the way the randomization is carried out, despite the form of the expected mean square for blocks, we do not test the hypothesis of equal block means. We are more concerned with the efficiency of the RCB (randomized complete block) design relative to the efficiency of the CR (completely randomized) design that might have been used for the same kn experimental units.

We can estimate the relative efficiency by

$$\text{Rel. eff. RCB to CR} = \frac{(n-1)B + n(k-1)E}{(kn-1)E} \times 100\% \quad \textbf{(12.39)}$$

where B and E are the block and error mean squares, respectively, from the analysis of variance of the RCB experiment. We see that when the block mean square is greater than the error mean square, the estimated experimental error for the RCB is less than that for the CR design. This will be the case only when we have an effective criterion for blocking.

EXAMPLE 1

An experiment station conducted a randomized complete block experiment in order to make comparisons among three varieties of barley. Six blocks were used. The yields in bushels per acre were as follows:

	Variety			
Block	1	2	3	Block totals
1	45	40	30	115
2	40	42	37	119
3	46	38	26	110
4	38	42	25	105
5	35	45	27	107
6	43	48	35	126
Variety totals	247	255	180	682
Means	41.2	42.5	30	37.9

The total sum of squares is:

$$(45)^2 + (40)^2 + (30)^2 + \cdots + (35)^2 - \frac{(682)^2}{18} = 843.78$$

the block sum of squares is

$$\tfrac{1}{3}[(115)^2 + (119)^2 + \cdots + (126)^2] - \frac{(682)^2}{18} = 105.11$$

the variety sum of squares is

$$\tfrac{1}{6}[(274)^2 + (255)^2 + (180)^2] - \frac{(682)^2}{18} = 565.44$$

and the error sum of squares, by subtraction, is

$$843.78 - (105.11 + 565.44) = 173.23$$

The analysis-of-variance table is as follows:

Source	df	SS	MS
Blocks	5	105.11	21.02
Varieties	2	565.44	282.72
Error	10	172.23	17.32
Total	17		

To test the hypothesis of equal mean yields for the three varieties we use

$$F_{2,10} = \frac{282.72}{17.32} = 16.32$$

From the F-table, $F_{.01,2,10}$ is found to equal 7.56; therefore, we reject the hypothesis of equal variety effects. We would now examine the variety means and make comparisons among them. We can see, in this case, that varieties 1 and 2 are about the same, and that most of the difference among the means is accounted for by the low mean for the third variety. As previously mentioned, one would use techniques for making comparisons among the means that are beyond the scope of this text.

The variance of a variety mean is estimated by

$$s_{\bar{X}.j}^2 = \frac{E}{n} = \frac{17.32}{6} = 2.89$$

Making use of equation (12.39) we estimate the efficiency of this experiment relative to a CR experiment on the same experimental plots as

$$\frac{5(21.02) + 12(17.32)}{17(17.32)} \times 100\% = 106\%$$

There is a gain of only 6% in efficiency. This could have been anticipated by looking at the block totals. It can be seen that the differences among them are not large, and therefore the blocking was not very effective.

12.12 NESTED CLASSIFICATIONS

Frequently, the treatments in an experiment require relatively large experimental units. When the time comes to obtain objective measures of the characteristic of interest, the experimental units sometimes are then too large for convenience, or the method of measurement is such that it can be applied to only a small part of the experimental unit. Bacteria counts on frozen meat pies would be made on only a small portion of the whole pie, moisture determinations at various depths in a field plot are made at only a few points in the plot, and so on. In such cases we make our determinations either on samples taken within the experimental units, or at randomly selected points within the unit. It is entirely possible that we would sample at several stages before reaching the level at which the actual observed value is obtained. We might, for example, perform a completely randomized experiment in which we have n experimental units per treatment, take a sample of m smaller units per experimental unit, select q portions from each sub-unit, and make r determinations on each portion. In such a case the sources of variation would be:

1. among treatments,
2. among experimental units within treatments,
3. among samples within experimental units,
4. among portions within samples,
5. among determinations within portions.

Situations of this sort, where every classification is nested within the next larger one, are called *nested* or *hierarchical classifications*. We shall consider here only the two-stage nested classification, in which we have individuals within subgroups and subgroups within groups, or samples within experimental units and experimental units within treatments.

Let us now consider a completely randomized experiment for comparing the effects of k treatments, when each treatment is applied to n experimental units and we take p samples from each experimental unit. Each observed value needs three subscripts for complete identification, one for each classification; hence, X_{ijm} is the observed value for the mth sample from the jth experimental unit to which the ith treatment was applied. The model we assume is

$$X_{ijm} = \mu + \tau_i + e_{ij} + \eta_{ijm} \qquad (12.40)$$

where $i = 1, 2, \ldots, k; j = 1, 2, \ldots, n$; and $m = 1, 2, \ldots, p$. The equation states that the observed value X_{ijm} is equal to the overall mean, plus the deviation of the ith treatment mean from the overall mean, plus the deviation of the (ij)th experimental unit from the treatment mean, plus the deviation of the observed value from the response of the experimental unit. For this model we assume that:

1. μ is an unknown constant or parameter.
2. The τ_i are unknown constants (so long as we are concerned with only these k treatments—so long as they are not randomly selected from a population of possible treatments).
3. The e_{ij} are normally and independently distributed with mean zero and variance σ_e^2.
4. The η_{ijm} are normally and independently distributed with mean zero and variance σ_η^2, and are distributed independently of the e_{ij}.

265

The data from such an experiment could be presented as in Table 12.8. In the table there are a total of knp observed values; therefore, the total sum of squares will have $knp - 1$ degrees of freedom. The machine formula for the total sum of squares is

FORMULA 1:   *Total SS:*

$$\sum_i \sum_j \sum_m X_{ijm}^2 - \frac{X_{...}^2}{knp}$$

The sum of squares among the k treatments will have $k - 1$ degrees of freedom. The machine formula is

FORMULA 2:   *Treatment SS:*

$$\frac{1}{np} \sum_i X_{i..}^2 - \frac{X_{...}^2}{knp}$$

Among the n experimental units within each of the k treatments there are $n - 1$ degrees of freedom, so the pooled sum of squares will have $k(n - 1)$ degrees of freedom.

FORMULA 3:   *Exp. unit/trt. SS:*

$$\frac{1}{p} \sum_i \sum_j X_{ij.}^2 - \frac{1}{np} \sum_i X_{i..}^2$$

Notice that the sum of squares for experimental units within treatments is the sum of squares among the kn experimental units *with treatments ignored*, minus the treatment sum of squares. This illustrates a general principle for calculating sums of squares: The sum of squares for any factor A within a second factor B is the among sum of squares for A minus the sum of squares among B. We may say that a *within* sum of squares is the difference between the corresponding *among* sums of squares.

Among the p individuals or samples within an experimental unit there are $p - 1$ degrees of freedom. Since there are, in all, kn experimental units, the pooled degrees of freedom among samples within units is $kn(p - 1)$. The sum of squares is

FORMULA 4:   *Samples/exp. units SS:*

$$\sum_i \sum_j \sum_m X_{ijm}^2 - \frac{1}{p} \sum_i \sum_j X_{ij.}^2$$

TABLE 12.8. Results of a Completely Randomized Experiment with Subsampling

Treatment	Experimental unit	Sample				Experimental unit total	Treatment total
		1	2	$\cdots$	p		
1	1	X_{111}	X_{112}	$\cdots$	X_{11p}	$X_{11.}$	
	2	X_{121}	X_{122}	$\cdots$	X_{12p}	$X_{12.}$	
	$\vdots$	$\vdots$				$\vdots$	
	n	X_{1n1}	X_{1n2}	$\cdots$	X_{1np}	$X_{1n.}$	$X_{1..}$
2	1	X_{211}	X_{212}	$\cdots$	X_{21p}	$X_{21.}$	
	2	X_{221}	X_{222}	$\cdots$	X_{22p}	$X_{22.}$	
	$\vdots$	$\vdots$				$\vdots$	
	n	X_{2n1}	X_{2n2}	$\cdots$	X_{2np}	$X_{2n.}$	$X_{2..}$
$\vdots$							
k	1	X_{k11}	X_{k12}	$\cdots$	X_{k1p}	$X_{k1.}$	
	2	X_{k21}	X_{k22}	$\cdots$	X_{k2p}	$X_{k2.}$	
	$\vdots$	$\vdots$				$\vdots$	
	n	X_{kn1}	X_{kn2}	$\cdots$	X_{knp}	$X_{kn.}$	$X_{k..}$
						Overall total	$X_{...}$

Here again we see that the within sum of squares is the difference between the corresponding among sums of squares—the sum of squares among samples minus the sum of squares among experimental units.

In connection with calculating sums of squares it should be observed that an among sum of squares is always found by squaring each total, dividing the squared total by the number of observations that make up the total, and then summing these quotients. For equal numbers we may divide the sum of the squared totals by the common number of observations. This procedure results in the uncorrected among sum of squares. To obtain the corrected sum of squares we subtract the correction term, the square of the overall total divided by the total number of observed values.

The analysis of variance, with the sums of squares expressed in terms of squared deviations, is shown in Table 12.9. The mean squares, of course, are the sums of squares divided by their degrees of freedom.

The expected mean squares may be justified in part as follows: The mean square among samples is an unbiased estimator for the variance among samples taken from the same experimental unit. Some of the variation among experimental units treated alike is due to the variation among the samples; hence, the expected mean square for experimental units treated alike contains this component in addition to the variance component for the experimental units. The coefficient of σ_e^2 is equal to the number of observed values for *each* experimental unit.

267

TABLE 12.9. Analysis of Variance for the Data of Table 12.8

Source	df	SS	MS	EMS
Treatments	$k-1$	$np \sum_i (\bar{X}_{i..} - \bar{X}_{...})^2$	T	$\sigma_\eta^2 + p\sigma_e^2 + np\kappa_\tau^2$
E.U./trts.	$k(n-1)$	$p \sum_i \sum_j (\bar{X}_{ij.} - \bar{X}_{i..})^2$	E	$\sigma_\eta^2 + p\sigma_e^2$
Samples/E.U.	$kn(p-1)$	$\sum_i \sum_j \sum_m (X_{ijm} - \bar{X}_{ij.})^2$	D	σ_η^2
Totals	$knp-1$	$\sum_i \sum_j \sum_m (X_{ijm} - \bar{X}_{...})^2$		

Since some of the variation among the treatment means can be attributed to sampling, and some to variation among experimental units, the expected mean square for treatments contains both these components plus the mean square deviation of the treatment effects. Again, the coefficient of κ_τ^2 is the number of *individual observations* on each treatment.

The mean square for experimental units within treatments provides our estimate of experimental error in this design. The estimated variance of any treatment mean in this equal-number case is the error mean square divided by the number of observations that went into each mean, that is,

$$s_{\bar{X}..}^2 = \frac{E}{np}$$

and the estimated variance of the difference between two treatment means is

$$s_{\bar{X}_{i..} - \bar{X}_{q..}}^2 = \frac{2E}{np}$$

Looking at the expected mean squares in Table 12.9, we see that, under the hypothesis of equal treatment means, the hypothesis H_0 that τ_i is 0 for all i, the mean squares for treatments and error (E.U./trts.) have the same expected value; therefore we test the hypothesis by an F-test where the calculated F is the ratio

$$F = \frac{T}{E}$$

with $k-1$ and $k(n-1)$ degrees of freedom.

The following example will illustrate the procedures outlined in this section.

EXAMPLE 1

A standard type, Type A, of electron tube is used in the radio frequency section of an airborne radio receiver and it is found that these tubes must be replaced too frequently. In an effort to increase service life, two new types, Type AW, a ruggedized version of Type A, and Type AR, a modification of Type A, are designed, and pilot runs of the new types are carried out. Before comparing the three types with respect to mean life under service conditions, we want to see whether or not they perform equally well so far as the sensitivity of the receiver is concerned. We select six tubes of each type at random, install them one at a time in random order in a receiver set up in the laboratory, and make four sensitivity measurements for each tube. The results, given in terms of the input signal strength in microvolts required to obtain a ten-decibel signal-to-noise ratio, are shown in Table 12.10.

The sums of squares are:

$$Total: \quad (2.0)^2 + (2.1)^2 + (1.9)^2 + \cdots + (1.6)^2 - \frac{(152.8)^2}{72} = 6.20$$

$$Among \ types: \quad \tfrac{1}{24}[(53.5)^2 + (54.7)^2 + (44.6)^2] - \frac{(152.8)^2}{72} = 2.53$$

$$Among \ tubes \ (types \ ignored): \quad \tfrac{1}{4}[(8.0)^2 + (8.8)^2 + \cdots + (6.7)^2]$$
$$- \frac{(152.8)^2}{72} = 5.65$$

Tubes/types: among-tubes SS − among-types SS = 5.65 − 2.53 = 3.12

Observations/tubes: total SS − among-tubes SS = 6.20 − 5.65 = .55

TABLE 12.10. Signal Strength in Microvolts Required for a Ten-decibel Signal-to-Noise Ratio

Type	Tube					Tube total	Type total
A	1	2.0	2.1	1.9	2.0	8.0	
	2	2.2	2.3	2.2	2.1	8.8	
	3	2.4	2.3	2.2	2.3	9.2	
	4	1.9	1.8	2.2	2.0	7.9	
	5	2.4	2.5	2.3	2.4	9.6	
	6	2.5	2.5	2.4	2.6	10.0	53.5
AW	1	2.4	2.3	2.4	2.1	9.2	
	2	2.0	2.1	1.9	1.9	7.9	
	3	2.2	2.2	2.4	2.3	9.1	
	4	2.6	2.5	2.5	2.7	10.3	
	5	1.8	2.0	2.1	1.9	7.8	
	6	2.5	2.6	2.6	2.7	10.4	54.7
AR	1	1.8	1.7	1.7	1.9	7.1	
	2	2.0	2.1	1.9	2.1	8.1	
	3	1.6	1.7	1.7	1.7	6.7	
	4	1.9	1.8	1.9	2.0	7.6	
	5	2.0	2.2	2.0	2.2	8.4	
	6	1.6	1.8	1.7	1.6	6.7	44.6
							152.8

The analysis of variance is given in Table 12.11. We assume the fixed model because we are interested in only the three types of tubes that were tested. Looking at the expected mean squares, we see that under the hypothesis of equal sensitivities for the three types the mean squares for types and for tubes within types estimate the same quantity; hence, the mean square for tubes within types is our experimental error for testing among types, and will be the basic estimate of variance we use to find the variance of a type mean.

TABLE 12.11. Analysis of Variance for the Data of Table 12.10

Source	df	SS	MS	EMS
Types	2	2.53	1.26	$\sigma_\eta^2 + 4\sigma_e^2 + 24\kappa_\tau^2$
Tubes/types	15	3.12	.21	$\sigma_\eta^2 + 4\sigma_e^2$
Observations/tubes	54	.55	.01	σ_η^2
Totals	71	6.20		

To test $H_0: \tau_i = 0$, $i = 1, 2, 3$, we find the F-ratio

$$F = \frac{1.26}{.21} = 6.0$$

By the F-table, $F_{.05,2,15}$ equals 3.68; therefore, at the 5% level we reject the hypothesis of equal mean sensitivities for the three types of tubes.

The means are

$$\text{Type } A: \overline{X}_{1..} = \frac{53.5}{24} = 2.23$$

$$\text{Type } AW: \overline{X}_{2..} = \frac{54.7}{24} = 2.28$$

$$\text{Type } AR: \overline{X}_{3..} = \frac{44.6}{24} = 1.86$$

The variances and standard deviations for the type means are the same for all types, because we had equal numbers of observations on each type.

$$s_{\overline{X}_{i..}}^2 = \frac{.21}{24} = .00875$$

$$s_{\overline{X}_{i..}} = \sqrt{.00875} = .094$$

$$s_{\overline{X}_{i..} - \overline{X}_{p..}}^2 = 2(.00875) = .0175$$

$$s_{\overline{X}_{i..} - \overline{X}_{p..}} = \sqrt{.0175} = .13$$

The F-test led us to conclude that there were differences among the type means. In order to inquire more closely into these differences we can use t-tests to compare each new type with the standard, Type A. Under the hypothesis of no difference, the ratio

$$t = \frac{\overline{X}_{i..} - \overline{X}_{p..}}{s_{\overline{X}_{i..} - \overline{X}_{p..}}}$$

has the t-distribution with 15 degrees of freedom. To compare Type AW with Type A we have

$$t = \frac{2.28 - 2.23}{.13} = \frac{.05}{.13} = .385$$

To compare Type AR with Type A we get

$$t = \frac{1.86 - 2.23}{.13} = \frac{-.37}{.13} = -2.846$$

From the t-table, $t_{.025(15)}$ is found to be 2.131, so that we conclude that Type AR is more sensitive than Type A, but have no reason to believe there is any difference in the sensitivities of Types A and AW.

The use of t-tests for making comparisons among means is quite common, but it is not an entirely satisfactory procedure for reasons similar to those discussed in connection with confidence intervals in Section 12.7. Recent techniques for making multiple comparisons among the means use a table based on the distribution of the range, and are discussed in the references previously cited.

If we were to assume that the k treatments employed in the experiment are a random sample from an infinite population of possible treatments, we should be assuming the random model for which the τ_i are random variables with variance σ_τ^2. In this case the expected mean square for treatments would be

$$\sigma_\eta^2 + p\sigma_e^2 + np\sigma_\tau^2$$

More detailed treatments of the nested classifications including the effects of unequal numbers at various stages may be found in the references listed at the end of this chapter.

12.13   SUBSAMPLING IN RANDOMIZED BLOCKS

The discussion of subsampling, or sampling from the experimental units, of the preceding section related to the completely randomized experiment, but the principle set forth can be extended with no difficulty to include subsampling in more complicated experiments.

271

For the randomized block experiment where p samples are selected at random for each experimental unit, the analysis-of-variance table may be summarized in the following form:

Source	df	MS	EMS
Blocks	$n - 1$	B	$\sigma_\eta^2 + p\sigma_e^2 + kp\kappa_\beta^2$
Treatments	$k - 1$	T	$\sigma_\eta^2 + p\sigma_e^2 + np\kappa_\tau^2$
Error	$(k - 1)(n - 1)$	E	$\sigma_\eta^2 + p\sigma_e^2$
Samples/exp. units	$kn(p - 1)$	D	σ_η^2
Total	$knp - 1$		

The total sums of squares, and the sums of squares for treatments and for samples within experimental units, are calculated as in Section 12.12. The new feature is the subdivision of the sum of squares *among* experimental units into those for blocks, treatments, and error. We find the sums of squares as follows:

FORMULA 1: *Block SS:*

$$\frac{1}{kp} \sum_i X_{i..}^2 - \frac{X_{...}^2}{knp}$$

FORMULA 2: *Treatment SS:*

$$\frac{1}{np} \sum_j X_{.j.}^2 - \frac{X_{...}^2}{knp}$$

FORMULA 3: *The error SS is equal to the experimental-units SS, minus the block SS, minus the treatment SS.*

Tests of hypotheses are carried out and confidence intervals are found exactly as before. The error mean square E is again our estimate of experimental error.

12.14   ESTIMATING COMPONENTS OF VARIANCE

In the analysis of variance, Table 12.9, the mean squares for the experimental units treated alike and samples within experimental units are given, along with their expected values, as:

Source	MS	EMS
Exp. units/treatments	E	$\sigma_\eta^2 + p\sigma_e^2$
Samples/exp. units	D	σ_η^2

We see that the mean square D is an unbiased estimate for σ_η^2. Using the conventional notation we could write our estimator for this variance component as:

$$s_\eta^2 = D \qquad \qquad (12.41)$$

If we now subtract D from E, the difference will be an unbiased estimate for

$$\sigma_\eta^2 + p\sigma_e^2 - \sigma_\eta^2 = p\sigma_e^2$$

Hence,

$$s_e^2 = \frac{E - D}{p} \qquad \qquad (12.42)$$

is an unbiased estimate for σ_e^2.

Similarly, if we assume the random model, the expected value of the treatment mean square T is

$$E(T) = \sigma_\eta^2 + p\sigma_e^2 + np\sigma_\tau^2$$

The difference between the treatment mean square T and the error mean square E will then have the expected value $np\sigma_\tau^2$, and

$$s_\tau^2 = \frac{T - E}{np}$$

will give an unbiased estimate for σ_τ^2.

For the example of Section 12.12 we had:

Source	MS	EMS
Types	1.26	$\sigma_\eta^2 + 4\sigma_e^2 + 24\kappa_\tau^2$
Tubes/types	.21	$\sigma_\eta^2 + 4\sigma_e^2$
Observations/tubes	.01	σ_η^2

Our estimates for the components of variance in this case are

$$s_\eta^2 = .01$$

and

$$s_e^2 = \frac{.21 - .01}{4} = .05$$

We do not ordinarily estimate κ_τ^2. If we had assumed the random model in this case, the estimate for σ_τ^2 would have been

$$s_\tau^2 = \frac{1.26 - .21}{24} = .044$$

With the hierarchical classifications, we can use our estimates for variance components to estimate the efficiency of the design we use to obtain the data, relative to the efficiency of an alternative design of similar structure but with different values for the numbers of subgroups within groups, sub-subgroups within subgroups, and so on. Discussions of variance components including estimates of relative efficiency may be found in the references.

PROBLEMS

1. Given the data in the following table,
   a. Construct the analysis-of-variance table. Use deviations from means to calculate the sums of squares.
   b. Recalculate the sums of squares by means of machine formulas.
   c. Write the expected mean squares.
   d. Find estimates for the group means and their variances.
   e. Write the model and list the assumptions.
   f. Test the hypothesis of equal group means.

		Group		
	1	*2*	*3*	*4*
	15	9	17	13
	17	12	20	12
	22	15	23	17

2. Given the data in the following table,
   a. Construct the analysis-of-variance table. Use deviations from means to calculate the sums of squares.
   b. Calculate the sums of squares using machine formulas.
   c. Write the expected mean squares.
   d. Write the model and state the assumptions.
   e. Estimate the variance of a mean.
   f. Test the hypothesis of equal population means.

	Group	
1	*2*	*3*
50	67	50
48	72	44
53	71	43
48	74	45
51	66	43

3. In a completely randomized experiment, six treatments were each applied to five experimental units.
   a. Complete the following analysis-of-variance table.
   b. Test the hypothesis of equal treatment effects. Let $\alpha = .01$.
   c. What is the variance of a treatment mean?
   d. Give the expected mean squares.

Source of variation	df	Sum of squares	Mean square
Treatments		200	
Error			
Totals		296	

4. Given an experiment in which each of five treatments was randomly assigned to six experimental units, and given that the pooled estimate for variance is 24,
   a. Complete the following table.
   b. Test the hypothesis of equal treatment effects.
   c. Find the standard deviation of a treatment mean.

Source of variation	df	Sum of squares	Mean square
Treatments			
Error			
Totals		1176	

5. Three packaging materials were tested for moisture retention by storing the same food product in each of them for a fixed period of time and then determining the moisture loss. Each material was used to wrap ten food samples. Given the following results,
   a. Construct the analysis-of-variance table.
   b. Can we reject the hypothesis that the materials are equally effective? Let $\alpha = .05$.
   c. Find a 95% confidence interval for the mean loss that results from using material 2.

	Material		
	1	*2*	*3*
Number of packages	10	10	10
Mean loss	224	232	228
$\sum (X_{ij} - \bar{X}_{i.})^2$	300	400	380

6. To study the effects of different pressures on the yield of a dye, five lots were produced under each of three pressures with the results given below.

	Lot				
Pressure	*1*	*2*	*3*	*4*	*5*
200 mm	32.4	32.6	32.1	32.4	32.3
500 mm	37.8	38.2	37.9	38.0	37.8
800 mm	30.3	30.5	30.0	30.1	29.7

a. Construct the analysis-of-variance table.

b. Estimate the mean yields and their standard deviations.

c. Test the hypothesis that the mean yields are equal for the three pressures. Let $\alpha = .01$.

d. Find 95% confidence intervals for each pressure mean.

7. Five treatments were each assigned to ten experimental units. The total sum of squares was 8550, and the variance of each treatment mean was 15. Reproduce the analysis-of-variance table and test the hypothesis of equal treatment means. Let $\alpha = .05$.

8. Six treatments were applied to each of eight experimental units. The standard deviation for the difference between two treatment means was equal to 4, and the calculated F-value for testing the hypothesis of equal treatment means was equal to 3. Reproduce the analysis-of-variance table.

9. To investigate the effects of four different types of plates on the extraction efficiency of a pulse column, five runs were made with each type of plate. The height in theoretical units was determined for each run, with the results given below.

a. Construct the analysis-of-variance table. Include the expected mean squares.

b. Estimate the means and their standard deviation.

c. Test the hypothesis of equal extraction efficiency. Let $\alpha = .025$.

d. Find 98% confidence intervals for the mean efficiency of each plate.

			Plate	
Run	*1*	*2*	*3*	*4*
1	4.0	7.2	3.9	7.3
2	3.2	6.9	5.2	6.5
3	3.9	8.3	4.2	6.0
4	4.7	7.5	5.4	5.8
5	3.8	6.8	4.5	5.9

10. Four animals were randomly assigned to each of four rations. They were individually fed and, after a period of time, a measure of damage to a given organ was obtained.

a. Construct the analysis-of-variance table.

b. Estimate the mean for each ration.

c. Test the hypothesis of equal damage resulting from these rations.

d. Find a 95% confidence interval for each mean.

		Ration	
1	*2*	*3*	*4*
7.2	4.5	9.7	7.1
6.8	6.0	8.4	6.1
6.0	4.6	8.8	7.2
6.3	5.3	9.9	6.4

11. In problem 9, the plate types differed in the number and size of perforations in the plates as follows:

> Type 1: Size of hole, h_1; number of holes, p_1.
>
> Type 2: Size of hole, h_2; number of holes, p_1.
>
> Type 3: Size of hole, h_1; number of holes, p_2.
>
> Type 4: Size of hole, h_2; number of holes, p_2.

To test the hypothesis that hole size, averaged over numbers of holes, has no effect, we test $H_0: \mu_2 - \mu_1 + \mu_4 - \mu_3 = 0$. To test the hypothesis that the number of holes has no effect, the appropriate hypothesis is $H_0: \mu_4 - \mu_2 + \mu_3 - \mu_1 = 0$.

  Using the data of problem 9, test these hypotheses. What conclusions do you reach? [*Hint:* $\bar{X}_{2.} - \bar{X}_{1.} + \bar{X}_{4.} - \bar{X}_{3.}$ estimates $\mu_2 - \mu_1 + \mu_4 - \mu_3$ unbiasedly, and has the estimated variance $4s^2/n$; hence,

$$\frac{\bar{X}_{2.} - \bar{X}_{1.} + \bar{X}_{4.} - \bar{X}_{3.}}{\sqrt{4s^2/n}}$$

has a t-distribution if $\mu_2 - \mu_1 + \mu_4 - \mu_3 = 0$.]

12. In problem 10 the rations may be described as follows, as regards source and level of fat:

> Ration 1: Vegetable fat, high level.
>
> Ration 2: Vegetable fat, low level.
>
> Ration 3: Animal fat, high level.
>
> Ration 4: Animal fat, low level.

  a. Test the hypothesis that there is no difference between the animal and vegetable fats. $H_0: \mu_3 + \mu_4 - \mu_1 - \mu_2 = 0$.
  b. Test the hypothesis that the levels of fat do not differ in their effects. $H_0: \mu_1 + \mu_3 - \mu_2 - \mu_4 = 0$.

13. Given the following data,
  a. Construct the analysis-of-variance table. Include the expected mean squares.
  b. Estimate the population means and estimate the standard deviation of each group mean.
  c. Find a 99% confidence interval for the difference between the means of the first and third groups.
  d. Test the hypothesis of equal group means. Let $\alpha = .05$.

	Group		
1	*2*	*3*	*4*
9	17	22	13
6	10	17	14
8	12	21	22
13			16
			10

14. The following are the hourly rates of pay for samples of workers in three different types of firms.
    a. Construct the analysis-of-variance table.
    b. Write the expected mean squares.
    c. Test the hypothesis of equal hourly pay scales.
    d. Estimate the standard deviations of the group means.
    e. Find a 95% confidence interval for $\mu_1 - \mu_3$.
    f. Test the hypothesis $H_0: \mu_1 = \mu_2$. Let $\alpha = .01$.

Type of firm

1	2	3
2.30	2.00	1.65
2.35	1.80	1.90
2.25	2.15	1.85
2.00	2.10	1.80
1.95	1.90	1.75
2.10	1.75	1.95
2.40		2.00
		1.90

15. In a completely randomized experiment, three treatments were assigned to $n_1 = 7$, $n_2 = 10$, and $n_3 = 8$ experimental units, respectively.
    a. Complete the following table.
    b. Write the model and state the assumptions.
    c. Test the hypothesis of equal treatment effects.

Source	df	SS	MS
Treatments			
Error			10
Totals		320	

16. Given that five treatments were randomly assigned to $n_1 = 5$, $n_2 = 8$, $n_3 = 10$, $n_4 = 13$, and $n_5 = 11$ experimental units, respectively, and the estimated standard deviation of $\bar{X}_2$ was 2:
    a. Complete the following table.
    b. Give the expected mean squares.
    c. Write the model and state the assumptions.
    d. Test the hypothesis of equal treatment effects.
    e. Given that $\bar{X}_5 = 50$, find a 99% confidence interval for $\mu + \tau_5$.

Source	df	SS	MS
Treatments			131.2
Error			
Totals			

17. In the course of a sample survey conducted in one county of a midwestern state, the educational backgrounds of randomly selected respondents were recorded with the following results.

   Urban: Sample size, $n_1 = 350$; mean number of years of school completed, $\bar{X}_1 = 11.4$.

   Rural-farm: Sample size, $n_2 = 200$; mean number of years of school completed, $\bar{X}_2 = 9.3$.

   Rural-nonfarm: Sample size, $n_3 = 150$; mean number of years of school completed, $\bar{X}_3 = 10.1$.

   The estimated standard deviation was ten years.
   a. Construct the analysis-of-variance table.
   b. Are there real differences in the educational backgrounds of the three groups? Let $\alpha = .01$.
   c. What is the combined mean number of years completed? Find a 95% confidence interval for the mean educational level in this county.

18. The following data show the number of persons currently employed and number of days lost from work by geographic region. Assume that the estimated standard deviation on a per-person basis is 2578.
   a. Construct the analysis of variance.
   b. Are there significant differences among the regions as regards mean numbers of days lost per person?
   c. Find 95% confidence intervals for the regional means and for the national mean.

		Region		
	Northeast	North Central	South	West
Days lost (thousands)	92,595	102,567	125,693	64,335
Population (thousands)	18,079	20,051	21,021	10,975

19. Given the following data for a randomized complete block experiment,
   a. Use the terms in the identity, equation (12.32), to calculate the sums of squares.
   b. Use machine formulas to calculate the sums of squares.
   c. Construct the analysis-of-variance table. Include the expected mean squares.
   d. Write the model and state the assumptions.

	Treatment		
Block	1	2	3
1	6	7	8
2	14	9	16

20. The following are the yields in kilograms per plot that resulted when four equally spaced levels of nitrogen, N_0, N_4, N_8, and N_{12}, were applied to a variety of a grain in a randomized block experiment. Blocking was based on level of irrigation.

a. Construct the analysis-of-variance table.

b. Test that there are no differences among the effects of the nitrogen levels.

c. Estimate the means and their standard deviations.

d. Is there a significant difference between the means for the highest and lowest levels of nitrogen?

	Treatment			
Block	N_0	N_4	N_8	N_{12}
1	4.37	4.50	4.41	4.92
2	6.72	8.80	7.82	8.05
3	8.32	8.73	8.91	9.40
4	8.03	8.31	9.62	9.28

21. In a service test of traffic paints, four different paints were tested at three different locations. The locations may be considered to be blocks. The following are measures of visibility taken after a period of exposure to weather and traffic.

a. Construct the analysis-of-variance table.

b. Test the hypothesis of equal serviceability for the four paints. Let $\alpha = .05$.

c. Given that paints numbered one and two were white, and that those numbered three and four were yellow, can we conclude that yellow paints have a higher visibility score? Use a t-test, or find a sum of squares for white versus yellow with a degree of freedom as:

$$\frac{(X_{1.} + X_{2.})^2}{n_1 + n_2} + \frac{(X_{3.} + X_{4.})^2}{n_3 + n_4} - \frac{X_{..}^2}{\sum n_i}$$

d. Find a 95% confidence interval for the difference between the visibilities of white and yellow paints.

	Paint			
Location	*1*	*2*	*3*	*4*
1	7.4	9.6	11.3	11.8
2	4.2	9.2	9.2	9.9
3	10.0	9.8	9.9	10.4

22. The following data are field weights in pounds of corn for 26-hill plots. The treatments were different methods of application of a fertilizer: (1)

check (no fertilizer), (2) 300 pounds per acre plowed under, and (3) 300 pounds per acre broadcast.

a. Construct the analysis-of-variance table.

b. Test the hypothesis of no differences among treatments.

c. Test the hypothesis that the mean yield resulting from the two fertilizer treatments is no greater than the mean yield with no fertilizer, i.e., $H_0: 2\tau_1 - \tau_2 - \tau_3 = 0$.

d. Can we conclude there is a difference between the two methods of fertilizer application?

	Block					
Treatment	*1*	*2*	*3*	*4*	*5*	*6*
1	45.1	46.6	51.2	49.3	52.4	44.2
2	56.7	57.3	54.6	55.0	60.1	58.2
3	53.3	55.0	54.7	58.2	55.2	57.2

23. In order to estimate the efficiency of a randomized complete block design relative to a completely randomized design, uniformity data were obtained—that is, all experimental units were treated in the same fashion and a measure of response under identical conditions obtained—with the following results.

109	142	124	90	135	126	107
102	112	123	148	111	120	130
84	89	111	103	123	152	150
84	69	79	115	110	108	110
96	45	100	140	159	75	100
152	125	133	114	132	160	120

a. Obtain an estimate for the variation among the experimental units ignoring rows and columns. This estimates the error variance for a completely randomized design.

b. Construct the analysis of variance using rows as blocks—the sources will be rows—and experimental units within rows. The mean square for units within rows estimates the error variance for a randomized complete block design.

c. Estimate the gain or loss in efficiency that would result from using the randomized blocks rather than the completely randomized design. Assume there would be either six blocks or six experimental units per treatment.

24. A type of transceiver was used in three different general kinds of service: fixed base, shipboard, and airborne. A record was kept of the number of tube removals for each socket for each equipment. The following data are the average transformed values for ten transceivers in each type of service. A square-root transformation was applied to the original data in an effort to achieve common variance. Analyze and interpret these results.

Socket	Type of service		
number	Fixed base	Shipboard	Airborne
1	3.33	5.61	9.30
2	3.33	4.85	9.57
3	1.87	2.12	5.15
4	2.12	2.55	7.52
5	1.58	.71	2.55
6	1.87	1.58	3.24
7	.71	1.87	2.92
8	1.22	2.55	2.74
9	2.12	.71	5.61
10	2.92	1.87	2.55
11	3.24	1.58	4.74
12	2.12	2.74	2.74
13	3.24	4.74	8.34
14	3.08	2.34	4.85
15	2.74	1.22	3.81

25. To compare the effects of four different oils on gas mileage, four cars were used. The randomization was restricted so that each oil was used once in each car and once in each season. The gas mileages are given below.
   a. Construct the analysis of variance. The sources of variation are: between cars, between seasons, between oils, and error (obtained by subtraction).
   b. Can we conclude that the oils differ in their effect on gas mileage?
   c. Find a 95% confidence interval for the difference between oils A and C.

	Car				Season
Season	I	II	III	IV	totals
Fall	A: 20.06	B: 14.59	C: 19.42	D: 14.93	69.00
Winter	B: 19.31	C: 14.19	D: 19.36	A: 12.96	65.82
Spring	C: 20.75	D: 15.10	A: 19.31	B: 13.73	68.89
Summer	D: 21.53	A: 15.39	B: 20.19	C: 15.80	72.91
Car totals	81.65	59.27	78.28	57.42	276.62
Oil totals	A: 67.72	B: 67.82	C: 70.16	D: 70.92	

26. To compare the efficiencies of four kinds of desk calculators, A, B, C, and D, four operators assisted in an experiment in which four different types of analyses were carried out. The experiment was planned in such a way that each machine was used once by each operator and once for each type of analysis. The design, an example of a *Latin square*, permits the removal of variation among operators and among analyses. Given the following data:
   a. Construct the analysis-of-variance table.
   b. Test the hypothesis that the machines are equally efficient.

	Operator			
Analysis	*1*	*2*	*3*	*4*
1	*B:* 44	*C:* 40	*D:* 30	*A:* 29
2	*C:* 38	*D:* 32	*A:* 26	*B:* 43
3	*D:* 35	*A:* 28	*B:* 41	*C:* 39
4	*A:* 24	*B:* 45	*C:* 39	*D:* 35

27. In order to get information that might help in designing an experiment to compare different methods of roasting turkey rolls, three turkeys were roasted under conditions as nearly identical as possible. A particular muscle was removed from each side of each bird and subjected to an objective measurement of tenderness. Three determinations were made on each muscle. The results are given in the following table.

	Turkey		
Side	*1*	*2*	*3*
1	2.8	3.5	4.5
	2.5	3.2	5.1
	2.3	3.6	4.2
2	1.8	3.5	4.1
	2.2	4.4	3.9
	2.4	4.3	4.3

a. Construct the analysis-of-variance table.
b. Write the expected mean squares, and estimate the variance components.
c. Is the variation among birds significantly greater than that between sides of the same bird? Let $\alpha = .05$.

28. For bacterial counts on meat pies, samples are homogenized with a diluent and, after blending, are usually allowed to sit for a few minutes to permit foam to subside. In a study to determine whether the time after homogenization has any effect on the bacterial count, ten samples were randomly assigned to each of four times, and two counts were made on each sample. The following data are the log counts. (A logarithmic transformation is used to stabilize the variance within groups.)
a. Construct the analysis-of-variance table.
b. Is there any reason to believe that time after blending has an effect on count?
c. What is the variance of a time mean?
d. Estimate the variance component for counts and for samples.

Time after blending (minutes)

Sample	1	2	3	4
1	3.73	3.72	3.59	2.78
	3.72	3.70	3.60	2.79
2	3.65	3.59	3.52	3.00
	3.67	3.59	3.55	3.00
3	3.34	3.78	3.38	3.24
	3.35	3.76	3.37	3.25
4	3.20	3.08	3.36	3.18
	3.20	3.10	3.37	3.20
5	3.76	3.28	3.14	3.11
	3.76	3.28	3.17	3.09
6	3.56	2.91	3.45	3.38
	3.55	2.94	3.44	3.39
7	3.63	3.52	3.04	3.30
	3.65	3.51	3.01	3.32
8	3.35	3.36	2.95	3.69
	3.34	3.35	2.92	3.71
9	3.73	3.58	3.43	3.21
	3.72	3.60	3.42	3.19
10	3.19	3.07	3.25	3.17
	3.20	3.05	3.23	3.17

29. In a lamb-feeding experiment, four lambs were randomly assigned to each of six lots. Three rations containing different percentages of corn were randomly assigned to the lots in such a way that each ration was used to feed two lots. The gains in weight over a three-month period are given below.
   a. Construct the analysis-of-variance table.
   b. Does it appear that there are differences among the mean gains under the three rations? Let $\alpha = .05$.
   c. What is the variance of a ration mean?
   d. Estimate the variance components.

Ration	30% Corn		40% Corn		50% Corn	
Lot	1	2	3	4	5	6
	14	17	19	17	18	12
	18	20	26	23	25	20
	12	16	22	25	20	23
	16	21	25	24	25	29

30. Six plants of a given variety were selected at random. Then one or more leaves were selected at random from each plant, and three determinations for ascorbic acid were made on each leaf. Construct the analysis-of-variance table, showing the partitioning of the degrees of freedom and sum of squares. Write the expected mean squares, and estimate the components of variance for determinations, leaves, and plants.

					Plant		
Leaf	*Det.*	*1*	*2*	*3*	*4*	*5*	*6*
1	1	9.12	15.58	12.98	15.43	10.78	12.83
	2	9.10	15.62	13.03	15.32	10.86	12.87
	3	9.08	15.64	12.94	15.34	10.71	12.79
2	1	8.36		14.23	10.68	8.95	9.46
	2	8.32		14.30	10.79	8.83	9.52
	3	8.29		14.18	10.67	9.00	9.40
3	1	7.31		9.95		7.02	11.63
	2	7.25		10.04		7.15	11.75
	3	7.28		9.98		7.11	11.92
4	1	8.63					13.20
	2	8.58					13.31
	3	8.67					13.27

31. The following data are the yields in grams for samples of oats treated with three different fertilizers. Treatments were randomly assigned within each of six blocks. Three samples of .0001 acre were taken from each plot. Analyze the data by means of the analysis-of-variance table, and:
a. Test the hypothesis of equal treatment effects.
b. Given that treatment A is a check (no fertilizer applied), compare treatments B and C with A by means of t-tests. What do you conclude?
c. Estimate the variance components.
d. Write the model and state all assumptions.

				Block		
Treatment	*1*	*2*	*3*	*4*	*5*	*6*
A	45	30	17	43	32	53
	50	40	57	23	39	46
	39	35	42	11	47	43
B	68	50	51	60	85	83
	40	84	83	64	74	74
	49	74	66	65	87	64
C	53	54	24	57	76	62
	46	63	85	33	48	57
	43	112	88	28	42	59

32. Five paints were tested for barnacle resistance in a randomized complete block design with the hulls of ships serving as blocks. After a period of time at sea, four one-foot-square sample areas were selected at random in each experimental section of each hull and scraped. The weight of barnacles removed from each sample area is given below.
    a. Write the model.
    b. Construct the analysis-of-variance table.
    c. Give the expected mean squares.
    d. Test the hypothesis that the paints are equally effective.
    e. Assuming that paint A is standard, use t-tests to compare each of the other paints with paint A. Which, if any, show a significantly lower encrustation?
    f. Which paint, if any, would you recommend?

| | | Paint | | | |
Ship	A	B	C	D	E
1	62	33	60	42	48
	66	42	53	51	53
	73	39	48	57	59
	65	35	57	50	45
2	89	58	70	68	60
	78	49	62	64	63
	85	47	77	70	58
	73	52	59	73	55
3	108	76	97	95	83
	95	70	89	84	85
	102	69	93	87	97
	97	80	100	91	92

33. For the following analysis of variance and assuming equal numbers at all stages,
    a. Describe the experiment and write the model.
    b. Write the expected mean squares.
    c. Test the hypothesis of equal treatment means. Let $\alpha = .01$.
    d. What is the variance of a treatment mean?
    e. Estimate the variance components.

Source	df	MS
Treatments	5	710
Experimental units within treatments	24	110
Determinations within experimental units	60	20

34. Given the following analysis of variance,
    a. Fill in the expected mean squares, assuming a given set of treatments and equal numbers at all stages.
    b. What is the variance of a treatment mean?
    c. If the mean of the first treatment is 100, find a 95% confidence interval for the true mean of treatment 1.
    d. Estimate all variance components in the expected mean squares.
    e. Test the hypothesis of equal treatment means.

Source of variation	df	MS
Treatments	3	775
Exp. units/treatments	20	175
Samples/exp. units	72	55
Determinations/samples	192	10

35. A study of daily calorie intake of women over age 25 resulted in the following analysis of variance. The areas are rural-farm, rural-nonfarm, and urban. Assume equal numbers at each stage.
   a. Estimate the variance components for individuals, for secondary sampling units, and for primary sampling units.
   b. Test the hypothesis that the variance component for secondary sampling units is zero.
   c. Test the hypothesis that calorie consumption is the same in all areas.

Source	df	Mean square
Areas	2	6,350,000
Primary units/areas	72	317,500
Secondary units/primary units	75	300,000
Individuals/secondary units	600	200,000

36. Given the following analysis of variance,
   a. Describe the experiment and write the model.
   b. Give the expected mean squares.
   c. Find the variance of a treatment mean.
   d. Estimate the variance components for samples within experimental units, and for experimental units.

Source	df	Mean square
Blocks	3	2860
Treatments	8	3340
Error	24	1780
Samples/exp. units	144	280

REFERENCES

12.1 COCHRAN, W. G., and GERTRUDE M. COX. *Experimental Designs*, 2nd edition. Wiley, New York, 1957. Chapters 2, 3, and 4.

12.2 DUNCAN, D. B. "Multiple range and multiple F tests," *Biometrics*, Vol. 11, 1955.

12.3 KEMPTHORNE, OSCAR. *The Design and Analysis of Experiments*. Wiley, New York, 1952. Chapters 6 and 7.

12.4 OSTLE, BERNARD. *Statistics in Research*, 2nd edition. Iowa State University Press, Ames, 1963. Chapters 10, 11, and 12.

12.5 SNEDECOR, GEORGE W., and WILLIAM G. COCHRAN. *Statistical Methods*, 6th edition. Iowa State University Press, Ames, 1967. Chapters 10 and 11.

13

Nonparametric Methods

13.1 INTRODUCTION

Many of the methods we have considered, such as those involving the *t*-test, apply only to normal populations. The need for techniques that apply more broadly has lead to the development of *nonparametric* methods. These do not require that the underlying populations be normal—or indeed that they have any single mathematical form—and some even apply to nonnumerical data. In place of parameters such as means and variances and their estimators, these methods use ranks and other measures of relative magnitude; hence the term "nonparametric."

13.2 THE WILCOXON TEST

The *median* of a continuous population is a number ξ such that an observation X from the population has probability .5 of being less than ξ and probability .5 of being greater than ξ. In symbols,

$$P(X < \xi) = P(X > \xi) = .5 \tag{13.1}$$

The sample quantity corresponding to ξ was considered in Section 3.6. The population is *symmetric* about its median ξ if, for each positive x, the observation X has the same probability of being less than $\xi - x$ as of being greater than $\xi + x$. In symbols,

$$P(X < \xi - x) = P(X > \xi + x) \tag{13.2}$$

Geometrically, this means that the shaded areas in Figure 13.1 are equal for each x, so that the frequency curve looks the same if viewed through a mirror. A normal curve with mean ξ has median ξ and is symmetric about ξ, but a nonnormal curve like the one in the figure can also have this property.

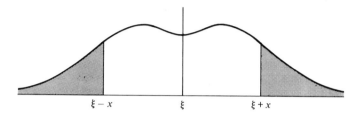

FIGURE 13.1.   *A frequency curve symmetric about its median* ξ

Consider the null hypothesis that the population median is 0 and the population is symmetric about 0, together with the alternative hypothesis that the population median ξ is positive and the population is symmetric about ξ:

$$\begin{cases} H_0: \xi = 0, \text{ symmetric} \\ H_a: \xi > 0, \text{ symmetric} \end{cases} \tag{13.3}$$

If the population is normal, the t-test applies to this problem. If the population may be nonnormal, another test is needed.

Let $X_1, X_2, \ldots, X_n$ be an independent sample from the population. The *Wilcoxon statistic W* is computed in three steps.

1. Arrange the observations $X_1, X_2, \ldots, X_n$ in order of increasing *absolute value*.
2. Write down the numbers $1, 2, \ldots, n$ in order, each with the algebraic sign of the observation in the corresponding position in the arrangement of step 1.
3. Compute the sum W of these numbers with their appropriate signs.

For example, suppose n is 4 and the observations are $+5.4$, -7.3, -3.8, and $+9.5$. Arranged in order of increasing absolute value, the observations are:

$$-3.8 \qquad +5.4 \qquad -7.3 \qquad +9.5 \tag{13.4}$$

Here $+5.4$ precedes -7.3 because $|+5.4| < |-7.3|$ (even though $+5.4 > -7.3$). The numbers 1, 2, 3, and 4 with the corresponding signs attached are

$$-1 \qquad +2 \qquad -3 \qquad +4 \tag{13.5}$$

The sum W is $-1 + 2 - 3 + 4$, or $+2$. The numbers 1, 2, 3, and 4 are the *ranks* of the quantities 3.8, 5.4, 7.3, and 9.5.

289

In the testing problem (13.3), we reject H_0 in favor of H_a if W is excessively large. If the population were normal, so that the t-test applied, we would compute the sample mean $\bar{X}$ and reject H_0 in case of an excessively large value of $\bar{X}$ (large relative to $s/\sqrt{n}$—compare the t-statistic (8.2) with a μ_0 of 0). The statistic W/n is analogous to the mean $\bar{X}$. For the four observations above, $\bar{X}$ is $(+5.4 - 7.3 - 3.8 + 9.5)/4$, or $+1.2$, and $W/4$ equals .5. These are the centers of gravity for the two dispositions of weights in Figure 13.2. To pass from the array (13.4) to the array (13.5) is in the arithmetic

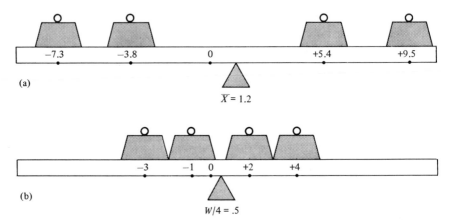

$$\bar{X} = 1.2$$

$$W/4 = .5$$

FIGURE 13.2. $\bar{X}$ and W/n compared

to pass from $\bar{X}$ to $W/4$ and is geometrically to pass from (a) to (b) in the figure. In (a), the center of gravity $\bar{X}$ exceeds 0 because the weights on the positive side overbalance those on the negative side. In (b), the center of gravity $W/4$ still exceeds 0 because $+9.5$ (farthest from 0 in (a)) has moved to $+4$ (farthest from 0 in (b)), -7.3 (next farthest from 0 in (a)) has moved to -3 (next farthest from 0 in (b)), and so on. The weights on the positive side still overbalance the others. Thus W/n is a kind of "nonparametric mean," and it accords with intuition in the testing problem (13.3) to reject H_0 in favor of H_a if W/n is large. Passing from $\bar{X}$ to W/n enables us to dispense with the assumption of normality.

For fixed n the distribution of W is the same for every population satisfying the null hypothesis H_0. There are published tables of this distribution for small values of n (see reference 13.2). In the examples here we shall use the normal approximation, which is accurate for an n of 10 or more. The mean and variance of W are

$$\mu_W = 0 \tag{13.6}$$

and

$$\sigma_W^2 = \frac{n(n + 1)(2n + 1)}{6} \tag{13.7}$$

Thus the standardized variable is W/σ_W. To test at the level α, we reject H_0 if W/σ_W exceeds the corresponding percentage point $t_{\alpha,\infty}$ on the normal curve. This is the Wilcoxon test. The problem and the rejection region are

$$\begin{cases} H_0: \xi = 0, \text{ symmetric} \\ H_a: \xi > 0, \text{ symmetric} \\ R: W/\sigma_W > t_{\alpha,\infty} \end{cases}$$

This testing problem can arise, for example, from paired comparisons, as in Section 9.6. We have n pairs of experimental units and two competing treatments (or a treatment and a nontreatment). Treatment 1 is given to a randomly selected element of pair i, which results in an observation Y_{i1}, and Treatment 2 is given to the other element of pair i, which results in an observation Y_{i2}. Under the null hypothesis that the two treatments have the same effect, the difference $Y_{i1} - Y_{i2}$, which we denote X_i, has median 0 and is symmetric about 0. Without the assumption of normality required for the t-test, we can use the Wilcoxon test.

EXAMPLE 1

In Example 1 of Section 9.6, p. 186, we used the t-test on the null hypothesis that a particular heat treatment has no effect on the number of bacteria in skim milk against the alternative that the treatment tends to reduce this number. Here X_i is the count (log DMC) for sample i before treatment minus the count after treatment. The twelve differences are:

.03　.14　1.17　.15　−.02　−.04　.44　.22　−.01　.13　.19　.70

Arranged in order of increasing absolute value, they are:

−.01　−.02　.03　−.04　.13　.14　.15　.19　.22　.44　.70　1.17

The numbers $1, 2, \ldots, 12$ with algebraic signs in the same pattern are:

−1　−2　+3　−4　+5　+6　+7　+8　+9　+10　+11　+12

The sum W of these comes to $+64$. By the formula (13.7),

$$\sigma_W = \sqrt{\frac{12 \cdot 13 \cdot 25}{6}} = \sqrt{650} = 25.5$$

so the standardized W-value, W/σ_W, is $64/25.5$, or 2.51. The upper 5 percentage point $t_{.05,\infty}$ on the normal curve being 1.645, we reject the null hypothesis of no effect.

The same method works for the opposite alternative

$$\begin{cases} H_0: \xi = 0, \text{ symmetric} \\ H_a: \xi < 0, \text{ symmetric} \\ R: W/\sigma_W < -t_{\alpha,\infty} \end{cases}$$

and for the two-sided alternative

$$\begin{cases} H_0 \colon \xi = 0, \text{ symmetric} \\ H_a \colon \xi \neq 0, \text{ symmetric} \\ R \colon |W/\sigma_W| > t_{\alpha/2,\infty} \end{cases}$$

The median in the null case need not be 0. To test, say, $\xi = 5$ against $\xi > 5$, we subtract 5 from each X_i and proceed as before. Ties (equal observations) can be dealt with by averaging adjacent ranks. If in Example 1 the ordered observations had been $-.01$, $-.02$, $.02$, $-.04$, etc., we would have used ranks 1, 2.5, 2.5, 4, etc. (instead of 1, 2, 3, 4, etc.) and signed ranks -1, -2.5, $+2.5$, -4, etc.

13.3 THE SIGN TEST

The Wilcoxon test cannot be used unless the population is symmetric about its median. In the absence of symmetry, we can use the *sign test* instead. The sign test, being less sensitive than the Wilcoxon test, should be used only if symmetry cannot be assumed.

On the basis of an independent sample $X_1, X_2, \ldots, X_n$, we are to test the null hypothesis that the population median ξ is 0 against the alternative that it exceeds 0:

$$\begin{cases} H_0 \colon \xi = 0 \\ H_a \colon \xi > 0 \end{cases} \tag{13.8}$$

The sign test is simple. We count the number Y of positive values among $X_1, X_2, \ldots, X_n$. Because of the definition (13.1) of the median, the distribution of Y under H_0 is binomial with $p = .5$, while under H_a it is binomial with $p > .5$. Thus we can use the methods of Section 8.3.

EXAMPLE 1

Twenty patients on a certain diet made these weight gains (in pounds):

$+7$	-6	$+3$	$+1$	$+6$	$+4$	$+9$	-5	$+9$	-7
-3	$+7$	-9	$+8$	$+6$	-4	$+4$	$+9$	-6	$+1$

We are to test at the 5% level the null hypothesis that the median weight gain is 0 against the alternative that it is positive. There are thirteen positive observations among the twenty: $Y = 13$. The mean and standard deviation of Y are

$$n \times .5 = 10$$

and

$$\sqrt{n \times .5 \times .5} = \sqrt{5} = 2.24$$

so the standardized variable is $(Y - 10)/2.24$, which has the value 1.34. The upper 5 percentage point $t_{.05,\infty}$ is 1.645, so the data favor the null hypothesis.

By an adaptation of the methods of Section 8.3, it is possible to test against a two-sided alternative ($\xi \neq 0$) as well. To test for a median of ξ_0 (not necessarily 0), we subtract ξ_0 from each X_i and then carry through the test as before.

13.4 THE RANK SUM TEST

The rank sum test stands to the Wilcoxon test as the two-sample t-test of Section 9.4 stands to the one-sample t-test of Section 8.2. The rank sum test can be used to check whether two populations have the same median, and it does not require the assumption of normality.

Let $X_{11}, X_{12}, \ldots, X_{1n_1}$ be a sample of size n_1 from Population 1, and let $X_{21}, X_{22}, \ldots, X_{2n_2}$ be a sample of size n_2 from Population 2. Let H_0 be the null hypothesis that the two populations are the same, and let H_a be the hypothesis that the frequency curve for Population 2 has the same shape as the curve for Population 1 but is shifted to the right as shown in Figure 13.3.

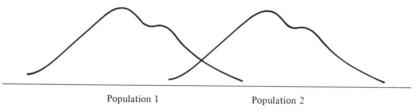

Population 1   Population 2

FIGURE 13.3.   *The alternative hypothesis H_a*

The statistic for this problem, the *rank sum*, is computed in four steps.

1. Combine the two samples into one, underlining the observations in the second sample to keep track of them.

2. Arrange the observations in the combined sample in order of increasing size, carrying along the lines under the observations in the second sample.

3. Write down the numbers $1, 2, \ldots, n_1 + n_2$ in order, underlining those for which the corresponding position in the arrangement of step 2 is occupied by an element of the second sample (that is, by an underlined number).

4. From the average of the underlined numbers subtract the average of the others. Call the difference V.

For example, suppose n_1 is 3, the observations being 3.1, -2.4, and 0.6; and suppose n_2 is 2, the observations being 7.7 and 2.8. The combined sample is:

$$3.1 \qquad -2.4 \qquad 0.6 \qquad \underline{7.7} \qquad \underline{2.8}$$

293

Arranged in increasing order, this is:

$$-2.4 \qquad 0.6 \qquad \underline{2.8} \qquad 3.1 \qquad \underline{7.7} \qquad\qquad \textbf{(13.9)}$$

The numbers 1, 2, 3, 4, and 5 ($n_1 + n_2 = 5$) with underlineations in the same pattern are:

$$1 \qquad 2 \qquad \underline{3} \qquad 4 \qquad \underline{5} \qquad\qquad \textbf{(13.10)}$$

The underlined numbers average to $(3 + 5)/2$, or 4, the others to $(1 + 2 + 4)/3$, or 2.33. The difference V of these averages is $4 - 2.33$, or 1.66.

If we were to compute the two-sample t-statistic (see formula (9.12) on p. 182), we would first form the average $\bar{X}_2$ of the underlined numbers in (13.9), then the average $\bar{X}_1$ of the others, and then the difference $\bar{X}_2 - \bar{X}_1$ (which we would then normalize). To compute V, we apply the same procedure to (13.10). Although the numbers in (13.10) are different from those in (13.9), they come in the same order. Therefore, in the same way as does a large value of $\bar{X}_2 - \bar{X}_1$, a large value of V indicates that observations from Population 2 tend to exceed those of Population 1—indicates, that is, that the data in the pair of samples favor H_a over H_0. The statistic V can be thought of as a "nonparametric difference of means."

For each n_1 and n_2, the distribution of V under H_0 has the desirable property that it does not depend on the shape of the frequency curve common to the two populations. Tables are available for small values of n_1 and n_2 (see reference 13.2). In the examples here, the normal approximation to this distribution can be used. The mean and variance of V are

$$\mu_V = 0 \qquad\qquad \textbf{(13.11)}$$

and

$$\sigma_V^2 = \frac{(n_1 + n_2)^2(n_1 + n_2 + 1)}{12 n_1 n_2} \qquad\qquad \textbf{(13.12)}$$

We reject H_0 in favor of H_a if V/σ_V exceeds $t_{\alpha,\infty}$.

EXAMPLE 1

Healthy and infected plants of a common strain achieved these heights (in inches):

Infected	40.1	37.5	46.3	44.2	35.1	48.2	41.7	37.3	50.3	43.9
Healthy	49.4	41.3	45.8	39.7	44.4	43.1	48.8	47.5		

We are to test at the 5% level the null hypothesis of no difference in heights against the alternative that healthy plants tend to be taller, and we are to do this without assuming normality. Here n_1 is 10 and n_2 is 8. The two samples merged into one and ordered are:

35.1	37.3	37.5	39.7	40.1	41.3	41.7	43.1	43.9
44.2	44.4	45.8	46.3	47.5	48.2	48.8	49.4	50.3

The numbers $1, 2, \ldots, 18$ $(n_1 + n_2 = 18)$ underlined in the same pattern are:

1 2 3 <u>4</u> 5 <u>6</u> 7 <u>8</u> 9 10 <u>11</u> <u>12</u> 13 <u>14</u> 15 <u>16</u> <u>17</u> 18

The ranks for the second sample (the underlined numbers) average to 88/8, or 11.0, and the ranks for the first sample (the remaining numbers) average to 83/10, or 8.3. The difference V is $11.0 - 8.3$, or 2.7. The standard deviation according to the formula (13.12) is

$$\sigma_V = \sqrt{\frac{18^2 \times 19}{12 \times 10 \times 8}} = 2.54$$

Thus the standardized statistic V/σ_V has the value 2.7/2.54, or 1.07. Since this is less than 1.645, the upper 5% point for the normal curve, the data favor the null hypothesis.

As in Section 13.2, ties are dealt with by averaging adjacent ranks. If in Example 1 the observation 37.5 were 39.7 instead, creating a tie for third from the bottom, the ranks 3 and 4 would each be replaced by 3.5.

Paired comparisons, as in Example 1 of Section 13.2, are preferable to the group method of this section if variation among pairs exceeds variation between units within the pairs, but not otherwise. The situation is just as in the parametric case; see Section 9.7.

13.5 ASSOCIATION

Suppose four students, A, B, C, and D, are ranked in two subjects, mathematics and history, with these results:

	Student			
	A	B	C	D
Mathematics	4	2	3	1
History	3	1	4	2

That is to say, in mathematics, student D is worst (rank 1), B is next worst (rank 2), C next (rank 3), and A is best (rank 4); while in history the ranking (worst to best) is B, D, A, C. To check whether there is a connection between performance in the two subjects, we want a measure of the extent to which these two rankings agree.

We can compute such a measure as follows: For each of the six possible pairs of students we check whether the ranks in the two subjects go in the same direction or in opposite directions and score a $+1$ or a -1 accordingly. Since student A did better than student B both in mathematics and in history (the ranks go in the same direction), the score for the pair AB is $+1$. Since A did better than C in mathematics but worse in history (the ranks go in opposite directions), the score for the pair AC is -1. The six pairs and the corresponding scores are:

Pair	AB	AC	AD	BC	BD	CD
Score	$+1$	-1	$+1$	$+1$	-1	$+1$

The sum of the six scores is $+2$. This sum provides a *measure of association* for the two rankings. That it is positive in this case indicates that high standing in mathematics tends to go with high standing in history. (The sum would be the same if the students were ranked best to worst instead of worst to best.)

For the rankings

	Student			
	A	B	C	D
Mathematics	1	2	3	4
History	1	2	3	4

the score is $+6$, there being a $+1$ for each of the six pairs of students. This, the highest possible value of the measure, indicates perfect agreement between the two rankings. For the rankings

	Student			
	A	B	C	D
Mathematics	1	2	3	4
History	4	3	2	1

the score is -6, there being a -1 for each pair. This, the lowest possible value of the measure, indicates perfect disagreement. The measure always lies between $+6$ and -6. If we divide it by 6, the new measure lies between $+1$ (the value for perfect agreement) and -1 (the value for perfect disagreement). For our original set of rankings it is $+2/6$, or $+.33$. This is Kendall's *rank correlation coefficient*, denoted by τ.

In the general case, we have n subjects (four students in the example) ranked in two ways (by standing in two subjects in the example). Thus we have two permutations of the numbers $1, 2, \ldots, n$. There are $\binom{n}{2}$ pairs of subjects, and for each pair we score $+1$ or -1 according as the two rankings go in the same or opposite directions. We then compute τ, the sum of these scores divided by $\binom{n}{2}$. A positive τ indicates *positive association*, a tendency for the rankings to agree, with a τ of $+1$ for perfect agreement. A negative τ indicates *negative association*, a tendency for the rankings to disagree, with a τ of -1 for complete disagreement. A τ of 0 indicates that the two rankings are independent of one another.

EXAMPLE 1

Ten students are tested before a course of study and again afterward. Their ranks in the tests are:

	\multicolumn{10}{c}{Student}

	A	B	C	D	E	F	G	H	I	J
Test 1	8	9	4	1	5	10	2	3	7	6
Test 2	9	1	8	3	4	2	10	5	6	7

The computation of τ is facilitated by rearranging the students so the ranks for the first test increase:

	\multicolumn{10}{c}{Student}

	D	G	H	C	E	J	I	A	B	F
Test 1	1	2	3	4	5	6	7	8	9	10
Test 2	3	10	5	8	4	7	6	9	1	2

(The identifications D, G, H, etc., are irrelevant to the computation.) The number of pairs is $\binom{10}{2}$, or 45. For each pair of numbers in the bottom row, we score $+1$ or -1 according as the right element of the pair does or does not exceed the left element, and we sum the scores. To put it another way, for each entry in the bottom row, we compute the number of entries to the right of it that are larger minus the number of entries to the right of it that are smaller, and we add up these differences. Here the sum is -9, so that τ is $-9/45$, or $-.2$.

As usual, the question arises whether a τ far removed from 0 is really significant—whether it may not be an accident of sampling. If the two rankings are independent in the sense that each is merely a random permutation of the other, then τ has mean 0 and variance

$$\sigma_\tau^2 = \frac{2(2n + 5)}{9n(n - 1)}$$

If n is 10 or more, τ has approximately a normal distribution.

In Example 1, n is 10, so that

$$\sigma_\tau = \sqrt{\frac{2 \times 25}{9 \times 10 \times 9}} = .25$$

The standardized statistic τ/σ_τ is $-.2/.25$, or $-.8$. This is not significant even at the 10% level ($-t_{.1,\infty}$ is -1.282).

PROBLEMS

1. Assume that the following measurements come from a population symmetric about its median ξ.

-12.6	-20.5	8.1	-17.3	-21.2	-29.4	5.5	-25.3
15.9	.3	-11.7	-9.3	-28.8	2.7	19.2	-27.1

   Test $H_0: \xi = 0$ against $H_a: \xi < 0$ at the 2.5% level.

2. Do part **a** of problem 23, Chapter 9, by the Wilcoxon test.

3. Use the sign test to test at the 5% level whether the following measurements come from a population with median 10.

13.6	8.0	15.8	12.2	3.5	17.3	9.5	11.4	2.8	10.7
7.1	12.7	13.9	11.4	7.5	16.3	13.2	17.0	12.1	6.3

4. Do problem 1 without the assumption of symmetry.

5. Use the rank sum test to check whether the following two samples come from the same population.

Sample 1	120	136	107	109	129	117	115	110	124
Sample 2	131	144	146	111	103	122	121	139	130
	133	132	135	128					

6. Do problem 17, Chapter 9, by the rank sum test.

7. Do problem 19, Chapter 9, by the rank sum test.

8. Ten children given two reading tests ranked as follows:

   Child

	A	B	C	D	E	F	G	H	I	J
Test 1	5	6	3	9	4	8	1	7	10	2
Test 2	3	4	1	8	5	10	6	7	9	2

   Compute the rank correlation coefficient. Is it significantly greater than 0 at the 2.5% level?

9. For the data in problem 21, Chapter 9, rank the ten older brothers and the ten younger brothers. Compute τ. Is it significant?

10. Rank the data in problem 27, Chapter 11, and compute τ. Is it significant?

REFERENCES

13.1 HOGG, ROBERT V., and ALLEN T. CRAIG. *Introduction to Mathematical Statistics*, 3rd edition. Macmillan, New York, 1970. Chapter 11.

13.2 KRAFT, CHARLES H., and CONSTANCE VAN EEDEN. *A Nonparametric Introduction to Statistics*. Macmillan, New York, 1968.

13.3 NOETHER, GOTTFRIED E. *Elements of Nonparametric Statistics*. John Wiley & Sons, New York, 1967.

Answers to Odd-numbered Problems

CHAPTER 2

1. **a.** 6 **b.** 9 **c.** 10 **d.** 12
3. **a.** 24.5, 28.5, 32.5, 36.5, 40.5 **b.** 26.5, 30.5, 34.5, 38.5
9. 6, 14, 18, 12
11. **a.** 3.00% **b.** .67 **c.** limits: 0, 1, 2, ..., 7; boundaries: $-.5, .5, 1.5, ..., 7.5$

CHAPTER 3

1. **a.** $X_1^3 f_1 + X_2^3 f_2 + X_3^3 f_3 + X_4^3 f_4 + X_5^3 f_5$
   c. $-Y_2^3 + Y_3^4 - Y_4^5 + Y_5^6$
   e. $Y_1^2 + Y_2^2 + Y_3^2 - 3$
3. **a.** 36 **c.** 1296 **e.** 2 **g.** 32

7.

	a	b	c	d	e	f
i	8	9	—	11	20	4.47
iii	8	8	4, 8, 10	12	16	4
v	0	0	$-4, 0, 2$	12	16	4
vii	14	15	—	22	64	8

9. **a.** .02129 **b.** .00003053 **c.** .0174 **d.** .005526
11. $\bar{X} = 2.53$, $m = 2$, $M = 1$, $s^2 = 4.8898$, $s = 2.21$
13. $\bar{X} = 64.4$, $m = 65.55$
15. 20.43

17. a. 11, 10   **b.** 18, 90   **c.** 23, 90
19. $\bar{X} = 16, s^2 = 1.6$
21. a. $\bar{X} = 103, s^2 = 36, s = 6$ **c.** $\bar{X} = 6879, s^2 = 4, s = 2$
23. $\bar{X} = 24.5, s^2 = 36, s = 6$
25. $\bar{U} = 1.9, s_U^2 = 24.7667, s_U = 4.98$
     $\bar{X} = 2.4819 \times 10^{-6}, s_X^2 = 2.477 \times 10^{-17}, s_X = 4.98 \times 10^{-9}$

27. Increased because $\dfrac{2.60}{2.54} = 1.024 > \dfrac{108.1}{106.7} = 1.013$

29. 1960: 100.0;   1965: 103.2;   1970: 105.0

CHAPTER 4

1. 8, 3, 4
3. 1/12, 1/4
5. 60
7. 725, 760
9. a. 120   **b.** 216   **c.** 60
11. 120
13. 635, 013, 559, 600
15. a. 100   **b.** 210   **c.** 205   **d.** 200
17. a. 123,552   **b.** 3744   **c.** 40   **d.** 624
19. 108, 12
21. a. 1/2   **b.** 1/2   **c.** 1/4   **d.** 3/4
23. .48, .08, .92
25. 1/13
27. 3/29
29. a. 1/221   **b.** 4/17   **c.** 1/17   **d.** 13/17   **e.** 25/51
31. a. .35   **b.** .15   **c.** .72   **d.** .35
33. 1/32, 1/32, 1/16
35. a. .7   **b.** .3   **c.** .1   **d.** .9   **e.** .2   **f.** .6   **g.** 1/7   **h.** 2/3
37. .00364
39. a. 1/7   **b.** 2/7   **c.** 8/35   **d.** 4/35
41. a. .423   **b.** .02113   **c.** .00392   **d.** .001965
43. .0590
45. a. 1/4   **b.** 11/16   **c.** 15/16
47. a. 1/256   **b.** 28/256   **c.** 255/256
49. a. .729   **b.** .972
51. 1/8, 1/4, 5/16, 5/16
53. 9/16, 7/16

CHAPTER 5

1. a. .50   **b.** .25   **c.** .50   **d.** .10
3. a. 4   **b.** .25   **c.** .50   **d.** .50   **e.** 1.6
5. $\mu = 2, \sigma^2 = 1$

7. b.

k	0	1	2	3
$P(X = k)$	$\frac{4}{35}$	$\frac{18}{35}$	$\frac{12}{35}$	$\frac{1}{35}$

    c. 9/7
9. **a.** 1/8 **b.** 15/16 **c.** 1/8
11. **a.** .34134 **b.** .15866 **c.** .68268 **d.** .84134
13. **a.** .97500 **b.** .04181 **c.** .27417 **d.** .54107
15. **a.** 1.96 **b.** -1.90 **c.** 1.96
17. **a.** .93319 **b.** .00621 **c.** .67307 **d.** .26702
19. **a.** .02275 **b.** .02784
21. 1.96
23. 71
25. **a.** .95254 **b.** .07966 **c.** .38292
27. **a.** 40/243 **b.** 11/243 **c.** 32/243 **d.** 211/243
29. **a.** .2916 **b.** .6561 **c.** .3439
31. .00009
33. **a.** .7554 **b.** .0076
35. .11
37. **a.** .135 **b.** .270 **c.** .595
39. .217, .699
41. .368, .368, .184, .061

CHAPTER 6

1. $E(\bar{X}) = 10$, $\text{Var}(\bar{X}) = .16$
3. 9992, 10,008
5. .06681, .00135, .97556

CHAPTER 7

1. **a.** $\bar{X} = 4$, $s^2 = 36$, $s = 6$, $s/\sqrt{n} = 2$
    c. $\bar{X} = 50$, $s^2 = 4$, $s = 2$, $s/\sqrt{n} = 2/3$
    e. $\bar{X} = 20$, $s^2 = 16$, $s = 4$, $s/\sqrt{n} = 1$
3. **a.** $f = .20$, $\quad nf(1 - f) = 4$, $\quad \sqrt{nf(1 - f)} = 2$, $\quad f(1 - f)/n = .0064$,
    $\sqrt{f(1 - f)/n} = .08$
    c. $f = .36$, $nf(1 - f) = 92.16$, $\sqrt{nf(1 - f)} = 9.6$, $f(1 - f)/n = .000576$,
    $\sqrt{f(1 - f)/n} = .024$
5. **a.** 18.04, 21.96 **b.** 46.848, 57.152 **c.** 113.42, 126.58
7. **a.** 2.771 **b.** 2.145 **c.** 1.684
9. **a.** $-.612$, 8.612 **c.** 48.463, 51.537 **e.** 17.869, 22.131
11. 2.99, 3.41
13. 9.438, 9.562
15. 0.8, 7.2
17. 5885.6, 5899.4

19. .01561, .02697
21. 29.66, 34.34
23. 37.8, 42.2
25. 21.8, 23.9
27. a. .35, .93 b. .00, .07 c. .15, .32 d. .54, .73 e. .54, .66 f. .04, .07
29. a. .53, .84 b. .03, .21 c. .46, .54 d. .14, .28
31. 26%, 32%
33. .06, .14
35. .19, .31
37. 14
39. 96
41. 2401

CHAPTER 8

1. a. 1/3 b. 1/2
3. 23/94
5. a. $t = 13.33$; $t_{.025, 24} = 2.064$; reject H_0
   b. $t = -2.5$; $-t_{.01, 24} = -2.492$; reject H_0
   c. $t = 2.3$; $t_{.025, 8} = 2.306$; accept H_0
7. $t = 2.5$; $t_{.01, 11} = 2.718$; accept $H_0: \mu \leq 2.0$
9. $z = 4$; $t_{.05, \infty} = 1.645$; reject $H_0: \mu = 60$
11. $t = 3$; $t_{.01, 24} = 2.492$; reject $H_0: \mu \leq 27$
13. $t = -2.5$; $-t_{.05, 8} = -1.860$; reject $H_0: \mu \geq 1600$
15. $t = -2.174$; $-t_{.025, 11} = -2.201$; accept $H_0: \mu \geq 150$
17. $t = 4.248$; $t_{.05, 9} = 1.833$; reject $H_0: \mu \leq 6.00$
19. $t = 1.597$; $t_{.005, 11} = 3.106$; accept $H_0: \mu = 180$
21. $z = -2.333$; $-t_{.025, \infty} = -1.96$; reject $H_0: p \geq .9$
23. $z = 3.000$; $t_{.005, \infty} = 2.576$; reject $H_0: p = .5$

CHAPTER 9

1. a. $\bar{X}_1 = 150$, $\bar{X}_2 - \bar{X}_1 = -30$, $s^2 = 550$, $s_{\bar{X}_1}^2, s_d^2 = 100$
   b. 135.25, 164.75; -50.86, -9.14
3. 1745, 2755
5. -2105, 11605. No. It contains zero.
7. -4.69, 36.69; 76, 116; 65, 95
9. $t = 2.000$, $t_{.05, 25} = 1.708$, reject $H_0: \delta \leq 0$
11. $t = -2.5$, $-t_{.05, 23} = -1.714$, reject $H_0: \delta \geq 0$
13. $t = -2.0$, $-t_{.025, 22} = -2.074$, accept $H_0: \delta \geq 5$
15. $t = 2.7$, $t_{.01, 23} = 2.500$, reject $H_0: \mu_2 = 54.2$
17. $t = .582$, $t_{.025, 14} = 2.145$, accept $H_0: \mu_A = \mu_B$
19. $t = 2.22$, $t_{.025, 30} = 2.042$, reject $H_0: \delta = 0$
21. $t = 1.50$. $t_{.05, 9} = 1.833$, accept $H_0: \delta \leq 0$
23. a. $t = 2.00$, $t_{.05, 8} = 1.860$, reject $H_0: \mu_A \leq \mu_B$
   b. -1.792, 9.792

25. **a.** $t = 1.82$, $t_{.025, 13} = 2.160$, accept $H_0: \mu_1 = \mu_2$
  b. $-.234, .952$
27. **a.** $.28, .46, .40$ **b.** $.057$ **c.** $.068, .360$ **d.** $z = 3.00$, $t_{.005, \infty} = 2.576$, reject
  $H_0: p_1 = p_2$
29. **a.** $.003, .197$ **b.** $z = 2.74$, $t_{.05, \infty} = 1.645$, reject $H_0: p_1 = p_2$
31. $z = 2.232$, $t_{.025, \infty} = 1.96$, reject $H_0: p_m \leq p_f$
33. $z = -1.366$, $-t_{.05, \infty} = -1.645$, accept $H_0: p_1 \geq p_2$

CHAPTER 10

1. $\chi^2 = 6.84$, $\chi^2_{.05, 4} = 9.49$, accept H_0
3. **a.** $.28, .32, .40$ **b.** $\chi^2 = 6.72$, $\chi^2_{.05, 2} = 5.99$, reject H_0 **c.** $\chi^2 = 3.84$,
  $\chi^2_{.01, 1} = 6.63$, accept H_0
5. $\chi^2 = 34.28$, $\chi^2_{.01, 10} = 23.21$, reject H_0: fair dice
7. $\chi^2 = .96$, $\chi^2_{.05, 1} = 3.84$, accept H_0
9. $\chi^2 = 3.01$, $\chi^2_{.05, 2} = 5.99$, accept H_0
11. $\chi^2 = 3.84$, $\chi^2_{.05, 1} = 3.84$, reject $H_0: p = .75$
13. $\chi^2 = 5.95$, $\chi^2_{.05, 4} = 9.49$, accept H_0: data are Poisson
15. $\chi^2 = 4.03$, $\chi^2_{.05, 7} = 14.07$, accept H_0
17. $\chi^2 = 2.49$, $\chi^2_{.05, 3} = 7.81$, accept H_0
19. $\chi^2 = 5.31$, $\chi^2_{.05, 5} = 11.07$, accept H_0
21. $\chi^2 = .9$, $\chi^2_{.05, 3} = 7.81$, accept H_0
23. $\chi^2 = 1.40$, $\chi^2_{.05, 2} = 5.99$, accept hypothesis of independence
25. $\chi^2 = 3.24$, $\chi^2_{.05, 1} = 3.84$, accept $H_0: p_1 = p_2$
27. $\chi^2 = 14.47$, $\chi^2_{.01, 4} = 13.28$, reject independence
29. $\chi^2 = 8.91$, $\chi^2_{.05, 2} = 5.99$, reject H_0
31. $\chi^2 = 4.67$, $\chi^2_{.05, 2} = 5.99$, accept hypothesis of no interaction

CHAPTER 11

1. **a.** $\hat{Y} = .2 + .8X$ **b.** 4.2
3. **a.** $\hat{Y} = 2X$ **b.** 16
5. $\hat{Y} = 4X - 58$
7. **a.** $\hat{Y} = 2.5 - 3X$ **b.** 2.5
  c. $t = -6.0$, $t_{.025, 28} = 2.048$, reject $H_0: B = 0$
9. **a.** $\hat{Y} = 2.9 - .3X$ **b.** $s^2 = 4$, $s_b^2 = .01$, $s_a^2 = .25$ **c.** $t = -3.0$, $t_{.005, 23} =$
  2.807, reject $H_0: B = 0$ **d.** $1.87, 3.93$
11. $144, 256, 10.24$
13. $t = 2.70$, $t_{.005, 15} = 2.947$, accept $H_0: B = 1$
15. $-6.29, 2.29$
17. **a.** $\hat{Y} = 4 + 4X$ **b.** 28 **c.** $20.92, 35.08$ **d.** $8.57, 47.43$
19. **b.** $\$10,640$
21. **a.** $\hat{Y} = -149.70 + .077X$ **b.** $.068, .086$ **c.** 99%
23. **a.** $\hat{Y} = 19.89 + .822X$ **b.** $t = -2.55$, $t_{.025, 18} = 2.101$, reject $H_0: B = 1$
  c. 88.5% **d.** 24.0 **e.** $23.97, 24.03$
25. **c.** $\hat{Y} = 9.92 + .148X$ **e.** 5.949 **g.** $s^2 = .3305$, $s_b^2 = .000225$, $s_b = .015$
  h. $.116, .179$ **i.** $t = 4.69$, $t_{.025, 18} = 2.101$, reject $H_0: B = 0$ **j.** $\hat{Y}_{X=50} =$
  17.3, $s^2_{\hat{Y}} = .0262$, $s_{\hat{Y}} = .162$ **k.** $18.4, 19.2$

27. **a.** $\hat{Y} = 42.26 - 3.89X$ **b.** $-4.93, -2.85$ **c.** $32.42, 36.54$ **d.** $r^2 = .91$
29. **a.** $r = .8$; $t = 4$, $t_{.025,9} = 2.262$, reject $H_0: \rho = 0$ **b.** $r = .6$; $t = 3$, $t_{.025,16} = 2.120$, reject $H_0: \rho = 0$
31. **a.** $r = -.6$; $t = 3$, $t_{.025,16} = 2.120$, reject $H_0: \rho = 0$ **b.** $r = .8$; $t = 4$, $t_{.025,9} = 2.262$, reject $H_0: \rho = 0$
33. $r = .70$; $t = 3.398$, $t_{.005,12} = 3.055$, reject $H_0: \rho = 0$
35. **a.** $.16, .74$ **b.** $-.84, -.62$ **c.** $.77, .89$
37. $t = -7.94$, $t_{.005,\infty} = 2.576$, reject $H_0: \rho = .9$
39. $t = 1.06$, $t_{.005,\infty} = 2.576$, accept $H_0: \rho = .5$

CHAPTER 12

1.

Source	df	SS	MS	EMS
Between groups	3	120	40.0	$\sigma^2 + 3\kappa_G^2$
Within groups	8	76	9.5	σ^2
Totals	11	196		

d. Means: 18, 12, 20, 14; $s_{\bar{X}_i}^2 = 3.17$
f. $F = 4.21$, $F_{.05,3,8} = 4.07$, reject H_0

3. **a.**

Source	df	SS	MS	EMS
Treatment	5	200	40	$\sigma^2 + 5\kappa_T^2$
Error	24	96	4	σ^2
Totals	29	296		

b. $F = 10$, $F_{.05,5,24} = 3.90$, reject
c. $s_{\bar{X}_i}^2 = .8$

5. **a.**

Source	df	SS	MS
Materials	2	320	160
Error	27	1080	40
Totals	29	1400	

b. $F = 4$, $F_{.05,2,27} = 3.35$, reject H_0
c. $227.9, 236.1$

7.

Source	df	SS	MS
Treatments	4	1800	450
Error	45	6750	150
Totals	49	8550	

$F = 3$, $F_{.05,4,45} = 2.56$, reject H_0

9. a.

Source	df	SS	MS	EMS
Plates	3	36.26	12.09	$\sigma^2 + 5\kappa_P^2$
Runs/plates	16	5.79	.36	σ^2
Totals	19	42.05		

b. 3.92, 7.34, 4.64, 6.30; .268

c. $F = 33.58$, $F_{.025, 3, 16} = 4.08$, reject H_0

d. 3.23, 4.61; 6.65, 8.03; 3.95, 5.33; 5.61, 6.99

11. $t = 9.46$, $t_{.005, 16} = 2.921$, reject $H_0: \mu_2 - \mu_1 + \mu_4 - \mu_3 = 0$; $t = -.596$, $t_{.005, 16} = 2.921$, accept $H_0: \mu_4 - \mu_2 + \mu_3 - \mu_1 = 0$

13. a.

Source	df	SS	MS
Groups	3	216	72.0
Error	11	146	13.3
Totals	14	362	

b.

Group	1	2	3	4
Mean	9	13	20	15
$s_{\bar{X}_i}$	1.82	2.10	2.10	1.63

c. 2.3, 19.7

d. $F = 5.41$, $F_{.05, 3, 11} = 3.59$, reject H_0

15. a.

Source	df	SS	MS
Treatments	2	100	50
Error	22	220	10
Totals	24	320	

c. $F = 5$, $F_{.05, 2, 22} = 3.44$, reject H_0

17. a.

Source	df	SS	MS
Groups	2	595	297
Error	697	69,700	100
Totals	699	70,295	

b. $F = 2.97$, $F_{.01, 2, \infty} = 4.61$, accept H_0

c. 10.52; 9.78, 11.26

19.

Source	df	SS	MS	EMS
Blocks	1	54	54	$\sigma^2 + 3\kappa_B^2$
Treatments	2	16	8	$\sigma^2 + 2\kappa_T^2$
Error	2	12	6	σ^2
Totals	5	82		

21. a.

Source	df	SS	MS
Locations	2	9.63	4.82
Paints	3	21.26	7.09
Error	6	11.66	1.94
Totals	11	42.55	

b. $F = 3.65$, $F_{.05,3,6} = 4.76$, accept H_0
c. Sum of squares $= 12.61$, $F = 6.5$, $F_{.05,1,6} = 5.99$, reject H_0
d. .08, 4.02

23. a. For CR design $s^2 = 648.3$

b.

Source	df	SS	MS
Blocks	5	6378	
Error	36	20,203	561.2
Totals	41	26,581	

c. Rel. eff. RCB to CR $= 115.5\%$. RCB 15.5% more efficient

25. a.

Source	df	SS	MS
Cars	3	118.7036	39.5679
Seasons	3	6.3292	2.1097
Oils	3	1.9917	.6639
Error	6	.5085	.0848
Total	15		

b. $F = 7.83$, $F_{.025,3,6} = 6.599$; yes, reject H_0
c. 1.94, 2.94

27. a.

Source	df	SS	MS	EMS
Turkeys	2	12.8677	6.4338	$\sigma_D^2 + 3\sigma_H^2 + 6\sigma_T^2$
Sides/turkeys	3	1.2167	.4056	$\sigma_D^2 + 3\sigma_H^2$
Det./sides	12	1.3867	.1156	σ_D^2
Totals	17	15.4711		

b. $s_D^2 = .1156$, $s_H^2 = .0967$, $s_T^2 = 1.0047$
c. $F = 15.86$, $F_{.05,2,3} = 9.55$; yes, reject H_0: $\sigma_T^2 = 0$

29. **a.**

Source	df	SS	MS
Rations	2	155.583	77.792
Lots/rations	3	111.625	37.208
Animals/lots	18	209.750	11.658
Totals	23	476.958	

b. $F = 2.09$, $F_{.05, 2, 3} = 9.55$; no, accept H_0
c. 1.457
d. $s_A^2 = 11.658$, $s_L^2 = 6.388$, $s_R^2 = 5.073$

31.

Source	df	SS	MS
Blocks	5	2,435.3	487.06
Treatments	2	7,973.4	3986.70
Error	10	2,538.8	253.88
Samples/exp. units	36	9,202.0	255.61
Totals	53	22,149.5	

a. $F = 15.70$, $F_{.01, 2, 10} = 7.56$, reject H_0
b. $t = 5.54$, $t_{.005, 10} = 3.169$, reject $H_0: \tau_B = \tau_A$; $t = 3.54$, $t_{.005, 10} = 3.169$, reject $H_0: \tau_C = \tau_A$
c. $s_{Samples}^2 = 255.61$, $s_E^2 = 0$, $s_T^2 = 207.38$
33. **a.** $X_{ijk} = \mu + \tau_i + e_{ij} + \eta_{ijk}$; $i = 1, 2, \ldots, 6; j = 1, 2, \ldots, 5; k = 1, 2, 3$
b. σ_D^2, $\sigma_D^2 + 3\sigma_E^2$, $\sigma_D^2 + 3\sigma_E^2 + 15\kappa_T^2$
c. $F = 6.45$, $F_{.01, 5, 24} = 3.895$, reject H_0
d. 7.33
e. $s_D^2 = 20$, $s_E^2 = 30$, $\kappa_T^2 = 40$
35. **a.** $s_{Ind.}^2 = 200,000$, $s_{S.U.}^2 = 20,000$, $s_{P.U.}^2 = 1750$
b. $F = 1.5$, $F_{.05, 75, 600} < 1.4$, reject $H_0: \sigma_{S.U.}^2 = 0$
c. $F = 20.0$, $F_{.01, 2, 72} < 4.98$, reject $H_0: \kappa_A^2 = 0$

CHAPTER 13

1. $W/\sigma_W = -2.3$, $-t_{.025, \infty} = -1.96$, reject H_0
3. $(Y - 10)/\sqrt{5} = 1.34$, accept H_0
5. $V/\sigma_V = 2.06$, $t_{.025, \infty} = 1.96$, with a two-sided alternative reject H_0 at the 5% level
7. $V/\sigma_V = 2.11$, $t_{.025, \infty} = 1.96$, reject H_0

9.

	Pair									
	1	*2*	*3*	*4*	*5*	*6*	*7*	*8*	*9*	*10*
Older	8	7	3	10	2	5	1	6	9	4
Younger	7	8	2	9	4	5	1	6	10	3

$\tau = .78$, $\tau/\sigma_\tau = 3.12$

Appendix

Thanks are due the late Professor Sir Ronald Fisher, Cambridge, Dr. Frank Yates, Rothamsted, and Messrs. Oliver and Boyd Ltd., Edinburgh, for permission to reprint Table III from their book *Statistical Tables for Biological, Agricultural, and Medical Research*; Professor George W. Snedecor and the Iowa State University Press for permission to reproduce Table IV; Professor George W. Snedecor for permission to reproduce Table VI; Dr. Bernard Ostle and the Iowa State University Press for permission to reproduce Table VII; and Professor E. S. Pearson and the *Biometrika* Office for permission to use the material presented in Tables V and IX.

TABLE I · Binomial Coefficients

TABLE I.   Binomial Coefficients $\binom{n}{r}$

n	r										
	0	1	2	3	4	5	6	7	8	9	10
0	1										
1	1	1									
2	1	2	1								
3	1	3	3	1							
4	1	4	6	4	1						
5	1	5	10	10	5	1					
6	1	6	15	20	15	6	1				
7	1	7	21	35	35	21	7	1			
8	1	8	28	56	70	56	28	8	1		
9	1	9	36	84	126	126	84	36	9	1	
10	1	10	45	120	210	252	210	120	45	10	1
11	1	11	55	165	330	462	462	330	165	55	11
12	1	12	66	220	495	792	924	792	495	220	66
13	1	13	78	286	715	1287	1716	1716	1287	715	286
14	1	14	91	364	1001	2002	3003	3432	3003	2002	1001
15	1	15	105	455	1365	3003	5005	6435	6435	5005	3003

TABLE II · Areas of the Standard Normal Distribution

TABLE II.   Areas of the Standard Normal Distribution[1]

A(Z) Is the Area under the Curve between Zero and Z.

Z	A(Z)	Z	A(Z)	Z	A(Z)
.00	.00000	.30	.11791	.60	.22575
.01	.00399	.31	.12172	.61	.22907
.02	.00798	.32	.12552	.62	.23237
.03	.01197	.33	.12930	.63	.23565
.04	.01595	.34	.13307	.64	.23891
.05	.01994	.35	.13683	.65	.24215
.06	.02392	.36	.14058	.66	.24537
.07	.02790	.37	.14431	.67	.24857
.08	.03188	.38	.14803	.68	.25175
.09	.03586	.39	.15173	.69	.25490
.10	.03983	.40	.15542	.70	.25804
.11	.04380	.41	.15910	.71	.26115
.12	.04776	.42	.16276	.72	.26424
.13	.05172	.43	.16640	.73	.26730
.14	.05567	.44	.17003	.74	.27035
.15	.05962	.45	.17364	.75	.27337
.16	.06356	.46	.17724	.76	.27637
.17	.06750	.47	.18082	.77	.27935
.18	.07142	.48	.18439	.78	.28230
.19	.07535	.49	.18793	.79	.28524
.20	.07926	.50	.19146	.80	.28814
.21	.08317	.51	.19497	.81	.29103
.22	.08706	.52	.19847	.82	.29389
.23	.09095	.53	.20194	.83	.29673
.24	.09483	.54	.20540	.84	.29955
.25	.09871	.55	.20884	.85	.30234
.26	.10257	.56	.21226	.86	.30511
.27	.10642	.57	.21566	.87	.30785
.28	.11026	.58	.21904	.88	.31057
.29	.11409	.59	.22240	.89	.31327

(*Continued*)

[1] Abridged from *Table of Probability Functions*, V. II, of the Federal Works Agency, Work Projects Administration for the City of New York, New York, 1942.

TABLE II · Areas of the Standard Normal Distribution

TABLE II (*Continued*)

Z	A(Z)	Z	A(Z)	Z	A(Z)
.90	.31594	1.20	.38493	1.50	.43319
.91	.31859	1.21	.38686	1.51	.43448
.92	.32121	1.22	.38877	1.52	.43574
.93	.32381	1.23	.39065	1.53	.43699
.94	.32639	1.24	.39251	1.54	.43822
.95	.32894	1.25	.39435	1.55	.43943
.96	.33147	1.26	.39617	1.56	.44062
.97	.33398	1.27	.39796	1.57	.44179
.98	.33646	1.28	.39973	1.58	.44295
.99	.33891	1.29	.40147	1.59	.44408
1.00	.34134	1.30	.40320	1.60	.44520
1.01	.34375	1.31	.40490	1.61	.44630
1.02	.34614	1.32	.40658	1.62	.44738
1.03	.34849	1.33	.40824	1.63	.44845
1.04	.35083	1.34	.40988	1.64	.44950
1.05	.35314	1.35	.41149	1.65	.45053
1.06	.35543	1.36	.41309	1.66	.45154
1.07	.35769	1.37	.41466	1.67	.45254
1.08	.35993	1.38	.41621	1.68	.45352
1.09	.36214	1.39	.41774	1.69	.45449
1.10	.36433	1.40	.41924	1.70	.45543
1.11	.36650	1.41	.42073	1.71	.45637
1.12	.36864	1.42	.42220	1.72	.45728
1.13	.37076	1.43	.42364	1.73	.45818
1.14	.37286	1.44	.42507	1.74	.45907
1.15	.37493	1.45	.42647	1.75	.45994
1.16	.37698	1.46	.42785	1.76	.46080
1.17	.37900	1.47	.42922	1.77	.46164
1.18	.38100	1.48	.43056	1.78	.46246
1.19	.38298	1.49	.43189	1.79	.46327

(*Continued*)

TABLE II · Areas of the Standard Normal Distribution

TABLE II (*Continued*)

Z	A(Z)	Z	A(Z)	Z	A(Z)
1.80	.46407	2.10	.48214	2.40	.49180
1.81	.46485	2.11	.48257	2.41	.49202
1.82	.46562	2.12	.48300	2.42	.49224
1.83	.46638	2.13	.48341	2.43	.49245
1.84	.46712	2.14	.48382	2.44	.49266
1.85	.46784	2.15	.48422	2.45	.49286
1.86	.46856	2.16	.48461	2.46	.49305
1.87	.46926	2.17	.48500	2.47	.49324
1.88	.46995	2.18	.48537	2.48	.49343
1.89	.47062	2.19	.48574	2.49	.49361
1.90	.47128	2.20	.48610	2.50	.49379
1.91	.47193	2.21	.48645	2.51	.49396
1.92	.47257	2.22	.48679	2.52	.49413
1.93	.47320	2.23	.48713	2.53	.49430
1.94	.47381	2.24	.48745	2.54	.49446
1.95	.47441	2.25	.48778	2.55	.49461
1.96	.47500	2.26	.48809	2.56	.49477
1.97	.47558	2.27	.48840	2.57	.49492
1.98	.47615	2.28	.48870	2.58	.49506
1.99	.47670	2.29	.48899	2.59	.49520
2.00	.47725	2.30	.48928	2.60	.49534
2.01	.47778	2.31	.48956	2.61	.49547
2.02	.47831	2.32	.48983	2.62	.49560
2.03	.47882	2.33	.49010	2.63	.49573
2.04	.47932	2.34	.49036	2.64	.49585
2.05	.47982	2.35	.49061	2.65	.49598
2.06	.48030	2.36	.49086	2.66	.49609
2.07	.48077	2.37	.49111	2.67	.49621
2.08	.48124	2.38	.49134	2.68	.49632
2.09	.48169	2.39	.49158	2.69	.49643

(*Continued*)

TABLE II · Areas of the Standard Normal Distribution

Table II (*Continued*)

Z	A(Z)	Z	A(Z)	Z	A(Z)
2.70	.49653	3.00	.49865	3.30	.49952
2.71	.49664	3.01	.49869	3.31	.49953
2.72	.49674	3.02	.49874	3.32	.49955
2.73	.49683	3.03	.49878	3.33	.49957
2.74	.49693	3.04	.49882	3.34	.49958
2.75	.49702	3.05	.49886	3.35	.49960
2.76	.49711	3.06	.49889	3.36	.49961
2.77	.49720	3.07	.49893	3.37	.49962
2.78	.49728	3.08	.49896	3.38	.49964
2.79	.49736	3.09	.49900	3.39	.49965
2.80	.49744	3.10	.49903	3.40	.49966
2.81	.49752	3.11	.49906	3.41	.49968
2.82	.49760	3.12	.49910	3.42	.49969
2.83	.49767	3.13	.49913	3.43	.49970
2.84	.49774	3.14	.49916	3.44	.49971
2.85	.49781	3.15	.49918	3.45	.49972
2.86	.49788	3.16	.49921	3.46	.49973
2.87	.49795	3.17	.49924	3.47	.49974
2.88	.49801	3.18	.49926	3.48	.49975
2.89	.49807	3.19	.49929	3.49	.49976
2.90	.49813	3.20	.49931	3.50	.49977
2.91	.49819	3.21	.49934	3.51	.49978
2.92	.49825	3.22	.49936	3.52	.49978
2.93	.49831	3.23	.49938	3.53	.49979
2.94	.49836	3.24	.49940	3.54	.49980
2.95	.49841	3.25	.49942	3.55	.49981
2.96	.49846	3.26	.49944	3.56	.49981
2.97	.49851	3.27	.49946	3.57	.49982
2.98	.49856	3.28	.49948	3.58	.49983
2.99	.49861	3.29	.49950	3.59	.49983

(*Continued*)

TABLE II · Areas of the Standard Normal Distribution

TABLE II (*Continued*)

Z	A(Z)	Z	A(Z)	Z	A(Z)
3.60	.49984	3.75	.49991	3.90	.49995
3.61	.49985	3.76	.49992	3.91	.49995
3.62	.49985	3.77	.49992	3.92	.49996
3.63	.49986	3.78	.49992	3.93	.49996
3.64	.49986	3.79	.49992	3.94	.49996
3.65	.49987	3.80	.49993	3.95	.49996
3.66	.49987	3.81	.49993	3.96	.49996
3.67	.49988	3.82	.49993	3.97	.49996
3.68	.49988	3.83	.49994	3.98	.49997
3.69	.49989	3.84	.49994	3.99	.49997
3.70	.49989	3.85	.49994	4.00	.49997
3.71	.49990	3.86	.49994		
3.72	.49990	3.87	.49995		
3.73	.49990	3.88	.49995		
3.74	.49991	3.89	.49995		

TABLE III · Values of t for Given Probability Levels

TABLE III.   Values of *t* for Given Probability Levels[1]

Use $\frac{z}{s}$ $\bar{\sigma}$
Use t

Degrees of Freedom	Probability of a Larger Value				
	.1	.05	.025	.01	.005
1	3.078	6.314	12.706	31.821	63.657
2	1.886	2.920	4.303	6.965	9.925
3	1.638	2.353	3.182	4.541	5.841
4	1.533	2.132	2.776	3.747	4.604
5	1.476	2.015	2.571	3.365	4.032
6	1.440	1.943	2.447	3.143	3.707
7	1.415	1.895	2.365	2.998	3.499
8	1.397	1.860	2.306	2.896	3.355
9	1.383	1.833	2.262	2.821	3.250
10	1.372	1.812	2.228	2.764	3.169
11	1.363	1.796	2.201	2.718	3.106
12	1.356	1.782	2.179	2.681	3.055
13	1.350	1.771	2.160	2.650	3.012
14	1.345	1.761	2.145	2.624	2.977
15	1.341	1.753	2.131	2.602	2.947
16	1.337	1.746	2.120	2.583	2.921
17	1.333	1.740	2.110	2.567	2.898
18	1.330	1.734	2.101	2.552	2.878
19	1.328	1.729	2.093	2.539	2.861
20	1.325	1.725	2.086	2.528	2.845
21	1.323	1.721	2.080	2.518	2.831
22	1.321	1.717	2.074	2.508	2.819
23	1.319	1.714	2.069	2.500	2.807
24	1.318	1.711	2.064	2.492	2.797
25	1.316	1.708	2.060	2.485	2.787
26	1.315	1.706	2.056	2.479	2.779
27	1.314	1.703	2.052	2.473	2.771
28	1.313	1.701	2.048	2.467	2.763
29	1.311	1.699	2.045	2.462	2.756
30	1.310	1.697	2.042	2.457	2.750
40	1.303	1.684	2.021	2.423	2.704
60	1.296	1.671	2.000	2.390	2.660
120	1.290	1.661	1.984	2.358	2.626
∞	1.282	1.645	1.960	2.326	2.576

NORMAL DISTR.

[1] Table III is abridged from Table III of Fisher and Yates: *Statistical Tables for Biological, Agricultural, and Medical Research*, published by Oliver and Boyd Limited, Edinburgh, by permission of the authors and publishers.

TABLE IV · 95% Confidence Intervals for Binomial Distributions

TABLE IV. 95% Confidence Intervals (Percent) for Binomial Distributions[1]

Number Observed X	Size of Sample, n 10	15	20	30	50	100	Fraction Observed X/n	Size of Sample 250	1000
0	0 31	0 22	0 17	0 12	0 07	0 4	.00	0 1	0 0
1	0 45	0 32	0 25	0 17	0 11	0 5	.01	0 4	0 2
2	3 56	2 40	1 31	1 22	0 14	0 7	.02	1 5	1 3
3	7 65	4 48	3 38	2 27	1 17	1 8	.03	1 6	2 4
4	12 74	8 55	6 44	4 31	2 19	1 10	.04	2 7	3 5
5	19 81	12 62	9 49	6 35	3 22	2 11	.05	3 9	4 7
6	26 88	16 68	12 54	8 39	5 24	2 12	.06	3 10	5 8
7	35 93	21 73	15 59	10 43	6 27	3 14	.07	4 11	6 9
8	44 97	27 79	19 64	12 46	7 29	4 15	.08	5 12	6 10
9	55 100	32 84	23 68	15 50	9 31	4 16	.09	6 13	7 11
10	69 100	38 88	27 73	17 53	10 34	5 18	.10	7 14	8 12
11		45 92	32 77	20 56	12 36	5 19	.11	7 16	9 13
12		52 96	36 81	23 60	13 38	6 20	.12	8 17	10 14
13		60 98	41 85	25 63	15 41	7 21	.13	9 18	11 15
14		68 100	46 88	28 .66	16 43	8 22	.14	10 19	12 16
15		78 100	51 91	31 69	18 44	9 24	.15	10 20	13 17
16			56 94	34 72	20 46	9 25	.16	11 21	14 18
17			62 97	37 75	21 48	10 26	.17	12 22	15 19
18			69 99	40 77	23 50	11 27	.18	13 23	16 21
19			75 100	44 80	25 53	12 28	.19	14 24	17 22
20			83 100	47 83	27 55	13 29	.20	15 26	18 23
21				50 85	28 57	14 30	.21	16 27	19 24
22				54 88	30 59	14 31	.22	17 28	19 25
23				57 90	32 61	15 32	.23	18 29	20 26
24				61 92	34 63	16 33	.24	19 30	21 27
25				65 94	36 64	17 35	.25	20 31	22 28
26				69 96	37 66	18 36	.26	20 32	23 29
27				73 98	39 68	19 37	.27	21 33	24 30
28				78 99	41 70	19 38	.28	22 34	25 31
29				83 100	43 72	20 39	.29	23 35	26 32
30				88 100	45 73	21 40	.30	24 36	27 33
31					47 75	22 41	.31	25 37	28 34
32					50 77	23 42	.32	26 38	29 35
33					52 79	24 43	.33	27 39	30 36
34					54 80	25 44	.34	28 40	31 37
35					56 82	26 45	.35	29 41	32 38
36					57 84	27 46	.36	30 42	33 39
37					59 85	28 47	.37	31 43	34 40
38					62 87	28 48	.38	32 44	35 41
39					64 88	29 49	.39	33 45	36 42
40					66 90	30 50	.40	34 46	37 43
41					69 91	31 51	.41	35 47	38 44
42					71 93	32 52	.42	36 48	39 45
43					73 94	33 53	.43	37 49	40 46
44					76 95	34 54	.44	38 50	41 47
45					78 97	35 55	.45	39 51	42 48
46					81 98	36 56	.46	40 52	43 49
47					83 99	37 57	.47	41 53	44 50
48					86 100	38 58	.48	42 54	45 51
49					89 100	39 59	.49	43 55	46 52
50					93 100	40 60	.50	44 56	47 53
						*		†	†

*If X exceeds 50, read 100 − X = number observed and subtract each confidence limit from 100.

†If X/n exceeds .50, read 1.00 − X/n = fraction observed and subtract each confidence limit from 100.

[1]Table IV is reproduced from Table 1.3.1 of George W. Snedecor's *Statistical Methods*, 6th edition, published by the Iowa State University Press, Ames, Iowa, by permission of the author and publishers.

TABLE V · Percentage Points of the Chi-Square Distribution

TABLE V. Percentage Points of the Chi-Square Distribution[1]

df	\multicolumn{8}{c}{Probability of a Larger Value}
	.995	.990	.975	.950	.050	.025	.010	.005
1	---	---	---	.004	3.84	5.02	6.63	7.88
2	.01	.02	.05	.10	5.99	7.38	9.21	10.60
3	.07	.11	.22	.35	7.81	9.35	11.34	12.84
4	.21	.30	.48	.71	9.49	11.14	13.28	14.86
5	.41	.55	.83	1.15	11.07	12.83	15.09	16.75
6	.68	.87	1.24	1.64	12.59	14.45	16.81	18.55
7	.99	1.24	1.69	2.17	14.07	16.01	18.48	20.28
8	1.34	1.65	2.18	2.73	15.51	17.53	20.09	21.96
9	1.73	2.09	2.70	3.33	16.92	19.02	21.67	23.59
10	2.16	2.56	3.25	3.94	18.31	20.48	23.21	25.19
11	2.60	3.05	3.82	4.57	19.68	21.92	24.72	26.76
12	3.07	3.57	4.40	5.23	21.03	23.34	26.22	28.30
13	3.57	4.11	5.01	5.89	22.36	24.74	27.69	29.82
14	4.07	4.66	5.63	6.57	23.68	26.12	29.14	31.32
15	4.60	5.23	6.26	7.26	25.00	27.49	30.58	32.80
16	5.14	5.81	6.91	7.96	26.30	28.85	32.00	34.27
17	5.70	6.41	7.56	8.67	27.59	30.19	33.41	35.72
18	6.26	7.01	8.23	9.39	28.87	31.53	34.81	37.16
19	6.84	7.63	8.91	10.12	30.14	32.85	36.19	38.58
20	7.43	8.26	9.59	10.85	31.41	34.17	37.57	40.00
21	8.03	8.90	10.28	11.59	32.67	35.48	38.93	41.40
22	8.64	9.54	10.98	12.34	33.92	36.78	40.29	42.80
23	9.26	10.20	11.69	13.09	35.17	38.08	41.64	44.18
24	9.89	10.86	12.40	13.85	36.42	39.36	42.98	45.56
25	10.52	11.52	13.12	14.61	37.65	40.65	44.31	46.93
26	11.16	12.20	13.84	15.38	38.89	41.92	45.64	48.29
27	11.81	12.88	14.57	16.15	40.11	43.19	46.96	49.64
28	12.46	13.56	15.31	16.93	41.34	44.46	48.28	50.99
29	13.12	14.26	16.05	17.71	42.56	45.72	49.59	52.34
30	13.79	14.95	16.79	18.49	43.77	46.98	50.89	53.67
40	20.71	22.16	24.43	26.51	55.76	59.34	63.69	66.77
50	27.99	29.71	32.36	34.76	67.50	71.42	76.15	79.49
60	35.53	37.48	40.48	43.19	79.08	83.30	88.38	91.95
70	43.28	45.44	48.76	51.74	90.53	95.02	100.43	104.22
80	51.17	53.54	57.15	60.39	101.88	106.63	112.33	116.32
90	59.20	61.75	65.65	69.13	113.14	118.14	124.12	128.30
100	67.33	70.06	74.22	77.93	124.34	129.56	135.81	140.17

[1] Table V is abridged from Thompson, Catherine M.: "Table of Percentage Points of the x^2 Distribution," *Biometrika*, Vol. 32 (1942), p. 187, by permission of Professor E. S. Pearson.

TABLE VI · Random Numbers

TABLE VI.   Random Numbers[1]

	00 04	05 09	10 14	15 19	20 24	25 29	30 34	35 39	40 44	45 49
00	39591	66082	48626	95780	55228	87189	75717	97042	19696	48613
01	46304	97377	43462	21739	14566	72533	60171	29024	77581	72760
02	99547	60779	22734	23678	44895	89767	18249	41702	35850	40543
03	06743	63537	24553	77225	94743	79448	12753	95986	78088	48019
04	69568	65496	49033	88577	98606	92156	08846	54912	12691	13170
05	68198	69571	34349	73141	42640	44721	30462	35075	33475	47407
06	27974	12609	77428	64441	49008	60489	66780	55499	80842	57706
07	50552	20688	02769	63037	15494	71784	70559	58158	53437	46216
08	74687	02033	98290	62635	88877	28599	63682	35566	03271	05651
09	49303	76629	71897	30990	62923	36686	96167	11492	90333	84501
10	89734	39183	52026	14997	15140	18250	62831	51236	61236	09179
11	74042	40747	02617	11346	01884	82066	55913	72422	13971	64209
12	84706	31375	67053	73367	95349	31074	36908	42782	89690	48002
13	83664	21365	28882	48926	45435	60577	85270	02777	06878	27561
14	47813	74854	73388	11385	99108	97878	32858	17473	07682	20166
15	00371	56525	38880	53702	09517	47281	15995	98350	25233	79718
16	81182	48434	27431	55806	25389	40774	72978	16835	65066	28732
17	75242	35904	73077	24537	81354	48902	03478	42867	04552	66034
18	96239	80246	07000	09555	55051	49596	44629	88225	28195	44598
19	82988	17440	85311	03360	38176	51462	86070	03924	84413	92363
20	77599	29143	89088	57593	60036	17297	30923	36224	46327	96266
21	61433	33118	53488	82981	44709	63655	64388	00498	14135	57514
22	76008	15045	45440	84062	52363	18079	33726	44301	86246	99727
23	26494	76598	85834	10844	56300	02244	72118	96510	98388	80161
24	46570	88558	77533	33359	07830	84752	53260	45655	36881	98535
25	73995	41532	87933	79930	14310	64833	49020	70067	99726	97007
26	93901	38276	75544	19679	82899	11365	22896	42118	77165	08734
27	41925	28215	40866	93501	45446	27913	21708	01788	81404	15119
28	80720	02782	24326	41328	10357	86883	80086	77138	57072	12100
29	92596	39416	50362	04423	04561	58179	54188	44978	14322	97056
30	39693	58559	45839	47278	38548	38885	19875	26829	86711	57005
31	86923	37863	14340	30929	04079	65274	03030	15106	09362	82972
32	99700	79237	18177	58879	56221	65644	33331	87502	32961	40996
33	60248	21953	52321	16984	03252	90433	97304	50181	71026	01946
34	29136	71987	03992	67025	31070	78348	47823	11033	13037	47732
35	57471	42913	85212	42319	92901	97727	04775	94396	38154	25238
36	57324	93847	03269	56096	95028	14039	76128	63747	27301	65529
37	56768	71694	63361	80836	30841	71875	40944	54827	01887	54822
38	70400	81534	02148	41441	26582	27481	84262	14084	42409	62950
39	05454	88418	48496	99565	36635	85496	18894	77271	26894	00889
40	80934	56136	47063	96311	19067	59790	08752	68050	85685	83076
41	06919	46237	50676	11238	75637	43086	95323	52867	06891	32089
42	00152	23997	41751	74756	50975	75365	70158	67663	51431	46375
43	88505	74625	71783	82511	13661	63178	39291	76796	74736	10980
44	64514	80967	33545	09582	86329	58152	05931	35961	70069	12142
45	25280	53007	99651	96366	49378	80971	10419	12981	70572	11575
46	71292	63716	93210	59312	39493	24252	54849	29754	41497	79228
47	49734	50498	08974	05904	68172	02864	10994	22482	12912	17920
48	43075	09754	71880	92614	99928	94424	86353	87549	94499	11459
49	15116	16643	03981	06566	14050	33671	03814	48856	41267	76252

(Continued)

[1] Reproduced from George W. Snedecor's *Everyday Statistics*, published by Wm. C. Brown Company, Dubuque, Iowa, (1950), by permission of the author and publishers.

TABLE VI · Random Numbers

TABLE VI (*Continued*)

	50 54	55 59	60 64	65 69	70 74	75 79	80 84	85 89	90 94	95 99
00	25178	77518	41773	39926	09843	29694	43801	69276	44707	23455
01	45803	95106	85816	33366	37383	76832	37024	06581	22587	24827
02	15532	30898	14922	13923	44987	45122	86515	55836	96165	19650
03	99068	35453	42152	12078	04913	06083	06645	93310	40016	85421
04	70983	88359	95583	79848	24101	67502	25692	42496	77732	19278
05	71181	48289	03153	18779	65702	03612	64608	84071	47588	09982
06	44052	59163	74033	86112	27731	46135	63092	59171	44816	12354
07	91555	87708	70964	43346	56811	08725	75139	77674	82467	41899
08	54307	12188	58089	73745	35569	97352	77301	37684	36823	69218
09	63631	23919	06785	13891	89918	76211	09362	34292	17640	65907
10	46832	30801	98898	28954	97793	20825	36775	71974	15574	09184
11	05944	82632	39310	74857	61725	50569	81937	16820	85446	51168
12	28199	90116	59501	49025	73005	84954	11587	97691	90415	34685
13	08391	05600	00624	95068	33776	44985	01505	76911	45539	32181
14	29634	13021	96568	15124	55092	44043	31073	92371	51288	33378
15	61509	18842	79201	46451	68594	98120	68110	91062	42095	61839
16	87888	23033	69837	65661	15130	44649	42515	83861	50721	36110
17	94585	15218	74838	61809	92293	85490	46934	08531	70107	65707
18	82033	93915	34898	79913	70013	27573	39256	35167	35070	47095
19	79131	10022	82199	78976	22702	37936	10445	96846	84927	69745
20	79344	39236	41333	11473	15049	47930	99029	97150	82275	55149
21	15384	44585	18773	89733	40779	59664	83328	25162	58758	17761
22	38802	90957	32910	97485	10358	88588	95310	22252	19143	69011
23	85874	18400	28151	29541	63706	43197	65726	94117	22169	91806
24	26200	72680	12364	46010	92208	59103	60417	45389	56122	85353
25	13772	75282	81418	42188	66529	47981	92548	10079	68179	40915
26	91876	07434	96946	98382	97374	34444	17992	42811	01579	48741
27	31721	21713	83632	40605	24227	53219	05482	86768	53239	24812
28	92570	53242	98133	84706	78048	29645	79336	66091	05793	25922
29	02880	29307	73734	66448	64739	74645	29562	13999	17492	49891
30	80982	14684	31038	85302	98349	57313	86371	33938	10768	60837
31	38000	43364	94825	32413	46781	09685	69058	56644	85531	55173
32	14218	94289	79484	61868	40034	22546	68726	14736	80844	13466
33	74358	21940	40280	22233	09123	49375	55094	46113	54046	51771
34	39049	14986	94000	26649	13037	34609	45186	89515	63214	66886
35	48727	06309	91486	67316	84576	11100	37580	49629	83224	46321
36	22719	29784	40682	96715	40745	57458	70048	48306	50270	87424
37	33980	36769	51977	03689	79071	20279	64787	48877	44063	93733
38	23885	66721	16542	12648	65986	43104	45583	75729	35118	58742
39	85190	44068	78477	69133	58983	96504	44232	74809	25266	73872
40	33453	36333	45814	78128	55914	89829	43251	41634	48488	49153
41	98236	11489	97240	01678	30779	75214	80039	68895	95271	19654
42	21295	53563	43609	48439	87427	88065	09892	58524	43815	31340
43	28335	79849	69842	71669	38770	54445	48736	03242	83181	85403
44	95449	35273	62581	85522	35813	34475	97514	72839	10387	31649
45	88167	03878	89405	55461	73248	48620	31732	47317	06252	54652
46	86131	62596	98785	02360	54271	26242	93735	20752	17146	18315
47	71134	90264	30126	08586	97497	61678	81940	00907	39096	02082
48	02664	53438	76839	52290	77999	05799	93744	16634	84924	31344
49	90664	96876	16663	25608	67140	84619	67167	13192	81774	58619

(*Continued*)

TABLE VI · Random Numbers

Table VI (*Continued*)

	00 04	05 09	10 14	15 19	20 24	25 29	30 34	35 39	40 44	45 49
50	03873	86558	72524	02542	73184	37905	05882	15596	73646	50798
51	08761	47547	02216	48086	56490	89959	69975	04500	23779	76697
52	61270	98773	40298	26077	80396	08166	35723	61933	13985	19102
53	73758	15578	95748	02967	35122	36539	72822	68241	34803	42457
54	17132	32196	60523	00544	73700	70122	27962	85597	36011	79971
55	26175	29794	44838	84414	82748	22246	70694	57953	39780	17791
56	06004	04516	06210	03536	84451	30767	37928	26986	07396	64611
57	34687	73753	36327	73704	61564	99434	90938	03967	97420	19913
58	27865	08255	57859	04746	79700	68823	16002	58115	07580	12675
59	89423	51114	90820	26786	77404	05795	49036	34686	98767	32284
60	99039	80312	69745	87636	10058	84834	89485	08775	19041	61375
61	02852	54339	45496	20587	85921	06763	68873	35367	42627	54973
62	10850	42788	94737	74549	74296	13053	46816	32141	02533	25648
63	38391	18507	33151	69434	80103	02603	61110	89395	67621	67025
64	48181	95478	62739	90148	00156	09338	44558	53271	87549	45974
65	23098	23720	76508	69083	56584	00423	21634	35990	09234	95116
66	25104	82019	21120	06165	44324	77577	15774	44091	69687	67576
67	22205	40198	86884	28103	57306	54915	03426	66700	45993	36668
68	64975	05064	29617	40622	20330	18518	45312	57921	23188	82361
69	58710	75278	47730	26093	16436	38868	76861	85914	14162	21984
70	12140	72905	26022	07675	16362	34504	47740	39923	04081	03162
71	73226	39840	47958	97249	14146	34543	76162	74158	59739	67447
72	12320	86217	66162	70941	58940	58006	80731	66680	02183	94678
73	41364	64156	23000	23188	64945	33815	32884	76955	56574	61666
74	97881	80867	70117	72041	03554	29087	19767	71838	80545	61402
75	88295	87271	82812	97588	09960	06312	03050	77332	25977	18385
76	95321	89836	78230	46037	72483	87533	74571	88859	26908	55626
77	24337	14264	30185	36753	22343	81737	62926	76494	93536	75502
78	00718	66303	75009	91431	64245	61863	16738	23127	89435	45109
79	38093	10328	96998	91386	34967	40407	48380	09115	59367	49596
80	87661	31701	29974	56777	66751	35181	63887	95094	20056	84990
81	87142	91818	51857	85061	17890	39057	44506	00969	32942	54794
82	60634	27142	21199	50437	04685	70252	91453	75952	66753	50664
83	73356	64431	05068	56334	34487	78253	67684	69916	63885	88491
84	29889	11378	65915	66776	95034	81557	98035	16815	68432	63020
85	48257	36438	48479	72173	31418	14035	84239	02032	40409	11715
86	38425	29462	79880	45713	90049	01136	72426	25077	64361	94284
87	48226	31868	38629	12135	28346	17552	03293	42618	44151	78438
88	80189	30031	15435	76730	58565	29817	36775	64007	47912	16754
89	33208	33475	95219	29832	74569	50667	90569	66717	46958	04820
90	19750	48564	49690	43352	53884	80125	47795	99701	06800	22794
91	62820	23174	71124	36040	34873	95650	79059	23894	58534	78296
92	95737	34362	81520	79481	26442	37826	76886	01850	83713	94272
93	64642	62961	37566	41064	69372	84369	92823	91391	61056	44495
94	77636	60163	14915	50744	95611	99346	38741	04407	72940	87936
95	43633	52102	93561	31010	11299	52661	79014	17910	88492	60753
96	93686	41960	61280	96529	52924	87371	34855	67125	40279	10186
97	23775	33402	28647	42314	51213	29116	26243	40243	32137	25177
98	91325	64698	58868	63107	08993	96000	66854	11567	80604	72299
99	58129	44367	31924	73586	24422	92799	28963	36444	01315	10226

(*Continued*)

TABLE VI · Random Numbers

TABLE VI (*Continued*)

	50 54	55 59	60 64	65 69	70 74	75 79	80 84	85 89	90 94	95 99
50	37686	78520	31209	83677	99115	94024	09286	58927	24078	16770
51	58108	29344	11825	51955	50618	99753	02200	50503	32466	50055
52	71545	42326	66429	93607	55276	85482	24449	41764	19884	46443
53	93303	90557	79166	90097	01627	96690	77434	06102	05379	59549
54	36731	37929	13079	83036	31525	35811	59131	65257	03731	86703
55	49781	31581	80391	84608	23390	30433	08210	85136	80060	43651
56	65995	94208	68785	04370	44192	91852	01129	28739	08705	54538
57	19663	09309	02836	10223	90814	92786	96747	46014	54765	76001
58	88479	24307	63812	47615	17220	27942	11785	49933	03923	35432
59	95407	95006	95421	20811	76761	47475	58865	06204	36543	81002
60	22789	87011	61926	97996	10604	80855	48714	52754	98279	96467
61	96783	18403	36729	18760	30810	73087	94565	68682	15792	60020
62	68933	05665	12264	23954	01583	75411	04460	83939	66528	22576
63	68794	13000	20066	98963	93483	51165	63358	12373	13877	37580
64	40537	31604	60323	51235	65546	85117	15647	09617	73520	48525
65	41249	42504	91773	81579	02882	74657	73765	10932	74607	83825
66	08813	84525	30329	33144	76884	89996	07834	67266	96820	15128
67	46609	30917	29996	10848	39555	09233	58988	82131	69232	76762
68	68543	69424	92072	57937	05563	80727	67053	35431	00881	56541
69	09926	84219	30089	08843	24998	27105	18397	79071	40738	73876
70	30515	76316	49597	37000	98604	05857	51729	19006	15239	27129
71	21611	26346	04877	71584	55724	39616	64648	36811	60915	34108
72	47410	83767	56454	96768	27001	83712	01245	27256	57991	75758
73	18572	31214	41015	64110	61807	72472	78059	69701	78681	17356
74	28078	02819	02459	33308	96540	15817	78694	81476	87856	99737
75	56644	50430	34562	75842	67724	02918	55603	55195	88219	39676
76	27331	48055	18928	47763	61966	64507	06559	81329	29481	03660
77	32080	21524	32929	07739	00836	39497	94476	27433	96857	52987
78	27027	69762	65362	90214	89572	52054	43067	73017	87664	03293
79	56471	68839	09969	45853	72627	71793	49920	64544	71874	74053
80	22689	19799	18870	49272	74783	38777	76176	40961	18089	32499
81	71263	82247	66684	90239	67686	48963	30842	59354	33551	87966
82	64084	57386	89278	27187	52142	96305	87393	80164	95518	82742
83	23121	10194	09911	37062	43446	09107	47156	70179	00858	92326
84	78906	48080	76745	65814	51167	87755	66884	12718	14951	47937
85	87257	26005	21544	37223	53288	72056	96396	67099	49416	91891
86	39529	98126	33694	29025	94308	24426	63072	51444	04718	49891
87	89632	11606	87159	89408	06295	31055	15530	46432	49871	37982
88	23708	98919	14407	53722	58779	92849	94176	24870	56688	25405
89	51445	46758	42024	27940	64237	10086	95601	53923	85209	79385
90	23849	65272	24743	39960	27313	99925	29743	87270	05773	21797
91	78613	15441	34568	57398	25872	61792	94599	60944	90908	38948
92	90694	27996	94181	87428	41135	29461	72716	68056	67871	72459
93	86772	86829	36403	40087	67456	21071	39039	91037	45280	00066
94	24527	40701	56894	56894	00789	97573	09303	41704	05772	95372
95	31596	70876	46807	06741	29352	23829	52465	00336	24155	61871
96	31613	99249	17260	05242	19535	52702	64761	66694	06150	13820
97	02911	09514	50864	80622	20017	59019	43450	75942	08567	40547
98	02484	74068	04671	19646	41951	05111	34013	57443	87481	48994
99	69259	75535	73007	15236	01572	44870	53280	25132	70276	87334

TABLE VII · Normal Population of 1000 Observations

TABLE VII. Normal Population of 1000 Observations with a Mean of 4000 and Variance of 1,000,000[1]

(Observations Ordered from Low to High)

Identification No.	Observation Value	Identification No.	Observation Value	Identification No.	Observation Value
000	642	030	2126	060	2449
001	1016	031	2141	061	2458
002	1187	032	2155	062	2466
003	1300	033	2168	063	2474
004	1386	034	2182	064	2482
005	1456	035	2194	065	2490
006	1515	036	2207	066	2498
007	1567	037	2220	067	2505
008	1613	038	2232	068	2513
009	1654	039	2243	069	2520
010	1692	040	2255	070	2528
011	1726	041	2266	071	2535
012	1758	042	2278	072	2543
013	1788	043	2289	073	2550
014	1816	044	2299	074	2557
015	1843	045	2310	075	2564
016	1868	046	2320	076	2571
017	1892	047	2330	077	2578
018	1914	048	2340	078	2585
019	1936	049	2350	079	2592
020	1956	050	2360	080	2598
021	1976	051	2370	081	2605
022	1995	052	2379	082	2612
023	2014	053	2388	083	2618
024	2031	054	2397	084	2625
025	2048	055	2406	085	2631
026	2065	056	2415	086	2637
027	2081	057	2424	087	2644
028	2097	058	2432	088	2650
029	2112	059	2441	089	2656

(Continued)

[1] Table VII is reproduced from Appendix 3 of Bernard Ostle's *Statistics in Research*, published by the Iowa State College Press, Ames Iowa, by permission of the author and publishers.

TABLE VII · Normal Population of 1000 Observations

TABLE VII (*Continued*)

Identification No.	Observation Value	Identification No.	Observation Value	Identification No.	Observation Value
090	2662	120	2828	150	2966
091	2668	121	2832	151	2970
092	2674	122	2837	152	2974
093	2680	123	2842	153	2978
094	2686	124	2847	154	2983
095	2692	125	2852	155	2987
096	2698	126	2857	156	2991
097	2704	127	2862	157	2995
098	2710	128	2866	158	2999
099	2716	129	2871	159	3003
100	2721	130	2876	160	3008
101	2727	131	2881	161	3012
102	2733	132	2885	162	3016
103	2738	133	2890	163	3020
104	2744	134	2895	164	3024
105	2749	135	2899	165	3028
106	2755	136	2904	166	3032
107	2760	137	2908	167	3036
108	2765	138	2913	168	3040
109	2771	139	2917	169	3044
110	2776	140	2922	170	3048
111	2781	141	2926	171	3052
112	2787	142	2931	172	3056
113	2792	143	2935	173	3060
114	2797	144	2940	174	3063
115	2802	145	2944	175	3067
116	2807	146	2948	176	3071
117	2812	147	2953	177	3075
118	2818	148	2957	189	3079
119	2822	149	2961	179	3083

(*Continued*)

TABLE VII · *Normal Population of 1000 Observations*

TABLE VII (*Continued*)

Identifi-cation No.	Observation Value	Identifi-cation No.	Observation Value	Identifi-cation No.	Observation Value
180	3086	210	3195	240	3295
181	3090	211	3199	241	3298
182	3094	212	3202	242	3302
183	3098	213	3206	243	3305
184	3102	214	3209	244	3308
185	3105	215	3212	245	3311
186	3109	216	3216	246	3314
187	3113	217	3219	247	3318
188	3117	218	3223	248	3321
189	3120	219	3226	249	3324
190	3124	220	3230	250	3327
191	3128	221	3233	251	3330
192	3131	222	3236	252	3333
193	3135	223	3240	253	3336
194	3139	224	3243	254	3340
195	3142	225	3246	255	3343
196	3146	226	3250	256	3346
197	3149	227	3253	257	3349
198	3153	228	3256	258	3352
199	3157	229	3260	259	3355
200	3160	230	3263	260	3358
201	3164	231	3266	261	3361
202	3167	232	3269	262	3364
203	3171	233	3273	263	3367
204	3174	234	3276	264	3370
205	3178	235	3279	265	3374
206	3181	236	3282	266	3377
207	3185	237	3286	267	3380
208	3188	238	3289	268	3383
209	3192	239	3292	269	3386

(*Continued*)

TABLE VII · *Normal Population of 1000 Observations*

TABLE VII (*Continued*)

Identification No.	Observation Value	Identification No.	Observation Value	Identification No.	Observation Value
270	3389	300	3477	330	3561
271	3392	301	3480	331	3564
272	3395	302	3483	332	3567
273	3398	303	3486	333	3570
274	3401	304	3488	334	3572
275	3404	305	3491	335	3575
276	3407	306	3494	336	3578
277	3410	307	3497	337	3581
278	3413	308	3500	338	3583
279	3416	309	3503	339	3586
280	3419	310	3506	340	3589
281	3422	311	3508	341	3592
282	3425	312	3511	342	3594
283	3428	313	3514	343	3597
284	3430	314	3517	344	3600
285	3433	315	3520	345	3602
286	3436	316	3522	346	3605
287	3439	317	3525	347	3608
288	3442	318	3528	348	3611
289	3445	319	3531	349	3613
290	3448	320	3534	350	3616
291	3451	321	3536	351	3619
292	3454	322	3539	352	3621
293	3457	323	3542	353	3624
294	3460	324	3545	354	3627
295	3463	325	3548	355	3629
296	3466	326	3550	356	3632
297	3468	327	3553	357	3635
298	3471	328	3556	358	3638
299	3474	329	3559	359	3640

(*Continued*)

TABLE VII · Normal Population of 1000 Observations

TABLE VII (*Continued*)

Identification No.	*Observation Value*	*Identification No.*	*Observation Value*	*Identification No.*	*Observation Value*
360	3643	390	3722	420	3799
361	3646	391	3725	421	3802
362	3648	392	3727	422	3804
363	3651	393	3730	423	3807
364	3643	394	3732	424	3810
365	3656	395	3735	425	3812
366	3659	396	3738	426	3815
367	3662	397	3740	427	3817
368	3664	398	3743	428	3820
369	3667	399	3745	429	3822
370	3669	400	3748	430	3825
371	3672	401	3750	431	3827
372	3675	402	3753	432	3830
373	3677	403	3756	433	3833
374	3680	404	3758	434	3835
375	3683	405	3761	435	3838
376	3685	406	3763	436	3840
377	3688	407	3766	437	3843
378	3691	408	3769	438	3845
379	3693	409	3771	439	3848
380	3696	410	3774	440	3850
381	3698	411	3776	441	3853
382	3701	412	3779	442	3855
383	3704	413	3781	443	3858
384	3706	414	3784	444	3860
385	3709	415	3787	445	3863
386	3712	416	3789	446	3866
387	3714	417	3792	447	3868
388	3717	418	3794	448	3871
389	3719	419	3797	449	3873

(*Continued*)

TABLE VII · Normal Population of 1000 Observations

TABLE VII (*Continued*)

Identifi-cation No.	Observation Value	Identifi-cation No.	Observation Value	Identifi-cation No.	Observation Value
450	3876	480	3951	510	4026
451	3878	481	3954	511	4029
452	3881	482	3956	512	4031
453	3883	483	3959	513	4034
454	3886	484	3961	514	4036
455	3888	485	3964	515	4039
456	3891	486	3966	516	4041
457	3893	487	3969	517	4044
458	3896	488	3971	518	4046
459	3898	489	3974	519	4049
460	3901	490	3976	520	4051
461	3903	491	3979	521	4054
462	3906	492	3981	522	4056
463	3908	493	3984	523	4059
464	3911	494	3986	524	4061
465	3913	495	3989	525	4064
466	3916	496	3991	526	4066
467	3918	497	3994	527	4069
468	3921	498	3996	528	4072
469	3923	499	3999	529	4074
470	3926	500	4001	530	4077
471	3928	501	4004	531	4079
472	3931	502	4006	532	4082
473	3934	503	4009	533	4084
474	3936	504	4011	534	4087
475	3939	505	4014	535	4089
476	3941	506	4016	536	4092
477	3944	507	4019	537	4094
478	3946	508	4021	538	4097
479	3949	509	4024	539	4099

(*Continued*)

TABLE VII · *Normal Population of 1000 Observations*

TABLE VII (*Continued*)

Identification No.	Observation Value	Identification No.	Observation Value	Identification No.	Observation Value
540	4102	570	4178	600	4255
541	4104	571	4180	601	4257
542	4107	572	4183	602	4260
543	4109	573	4185	603	4262
544	4112	574	4188	604	4265
545	4114	575	4190	605	4268
546	4117	576	4193	606	4270
547	4119	577	4196	607	4273
548	4122	578	4198	608	4275
549	4124	579	4201	609	4278
550	4127	580	4203	610	4281
551	4129	581	4206	611	4283
552	4132	582	4208	612	4286
553	4134	583	4211	613	4288
554	4137	584	4213	614	4291
555	4140	585	4216	615	4294
556	4142	586	4219	616	4296
557	4145	587	4221	617	4299
558	4147	588	4224	618	4302
559	4150	589	4226	619	4304
560	4152	590	4229	620	4307
561	4155	591	4231	621	4309
562	4157	592	4234	622	4312
563	4160	593	4237	623	4315
564	4162	594	4239	624	4317
565	4165	595	4242	625	4320
566	4167	596	4244	626	4323
567	4170	597	4247	627	4325
568	4173	598	4250	628	4328
569	4175	599	4252	629	4331

(*Continued*)

TABLE VII · Normal Population of 1000 Observations

TABLE VII (*Continued*)

Identifi-cation No.	Observation Value	Identifi-cation No.	Observation Value	Identifi-cation No.	Observation Value
630	4333	660	4414	690	4497
631	4336	661	4417	691	4500
632	4338	662	4419	692	4503
633	4341	663	4422	693	4506
634	4344	664	4425	694	4509
635	4346	665	4428	695	4512
636	4349	666	4430	696	4514
637	4352	667	4433	697	4517
638	4354	668	4436	698	4520
639	4357	669	4439	699	4523
640	4360	670	4441	700	4526
641	4362	671	4444	701	4529
642	4365	672	4447	702	4532
643	4368	673	4450	703	4534
644	4371	674	4452	704	4537
645	4373	675	4455	705	4540
646	4376	676	4458	706	4543
647	4379	677	4461	707	4546
648	4381	678	4464	708	4549
649	4384	679	4466	709	4552
650	4387	680	4469	710	4555
651	4389	681	4472	711	4558
652	4392	682	4475	712	4561
653	4395	683	4478	713	4564
654	4398	684	4480	714	4567
655	4400	685	4483	715	4570
656	4403	686	4486	716	4572
657	4406	687	4489	717	4575
658	4408	688	4492	718	4578
659	4411	689	4494	719	4581

(*Continued*)

TABLE VII · *Normal Population of 1000 Observations*

TABLE VII (*Continued*)

Identifi-cation No.	Observation Value	Identifi-cation No.	Observation Value	Identifi-cation No.	Observation Value
720	4584	750	4676	780	4774
721	4587	751	4679	781	4777
722	4590	752	4682	782	4781
723	4593	753	4686	783	4784
724	4596	754	4689	784	4788
725	4599	755	4692	785	4791
726	4602	756	4695	786	4794
727	4605	757	4698	787	4798
728	4608	758	4702	788	4801
729	4611	759	4705	789	4805
730	4614	760	4708	790	4808
731	4617	761	4711	791	4812
732	4620	762	4714	792	4815
733	4623	763	4718	793	4819
734	4626	764	4721	794	4822
735	4630	765	4724	795	4826
736	4633	766	4727	796	4829
737	4636	767	4731	797	4833
738	4639	768	4734	798	4836
739	4642	769	4737	799	4840
740	4645	770	4740	800	4843
741	4648	771	4744	801	4847
742	4651	772	4747	802	4851
743	4654	773	4750	803	4854
744	4657	774	4754	804	4858
745	4660	775	4757	805	4861
746	4664	776	4760	806	4865
747	4667	777	4764	807	4869
748	4670	778	4767	808	4872
749	4673	779	4770	809	4876

(*Continued*)

TABLE VII · Normal Population of 1000 Observations

TABLE VII (*Continued*)

Identifi-cation No.	Observation Value	Identifi-cation No.	Observation Value	Identifi-cation No.	Observation Value
810	4880	840	4997	870	5129
811	4883	841	5001	871	5134
812	4887	842	5005	872	5138
813	4891	843	5009	873	5143
814	4895	844	5013	874	5148
815	4898	845	5017	875	5153
816	4902	846	5022	876	5158
817	4906	847	5026	877	5163
818	4910	848	5030	878	5168
819	4914	849	5034	879	5172
820	4917	850	5039	880	5178
821	4921	851	5043	881	5182
822	4925	852	5047	882	5188
823	4929	853	5052	883	5193
824	4933	854	5056	884	5198
825	4937	855	5060	885	5203
826	4940	856	5065	886	5208
827	4944	857	5069	887	5213
828	4948	858	5074	888	5219
829	4952	859	5078	889	5224
830	4956	860	5083	890	5229
831	4960	861	5087	891	5235
832	4964	862	5092	892	5240
833	4968	863	5096	893	5245
834	4972	864	5101	894	5251
835	4976	865	5105	895	5256
836	4980	866	5110	896	5262
837	4984	867	5115	897	5267
838	4988	868	5119	898	5273
839	4992	869	5124	899	5279

(*Continued*)

TABLE VII · Normal Population of 1000 Observations

TABLE VII (*Continued*)

Identifi-cation No.	Observation Value	Identifi-cation No.	Observation Value	Identifi-cation No.	Observation Value
900	5284	935	5518	970	5888
901	5290	936	5526	971	5903
902	5296	937	5534	972	5919
903	5302	938	5542	973	5935
904	5308	939	5551	974	5952
905	5314	940	5559	975	5969
906	5320	941	5568	976	5986
907	5326	942	5576	977	6005
908	5332	943	5585	978	6024
909	5338	944	5594	979	6044
910	5344	945	5603	980	6064
911	5350	946	5612	981	6086
912	5356	947	5621	982	6108
913	5363	948	5630	983	6132
914	5369	949	5640	984	6157
915	5375	950	5650	985	6184
916	5382	951	5660	986	6212
917	5388	952	5670	987	6242
918	5395	953	5680	988	6274
919	5402	954	5690	989	6308
920	5408	955	5701	990	6346
921	5415	956	5711	991	6387
922	5422	957	5722	992	6433
923	5429	958	5734	993	6485
924	5436	959	5745	994	6544
925	5443	960	5757	995	6614
926	5450	961	5768	996	6700
927	5457	962	5780	997	6813
928	5465	963	5793	998	6984
929	5472	964	5806	999	7358
930	5480	965	5818		
931	5487	966	5832		
932	5495	967	5845		
933	5502	968	5859		
934	5510	969	5874		

TABLE VIII · Relationship between z and r

TABLE VIII. Relationship between z and r (or μ_z and ρ)*

z	.00	.01	.02	.03	.04	.05	.06	.07	.08	.09
.0	.0000	.0100	.0200	.0300	.0400	.0500	.0599	.0699	.0798	.0898
.1	.0997	.1096	.1194	.1293	.1391	.1489	.1587	.1684	.1781	.1878
.2	.1974	.2070	.2165	.2260	.2355	.2449	.2543	.2636	.2729	.2821
.3	.2913	.3004	.3095	.3185	.3275	.3364	.3452	.3540	.3627	.3714
.4	.3800	.3885	.3969	.4053	.4136	.4219	.4301	.4382	.4462	.4542
.5	.4621	.4700	.4777	.4854	.4930	.5005	.5080	.5154	.5227	.5299
.6	.5370	.5441	.5511	.5581	.5649	.5717	.5784	.5850	.5915	.5980
.7	.6044	.6107	.6169	.6231	.6291	.6352	.6411	.6469	.6527	.6584
.8	.6640	.6696	.6751	.6805	.6858	.6911	.6963	.7014	.7064	.7114
.9	.7163	.7211	.7259	.7306	.7352	.7398	.7443	.7487	.7531	.7574
1.0	.7616	.7658	.7699	.7739	.7779	.7818	.7857	.7895	.7932	.7969
1.1	.8005	.8041	.8076	.8110	.8144	.8178	.8210	.8243	.8275	.8306
1.2	.8337	.8367	.8397	.8426	.8455	.8483	.8511	.8538	.8565	.8591
1.3	.8617	.8643	.8668	.8693	.8717	.8741	.8764	.8787	.8810	.8832
1.4	.8854	.8875	.8896	.8917	.8937	.8957	.8977	.8996	.9015	.9033
1.5	.9052	.9069	.9087	.9104	.9121	.9138	.9154	.9170	.9186	.9202
1.6	.9217	.9232	.9246	.9261	.9275	.9289	.9302	.9316	.9329	.9342
1.7	.9354	.9367	.9379	.9391	.9402	.9414	.9425	.9436	.9447	.9458
1.8	.9468	.9478	.9498	.9488	.9508	.9518	.9527	.9536	.9545	.9554
1.9	.9562	.9571	.9579	.9587	.9595	.9603	.9611	.9619	.9626	.9633
2.0	.9640	.9647	.9654	.9661	.9668	.9674	.9680	.9687	.9693	.9699
2.1	.9705	.9710	.9716	.9722	.9727	.9732	.9738	.9743	.9748	.9753
2.2	.9757	.9762	.9767	.9771	.9776	.9780	.9785	.9789	.9793	.9797
2.3	.9801	.9805	.9809	.9812	.9816	.9820	.9823	.9827	.9830	.9834
2.4	.9837	.9840	.9843	.9846	.9849	.9852	.9855	.9858	.9861	.9863
2.5	.9866	.9869	.9871	.9874	.9876	.9879	.9881	.9884	.9886	.9888
2.6	.9890	.9892	.9895	.9897	.9899	.9901	.9903	.9905	.9906	.9908
2.7	.9910	.9912	.9914	.9915	.9917	.9919	.9920	.9922	.9923	.9925
2.8	.9926	.9928	.9929	.9931	.9932	.9933	.9935	.9936	.9937	.9938
2.9	.9940	.9941	.9942	.9943	.9944	.9945	.9946	.9947	.9949	.9950
3.0	.9951									
4.0	.9993									
5.0	.9999									

* r-values appear in the body of the table, the z-values in scales at the left and above the table.

TABLE IX · *Percentage Points of the F-Distribution*

TABLE IX. Percentage Points of the *F*-Distribution*

F-distribution: 5 percent points

ν_2 \ ν_1	1	2	3	4	5	6	7	8	9
1	161.45	199.50	215.71	224.58	230.16	233.99	236.77	238.88	240.54
2	18.513	19.000	19.164	19.247	19.296	19.330	19.353	19.371	19.385
3	10.128	9.5521	9.2766	9.1172	9.0135	8.9406	8.8868	8.8452	8.8123
4	7.7086	6.9443	6.5914	6.3883	6.2560	6.1631	6.0942	6.0410	5.9988
5	6.6079	5.7861	5.4095	5.1922	5.0503	4.9503	4.8759	4.8183	4.7725
6	5.9874	5.1433	4.7571	4.5337	4.3874	4.2839	4.2066	4.1468	4.0990
7	5.5914	4.7374	4.3468	4.1203	3.9715	3.8660	3.7870	3.7257	3.6767
8	5.3177	4.4590	4.0662	3.8378	3.6875	3.5806	3.5005	3.4381	3.3881
9	5.1174	4.2565	3.8626	3.6331	3.4817	3.3738	3.2927	3.2296	3.1789
10	4.9646	4.1028	3.7083	3.4780	3.3258	3.2172	3.1355	3.0717	3.0204
11	4.8443	3.9823	3.5874	3.3567	3.2039	3.0946	3.0123	2.9480	2.8962
12	4.7472	3.8853	3.4903	3.2592	3.1059	2.9961	2.9134	2.8486	2.7964
13	4.6672	3.8056	3.4105	3.1791	3.0254	2.9153	2.8321	2.7669	2.7144
14	4.6001	3.7389	3.3439	3.1122	2.9582	2.8477	2.7642	2.6987	2.6458
15	4.5431	3.6823	3.2874	3.0556	2.9013	2.7905	2.7066	2.6408	2.5876
16	4.4940	3.6337	3.2389	3.0069	2.8524	2.7413	2.6572	2.5911	2.5377
17	4.4513	3.5915	3.1968	2.9647	2.8100	2.6987	2.6143	2.5480	2.4943
18	4.4139	3.5546	3.1599	2.9277	2.7729	2.6613	2.5767	2.5102	2.4563
19	4.3808	3.5219	3.1274	2.8951	2.7401	2.6283	2.5435	2.4768	2.4227
20	4.3513	3.4928	3.0984	2.8661	2.7109	2.5990	2.5140	2.4471	2.3928
21	4.3248	3.4668	3.0725	2.8401	2.6848	2.5757	2.4876	2.4205	2.3661
22	4.3009	3.4434	3.0491	2.8167	2.6613	2.5491	2.4638	2.3965	2.3419
23	4.2793	3.4221	3.0280	2.7955	2.6400	2.5277	2.4422	2.3748	2.3201
24	4.2597	3.4028	3.0088	2.7763	2.6207	2.5082	2.4226	2.3551	2.3002
25	4.2417	3.3852	2.9912	2.7587	2.6030	2.4904	2.4047	2.3371	2.2821
26	4.2252	3.3690	2.9751	2.7426	2.5868	2.4741	2.3883	2.3205	2.2655
27	4.2100	3.3541	2.9604	2.7278	2.5719	2.4591	2.3732	2.3053	2.2501
28	4.1960	3.3404	2.9467	2.7141	2.5581	2.4453	2.3593	2.2913	2.2360
29	4.1830	3.3277	2.9340	2.7014	2.5454	2.4324	2.3463	2.2782	2.2229
30	4.1709	3.3158	2.9223	2.6896	2.5336	2.4205	2.3343	2.2662	2.2107
40	4.0848	3.2317	2.8387	2.6060	2.4495	2.3359	2.2490	2.1802	2.1240
60	4.0012	3.1504	2.7581	2.5252	2.3683	2.2540	2.1665	2.0970	2.0401
120	3.9201	3.0718	2.6802	2.4472	2.2900	2.1750	2.0867	2.0164	1.9588
∞	3.8415	2.9957	2.6049	2.3719	2.2141	2.0986	2.0096	1.9384	1.8799

(Continued)

* Reproduced from Merrington, Maxine, and Thompson, Catherine M.: "Tables of percentage points of the inverted Beta (*F*) distribution," *Biometrika*, Vol. 33 (1943), pp. 73–88, by permission of Professor E. S. Pearson.

TABLE IX · Percentage Points of the F-Distribution

TABLE IX (*Continued*)

F-distribution: 5 percent points

ν_1 / ν_2	10	12	15	20	24	30	40	60	120	∞
1	241.88	243.91	245.95	248.01	249.05	250.09	251.14	252.20	253.25	254.32
2	19.396	19.413	19.429	19.446	19.454	19.462	19.471	19.479	19.487	19.496
3	8.7855	8.7446	8.7029	8.6602	8.6385	8.6166	8.5944	8.5720	8.5494	8.5265
4	5.9644	5.9117	5.8578	5.8025	5.7744	5.7459	5 7170	5.6878	5.6581	5.6281
5	4.7351	4.6777	4.6188	4.5581	4.5272	4.4957	4.4638	4.4314	4.3984	4.3650
6	4.0600	3.9999	3.9381	3.8742	3.8415	3.8082	3.7743	3.7398	3.7047	3.6688
7	3.6365	3.5747	3.5108	3.4445	3.4105	3.3758	3.3404	3.3043	3.2674	3.2298
8	3.3472	3.2840	3.2184	3.1503	3.1152	3.0794	3.0428	3.0053	2.9669	2.9276
9	3.1373	3.0729	3.0061	2.9365	2.9005	2.8637	2.8259	2.7872	2.7475	2.7067
10	2.9782	2.9130	2.8450	2.7740	2.7372	2.6996	2.6609	2.6211	2.5801	2.5379
11	2.8536	2.7876	2.7186	2.6464	2.6090	2.5705	2.5309	2.4901	2.4480	2.4045
12	2.7534	2.6866	2.6169	2.5436	2.5055	2.4663	2.4259	2.3842	2.3410	2.2962
13	2.6710	2.6037	2.5331	2.4589	2.4202	2.3803	2.3392	2.2966	2.2524	2.2064
14	2.6021	2.5342	2.4630	2.3879	2.3487	2.3082	2.2664	2.2230	2.1778	2.1307
15	2.5437	2.4753	2.4035	2.3275	2.2878	2.2468	2.2043	2.1601	2.1141	2.0658
16	2.4935	2.4247	2.3522	2.2756	2.2354	2.1938	2.1507	2.1058	2.0589	2.0096
17	2.4499	2.3807	2.3077	2.2304	2.1898	2.1477	2.1040	2.0584	2.0107	1.9604
18	2.4117	2.3421	2.2686	2.1906	2.1497	2.1071	2.0629	2.0166	1.9681	1.9168
19	2.3779	2.3080	2.2341	2.1555	2.1141	2.0712	2.0264	1.9796	1.9302	1.8780
20	2.3479	2.2776	2.2033	2.1242	2.0825	2.0391	1.9938	1.9464	1.8963	1.8432
21	2.3210	2.2504	2.1757	2.0960	2.0540	2.0102	1.9645	1.9165	1.8657	1.8117
22	2.2967	2.2258	2.1508	2.0707	2.0283	1.9842	1.9380	1.8895	1.8380	1.7831
23	2.2747	2.2036	2.1282	2.0476	2.0050	1.9605	1.9139	1.8649	1.8128	1.7570
24	2.2547	2.1834	2.1077	2.0267	1.9838	1.9390	1.8920	1.8424	1.7897	1.7331
25	2.2365	2.1649	2.0889	2.0075	1.9643	1.9192	1.8718	1.8217	1.7684	1.7110
26	2.2197	2.1479	2.0716	1.9898	1.9464	1.9010	1.8533	1.8027	1.7488	1.6906
27	2.2043	2.1323	2.0558	1.9736	1.9299	1.8842	1.8361	1.7851	1.7307	1.6717
28	2.1900	2.1179	2.0411	1.9586	1.9147	1.8687	1.8203	1.7689	1.7138	1.6541
29	2.1768	2.1045	2.0275	1.9446	1.9005	1.8543	1.8055	1.7537	1.6981	1.6377
30	2.1646	2.0921	2.0148	1.9317	1.8874	1.8409	1.7918	1.7396	1.6835	1.6223
40	2.0772	2.0035	1.9245	1.8389	1.7929	1.7444	1.6928	1.6373	1.5766	1.5089
60	1.9926	1.9174	1.8364	1.7480	1.7001	1.6491	1.5943	1.5343	1.4673	1.3893
120	1.9105	1.8337	1.7505	1.6587	1.6084	1.5543	1.4952	1.4290	1.3519	1.2539
∞	1.8307	1.7522	1.6664	1.5705	1.5173	1.4591	1.3940	1.3180	1.2214	1.0000

(*Continued*)

TABLE IX · Percentage Points of the F-Distribution

TABLE IX (*Continued*)

F-distribution: 2.5 percent points

ν_2 \ ν_1	1	2	3	4	5	6	7	8	9
1	647.79	799.50	864.16	899.58	921.85	937.11	948.22	956.66	963.28
2	38.506	39.000	39.165	39.248	29.298	39.331	39.355	39.373	39.387
3	17.443	16.044	15.439	15.101	14.885	14.735	14.624	14.540	14.473
4	12.218	10.649	9.9792	9.6045	9.3645	9.1973	9.0741	8.9796	8.9047
5	10.007	8.4336	7.7636	7.3879	7.1464	6.9777	6.8531	6.7572	6.6810
6	8.8131	7.2598	6.5988	6.2272	5.9876	5.8197	5.6955	5.5996	5.5234
7	8.0727	6.5415	5.8898	5.5226	5.2852	5.1186	4.9949	4.8994	4.8232
8	7.5709	6.0595	5.4160	5.0526	4.8173	4.6517	4.5286	4.4332	4.3572
9	7.2093	5.7147	5.0781	4.7181	4.4844	4.3197	4.1971	4.1020	4.0260
10	6.9367	5.4564	4.8256	4.4683	4.2361	4.0721	3.9498	3.8549	3.7790
11	6.7241	5.2559	4.6300	4.2751	4.0440	3.8807	3.7586	3.6638	3.5879
12	6.5538	5.0959	4.4742	4.1212	3.8911	3.7283	3.6065	3.5118	3.4358
13	6.4143	4.9653	4.3472	3.9959	3.7667	3.6043	3.4827	3.3880	3.3120
14	6.2979	4.8567	4.2417	3.8919	3.6634	3.5014	3.3799	3.2853	3.2093
15	6.1995	4.7650	4.1528	3.8043	3.5764	3.4147	3.2934	3.1987	3.1227
16	6.1151	4.6867	4.0768	3.7294	3.5021	3.3406	3.2194	3.1248	3.0488
17	6.0420	4.6189	4.0112	3.6648	3.4379	3.2767	3.1556	3.0610	2.9849
18	5.9781	4.5597	3.9539	3.6083	3.3820	3.2209	3.0999	3.0053	2.9291
19	5.9216	4.5075	3.9034	3.5587	3.3327	3.1718	3.0509	2.9563	2.8800
20	5.8715	4.4613	3.8587	3.5147	3.2891	3.1283	3.0074	2.9128	2.8365
21	5.8266	4.4199	3.8188	3.4754	3.2501	3.0895	2.9686	2.8740	2.7977
22	5.7863	4.3828	3.7829	3.4401	3.2151	3.0546	2.9338	2.8392	2.7628
23	5.7498	4.3492	3.7505	3.4083	3.1835	3.0232	2.9024	2.8077	2.7313
24	5.7167	4.3187	3.7211	3.3794	3.1548	2.9946	2.8738	2.7791	2.7027
25	5.6864	4.2909	3.6943	3.3530	3.1287	2.9685	2.8478	2.7531	2.6766
26	5.6586	4.2655	3.6697	3.3289	3.1048	2.9447	2.8240	2.7293	2.6528
27	5.6331	4.2421	3.6472	3.3067	3.0828	2.9228	2.8021	2.7074	2.6309
28	5.6096	4.2205	3.6264	3.2863	3.0625	2.9027	2.7820	2.6872	2.6106
29	5.5878	4.2006	3.6072	3.2674	3.0438	2.8840	2.7633	2.6686	2.5919
30	5.5675	4.1821	3.5894	3.2499	3.0265	2.8667	2.7460	2.6513	2.5746
40	5.4239	4.0510	3.4633	3.1261	2.9037	2.7444	2.6238	2.5289	2.4519
60	5.2857	3.9253	3.3425	3.0077	2.7863	2.6274	2.5068	2.4117	2.3344
120	5.1524	3.8046	3.2270	2.8943	2.6740	2.5154	2.3948	2.2994	2.2217
∞	5.0239	3.6889	3.1161	2.7858	2.5665	2.4082	2.2875	2.1918	2.1136

(*Continued*)

TABLE IX · Percentage Points of the F-Distribution

TABLE IX (*Continued*)

F-distribution: 2.5 percent points

ν_1 / ν_2	10	12	15	20	24	30	40	60	120	∞
1	968.63	976.71	984.87	993.10	997.25	1001.4	1005.6	1009.8	1014.0	1018.3
2	39.398	39.415	39.431	39.448	39.456	39.465	39.473	39.481	39.490	39.498
3	14.419	14.337	14.253	14.167	14.124	14.081	14.037	13.992	13.947	13.902
4	8.8439	8.7512	8.6565	8.5599	8.5109	8.4613	8.4111	8.3604	8.3092	8.2573
5	6.6192	6.5246	6.4277	6.3285	6.2780	6.2269	6.1751	6.1225	6.0693	6.0153
6	5.4613	5.3662	5.2687	5.1684	5.1172	5.0652	5.0125	4.9589	4.9045	4.8491
7	4.7611	4.6658	4.5678	4.4667	4.4150	4.3624	4.3089	4.2544	4.1989	4.1423
8	4.2951	4.1997	4.1012	3.9995	3.9472	3.8940	3.8398	3.7844	3.7279	3.6702
9	3.9639	3.8682	3.7694	3.6669	3.6142	3.5604	3.5055	3.4493	3.3918	3.3329
10	3.7168	3.6209	3.5217	3.4186	3.3654	3.3110	3.2554	3.1984	3.1399	3.0798
11	3.5257	3.4296	3.3299	3.2261	3.1725	3.1176	3.0613	3.0035	2.9441	2.8828
12	3.3736	3.2773	3.1772	3.0728	3.0187	2.9633	2.9063	2.8478	2.7874	2.7249
13	3.2497	3.1532	3.0527	2.9477	2.8932	2.8373	2.7797	2.7204	2.6590	2.5955
14	3.1469	3.0501	2.9493	2.8437	2.7888	2.7324	2.6742	2.6142	2.5519	2.4872
15	3.0602	2.9633	2.8621	2.7559	2.7006	2.6437	2.5850	2.5242	2.4611	2.3953
16	2.9862	2.8890	2.7875	2.6808	2.6252	2.5678	2.5085	2.4471	2.3831	2.3163
17	2.9222	2.8249	2.7230	2.6158	2.5598	2.5021	2.4422	2.3801	2.3153	2.2474
18	2.8664	2.7689	2.6667	2.5590	2.5027	2.4445	2.3842	2.3214	2.2558	2.1869
19	2.8173	2.7196	2.6171	2.5089	2.4523	2.3937	2.3329	2.2695	2.2032	2.1333
20	2.7737	2.6758	2.5731	2.4645	2.4076	2.3486	2.2873	2.2234	2.1562	2.0853
21	2.7348	2.6368	2.5338	2.4247	2.3675	2.3082	2.2465	2.1819	2.1141	2.0422
22	2.6998	2.6017	2.4984	2.3890	2.3315	2.2718	2.2097	2.1446	2.0760	2.0032
23	2.6682	2.5699	2.4665	2.3567	2.2989	2.2389	2.1763	2.1107	2.0415	1.9677
24	2.6396	2.5412	2.4374	2.3273	2.2693	2.2090	2.1460	2.0799	2.0099	1.9353
25	2.6135	2.5149	2.4110	2.3005	2.2422	2.1816	2.1183	2.0517	1.9811	1.9055
26	2.5895	2.4909	2.3867	2.2759	2.2174	2.1565	2.0928	2.0257	1.9545	1.8781
27	2.5676	2.4688	2.3644	2.2533	2.1946	2.1334	2.0693	2.0018	1.9299	1.8527
28	2.5473	2.4484	2.3438	2.2324	2.1735	2.1121	2.0477	1.9796	1.9072	1.8291
29	2.5286	2.4295	2.3248	2.2131	2.1540	2.0923	2.0276	1.9591	1.8861	1.8072
30	2.5112	2.4120	2.3072	2.1952	2.1359	2.0739	2.0089	1.9400	1.8664	1.7867
40	2.3882	2.2882	2.1819	2.0677	2.0069	1.9429	1.8752	1.8028	1.7242	1.6371
60	2.2702	2.1692	2.0613	1.9445	1.8817	1.8152	1.7440	1.6668	1.5810	1.4822
120	2.1570	2.0548	1.9450	1.8249	1.7597	1.6899	1.6141	1.5299	1.4327	1.3104
∞	2.0483	1.9447	1.8326	1.7085	1.6402	1.5660	1.4835	1.3883	1.2684	1.0000

(*Continued*)

TABLE IX · Percentage Points of the F-Distribution

TABLE IX (*Continued*)

F-distribution: 1 percent points

ν_1 / ν_2	1	2	3	4	5	6	7	8	9
1	4052.2	4999.5	5403.3	5624.6	5763.7	5859.0	5928.3	5981.6	6022.5
2	98.503	99.000	99.166	99.249	99.299	99.332	99.356	99.374	99.388
3	34.116	30.817	29.457	28.710	28.237	27.911	27.672	27.489	27.345
4	21.198	18.000	16.694	15.977	15.522	15.207	14.976	14.799	14.659
5	16.258	13.274	12.060	11.392	10.967	10.672	10.456	10.289	10.158
6	13.745	10.925	9.7795	9.1483	8.7459	8.4661	8.2600	8.1016	7.9761
7	12.246	9.5466	8.4513	7.8467	7.4604	7.1914	6.9928	6.8401	6.7188
8	11.259	8.6491	7.5910	7.0060	6.6318	6.3707	6.1776	6.0289	5.9106
9	10.561	8.0215	6.9919	6.4221	6.0569	5.8018	5.6129	5.4671	5.3511
10	10.044	7.5594	6.5523	5.9943	5.6363	5.3858	5.2001	5.0567	4.9424
11	9.6460	7.2057	6.2167	5.6683	5.3160	5.0692	4.8861	4.7445	4.6315
12	9.3302	6.9266	5.9526	5.4119	5.0643	4.8206	4.6395	4.4994	4.3875
13	9.0738	6.7010	5.7394	5.2053	4.8616	4.6204	4.4410	4.3021	4.1911
14	8.8616	6.5149	5.5639	5.0354	4.6950	4.4558	4.2779	4.1399	4.0297
15	8.6831	6.3589	5.4170	4.8932	4.5556	4.3183	4.1415	4.0045	3.8948
16	8.5310	6.2262	5.2922	4.7726	4.4374	4.2016	4.0259	3.8896	3.7804
17	8.3997	6.1121	5.1850	4.6690	4.3359	4.1015	3.9267	3.7910	3.6822
18	8.2854	6.0129	5.0919	4.5790	4.2479	4.0146	3.8406	3.7054	3.5971
19	8.1850	5.9259	5.0103	4.5003	4.1708	3.9386	3.7653	3.6305	3.5225
20	8.0960	5.8489	4.9382	4.4307	4.1027	3.8714	3.6987	3.5644	3.4567
21	8.0166	5.7804	4.8740	4.3688	4.0421	3.8117	3.6396	3.5056	3.3981
22	7.9454	5.7190	4.8166	4.3134	3.9880	3.7583	3.5867	3.4530	3.3458
23	7.8811	5.6637	4.7649	4.2635	3.9392	3.7102	3.5390	3.4057	3.2986
24	7.8229	5.6136	4.7181	4.2184	3.8951	3.6667	3.4959	3.3629	3.2560
25	7.7698	5.5680	4.6755	4.1774	3.8550	3.6272	3.4568	3.3239	3.2172
26	7.7213	5.5263	4.6366	4.1400	3.8183	3.5911	3.4210	3.2884	3.1818
27	7.6767	5.4881	4.6009	4.1056	3.7848	3.5580	3.3882	3.2558	3.1494
28	7.6356	5.4529	4.5681	4.0740	3.7539	3.5276	3.3581	3.2259	3.1195
29	7.5976	5.4205	4.5378	4.0449	3.7254	3.4995	3.3302	3.1982	3.0920
30	7.5625	5.3904	4.5097	4.0179	3.6990	3.4735	3.3045	3.1726	3.0665
40	7.3141	5.1785	4.3126	3.8283	3.5138	3.2910	3.1238	2.9930	2.8876
60	7.0771	4.9774	4.1259	3.6491	3.3389	3.1187	2.9530	2.8233	2.7185
120	6.8510	4.7865	3.9493	3.4796	3.1735	2.9559	2.7918	2.6629	2.5586
∞	6.6349	4.6052	3.7816	3.3192	3.0173	2.8020	2.6393	2.5113	2.4073

(*Continued*)

TABLE IX · *Percentage Points of the F-Distribution*

TABLE IX (*Continued*)

F-distribution: 1 percent points

ν_2 \ ν_1	10	12	15	20	24	30	40	60	120	∞
1	6055.8	6106.3	6157.3	6208.7	6234.6	6260.7	6286.8	6313.0	6339.4	6366.0
2	99.399	99.416	99.432	99.449	99.458	99.466	99.474	99.483	99.491	99.501
3	27.229	27.052	26.872	26.690	26.598	26.505	26.411	26.316	26.221	26.125
4	14.546	14.374	14.198	14.020	13.929	13.838	13.745	13.652	13.558	13.463
5	10.051	9.8883	9.7222	9.5527	9.4665	9.3793	9.2912	9.2020	9.1118	9.0204
6	7.8741	7.7183	7.5590	7.3958	7.3127	7.2285	7.1432	7.0568	6.9690	6.8801
7	6.6201	6.4691	6.3143	6.1554	6.0743	5.9921	5.9084	5.8236	5.7372	5.6495
8	5.8143	5.6668	5.5151	5.3591	5.2793	5.1981	5.1156	5.0316	4.9460	4.8588
9	5.2565	5.1114	4.9621	4.8080	4.7290	4.6486	4.5667	4.4831	4.3978	4.3105
10	4.8492	4.7059	4.5582	4.4054	4.3269	4.2469	4.1653	4.0819	3.9965	3.9090
11	4.5393	4.3974	4.2509	4.0990	4.0209	3.9411	3.8596	3.7761	3.6904	3.6025
12	4.2961	4.1553	4.0096	3.8584	3.7805	3.7008	3.6192	3.5355	3.4494	3.3608
13	4.1003	3.9603	3.8154	3.6646	3.5868	3.5070	3.4253	3.3413	3.2548	3.1654
14	3.9394	3.8001	3.6557	3.5052	3.4274	3.3476	3.2656	3.1813	3.0942	3.0040
15	3.8049	3.6662	3.5222	3.3719	3.2940	3.2141	3.1319	3.0471	2.9595	2.8684
16	3.6909	3.5527	3.4089	3.2588	3.1808	3.1007	3.0182	2.9330	2.8447	2.7528
17	3.5931	3.4552	3.3117	3.1615	3.0835	3.0032	2.9205	2.8348	2.7459	2.6530
18	3.5082	3.3706	3.2273	3.0771	2.9990	2.9185	2.8354	2.7493	2.6597	2.5660
19	3.4338	3.2965	3.1533	3.0031	2.9249	2.8422	2.7608	2.6742	2.5839	2.4893
20	3.3682	3.2311	3.0880	2.9377	2.8594	2.7785	2.6947	2.6077	2.5168	2.4212
21	3.3098	3.1729	3.0299	2.8796	2.8011	2.7200	2.6359	2.5484	2.4568	2.3603
22	3.2576	3.1209	2.9780	2.8274	2.7488	2.6675	2.5831	2.4951	2.4029	2.3055
23	3.2106	3.0740	2.9311	2.7805	2.7017	2.6202	2.5355	2.4471	2.3542	2.2559
24	3.1681	3.0316	2.8887	2.7380	2.6591	2.5773	2.4923	2.4035	2.3099	2.2107
25	3.1294	2.9931	2.8502	2.6993	2.6203	2.5383	2.4530	2.3637	2.2695	2.1694
26	3.0941	2.9579	2.8150	2.6640	2.5848	2.5026	2.4170	2.3273	2.2325	2.1315
27	3.0618	2.9256	2.7827	2.6316	2.5522	2.4699	2.3840	2.2938	2.1984	2.0965
28	3.0320	2.8959	2.7530	2.6017	2.5223	2.4397	2.3535	2.2629	2.1670	2.0642
29	3.0045	2.8685	2.7256	2.5742	2.4946	2.4118	2.3253	2.2344	2.1378	2.0342
30	2.9791	2.8431	2.7002	2.5487	2.4689	2.3860	2.2992	2.2079	2.1107	2.0062
40	2.8005	2.6648	2.5216	2.3689	2.2880	2.2034	2.1142	2.0194	1.9172	1.8047
60	2.6318	2.4961	2.3523	2.1978	2.1154	2.0285	1.9360	1.8363	1.7263	1.6006
120	2.4721	2.3363	2.1915	2.0346	1.9500	1.8600	1.7628	1.6557	1.5330	1.3805
∞	2.3209	2.1848	2.0385	1.8783	1.7908	1.6964	1.5923	1.4730	1.3246	1.0000

(*Continued*)

TABLE IX · Percentage Points of the F-Distribution

TABLE IX (*Continued*)

F-distribution: .5 percent points

ν_1 / ν_2	1	2	3	4	5	6	7	8	9
1	16211	20000	21615	22500	23056	23437	23715	23925	24091
2	198.50	199.00	199.17	199.25	199.30	199.33	199.36	199.37	199.39
3	55.552	49.799	47.467	46.195	45.392	44.838	44.434	44.126	43.882
4	31.333	26.284	24.259	23.155	22.456	21.975	21.622	21.352	21.139
5	22.785	18.314	16.530	15.556	14.940	14.513	14.200	13.961	13.772
6	18.635	14.544	12.917	12.028	11.464	11.073	10.786	10.566	10.391
7	16.236	12.404	10.882	10.050	9.5221	9.1554	8.8854	8.6781	8.5138
8	14.688	11.042	9.5965	8.8051	8.3018	7.9520	7.6942	7.4960	7.3386
9	13.614	10.107	8.7171	7.9559	7.4711	7.1338	6.8849	6.6933	6.5411
10	12.826	9.4270	8.0807	7.3428	6.8723	6.5446	6.3025	6.1159	5.9676
11	12.226	8.9122	7.6004	6.8809	6.4217	6.1015	5.8648	5.6821	5.5368
12	11.754	8.5096	7.2258	6.5211	6.0711	5.7570	5.5245	5.3451	5.2021
13	11.374	8.1865	6.9257	6.2335	5.7910	5.4819	5.2529	5.0761	4.9351
14	11.060	7.9217	6.6803	5.9984	5.5623	5.2574	5.0313	4.8566	4.7173
15	10.798	7.7008	6.4760	5.8029	5.3721	5.0708	4.8473	4.6743	4.5364
16	10.575	7.5138	6.3034	5.6378	5.2117	4.9134	4.6920	4.5207	4.3838
17	10.384	7.3536	6.1556	5.4967	5.0746	4.7789	4.5594	4.3893	4.2535
18	10.218	7.2148	6.0277	5.3746	4.9560	4.6627	4.4448	4.2759	4.1410
19	10.073	7.0935	5.9161	5.2681	4.8526	4.5614	4.3448	4.1770	4.0428
20	9.9439	6.9865	5.8177	5.1743	4.7616	4.4721	4.2569	4.0900	3.9564
21	9.8295	6.8914	5.7304	5.0911	4.6808	4.3931	4.1789	4.0128	3.8799
22	9.7271	6.8064	5.6524	5.0168	4.6088	4.3225	4.1094	3.9440	3.8116
23	9.6348	6.7300	5.5823	4.9500	4.5441	4.2591	4.0469	3.8822	3.7502
24	9.5513	6.6610	5.5190	4.8898	4.4857	4.2019	3.9905	3.8264	3.6949
25	9.4753	6.5982	5.4615	4.8351	4.4327	4.1500	3.9394	3.7758	3.6447
26	9.4059	6.5409	5.4091	4.7852	4.3844	4.1027	3.8928	3.7297	3.5989
27	9.3423	6.4885	5.3611	4.7396	4.3402	4.0594	3.8501	3.6875	3.5571
28	9.2838	6.4403	5.3170	4.6977	4.2996	4.0197	3.8110	3.6487	3.5186
29	9.2297	6.3958	5.2764	4.6591	4.2622	3.9830	3.7749	3.6130	3.4832
30	9.1797	6.3547	5.2388	4.6233	4.2276	3.9492	3.7416	3.5801	3.4505
40	8.8278	6.0664	4.9759	4.3738	3.9860	3.7129	3.5088	3.3498	3.2220
60	8.4946	5.7950	4.7290	4.1399	3.7600	3.4918	3.2911	3.1344	3.0083
120	8.1790	5.5393	4.4973	3.9207	3.5482	3.2849	3.0874	2.9330	2.8083
∞	7.8794	5.2983	4.2794	3.7151	3.3499	3.0913	2.8968	2.7444	2.6210

(*Continued*)

TABLE IX · *Percentage Points of the F-Distribution*

TABLE IX (*Continued*)

F-distribution: .5 percent points

ν_1 / ν_2	10	12	15	20	24	30	40	60	120	∞
1	24224	24426	24630	24836	24940	25044	25148	25253	25359	25465
2	199.40	199.42	199.43	199.45	199.46	199.47	199.47	199.48	199.49	199.51
3	43.686	43.387	43.085	42.778	42.622	42.466	42.308	42.149	41.989	41.829
4	20.967	20.705	20.438	20.167	20.030	19.892	19.752	19.611	19.468	19.325
5	13.618	13.384	13.146	12.903	12.780	12.656	12.530	12.402	12.274	12.144
6	10.250	10.034	9.8140	9.5888	9.4741	9.3583	9.2408	9.1219	9.0015	8.8793
7	8.3803	8.1764	7.9678	7.7540	7.6450	7.5345	7.4225	7.3088	7.1933	7.0760
8	7.2107	7.0149	6.8143	6.6082	6.5029	6.3961	6.2875	6.1772	6.0649	5.9505
9	6.4171	6.2274	6.0325	5.8318	5.7292	5.6248	5.5186	5.4104	5.3001	5.1875
10	5.8467	5.6613	5.4707	5.2740	5.1732	5.0705	4.9659	4.8592	4.7501	4.6385
11	5.4182	5.2363	5.0489	4.8552	4.7557	4.6543	4.5508	4.4450	4.3367	4.2256
12	5.0855	4.9063	4.7214	4.5299	4.4315	4.3309	4.2282	4.1229	4.0149	3.9039
13	4.8199	4.6429	4.4600	4.2703	4.1726	4.0727	3.9704	3.8655	3.7577	3.6465
14	4.6034	4.4281	4.2468	4.0585	3.9614	3.8619	3.7600	3.6553	3.5473	3.4359
15	4.4236	4.2498	4.0698	3.8826	3.7859	3.6867	3.5850	3.4803	3.3722	3.2602
16	4.2719	4.0994	3.9205	3.7342	3.6378	3.5388	3.4372	3.3324	3.2240	3.1115
17	4.1423	3.9709	3.7929	3.6073	3.5112	3.4124	3.3107	3.2058	3.0971	2.9839
18	4.0305	3.8599	3.6827	3.4977	3.4017	3.3030	3.2014	3.0962	2.9871	2.8732
19	3.9329	3.7631	3.5866	3.4020	3.3062	3.2075	3.1058	3.0004	2.8908	2.7762
20	3.8470	3.6779	3.5020	3.3178	3.2220	3.1234	3.0215	2.9159	2.8058	2.6904
21	3.7709	3.6024	3.4270	3.2431	3.1474	3.0488	2.9467	2.8408	2.7302	2.6140
22	3.7030	3.5350	3.3600	3.1764	3.0807	2.9821	2.8799	2.7736	2.6625	2.5455
23	3.6420	3.4745	3.2999	3.1165	3.0208	2.9221	2.8198	2.7132	2.6016	2.4837
24	3.5870	3.4199	3.2456	3.0624	2.9667	2.8679	2.7654	2.6585	2.5463	2.4276
25	3.5370	3.3704	3.1963	3.0133	2.9176	2.8187	2.7160	2.6088	2.4960	2.3765
26	3.4916	3.3252	3.1515	2.9685	2.8728	2.7738	2.6709	2.5633	2.4501	2.3297
27	3.4499	3.2839	3.1104	2.9275	2.8318	2.7327	2.6296	2.5217	2.4078	2.2867
28	3.4117	3.2460	3.0727	2.8899	2.7941	2.6949	2.5916	2.4834	2.3689	2.2469
29	3.3765	3.2111	3.0379	2.8551	2.7594	2.6601	2.5565	2.4479	2.3330	2.2102
30	3.3440	3.1787	3.0057	2.8230	2.7272	2.6278	2.5241	2.4151	2.2997	2.1760
40	3.1167	2.9531	2.7811	2.5984	2.5020	2.4015	2.2958	2.1838	2.0635	1.9318
60	2.9042	2.7419	2.5705	2.3872	2.2898	2.1874	2.0789	1.9622	1.8341	1.6885
120	2.7052	2.5439	2.3727	2.1881	2.0890	1.9839	1.8709	1.7469	1.6055	1.4311
∞	2.5188	2.3583	2.1868	1.9998	1.8983	1.7891	1.6691	1.5325	1.3637	1.0000

TABLE X · Square Roots

Table X. Square Roots

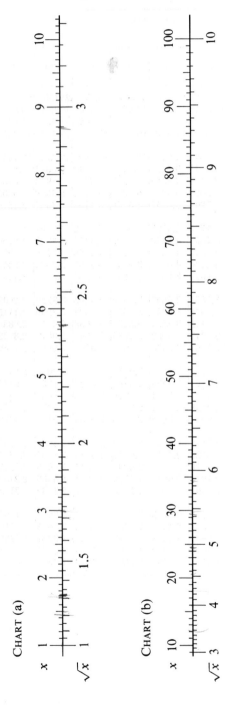

To find with slide-rule accuracy the square root of any value x in the range 1 to 100, locate x on the upper scale of chart (a) or (b) and read off $\sqrt{x}$ at that point on the lower scale of the chart. If x is outside this range, move its decimal point an even number of places left or right to get a y between 1 and 100, find $\sqrt{y}$ from the chart, and in $\sqrt{y}$ move the decimal point back half the original number of places to get $\sqrt{x}$.

Examples:

To find the root of 66,800, move the decimal four places left to get 6.68, find $\sqrt{6.68} = 2.58$ by chart (a), and move the decimal back two places right to get $258 = \sqrt{66{,}800}$. To find the root of .538, move the decimal two places right to get 53.8, find $\sqrt{53.8} = 7.33$ by chart (b), and move the decimal back one place left to get .733 = $\sqrt{.538}$.

Index